One-Dish
Meals
Cookbook

One-Dish Meals Cookbook

More Than 300 Recipes for Casseroles, Skillet Dishes and Slow-Cooker Meals

The Pillsbury Company

Clarkson Potter/Publishers
New York

Credits

Pillsbury Publications
The Pillsbury Company

Publisher: Sally Peters
Associate Publisher: Diane B. Anderson
Senior Editor: Maureen Rosener
Senior Food Editor: Andi Bidwell
Managing Editor: Karen Goodsell
Recipe Editor: Nancy A. Lilleberg
Contributing Editor: Ginger Hope
Contributing Writer: Mary Caldwell
Photography: Graham Brown Photography,
    Tad Ware Photography
Food Stylists: Sue Brosious, Sue Brue, JoAnn
    Cherry, Sue Finley, Sharon Harding, Cindy
    Ojczyk, Lisa Golden Schroeder, Barb Standal
Recipe Typists: Michelle Barringer, Jackie
    Ranney
Nutrition Information: Margaret Reinhardt,
    M.P.H., LN, Gayle M. Smith

Clarkson Potter/Publishers

The Crown Publishing Group

President and Publisher: Chip Gibson
Vice President–Editorial Director: Lauren Shakely
Senior Editor: Katie Workman
Editorial Assistant: Julia Coblentz
Designer: Lauren Monchik
Executive Managing Editor: Laurie Stark
Managing Editor: Amy Boorstein
Senior Production Editor: Liana Faughnan
Senior Production Manager: Jane Searle
Publicist: Wendy Schuman

Cover: Chuck Wagon Skillet Dinner, page 122.

Contents page (from top to bottom): Crescent Chicken Newburg, page 64; Vegetable Fiesta Skillet Supper, page 228; Slow-Cooked Hamburger and Noodle Soup, page 260.

Pillsbury Publications

Publisher: Sally Peters
Associate Publishers: Diane B. Anderson,
    William Monn
Senior Editors: Maureen Rosener, Jackie
    Sheehan
Senior Food Editor: Andi Bidwell
Test Kitchen Coordinator: Jill Crum
Circulation Manager: Karen Goodsell
Circulation Coordinator: Rebecca Bogema
Recipe Typists: Bev Gustafson, Mary Prokott,
    Renee Axtell
Publications Secretary: Jackie Ranney

Bake-Off® is a registered trademark of
    The Pillsbury Company.
Bundt® is a registered trademark of Northland
    Aluminum Company.
Crock-Pot® Slow Cooker is a registered
    trademark of The Rival Company,
    Kansas City, Missouri.

Published by Clarkson N. Potter, 201 East 50th Street, New York, New York 10022. Member of the Crown Publishing Group.

Random House, Inc. New York, Toronto, London, Sydney, Auckland
www.randomhouse.com

CLARKSON N. POTTER, POTTER, and colophon are registered trademarks of Random House, Inc.

Printed in Japan

Design by Lauren Monchik

Library of Congress Cataloging-in-Publication Data
Pillsbury, one-dish meals cookbook: more than 300 recipes for casseroles, skillet dishes and slow-cooker meals / by The Pillsbury
Company. — 1st ed.
Includes index.
1. Casserole cookery. I. Pillsbury Company.
TX693.P545   1999
641.8'21—dc21   99-14444

ISBN 0-609-60282-9

10 9 8 7 6 5 4 3 2 1

First Edition

contents

introduction

One-dish cooking has long been the first and last word in family meals that are convenient and satisfying. This collection gives you more than 300 ways to combine old-fashioned warmth and comfort with flavorful innovation—and the ease and simplicity of a single dish.

The first chapter concentrates on oven-baked casseroles, with a wide selection of entrees. Chapter 2 presents stove-top meals prepared in a wok, skillet or Dutch oven. The slow-cooker recipes in Chapter 3 will fill your kitchen with a savory aroma as they simmer.

Sweet and Hot Pork and Pineapple Stir-Fry, page 160

One-Dish Basics

Knowing a few fundamentals will help you get the most out of *Pillsbury: One-Dish Meals Cookbook*.

At the heart of many meals in this book, as in family recipes from around the world, are rice, pasta or beans. These beloved basics are hearty, satisfying and inexpensive; their mild flavor combines well with many seasonings and ingredients.

1. Instant Brown Rice 2. Arborio Rice 3. Bulgar (Cracked Wheat) 4. Wild Rice 5. Basmati 6. *Couscous 7. Instant White Rice 8. Regular White Rice

Couscous is actually a pasta but cooks like rice.

About Rice

WHITE RICE has had the husk, bran and germ removed. Regular white rice is sometimes referred to as polished rice. It cooks in about 20 minutes on the stove top. To prepare white rice, add 1 cup of rice to 2 cups of boiling, salted water; you can also add 1 tablespoon of butter, margarine or oil. Reduce heat to a bare simmer and cook the rice, tightly covered, for about 20 minutes, until the liquid has been absorbed and the grains are tender.

BROWN RICE is the whole grain with only the inedible outer husk removed. The high-fiber bran coating gives brown rice its tan color and nutlike flavor. It takes about 45 minutes for brown rice to cook on the stove top.

CONVERTED RICE is white rice that has been parboiled, then dried. When cooked to completion, the kernels are fluffier and more separated than those of regular white rice. Cooking time is similar to that of regular white rice.

INSTANT OR QUICK RICE has been partially cooked and dehydrated. Both white and brown varieties cook quickly, usually in about 5 minutes.

WILD RICE is not actually a rice but a type of marsh grass seed, native to the northern Great Lakes. Its flavor is nutty. During cooking, which takes 45 to 60 minutes, the dark seeds burst, giving the cooked rice an attractive dark and light appearance.

To give your rice dish a slightly different character try:

FRAGRANT JASMINE RICE, available at Asian markets and specialty food shops.
BASMATI (OR TEXMATI) RICE, sold in supermarkets, Indian groceries and gourmet food stores.
ARBORIO RICE, a short-grained Italian rice, available in Italian markets and specialty food shops.

- Store rice in an airtight container in a cool, dark, dry place. White rice will keep almost indefinitely. Brown rice, which contains oil in the bran, should be used within six months to prevent it from becoming rancid.
- Leftover rice can be refrigerated or frozen. Freeze cooked rice in resealable plastic freezer bags. It's not necessary to thaw frozen rice before reheating it.
- Reheat refrigerated rice in a covered saucepan on the stove or in a covered, microwave-safe casserole in the microwave oven. Microwave it on HIGH power for about 2 minutes per cup, stirring it halfway through cooking. Add 1 to 2 tablespoons of water or broth to restore the fluffiness before microwaving.

About Pasta

About Beans

1. Bow Tie Pasta 2. Manicotti 3. Pasta Nuggets (Radiatore) 4. Mini Lasagna Noodles (Mafalda) 5. Tortellini 6. Mostaccioli or Penne 7. Angel Hair 8. Wagon Wheel Pasta 9. Fettuccine 10. Vermicelli 11. Rotini

1. Pinto Beans 2. Lentils 3. Black-eyed Peas 4. Split Peas 5. Lima Beans 6. Great Northern Beans 7. Black Beans 8. Kidney Beans 9. Garbanzo Beans

The last generation of casseroles relied on elbow macaroni and flat egg noodles. Today, choices are more varied. If your pantry lacks the shape specified in a recipe, substitute with one of the pasta types pictured here.

Dried pasta is usually made with semolina, a flour made from hard durum wheat that is more durable and holds up better when boiled. Egg noodles have a light golden color from the addition of yolk in the dough and are usually more tender.

Colored pasta gains its hues from ingredients such as carrot, tomato or spinach. The color is usually more pronounced than the flavor, and the added vegetables do not change the pasta's nutritional profile.

Fresh pastas, sold in the refrigerator case of the grocery store, are softer textured and cook more quickly. They usually are not the best choice for an oven-baked casserole, though they make a fine base for a stew or a skillet meal.

Beans are high in fiber and vitamins, low in fat and a good source of vegetable protein. Beans can in fact be purchased fresh, usually in specialty markets or from farm stands, but are far more common in dried form.

Dried beans, packaged in plastic bags or sold in bulk, must be reconstituted before they are tender enough to eat. Overnight soaking in water is a common method; use about twice as much water as dried beans, since the beans absorb a lot of liquid. A quicker method is to bring the dried beans to a boil for a few minutes, then let them soak for an hour. In either method, drain the beans before using them in recipes. Don't add salt or tomato products called for in recipes until the end because they toughen the beans.

Canned beans are the easiest to use. Most canned beans vary more in color, size, shape and texture than in flavor. You can usually substitute one kind for another without hurting the results.

Freezer-Friendly Foods

Many one-dish meals have an added convenience: You can make them ahead and place them in the freezer. Look for the ✳ **Make-Ahead Directions** throughout Chapter 1, Casseroles. It marks recipes that freeze especially well.

For best results when freezing one-dish meals, follow these general rules:

• **A dish baked from the frozen state will need additional baking time. Check your dish during baking and adjust the time accordingly.**
• **Recipes with a low-fat sauce or condensed-soup base usually freeze well.**
• **You can freeze casseroles baked or unbaked.**
• **For recipes with sour cream, add it after thawing and reheating the dish.**
• **Potatoes do not freeze well.**
• **Add any crisp topping, such as nuts, after thawing the dish.**
• **Cook meats, vegetables, pasta and grains just until tender to avoid overcooking during reheating.**
• **Cool foods before packaging them for the freezer.**
• **Freeze foods in meal-size packages, either individual servings or enough for one family meal.**
• **Use airtight containers that are suitable for microwave or oven reheating.**
• **Label packages with the contents, date, cooking time and temperature.**
• **Store frozen meals at 0°F. or colder.**
• **For best quality, use frozen casseroles within three months.**

Freezing Tip

Tuck a casserole or two away in your freezer for those inevitable rushed-day dinners. Here's a super-simple way to freeze a one-dish meal in aluminum foil so that you don't tie up your baking dishes.

STEP **1.** Lightly grease an ovenproof casserole or baking dish. Line the dish with a sheet of foil large enough to bring the edges together to fold and seal. Place the casserole mixture in the foil-lined dish. Bake it according to the recipe directions, or leave it unbaked.

STEP **2.** After the casserole or stew has cooled, bring the edges of foil together and seal tightly, making sure the foil touches the top of the mixture to shut out any air. Freeze it until firm.

STEP **3.** Lift the frozen casserole from the dish. For additional protection, wrap the casserole in another layer of foil or place it in a freezer bag. Label the outer wrap with casserole name, date frozen, use-by date, number of servings and reheating or baking instructions. Return the labeled casserole to the freezer.

STEP **4.** When ready to use the casserole, place it in the original baking dish. Thaw in refrigerator; reheat or bake. (If baking directly from freezer to oven, add additional baking time; see individual recipes for specific baking time.) (Note: When using a microwave oven to bake or reheat, remove the foil first.)

Tips for Reducing Fat

One-dish cooking is not only convenient but can also be a healthy choice. Follow these simple tips to reduce the fat in one-dish cooking.

- **Use nonstick cookware.**
- **Use nonstick cooking spray, which is real oil in a pressurized can that disperses it in an ultra-thin layer. You can buy refillable spray canisters at kitchenware shops and use your own cooking oil.**
- **Use nonfat or reduced-fat dairy products, including nonfat milk, nonfat plain yogurt and reduced-fat cheeses.**
- **Reduce the amount of cheese and nuts in recipes. Try sprinkling these ingredients on top rather than mixing them in, for greater impact with a smaller quantity.**
- **Use egg whites or nonfat egg product (made of egg whites and flavorings) instead of whole eggs.**
- **Reduce the amount of meat in a recipe but keep the portion size the same by increasing the amount of beans, rice, vegetables and so on.**

Lowering the Fat in Ground Beef Recipes

By simply blotting and rinsing ground beef after cooking, you can wash away half or more of the fat. For 3 ounces of 70% lean ground beef, this technique reduces the fat from 18 grams to about 6 grams. This is how to do it:

1. **Brown the ground beef until the pink is gone.**
2. **Transfer the crumbles with a slotted spoon onto a plate lined with three layers of paper towels.**
3. **Gently press the meat with additional paper towels to remove more of the fat.**
4. **Transfer the crumbles to a strainer or colander and pour hot water over the meat; drain for 5 minutes.**

How to Chop, Cube, Dice . . . and More

Here is an easy guide to the commonly used preparation steps in this book.

To Chop
Cut the ingredient into pieces of random size. The food may be finely or coarsely chopped.

To Cube
Cut the ingredient into pieces of uniform size and shape— usually ½ inch or larger.

To Dice
Cut the ingredient into pieces of uniform size and shape— usually about ¼ inch.

To Grate
Rub the ingredient with a repeated downward motion against a grater. The food may be finely or coarsely grated.

To Julienne (Cut into matchsticks)
Cut the ingredient into 2x¼x¼-inch strips.

To Mince
Cut the ingredient into very small pieces.

To Shred
Cut the ingredient into thin slivers using a grater or knife.

Safe Handling of Meat, Poultry and Seafood

Fresh meat, poultry and seafood are all highly perishable and should be handled with care and common sense. At the market, check the "sell-by" date on the package; bring meats directly home and store them in the coldest part of your refrigerator (usually the bottom shelf), double-wrapped in plastic or set into a pan to catch any potential drips. Frozen products should be solid to the touch with no sign of ice crystals, freezer burn or discolored packaging.

- **Use or freeze fresh ground beef, other raw meats and poultry within two days. Seafood is best purchased and cooked the same day. If any meat or seafood becomes discolored or slimy or develops an "off" odor, discard it.**
- **During preparation, keep raw meat and seafood separate from foods that will be served uncooked. Thoroughly wash cutting boards, knives and other utensils used for raw meat in hot soapy water after each use.**
- **Keep meat and seafood cold or hot. Do not partially cook any kind of meat and finish cooking later. The in-between temperature may promote the growth of harmful bacteria. This goes for microwave defrosting, too. In the microwave, some spots may get hot while others remain partially frozen. Immediately cook meats thawed in the microwave.**
- **If you are taking prepared food to a potluck, keep the food hot (above 140° F.) or chilled (below 40° F.).**
- **Refrigerate leftovers as soon as possible.**

Buying Chicken

Boneless, skinless chicken breasts are the cut used most often in this book. You can buy them on sale, wrap them individually in plastic and freeze the pieces in a freezer bag. This makes it easy to defrost just as many as you need.

Fresh, uncooked chicken should be firm and moist, but not slimy. The skin color may range from yellow to white; this reflects the chicken's diet, not quality or flavor. All poultry should smell fresh. The skin and flesh should be free of tears and bruises.

Buying Beef

Boneless sirloin is easy to slice for casseroles and tender enough for quick cooking methods such as stir-frying. Look for a deep red color and a fine-grained, firm texture. Any fat should be creamy white. Less tender cuts of meat such as rump roast are more suited for slow-cooker cooking.

Many one-dish meals use ground beef. The price varies according to the cut of meat and the percentage of fat in the mixture. High-fat mixtures cost less but shrink more when cooked.

- **70 to 75% lean ground beef is suitable when the recipe calls for browning, then draining the beef.**
- **75 to 80% lean ground beef should be used when you want the meat to hold its shape and be juicy.**
- **80 to 85% lean ground beef lowers the fat and calorie content of the recipe.**

Buying Pork

The cut used most often in these recipes is pork tenderloin, a narrow cylindrical cut that is extremely tender. Boneless pork chops may be substituted.

Choose pork that is light pink to rose in color with firm, fine-grained texture. Any fat should be firm and white in color; the bone should be pinkish.

Buying Seafood

Even if you're not buying a whole fish, look at the whole fish in the fresh seafood display case for a clue to the quality of all the seafood. Fish eyes should look bright, clear and bulging, without a filmy or sunken appearance, and the gills should be bright red, not brownish or slimy.

Fish flesh should look firm and elastic; skin should look bright and shiny but not slimy. Seafood should have a fresh, perhaps faintly oceanlike smell, not a strong "fishy" or ammonia odor.

Using Soup or Stock in Recipes

Many of the dishes in this book use canned, condensed creamy soups instead of white sauce or cheese sauce made from scratch. Compare soup labels; fat, sodium and sugar content vary among brands.

Some recipes call for stock or broth to moisten ingredients and add flavor. Here are some equivalents in case you have a different form on hand than that specified in the recipe:

- A 14½-ounce can of ready-to-serve beef or chicken broth equals 1¾ cups of broth.
- A 10½-ounce can of condensed beef broth or a 10½-ounce can of condensed chicken broth diluted with 1 soup can of water equals 2⅔ cups of broth.
- 1 bouillon cube or 1 teaspoon of instant bouillon dissolved in 1 cup of water equals 1 cup of broth.
- 1 teaspoon of beef or chicken base diluted with 1 cup water equals 1 cup of broth.

Ten Tasty Toppings

Sprinkle one of the following ingredients on a casserole, either before or after baking:

1. Bread crumbs or croutons
2. Shredded cheese
3. Minced fresh herbs
4. Sliced ripe olives
5. Homemade or purchased salsa
6. Minced tomatoes
7. Toasted nuts
8. French fried onions
9. Crushed crackers or tortilla chips
10. Crumbled, cooked bacon

1

casseroles

Oven casseroles are among the most satisfying and comforting of meals, evoking cozy family suppers and shared meals with good friends. One of the beauties of a casserole is that you can assemble it ahead of time, set it to bake and forget about it for an hour or so. The time is yours to whip up dessert, catch up with other activities, enjoy an unhurried conversation or relax.

Chicken Divan, page 62

Casserole Cookware

In the strict sense of the word, "casserole" usually refers to a dish that is deep, round, ovenproof and equipped with a lid. A "baking dish," while also ovenproof, is usually shallow and can be topped with foil when a covering is needed.

Most recipes in this chapter call for one of these standard-size dishes, presented along with their volume equivalents:

8-inch square baking dish (2-quart casserole)
12x8-inch oblong baking dish (2-quart casserole)
13x9-inch oblong baking dish (3-quart casserole)

You'll have best results with the size specified in the recipe. If you must substitute, choose a dish slightly larger than the one specified. The cooking time may change slightly.

The capacity is sometimes stamped or printed on the bottom of the dish or under the handles. If you're not sure, measure how much water it takes to fill the casserole to the brim.

With the exception of lasagna, which is best made in an oblong pan to accommodate the long noodles, it rarely matters whether you use a square or round dish of equal capacity.

Casserole dishes now come in many colors, shapes and materials. The good news: Unlike in stove-top cooking, variations in casserole cookware have relatively little influence on the speed and success of cooking.

Casserole Cookware

1. Tempered glass (clear or tinted)

Glass is economical and practical. Its simple, neutral design coordinates well with any tableware. Most glass bakeware can go from freezer to oven and is both microwave and dishwasher safe. Glass retains heat well.

2. Ceramic or stoneware

Ceramic bakeware is widely available in many styles and motifs. Most can go from freezer to microwave or oven to dishwasher. Ceramic also retains heat well.

3. Handmade ceramic or pottery

Beautiful and distinctive, this bakeware is handy for oven-to-table serving. It may not withstand oven temperatures as high as those tolerated by tempered glass or commercial ceramic. It's probably not dishwasher safe. Most handmade ceramic or pottery bakeware is suitable for the freezer or microwave.

4. Enameled stainless steel or cast iron

Enameled bakeware offers colorful options. The flameproof and ovenproof design allows for browning ingredients on the stove top before baking. It's durable (however, the enamel can chip), and is fine in the freezer but not the microwave.

5. Aluminum

Aluminum conducts heat well but can react with acidic ingredients. It's inexpensive but not the most attractive for serving at table. Aluminum is fine for the freezer but not the microwave.

6. Anodized aluminum

Anodized aluminum has a silver-gray appearance. It can go from stove top to oven. The coated surface does not react with acidic ingredients. Anodized aluminum is fine for the freezer but not the microwave.

Brunch Specialties

Brew good coffee, make fresh orange juice and offer one or more of these casseroles for a brunch buffet:

Asparagus Egg Bake with Mornay Sauce, page 23
Black Bean and Corn Enchilada Egg Bake, page 110
Broccoli-Rice Quiche, page 105
Celebration Brunch Strata, page 95
Confetti Egg Bake, page 75
Crescent Brunch Dish, page 26
Overnight Southwestern Egg Bake, page 105
Southwestern Egg Bake, page 22
Turkey Sausage Strata, page 74

Celebration Brunch Strata, page 95

Kids' Favorites

Children love the familiar flavors of cheese, noodles and other standards in these recipes:

Bacon Cheeseburger Upside-Down Pizza, page 10
Baked Macaroni, Ham and Cheese, page 27
Cheesy Noodle Turkey Casserole, page 76
Ham and Cheese Potato Bake, page 29
Old-Time Tuna Bake, page 80
Pepperoni Pizza Pasta, page 31
Roasted Chicken and Vegetables, page 63
Sloppy Joe Casserole, page 10
Tater Nugget Hot Dish, page 7
Three-Color Macaroni and Cheese, page 95

Cheesy Noodle Turkey Casserole, page 76

Easy Entertaining

These casseroles are good choices for a formal buffet or sit-down meal:

Artichoke Cheese 'n Rice Casserole, page 99
Basil Ravioli with Red and White Sauce, page 98
Broccoli-Shrimp Fettuccine, page 86
Chicken and Cashew Bake, page 57
Chicken, Artichoke and Rice Casserole, page 58
Chicken Puff Pie, page 50
Citrus-Plum Orange Roughy, page 82
Crescent Chicken Newburg, page 64
Lasagna with Golden Flaky Topping, page 40
Light Crab Linguine, page 91
Penne and Spinach Bake, page 98
Prosciutto Basil Pasta Shells, page 33
Seafood Almond Casserole, page 90
Swiss Party Chicken, page 63

Lasagna with Golden Flaky Topping, page 40

Tried and True Family Favorites

Your family will recognize the flavors in these updated traditional favorites. You'll appreciate how easy they are to make:

Baked Ravioli and Meatballs, page 48
Chicken Pot Pies, page 51
Chicken Tetrazzini Bake, page 56
De-Lightful Tuna Casserole, page 84
Easy Taco Casserole, page 7
Grown-Up Mac and Cheese, page 96
Italian Classic Lasagna, page 42
Make-Ahead Spaghetti and Meatball Casserole, page 31
Western Beef Casserole au Gratin, page 11
Winter Warm-Up Beef Pot Pie, page 18

De-lightful Tuna Casserole, page 84

Sunburst Ground Beef Casserole

Prep Time: 25 minutes (Ready in 55 minutes)

Yield: 6 servings

1   lb. ground beef
¼   cup chopped onion
1   (14½-oz.) can cut green
     beans, drained
2   (8-oz.) cans tomato sauce
¼   teaspoon dried basil leaves
⅛   teaspoon pepper
1   (7-oz.) can refrigerated
     buttermilk biscuits
4   oz. Cheddar cheese, cut into
     ½-inch cubes (1 cup)
2   tablespoons margarine or
     butter, melted
1   tablespoon sesame seed

1. Heat oven to 375°F. In 10-inch ovenproof skillet, brown ground beef and onion until beef is thoroughly cooked. Drain. Add green beans, tomato sauce, basil and pepper; mix well. Simmer while preparing biscuits.

2. Separate dough into 10 biscuits. Cut hole in center of each biscuit. Fold cheese cubes into hot meat mixture. Pull edges of biscuit rings to form oval; place around outer edge of skillet. Place biscuit holes in center of skillet. Brush biscuit pieces with margarine; sprinkle with sesame seed.

3. Bake at 375°F. for 23 to 28 minutes or until golden brown.

Nutrition Information Per Serving: Serving Size: ⅙ of Recipe • Calories 400 • Calories from Fat 220 • % Daily Value • Total Fat 24 g 37% • Saturated 10 g 50% • Cholesterol 65 mg 22% • Sodium 1080 mg 45% • Total Carbohydrate 24 g 8% • Dietary Fiber 3 g 12% • Sugars 6 g • Protein 21 g • Vitamin A 25% • Vitamin C 15% • Calcium 20% • Iron 20%
Dietary Exchanges: 1½ Starch, 1 Vegetable, 2 Medium-Fat Meat, 2½ Fat OR 1½ Carbohydrate, 1 Vegetable, 2 Medium-Fat Meat, 2½ Fat

Deep-Dish Spaghetti Pie

Prep Time: 35 minutes (Ready in 1 hour 5 minutes)

Yield: 6 servings

6   oz. uncooked spaghetti
2   eggs, slightly beaten
¼   cup grated Parmesan cheese
1   lb. ground beef
¼   cup chopped onion
1   (14-oz.) jar spaghetti sauce
1   (11-oz.) can vacuum-packed
     whole kernel corn, drained
1   small green bell pepper, cut
     into rings
4   oz. (1 cup) shredded
     mozzarella cheese

1. Cook spaghetti to desired doneness as directed on package. Drain; rinse with hot water.

2. Heat oven to 350°F. Grease 10-inch pie pan or 9-inch square pan. Combine cooked spaghetti, eggs and Parmesan cheese; toss lightly. Place in greased pan. Press evenly over bottom and up sides of pan to form crust. Set aside.

3. In large skillet, brown ground beef with onion until beef is thoroughly cooked. Drain. Stir in spaghetti sauce and corn. Spoon evenly over crust. Top with bell pepper rings; sprinkle with cheese.

4. Bake at 350°F. for 25 to 30 minutes. Let stand 5 minutes before serving.

Nutrition Information Per Serving: Serving Size: ⅙ of Recipe • Calories 440 • Calories from Fat 170 • % Daily Value • Total Fat 19 g 29% • Saturated 8 g 40% • Cholesterol 130 mg 43% • Sodium 700 mg 29% • Total Carbohydrate 39 g 13% • Dietary Fiber 3 g 12% • Sugars 5 g • Protein 27 g • Vitamin A 10% • Vitamin C 15% • Calcium 25% • Iron 20%
Dietary Exchanges: 2 Starch, ½ Fruit, 3 Medium-Fat Meat, ½ Fat OR 2½ Carbohydrate, 3 Medium-Fat Meat, ½ Fat

Tater Nugget Hot Dish

Prep Time: 20 minutes (Ready in 1 hour 10 minutes)

Yield: 6 (1¼-cup) servings

1 lb. ground beef
¾ cup chopped onions
½ cup chopped celery
1 (10¾-oz.) can condensed 98% fat-free cream of mushroom soup with 30% less sodium
1 (10¾-oz.) can condensed 98% fat-free cream of chicken soup with 30% less sodium
⅛ teaspoon garlic powder
⅛ teaspoon pepper
1 cup frozen cut green beans, thawed, drained
1 (16-oz.) pkg. frozen potato nuggets

1. Heat oven to 375°F. In large saucepan, brown ground beef, onions and celery until beef is thoroughly cooked. Drain well.

2. Stir in soups, garlic powder, pepper and green beans. Spoon into ungreased 2-quart casserole; top with potato nuggets.

3. Bake at 375°F. for 40 to 50 minutes or until casserole is bubbly and potato nuggets are golden brown.

✳ **Make-Ahead Directions:** Prepare recipe as directed above; do not bake. Cover with foil; freeze. When ready to use, do not thaw; bake, covered, at 375°F. for 1½ hours. Uncover; bake an additional 10 minutes or until mixture is thoroughly heated and potato nuggets are golden brown.

Nutrition Information Per Serving: Serving Size: 1¼ Cups • Calories 400 • Calories from Fat 190 • % Daily Value • Total Fat 21 g 32% • Saturated 9 g 45% • Cholesterol 50 mg 17% • Sodium 1020 mg 43% • Total Carbohydrate 36 g 12% • Dietary Fiber 4 g 16% • Sugars 4 g • Protein 17 g • Vitamin A 6% • Vitamin C 10% • Calcium 10% • Iron 15%
Dietary Exchanges: 2½ Starch, 1½ Medium-Fat Meat, 2 Fat OR 2½ Carbohydrate, 1½ Medium-Fat Meat, 2 Fat

Easy Taco Casserole

Prep Time: 30 minutes (Ready in 55 minutes)

Yield: 6 servings

1 lb. ground beef
¾ cup chopped onions
1 (1¼-oz.) pkg. taco seasoning mix with 40% less sodium
¾ cup water
1 (16-oz.) can refried beans
1 (8-oz.) jar taco sauce
2½ cups crushed tortilla chips
7 oz. (1¾ cups) shredded Cheddar cheese
1½ cups shredded lettuce
½ cup chopped tomatoes

1. Heat oven to 400°F. In medium skillet, cook ground beef and onions over medium-high heat until beef is thoroughly cooked. Drain. Stir in taco seasoning mix and water; simmer 10 minutes.

2. In medium bowl, combine refried beans and taco sauce. In ungreased 8-inch square (2-quart) baking dish, layer ½ the bean mixture, ½ the beef mixture, 2 cups tortilla chips and 1 cup of the cheese. Top with remaining bean mixture and beef mixture.

3. Bake at 400°F. for 25 minutes. Remove from oven. Top with remaining tortilla chips and cheese. Return to oven; bake an additional 3 to 5 minutes or until cheese is melted. Serve with lettuce and tomatoes.

Nutrition Information Per Serving: Serving Size: ⅙ of Recipe • Calories 500 • Calories from Fat 250 • % Daily Value • Total Fat 28 g 43% • Saturated 12 g 60% • Cholesterol 80 mg 27% • Sodium 1280 mg 53% • Total Carbohydrate 36 g 12% • Dietary Fiber 6 g 24% • Sugars 3 g • Protein 26 g • Vitamin A 15% • Vitamin C 6% • Calcium 30% • Iron 20%
Dietary Exchanges: 2½ Starch, 2½ Medium-Fat Meat, 3 Fat OR 2½ Carbohydrate, 2½ Medium-Fat Meat, 3 Fat

Biscuit-Topped Fiesta Supper

Prep Time: 25 minutes (Ready in 45 minutes)

Yield: 5 servings

MEAT MIXTURE

1	lb. ground beef
½	cup chopped onion
¾	cup picante sauce
1	(11-oz.) can vacuum-packed whole kernel corn with red and green peppers, drained
1	(8-oz.) can tomato sauce
1	teaspoon sugar
½	teaspoon garlic powder
½	teaspoon chili powder
⅛	teaspoon pepper
4	oz. (1 cup) shredded Cheddar cheese

BISCUIT TOPPING

2	tablespoons yellow cornmeal
½	teaspoon paprika
⅛	teaspoon garlic powder
1	(12-oz.) can refrigerated flaky biscuits
1	tablespoon margarine or butter, melted

1. Heat oven to 375°F. In large ovenproof skillet, brown ground beef and onion until thoroughly cooked. Drain. Stir in picante sauce, corn, tomato sauce, sugar, garlic powder, chili powder and pepper. Bring to a boil. Reduce heat to low; simmer, uncovered, 10 to 15 minutes or until most of liquid is absorbed.

2. Meanwhile, in small bowl, combine cornmeal, paprika and garlic powder; mix well.

3. Separate dough into 10 biscuits. Cut each biscuit in half. Arrange biscuits around outer edge of hot beef mixture. Brush biscuits with margarine; sprinkle with cornmeal mixture. Sprinkle cheese in center of ground beef mixture.

4. Bake at 375°F. for 15 to 20 minutes or until biscuits are golden brown.

Nutrition Information Per Serving: Serving Size: ⅕ of Recipe • Calories 610 • Calories from Fat 300 • % Daily Value • Total Fat 33 g 51% • Saturated 12 g 60% • Cholesterol 80 mg 27% • Sodium 1800 mg 75% • Total Carbohydrate 50 g 17% • Dietary Fiber 4 g 16% • Sugars 11 g • Protein 27 g • Vitamin A 20% • Vitamin C 40% • Calcium 20% • Iron 25%
Dietary Exchanges: 3½ Starch, 2½ High-Fat Meat, 2 Fat OR 3½ Carbohydrate, 2½ High-Fat Meat, 2 Fat

Biscuit-Topped Fiesta Supper

Bacon Cheeseburger Upside-Down Pizza

Prep Time: 20 minutes (Ready in 50 minutes)

Yield: 6 servings

FILLING

- 6 slices bacon
- 1 lb. lean ground beef
- 1 medium onion, quartered, sliced
- 1 medium bell pepper (any color), cut into bite-sized strips
- 1 (14½-oz.) can chunky pizza sauce
- 2 to 3 Italian plum tomatoes, chopped
- 4 oz. (6 thin slices) Cheddar cheese

TOPPING

- 2 slices bacon
- 2 eggs
- 1 cup milk
- 1 tablespoon oil
- 1 cup all-purpose flour
- ¼ teaspoon salt

1. Heat oven to 400° F. Cook all bacon needed (8 slices) until crisp. Drain on paper towels; set aside.

2. In large saucepan, brown ground beef with onion and bell pepper until beef is thoroughly cooked. Drain. Crumble 6 slices of bacon. Add crumbled bacon and pizza sauce to ground beef mixture; mix well. Spoon into ungreased 13x9-inch (3-quart) baking dish. Sprinkle evenly with tomatoes; top with cheese slices.

3. In medium bowl, beat eggs slightly. Add milk and oil; mix well. Add flour and salt; beat 2 minutes at medium speed. Pour evenly over cheese slices. Crumble remaining 2 slices bacon; sprinkle over top.

4. Bake at 400° F. for 20 to 30 minutes or until topping is slightly puffed and deep golden brown.

Nutrition Information Per Serving: Serving Size: ⅙ of Recipe • Calories 460 • Calories from Fat 240 • % Daily Value • Total Fat 27 g 42% • Saturated 11 g 55% • Cholesterol 150 mg 50% • Sodium 870 mg 36% • Total Carbohydrate 26 g 9% • Dietary Fiber 2 g 8% • Sugars 8 g • Protein 27 g • Vitamin A 15% • Vitamin C 25% • Calcium 20% • Iron 20%
Dietary Exchanges: 2 Starch, 3 Medium-Fat Meat, 2 Fat OR 2 Carbohydrate, 3 Medium-Fat Meat, 2 Fat

Sloppy Joe Casserole

Prep Time: 15 minutes (Ready in 35 minutes)

Yield: 4 servings

- 1 lb. lean ground beef
- ½ cup sliced green onions
- 1 (15½-oz.) can sloppy joe sandwich sauce
- 1 (11-oz.) can vacuum-packed whole kernel corn with red and green peppers, undrained
- 1 (6-oz.) can refrigerated buttermilk flaky biscuits

1. Heat oven to 375° F. In large skillet, brown ground beef with green onions until beef is thoroughly cooked. Drain. Stir in sandwich sauce and corn. Cook 2 to 3 minutes or until thoroughly heated, stirring occasionally. Spoon mixture into ungreased 1- to 1½-quart casserole.

2. Separate dough into 5 biscuits; cut each in half. Arrange, cut side down, around outside edge of hot mixture with sides of biscuits touching.

3. Bake at 375° F. for 15 to 20 minutes or until biscuits are deep golden brown.

Nutrition Information Per Serving: Serving Size: ¼ of Recipe • Calories 480 • Calories from Fat 190 • % Daily Value • Total Fat 21 g 32% • Saturated 8 g 40% • Cholesterol 70 mg 23% • Sodium 1620 mg 68% • Total Carbohydrate 45 g 15% • Dietary Fiber 4 g 16% • Sugars 19 g • Protein 27 g • Vitamin A 45% • Vitamin C 4% • Calcium 2% • Iron 25%
Dietary Exchanges: 2 Starch, 1 Fruit, 3 Lean Meat, 2 Fat OR 3 Carbohydrate, 3 Lean Meat, 2 Fat

Western Beef Casserole au Gratin

Prep Time: 25 minutes (Ready in 1 hour)
Yield: 6 servings

½ lb. ground beef
⅓ cup chopped onion
1 (8-oz.) can tomato sauce
¼ teaspoon garlic powder
⅛ teaspoon pepper
1 (15¼-oz.) can whole kernel corn, drained
1½ cups water
¾ cup milk
2 cups mashed potato flakes
8 oz. (2 cups) shredded Cheddar cheese
1 (4½-oz.) can chopped green chiles, drained
1 medium tomato, chopped

1. Heat oven to 350° F. Spray 12x8-inch (2-quart) baking dish with nonstick cooking spray. In large skillet, brown ground beef and onion until beef is thoroughly cooked. Drain. Stir in tomato sauce, garlic powder and pepper. Spoon into sprayed baking dish. Spoon corn evenly over meat mixture.

2. Bring water to a boil in medium saucepan. Remove from heat; stir in milk and potato flakes with fork. Spread potato mixture evenly over corn; sprinkle with cheese. Top with green chiles.

3. Bake at 350° F. for 30 to 35 minutes or until bubbly around edges and cheese is melted. Let stand 5 minutes. Top with chopped tomato.

✳ **Make-Ahead Directions:** Prepare recipe as directed above except omit Cheddar cheese and green chiles; do not bake. Cover with foil; freeze. When ready to use, do not thaw; bake, covered, at 350° F. for 1 hour 20 minutes. Uncover, sprinkle with Cheddar cheese and green chiles. Bake an additional 10 minutes or until mixture is thoroughly heated and cheese is melted. Let stand 5 minutes before serving.

Nutrition Information Per Serving: Serving Size: ⅙ of Recipe • Calories 400 • Calories from Fat 180 • % Daily Value • Total Fat 20 g 31% • Saturated 11 g 55% • Cholesterol 65 mg 22% • Sodium 720 mg 30% • Total Carbohydrate 34 g 11% • Dietary Fiber 4 g 16% • Sugars 6 g • Protein 20 g • Vitamin A 20% • Vitamin C 25% • Calcium 35% • Iron 10%
Dietary Exchanges: 2½ Starch, 2 High-Fat Meat OR 2½ Carbohydrate, 2 High-Fat Meat

Garlic Potato-Topped Beef Cacciatore

Prep Time: 20 minutes (Ready in 55 minutes)

Yield: 4 (1½-cup) servings

CACCIATORE

- 1 lb. boneless beef sirloin steak, cut into 1½ x ½-inch strips
- 1 tablespoon oil
- 1 cup sliced onions
- 1 medium green bell pepper, cut into strips
- 1 (24½ to 28-oz.) jar cacciatore simmer sauce or spaghetti sauce

POTATOES

- 1½ cups water
- 3 tablespoons margarine or butter
- 2 garlic cloves, minced
- ¾ cup milk
- 2¼ cups mashed potato flakes
- ½ cup grated Parmesan cheese
- 1 egg, slightly beaten

1. Heat oven to 325° F. In large skillet, cook beef in oil over medium-high heat until lightly browned. Add onions and bell pepper; cook and stir 4 to 5 minutes or until vegetables are crisp-tender and beef is no longer pink. Stir in sauce. Cook until thoroughly heated. Spoon into ungreased 12 x 8-inch (2-quart) baking dish.

2. In medium saucepan, bring water, margarine and garlic to a boil. Remove from heat; add milk. Stir in potato flakes and cheese. Add egg; blend well. Spoon or pipe potato mixture around edges of baking dish over hot beef mixture.

3. Bake at 325° F. for 25 to 35 minutes or until potatoes are set and light golden brown.

Nutrition Information Per Serving: Serving Size: 1½ Cups • Calories 600 • Calories from Fat 230 • % Daily Value • Total Fat 25 g 38% • Saturated 8 g 40% • Cholesterol 125 mg 42% • Sodium 1220 mg 51% • Total Carbohydrate 58 g 19% • Dietary Fiber 6 g 24% • Sugars 17 g • Protein 35 g • Vitamin A 25% • Vitamin C 30% • Calcium 30% • Iron 70%
Dietary Exchanges: 3 Starch, 1 Fruit, 3½ Lean Meat, 2½ Fat OR 4 Carbohydrate, 3½ Lean Meat, 2½ Fat

Garlic Potato-Topped Beef Cacciatore

Keep It Hot

Prepared food should be maintained at 140° F. for food safety. If your gathering is far away, carry the casserole cold and heat it when you get there. For a shorter jaunt (up to one hour), keep your casserole hot en route with one of the following techniques:

- Set the casserole, with the lid tightly secured, into an empty picnic cooler. The insulated sides can keep in heat as well as cold.

- Set the casserole into a turkey roasting pan and surround it with clean kitchen towels for padding and insulation. Replace the roaster lid and cover the whole pan with a heavy bath towel.

- Line a heavy-duty paper shopping bag with several layers of folded newspaper. Set the casserole in the bag and pad with additional newspaper on the sides and top.

Baked Beef and Ravioli

Prep Time: 30 minutes (Ready in 55 minutes or 1 hour)
Yield: 4 servings

1 (9-oz.) pkg. refrigerated
    cheese-filled ravioli
1 lb. lean ground beef
1 (14-oz.) jar spaghetti sauce
1 (9-oz.) pkg. frozen spinach
    in a pouch, thawed,
    squeezed to drain*
4 oz. (1 cup) shredded
    mozzarella cheese

1. Heat oven to 350° F. Cook ravioli to desired doneness as directed on package. Drain.

2. Meanwhile, in large skillet, brown ground beef until thoroughly cooked. Drain. Stir in spaghetti sauce and spinach.

3. Spoon and spread ½ the beef mixture into ungreased 8-inch square (2-quart) baking dish. Arrange cooked ravioli over beef layer. Spoon and spread remaining beef mixture over ravioli. Cover with foil.

4. Bake at 350° F. for 20 minutes. Uncover; sprinkle with cheese. Bake uncovered for an additional 5 to 10 minutes or until casserole is bubbly and cheese is melted.

Tip: *To quickly thaw spinach, cut small slit in center of pouch; microwave on HIGH for 2 to 3 minutes or until thawed. Remove spinach from pouch; squeeze dry with paper towels.

Nutrition Information Per Serving: Serving Size: ¼ of Recipe • Calories 570 • Calories from Fat 260 • % Daily Value • Total Fat 29 g 45% • Saturated 13 g 65% • Cholesterol 140 mg 47% • Sodium 1010 mg 42% • Total Carbohydrate 37 g 12% • Dietary Fiber 4 g 16% • Sugars 2 g • Protein 41 g • Vitamin A 60% • Vitamin C 25% • Calcium 45% • Iron 25%
Dietary Exchanges: 2½ Starch, 4½ Medium-Fat Meat, 1 Fat OR 2½ Carbohydrate, 4½ Medium-Fat Meat, 1 Fat

Mexican Beef and Rice

Prep Time: 25 minutes (Ready in 40 minutes)

Yield: 4 servings

½ lb. boneless beef sirloin steak, cut into ¾-inch cubes
½ cup chopped onion
2 tablespoons 40% less sodium taco seasoning mix (from 1¼-oz. pkg.)
1½ cups uncooked instant rice
2½ cups water
1 (15½- or 15-oz.) can red kidney beans, drained, rinsed
2 medium tomatoes, chopped
1 oz. (¼ cup) shredded reduced-fat Cheddar cheese
¼ teaspoon chili powder

1. Heat oven to 350° F. Spray large nonstick skillet with nonstick cooking spray. Heat over medium-high heat until hot. Add beef and onion; cook and stir 3 to 4 minutes or until browned.

2. Add seasoning mix, rice and water; mix well. Bring to a boil. Reduce heat; cover and simmer 5 minutes.

3. Remove skillet from heat; stir in kidney beans and tomatoes. Divide mixture evenly into 4 ungreased 2-cup individual casseroles. Top each with cheese; sprinkle with chili powder.

4. Bake at 350° F. for 10 to 15 minutes or until casseroles are thoroughly heated and cheese is melted.

Nutrition Information Per Serving: Serving Size: ¼ of Recipe • Calories 340 • Calories from Fat 45 • % Daily Value • Total Fat 5 g 8% • Saturated 2 g 10% • Cholesterol 35 mg 12% • Sodium 470 mg 20% • Total Carbohydrate 52 g 17% • Dietary Fiber 6 g 24% • Sugars 4 g • Protein 21 g • Vitamin A 15% • Vitamin C 15% • Calcium 10% • Iron 25%
Dietary Exchanges: 3 Starch, 1 Vegetable, 1½ Lean Meat OR 3 Carbohydrate, 1 Vegetable, 1½ Lean Meat

Spaghetti and Meatball Casserole

Prep Time: 50 minutes (Ready in 1 hour 40 minutes)

Yield: 12 servings

MEATBALLS
1 lb. ground beef
1 lb. bulk mild Italian sausage
¼ cup Italian-style dry bread crumbs
1 egg, beaten

SPAGHETTI
1 lb. uncooked spaghetti, broken into fourths
½ cup chopped green onions
1 (30-oz.) jar spaghetti sauce
1 (4½-oz.) jar sliced mushrooms, drained
¼ to ½ cup shredded fresh Parmesan cheese

1. Heat oven to 350° F. In medium bowl, combine all meatball ingredients; mix well. Shape into 24 (1½-inch) meatballs. Place in ungreased 13x9-inch (3-quart) baking dish.

2. Bake at 350° F. for 30 to 35 minutes or until no longer pink. Remove meatballs from baking dish; set aside. Drain dish.

3. Meanwhile, cook spaghetti to desired doneness as directed on package. Drain.

4. Place spaghetti in same baking dish. Stir in green onions, spaghetti sauce and mushrooms. Top with cooked meatballs. Cover with foil.

5. Bake at 350° F. for 45 to 50 minutes or until thoroughly heated. Sprinkle with Parmesan cheese. Cover; let stand 5 minutes before serving.

Nutrition Information Per Serving: Serving Size: 1/12 of Recipe • Calories 370 • Calories from Fat 140 • % Daily Value • Total Fat 16 g 25% • Saturated 6 g 30% • Cholesterol 65 mg 22% • Sodium 720 mg 30% • Total Carbohydrate 37 g 12% • Dietary Fiber 2 g 8% • Sugars 2 g • Protein 20 g • Vitamin A 6% • Vitamin C 8% • Calcium 10% • Iron 20%
Dietary Exchanges: 2½ Starch, 2 High-Fat Meat OR 2½ Carbohydrate, 2 High-Fat Meat

Layered Cheese and Beef Casserole

Prep Time: 45 minutes (Ready in 1 hour 20 minutes)

Yield: 8 servings

8 oz. (4½ cups) uncooked medium egg noodles
1 lb. ground beef
¼ cup chopped onion
2 (8-oz.) cans tomato sauce
1 teaspoon salt
½ teaspoon garlic powder
¼ teaspoon pepper
1 cup cottage cheese
1 (8-oz.) pkg. cream cheese, softened
¼ cup thinly sliced green onions
¼ cup chopped green bell pepper
½ cup grated Parmesan cheese
Additional grated Parmesan cheese, if desired

1. Cook noodles to desired doneness as directed on package. Drain.

2. Meanwhile, in medium skillet, brown ground beef and onion over medium-high heat until beef is thoroughly cooked. Drain. Add tomato sauce, salt, garlic powder and pepper; mix well. Reduce heat; simmer 15 minutes.

3. Heat oven to 350°F. In medium bowl, combine cottage cheese, cream cheese, green onions, bell pepper and ½ cup Parmesan cheese; mix well.

4. In ungreased 13x9-inch (3-quart) baking dish, layer ½ each of cooked noodles, beef sauce and cheese mixture; repeat layers. Sprinkle additional Parmesan cheese over top if desired.

5. Bake at 350°F. for 30 to 35 minutes or until thoroughly heated.

✳ **Make-Ahead Directions:** Prepare recipe as directed above; do not bake. Cover with foil; freeze. When ready to use, do not thaw; bake, covered, at 350°F. for 1 hour 20 minutes. Uncover; bake an additional 5 minutes or until mixture is thoroughly heated.

Nutrition Information Per Serving: Serving Size: ⅛ of Recipe • Calories 420 • Calories from Fat 220 • % Daily Value • Total Fat 24 g 37% • Saturated 12 g 60% • Cholesterol 105 mg 35% • Sodium 990 mg 41% • Total Carbohydrate 28 g 9% • Dietary Fiber 2 g 8% • Sugars 5 g • Protein 23 g • Vitamin A 20% • Vitamin C 15% • Calcium 20% • Iron 20%
Dietary Exchanges: 1½ Starch, 1 Vegetable, 2½ Medium-Fat Meat, 2 Fat OR 1½ Carbohydrate, 1 Vegetable, 2½ Medium-Fat Meat, 2 Fat

Chili Cornbread Bake

Prep Time: 25 minutes (Ready in 1 hour 5 minutes)
Yield: 8 servings

CHILI

1	lb. ground beef
1	cup chopped onions
½	cup chopped green bell pepper
1	garlic clove, minced
1	(15½- or 15-oz.) can light red kidney beans, drained, rinsed
1	(8-oz.) can tomato sauce
1	(1¼-oz.) pkg. taco seasoning mix

CORNBREAD

1	cup all-purpose flour
1	cup yellow cornmeal
2	tablespoons sugar
3	teaspoons baking powder
½	teaspoon salt
1	(8½-oz.) can cream-style corn, undrained
½	cup milk
1	egg
4	oz. (1 cup) shredded Cheddar cheese

1. Heat oven to 350°F. Grease 2-quart casserole. In large skillet, cook ground beef, onions, bell pepper and garlic over medium–high heat until beef is thoroughly cooked. Drain. Stir in kidney beans, tomato sauce and taco seasoning mix. Reduce heat; simmer 10 minutes.

2. Meanwhile, in medium bowl, combine flour, cornmeal, sugar, baking powder and salt; mix well. In small bowl, combine corn, milk and egg; beat well. Add to dry ingredients; stir just until moistened.

3. Spoon ½ the cornbread mixture into greased casserole; sprinkle with ½ the cheese. Spoon chili over cheese; sprinkle with remaining cheese. Spoon remaining cornbread mixture evenly over cheese, spreading gently to cover.

4. Bake at 350°F. for 30 to 40 minutes or until top is golden brown. Let stand 5 minutes before serving.

High Altitude (above 3,500 feet): No change.

Nutrition Information Per Serving: Serving Size: ⅛ of Recipe • Calories 420 • Calories from Fat 140 • % Daily Value • Total Fat 16 g 25% • Saturated 7 g 35% • Cholesterol 75 mg 25% • Sodium 1110 mg 46% • Total Carbohydrate 47 g 16% • Dietary Fiber 6 g 24% • Sugars 11 g • Protein 21 g • Vitamin A 20% • Vitamin C 25% • Calcium 40% • Iron 35%
Dietary Exchanges: 3 Starch, 1½ Medium-Fat Meat, 1½ Fat OR 3 Carbohydrate, 1½ Medium-Fat Meat, 1½ Fat

Chili Cornbread Bake

Creamy Spinach and Beef Layered Casserole

Prep Time: 40 minutes (Ready in 1 hour 20 minutes)

Yield: 8 servings

8 oz. (4 cups) uncooked mini-lasagna noodles (mafalda) or medium egg noodles
1 lb. ground beef
1 cup chopped onions
1 garlic clove, minced
1 (10¾-oz.) can condensed cream of mushroom soup
1 (4-oz.) can mushroom pieces and stems, drained
1 (1-lb.) pkg. frozen cut leaf spinach, thawed, squeezed to drain*
1 (24-oz.) container (3 cups) cottage cheese
3 eggs
1 (8-oz.) container soft cream cheese with chives
1 (2.8-oz.) can french-fried onions

1. Grease 13x9-inch (3-quart) baking dish. Cook noodles to desired doneness as directed on package. Drain.

2. Meanwhile, in medium skillet, cook ground beef, onions and garlic over medium-high heat until beef is thoroughly cooked. Drain, if necessary. Add soup and mushrooms; mix well.

3. In large bowl, combine spinach, 2 cups of the cottage cheese and 2 of the eggs; mix well. In another large bowl, combine cooked noodles, remaining 1 cup cottage cheese, soft cream cheese and remaining egg; toss gently.

4. Heat oven to 350°F. In greased dish, layer ½ each of the noodle mixture, spinach mixture and beef mixture; repeat layers. Cover with foil.**

5. Bake at 350°F. for 35 to 40 minutes or until thoroughly heated. Uncover; sprinkle with french-fried onions. Bake an additional 3 minutes. Let stand 5 minutes before serving.

✳ **Make-Ahead Directions:** Prepare recipe as directed above except omit french-fried onions; do not bake. Cover with foil; freeze. When ready to use, do not thaw; bake, covered, at 350°F. for 1 hour. Uncover; bake an additional 45 to 50 minutes or until mixture is thoroughly heated. Sprinkle with french-fried onions; bake an additional 3 minutes.

Tips: *To quickly thaw spinach, place in colander or strainer; rinse with warm water until thawed. Squeeze dry with paper towels.

**A 10-inch springform pan can be substituted for the baking dish. Layer ingredients as directed in greased 10-inch springform pan. Cover with foil; place springform pan on cookie sheet. Bake at 350°F. for 50 to 55 minutes or until thoroughly heated. Uncover; sprinkle with french-fried onions. Bake an additional 3 minutes. Let stand 15 minutes. Run knife around sides of pan to loosen. Remove sides of pan; cut into wedges to serve.

Nutrition Information Per Serving: Serving Size: ⅛ of Recipe • Calories 560 • Calories from Fat 290 • % Daily Value • Total Fat 32 g 49% • Saturated 15 g 75% • Cholesterol 160 mg 53% • Sodium 960 mg 40% • Total Carbohydrate 37 g 12% • Dietary Fiber 4 g 16% • Sugars 4 g • Protein 32 g • Vitamin A 60% • Vitamin C 0% • Calcium 20% • Iron 25%
Dietary Exchanges: 2½ Starch, 3½ Lean Meat, 4 Fat OR 2½ Carbohydrate, 3½ Lean Meat, 4 Fat

Winter Warm-Up Beef Pot Pie

Prep Time: 40 minutes (Ready in 1 hour 20 minutes)

Yield: 6 servings

1	(15-oz.) pkg. refrigerated pie crusts
¾	lb. beef sirloin steak, cut into ½-inch cubes
2	small onions, cut into eighths
1½	cups cubed (¾-inch) peeled baking potatoes
¾	cup cut (1 x ½ x ½-inch) carrot
½	cup frozen sweet peas
1	(4½-oz.) jar whole mushrooms, drained
1	(12-oz.) jar brown gravy
2	tablespoons cornstarch
½	to 1 teaspoon dried thyme leaves
½	teaspoon salt
1	egg yolk
2	teaspoons water
1	teaspoon sesame seed

1. Heat oven to 425° F. Prepare pie crusts as directed on package for *two-crust pie* using 9-inch pie pan.

2. In large nonstick skillet, cook beef and onions over medium-high heat for 4 to 6 minutes or until beef is browned. Stir in potatoes, carrot, peas and mushrooms.

3. In small bowl, combine gravy, cornstarch, thyme and salt; mix well. Stir into beef mixture; cook until thoroughly heated. Spoon into crust-lined pan. Top with second crust; seal edges and flute. Cut small slits in several places in top crust.

4. In another small bowl, combine egg yolk and water; blend well. Brush top crust with egg mixture; sprinkle with sesame seed.

5. Bake at 425° F. for 30 to 40 minutes or until crust is golden brown and filling is bubbly. Cover edge of crust with strips of foil after 10 to 15 minutes of baking to prevent excessive browning. Cool 10 minutes before serving.

Nutrition Information Per Serving: Serving Size: ⅙ of Recipe • Calories 480 • Calories from Fat 210 • % Daily Value • Total Fat 23 g 35% • Saturated 9 g 45% • Cholesterol 85 mg 28% • Sodium 690 mg 29% • Total Carbohydrate 52 g 17% • Dietary Fiber 3 g 12% • Sugars 6 g • Protein 16 g • Vitamin A 90% • Vitamin C 10% • Calcium 4% • Iron 15%
Dietary Exchanges: 3 Starch, 1 Vegetable, 1 Lean Meat, 3½ Fat OR 3 Carbohydrate, 1 Vegetable, 1 Lean Meat, 3½ Fat

Spinach and Sausage Phyllo Bake

Prep Time: 50 minutes (Ready in 1 hour 50 minutes)
Yield: 8 servings

1	lb. bulk pork or mild Italian sausage
½	cup thinly sliced roasted red bell peppers (from 7¼-oz. jar)
1	(2¼-oz.) can sliced ripe olives, drained
4	oz. (1 cup) shredded mozzarella cheese
5	eggs, beaten
4	oz. (1 cup) shredded Cheddar cheese
1	cup ricotta cheese
1	(9-oz.) pkg. frozen spinach in a pouch, thawed, squeezed to drain*
16	(17 x 12-inch) sheets frozen phyllo (filo) pastry, thawed
½	cup butter, melted

1. Heat oven to 350°F. In large skillet, brown sausage over medium heat. Drain. Cool slightly. Stir in roasted peppers, olives, mozzarella cheese and eggs; mix well.

2. In medium bowl, combine Cheddar cheese, ricotta cheese and spinach; mix well.

3. Unroll phyllo pastry; cover with plastic wrap or towel. Place 1 sheet of phyllo in ungreased 13 x 9-inch (3-quart) baking dish, folding to fit. Brush lightly with melted butter. Continue layering and brushing with butter using 3 additional sheets of phyllo.

4. Spoon ½ the sausage mixture over phyllo in baking dish. Layer and brush with butter 4 more phyllo sheets. Top with spinach mixture. Layer and brush with butter 4 more phyllo sheets. Top with remaining sausage mixture. Layer and brush with butter 4 more phyllo sheets. Score top of phyllo in diamond shapes.

5. Bake at 350°F. for 50 to 60 minutes or until puffed and golden brown. Let stand 5 minutes before serving.

Tip: *To quickly thaw spinach, cut small slit in center of pouch; microwave on HIGH for 2 to 3 minutes or until thawed. Remove spinach from pouch; squeeze dry with paper towels.

Nutrition Information Per Serving: Serving Size: ⅛ of Recipe • Calories 550 • Calories from Fat 340 • % Daily Value • Total Fat 38 g 58% • Saturated 19 g 95% • Cholesterol 230 mg 77% • Sodium 1070 mg 45% • Total Carbohydrate 25 g 8% • Dietary Fiber 2 g 8% • Sugars 2 g • Protein 27 g • Vitamin A 50% • Vitamin C 25% • Calcium 35% • Iron 20%
Dietary Exchanges: 1½ Starch, 1 Vegetable, 3 High-Fat Meat, 2½ Fat OR 1½ Carbohydrate, 1 Vegetable, 3 High-Fat Meat, 2½ Fat

Oven-Roasted Pork 'n Vegetables

Prep Time: 20 minutes (Ready in 1 hour)

Yield: 8 servings

2	to 3 pork tenderloins (about 1½ lb.)
16	to 20 new potatoes (about 2 lb.), cut in half
6	to 8 carrots (about 1 lb.), peeled, cut into 2-inch pieces
1	medium onion, cut into wedges
1	tablespoon olive oil
2	teaspoons dried rosemary leaves, crushed
1	teaspoon dried sage leaves, crushed
¼	teaspoon pepper

1. Heat oven to 450° F. Generously spray roasting pan with nonstick cooking spray. Place pork tenderloins in sprayed pan. Insert meat thermometer into thickest part of 1 tenderloin.

2. Place potatoes, carrots and onion around tenderloin. Drizzle oil evenly over tenderloin and vegetables. Sprinkle with rosemary, sage and pepper.

3. Bake at 450° F. for 30 to 40 minutes or until meat thermometer reaches 165° F. and vegetables are tender, stirring vegetables occasionally.

Nutrition Information Per Serving: Serving Size: ⅛ of Recipe • Calories 270 • Calories from Fat 45 • % Daily Value • Total Fat 5 g 8% • Saturated 1 g 5% • Cholesterol 50 mg 17% • Sodium 65 mg 3% • Total Carbohydrate 36 g 12% • Dietary Fiber 5 g 20% • Sugars 5 g • Protein 21 g • Vitamin A 320% • Vitamin C 25% • Calcium 4% • Iron 15%
Dietary Exchanges: 2 Starch, 1 Vegetable, 2 Lean Meat OR 2 Carbohydrate, 1 Vegetable, 2 Lean Meat

Stock the Pantry

Keep some basic convenience products on hand for casseroles:

♦ Canned soup, especially cream of mushroom, cream of celery and chicken broth

♦ Canned kidney beans, diced tomatoes and other vegetables

♦ Ready-to-use fresh vegetables from the produce aisle, such as coleslaw blend and peeled, washed baby carrots

♦ International ingredients such as canned or jarred chile peppers, prepared salsa, cans of baby corn or water chestnuts

Oven-Roasted Pork 'n Vegetables

Southwestern Egg Bake

Prep Time: 40 minutes (Ready in 1 hour 40 minutes)

Yield: 6 servings

¾ lb. bulk spicy pork sausage
½ cup chopped onion
½ cup chopped green bell
    pepper
4 cups refrigerated or frozen
    hash-brown potatoes,
    thawed
6 oz. (1½ cups) shredded
    Cheddar cheese
4 eggs
¾ cup milk
1 cup chunky-style salsa

1. Heat oven to 350° F. Grease 8-inch square (2-quart) baking dish. In medium skillet, brown sausage with onion and bell pepper. Drain.

2. Arrange potatoes in bottom of greased baking dish. Top with ½ the cheese, all of the sausage mixture and the remaining cheese.

3. In small bowl, beat eggs slightly. Beat in milk. Pour over mixture in dish. Cover with foil.

4. Bake at 350° F. for 1 hour. Uncover; bake an additional 10 to 15 minutes or until knife inserted near center comes out clean. Let stand 5 minutes before serving. Serve topped with salsa.

Nutrition Information Per Serving: Serving Size: ⅙ of Recipe • Calories 410 • Calories from Fat 230 • % Daily Value • Total Fat 25 g 38% • Saturated 11 g 55% • Cholesterol 205 mg 68% • Sodium 990 mg 41% • Total Carbohydrate 24 g 8% • Dietary Fiber 2 g 8% • Sugars 5 g • Protein 23 g • Vitamin A 15% • Vitamin C 20% • Calcium 30% • Iron 15%
Dietary Exchanges: 1½ Starch, 2½ High-Fat Meat, 1 Fat OR 1½ Carbohydrate, 2½ High-Fat Meat, 1 Fat

Wild Rice Egg Bake

Prep Time: 45 minutes (Ready in 1 hour 25 minutes)

Yield: 8 servings

1   cup uncooked wild rice
2½ cups water
1   cup chopped onions
1   (12-oz.) pkg. frozen bulk
     pork sausage, thawed
1   (8-oz.) pkg. (3 cups) sliced
     fresh mushrooms
8   eggs
1   cup milk
2   tablespoons all-purpose flour
8   oz. (2 cups) shredded Swiss
     cheese
3   tablespoons chopped fresh
     parsley

1. Cook wild rice in water as directed on package. Drain.

2. Meanwhile, heat oven to 350° F. Grease 13x9-inch (3-quart) baking dish. In large skillet, cook onions, sausage and mushrooms over medium-high heat until sausage is no longer pink. Drain.

3. Combine cooked wild rice and sausage mixture in greased baking dish. With back of large spoon, make 8 evenly spaced indentations in mixture. Crack 1 egg into each indentation. Pierce egg yolks but do not stir. In small bowl, combine milk and flour; blend well. Pour over rice, avoiding eggs.

4. Bake at 350° F. for 30 to 40 minutes or until eggs are set. Sprinkle with cheese; bake an additional 2 to 3 minutes or until cheese is melted. Sprinkle with parsley.

Nutrition Information Per Serving: Serving Size: ⅛ of Recipe • Calories 360 • Calories from Fat 180 • % Daily Value • Total Fat 20 g 31% • Saturated 9 g 45% • Cholesterol 255 mg 85% • Sodium 420 mg 18% • Total Carbohydrate 21 g 7% • Dietary Fiber 2 g 8% • Sugars 4 g • Protein 23 g • Vitamin A 15% • Vitamin C 6% • Calcium 35% • Iron 10%
Dietary Exchanges: 1½ Starch, 2½ Medium-Fat Meat, 1½ Fat OR 1½ Carbohydrate, 2½ Medium-Fat Meat, 1½ Fat

Asparagus Egg Bake with Mornay Sauce

Prep Time: 30 minutes (Ready in 55 minutes)

Yield: 8 servings

EGGS

¼	cup chopped onion
2	tablespoons margarine or butter
1	cup cubed cooked ham
8	eggs, beaten

SAUCE

2	tablespoons margarine or butter
2	tablespoons all-purpose flour
1	teaspoon chicken-flavor instant bouillon
1¼	cups milk
2	oz. (½ cup) shredded Swiss cheese
¼	cup grated Parmesan cheese

TOPPING

1	(15-oz.) can extra-long tender asparagus spears, drained
2	tablespoons unseasoned dry bread crumbs
1	teaspoon margarine or butter, melted

1. Heat oven to 350° F. Grease 12x8-inch (2-quart) baking dish. In large skillet, cook onion in 2 tablespoons margarine until onion is crisp-tender. Add ham and eggs; cook just until eggs are set, stirring occasionally.

2. Melt 2 tablespoons margarine in medium saucepan. Blend in flour and bouillon; cook until smooth and bubbly. Gradually add milk; cook until mixture boils and thickens, stirring constantly. Add cheeses; stir until smooth. Carefully fold sauce into scrambled eggs. Pour into greased baking dish.*

3. Bake at 350° F. for 20 to 25 minutes or until eggs are thoroughly heated.

4. Remove from oven. Arrange asparagus spears over baked eggs. Combine bread crumbs and 1 teaspoon melted margarine; sprinkle over top. Return to oven; bake an additional 5 minutes.

Tip: *To make ahead, prepare as directed to this point. Cover; refrigerate up to 3 hours before baking. Uncover; bake as directed above.

Nutrition Information Per Serving: Serving Size: ⅛ of Recipe • Calories 240 • Calories from Fat 140 • % Daily Value • Total Fat 16 g 25% • Saturated 5 g 25% • Cholesterol 235 mg 78% • Sodium 660 mg 28% • Total Carbohydrate 7 g 2% • Dietary Fiber 1 g 3% • Sugars 3 g • Protein 16 g • Vitamin A 20% • Vitamin C 8% • Calcium 20% • Iron 10%
Dietary Exchanges: ½ Starch, 2 Lean Meat, 2 Fat OR ½ Carbohydrate, 2 Lean Meat, 2 Fat

Cheesy Hot Dog Casserole

Prep Time: 25 minutes (Ready in 1 hour 10 minutes)

Yield: 6 (1¼-cup) servings

CASSEROLE

½	lb. hot dogs, sliced
1	(10¾-oz.) can condensed Cheddar cheese soup
1	(7-oz.) can vacuum-packed whole kernel corn, drained
2	tablespoons finely chopped onion

TOPPING

1	cup water
2	tablespoons margarine or butter
1½	cups mashed potato flakes
½	cup milk
1	egg, slightly beaten
2	oz. (½ cup) shredded Cheddar cheese
	Paprika

1. Heat oven to 350°F. In large bowl, combine all casserole ingredients; mix well. Spoon into ungreased 2-quart casserole; set aside.

2. In medium saucepan, bring water and margarine to a boil. Remove from heat. Stir in potato flakes and milk. Add egg; blend well. Spoon and spread over casserole.

3. Bake at 350°F. for 35 to 45 minutes or until thoroughly heated. Sprinkle with cheese and paprika. Bake an additional 3 minutes or until cheese is melted.

✳ **Make-Ahead Directions:** Prepare recipe as directed above except omit Cheddar cheese and paprika; do not bake. Cover with foil; freeze. When ready to use, do not thaw; bake, covered, at 350°F. for 1 hour 35 minutes. Uncover; bake an additional 15 to 20 minutes or until mixture is thoroughly heated. Sprinkle with Cheddar cheese and paprika; bake an additional 3 minutes or until cheese is melted.

Nutrition Information Per Serving: Serving Size: 1¼ Cups • Calories 350 • Calories from Fat 220 • % Daily Value • Total Fat 24 g 37% • Saturated 10 g 50% • Cholesterol 80 mg 27% • Sodium 1020 mg 43% • Total Carbohydrate 21 g 7% • Dietary Fiber 2 g 8% • Sugars 5 g • Protein 12 g • Vitamin A 20% • Vitamin C 15% • Calcium 15% • Iron 6%
Dietary Exchanges: 1½ Starch, 1 High-Fat Meat, 3 Fat OR 1½ Carbohydrate, 1 High-Fat Meat, 3 Fat

Easy Ham 'n Noodle Casserole

Prep Time: 25 minutes (Ready in 1 hour)

Yield: 4 (1½-cup) servings

4	oz. (2½ cups) uncooked egg noodles
1	cup sour cream
1	(10¾-oz.) can condensed cream of mushroom soup
1	tablespoon instant minced onion
	Dash pepper
1	(1-lb.) pkg. frozen broccoli florets, carrots and cauliflower, thawed
2	cups cubed cooked ham
¼	cup cornflake crumbs
2	tablespoons margarine or butter, melted

1. Cook noodles to desired doneness as directed on package. Drain.

2. Meanwhile, heat oven to 350°F. Grease 2½-quart casserole. In small bowl, combine sour cream, soup, onion and pepper.

3. In greased casserole, combine cooked noodles, vegetables and ham. Pour soup mixture over noodle mixture; blend well. In small bowl, combine cornflake crumbs and melted margarine; mix well. Sprinkle evenly over casserole.

4. Bake at 350°F. for 30 to 35 minutes or until bubbly.

Nutrition Information Per Serving: Serving Size: 1½ Cups • Calories 510 • Calories from Fat 260 • % Daily Value • Total Fat 29 g 45% • Saturated 12 g 60% • Cholesterol 85 mg 28% • Sodium 1730 mg 72% • Total Carbohydrate 40 g 13% • Dietary Fiber 4 g 16% • Sugars 8 g • Protein 23 g • Vitamin A 70% • Vitamin C 35% • Calcium 15% • Iron 25%
Dietary Exchanges: 2½ Starch, 1 Vegetable, 2 Lean Meat, 4 Fat OR 2½ Carbohydrate, 1 Vegetable, 2 Lean Meat, 4 Fat

Cheesy Hot Dog Casserole

Crescent Brunch Dish

Prep Time: 35 minutes (Ready in 1 hour)

Yield: 8 servings

6   eggs
2   (8-oz.) cans refrigerated
      crescent dinner rolls
¼   cup margarine or butter
½   cup chopped green onions or
      onion
⅓   cup all-purpose flour
¼   teaspoon dried thyme leaves
¼   teaspoon pepper
1   (14½-oz.) can ready-to-serve
      chicken broth with ⅓ less
      sodium
1½ cups frozen mixed
      vegetables
2   cups diced cooked ham
1   egg, beaten
1   to 2 teaspoons sesame seed

1. Place eggs in medium saucepan; cover with cold water. Bring to a boil. Reduce heat; simmer about 15 minutes. Immediately drain; run cold water over eggs to stop cooking. Peel eggs; chop. Set aside.

2. Meanwhile, heat oven to 375°F. Separate 1 can of dough into 2 long rectangles. Keep remaining can refrigerated. Press rectangles over bottom and ½ inch up sides of ungreased 13x9-inch (3-quart) baking dish. Bake at 375°F. for 8 to 13 minutes or until light golden brown.

3. Melt margarine in medium saucepan over medium heat. Add green onions; cook and stir until crisp-tender. Stir in flour, thyme, pepper and broth. Cook 3 to 4 minutes or until mixture boils and thickens, stirring constantly. Reduce heat to low. Stir in vegetables; cook 4 to 6 minutes or until vegetables are crisp-tender.

4. Stir in ham and hard-cooked eggs; cook 3 to 5 minutes or until thoroughly heated. Spoon vegetable mixture over partially baked crust.

5. On sheet of waxed paper, unroll remaining can of dough into 2 long rectangles. Overlap long sides ½ inch; firmly press edges and perforations to seal. Press or roll to form 13x9-inch rectangle. Using small star-shaped cookie cutter, cut shapes out of dough; reserve cutouts to place on top. Invert dough rectangle over hot filling; remove waxed paper. Place star cutouts on top of dough. Brush with beaten egg; sprinkle with sesame seed.

6. Bake at 375°F. for 20 to 25 minutes or until deep golden brown.

Nutrition Information Per Serving: Serving Size: ⅛ of Recipe • Calories 410 • Calories from Fat 220 • % Daily Value • Total Fat 24 g 37% • Saturated 6 g 30% • Cholesterol 200 mg 67% • Sodium 1180 mg 49% • Total Carbohydrate 31 g 10% • Dietary Fiber 2 g 8% • Sugars 6 g • Protein 18 g • Vitamin A 20% • Vitamin C 4% • Calcium 6% • Iron 15%
Dietary Exchanges: 2 Starch, 1½ Medium-Fat Meat, 3 Fat OR 2 Carbohydrate, 1½ Medium-Fat Meat, 3 Fat

Baked Macaroni, Ham and Cheese

Prep Time: 30 minutes (Ready in 1 hour)

Yield: 4 servings

8   oz. (3½ cups) uncooked bow tie pasta (farfalle)
¼   cup butter
1   small garlic clove, minced
¼   cup all-purpose flour
2   cups milk
6   oz. (1½ cups) shredded extra-sharp Cheddar cheese
4   drops hot pepper sauce
1   cup julienne-cut (1½ x ¼ x ¼-inch) cooked ham

1. Heat oven to 375° F. Spray 1½-quart casserole with nonstick cooking spray.

2. Cook pasta to desired doneness as directed on package. Drain; return to saucepan.

3. Meanwhile, melt butter in medium saucepan over medium heat. Add garlic; cook 1 minute. With wire whisk, blend in flour; cook and stir 1 minute. Add milk; cook until mixture boils and thickens, stirring occasionally. Reduce heat to low. Add cheese; stir until melted.

4. Stir in hot pepper sauce. If desired, add salt and pepper to taste. Add ham; mix well. Add cheese sauce to cooked pasta; stir until well mixed. Spoon into sprayed casserole.

5. Bake at 375° F. for 25 to 30 minutes or until lightly browned and bubbly.

✳ **Make-Ahead Directions:** These make-ahead directions work best if you substitute an 8-inch square (2-quart) baking dish for the 1½-quart casserole. Prepare recipe as directed above; do not bake. Cover with foil; freeze. When ready to use, do not thaw; bake, covered, at 350° F. for 1½ hours. Uncover; bake an additional 10 minutes or until lightly browned and mixture is bubbly.

Nutrition Information Per Serving: Serving Size: ¼ of Recipe • Calories 620 • Calories from Fat 280 • % Daily Value • Total Fat 31 g 48% • Saturated 18 g 90% • Cholesterol 100 mg 33% • Sodium 950 mg 40% • Total Carbohydrate 55 g 18% • Dietary Fiber 2 g 8% • Sugars 9 g • Protein 30 g • Vitamin A 25% • Vitamin C 0% • Calcium 45% • Iron 20%

Dietary Exchanges: 3½ Starch, 3 High-Fat Meat, 1 Fat OR 3½ Carbohydrate, 3 High-Fat Meat, 1 Fat

Country Ham and Corn Casserole

Prep Time: 20 minutes (Ready in 1 hour 15 minutes)
Yield: 6 servings

2 cups cubed cooked ham
½ cup chopped green onions
½ cup margarine or butter, melted
3 eggs, well beaten
1 (15-oz.) can cream-style corn
1 (11-oz.) can vacuum-packed whole kernel corn with red and green peppers, drained
1 (7- to 8½-oz.) pkg. corn muffin mix
4 oz. (1 cup) shredded Cheddar cheese

1. Heat oven to 350°F. Grease 12x8-inch (2-quart) baking dish. In large bowl, combine all ingredients except cheese. Pour into greased baking dish.

2. Bake at 350°F. for 45 to 55 minutes or until golden brown and set. Sprinkle with cheese. Bake an additional 1 to 2 minutes or until cheese is melted. Let stand 5 minutes before serving. Cut into squares.

✳ **Make-Ahead Directions:** Prepare recipe as directed above except omit Cheddar cheese; do not bake. Cover with foil; freeze. When ready to use, do not thaw; bake, covered, at 350°F. for 1 hour 20 minutes. Uncover; sprinkle with Cheddar cheese. Bake an additional 25 minutes or until cheese is melted.

Nutrition Information Per Serving: Serving Size: ⅙ of Recipe • Calories 550 • Calories from Fat 270 • % Daily Value • Total Fat 30 g 46% • Saturated 9 g 45% • Cholesterol 150 mg 50% • Sodium 1610 mg 67% • Total Carbohydrate 50 g 17% • Dietary Fiber 3 g 12% • Sugars 16 g • Protein 21 g • Vitamin A 25% • Vitamin C 4% • Calcium 25% • Iron 10%
Dietary Exchanges: 3½ Starch, 1½ Medium-Fat Meat, 3½ Fat OR 3½ Carbohydrate, 1½ Medium-Fat Meat, 3½ Fat

Country Ham and Corn Casserole

Ham and Cheese Potato Bake

Ham and Cheese Potato Bake

Prep Time: 20 minutes (Ready in 40 minutes)
Yield: 8 (1-cup) servings

1½	cups skim milk
¼	cup all-purpose flour
½	teaspoon salt
¼	teaspoon pepper
8	cups frozen potatoes O'Brien with onions and peppers (from two 24-oz. pkg.), thawed, patted dry with paper towels
1½	cups (about 8 oz.) chopped 97% fat-free cooked ham
1	cup nonfat sour cream
6	oz. (1½ cups) shredded reduced-fat colby cheese

1. Heat oven to 400°F. Spray 13x9-inch (3-quart) baking dish with nonstick cooking spray.

2. In medium saucepan, combine milk, flour, salt and pepper; blend well. Cook and stir over medium-high heat until bubbly and thickened.

3. In large bowl, combine potatoes, ham, sour cream, cooked sauce and 1 cup of the cheese; mix well. Spoon potato mixture into sprayed baking dish. Sprinkle top with remaining ½ cup cheese.

4. Bake at 400°F. for 15 to 20 minutes or until casserole is bubbly and cheese is melted. Let stand 5 minutes before serving.

✳ **Make-Ahead Directions:** Prepare recipe as directed above except do not thaw potatoes and omit colby cheese; do not bake. Cover with foil; freeze. When ready to use, do not thaw; bake, covered, at 400°F. for 1 hour 20 minutes. Uncover, sprinkle with colby cheese. Bake an additional 25 minutes or until cheese is melted and mixture is bubbly.

Nutrition Information Per Serving: Serving Size: 1 Cup • Calories 230 • Calories from Fat 50 • % Daily Value • Total Fat 6 g 9% • Saturated 3 g 15% • Cholesterol 30 mg 10% • Sodium 670 mg 28% • Total Carbohydrate 28 g 9% • Dietary Fiber 2 g 8% • Sugars 6 g • Protein 16 g • Vitamin A 15% • Vitamin C 15% • Calcium 25% • Iron 8%
Dietary Exchanges: 2 Starch, 1½ Lean Meat OR 2 Carbohydrate, 1½ Lean Meat

Cooking Pasta

Al dente—literally, "to the tooth"—refers to the perfect stage of doneness when the pasta retains just the slightest bit of resistance at the center.

1. Bring a large, covered pot of water to a boil over high heat. When it comes to a full rolling boil, salt generously and add the pasta.

2. Stir the pasta at the beginning and periodically throughout cooking to prevent it from clumping together.

3. To test for doneness, remove a noodle from the pot with a slotted spoon. Run it under cold water just long enough to prevent you from burning your mouth when you taste it. For casseroles, noodles are perfect when the outside is cooked and tender but the inside still retains just a bit more crunch than you want in the finished dish.

4. Drain the pasta with a colander set into a sink, shaking occasionally to shed all the moisture. If you will not mix the noodles with other ingredients until later, toss with a little cooking oil to prevent the pasta from sticking together.

Bacon-Spaghetti Casserole

Prep Time: 30 minutes (Ready in 1 hour 30 minutes)

Yield: 5 (1½-cup) servings

1	(7-oz.) pkg. uncooked spaghetti, broken into thirds
½	lb. bacon, cut into 1-inch pieces
½	cup chopped onion
½	cup chopped green bell pepper
1	(28-oz.) can whole tomatoes, undrained, cut up
8	oz. (2 cups) shredded American cheese

1. Heat oven to 325° F. Cook spaghetti to desired doneness as directed on package. Drain; rinse with hot water.

2. Meanwhile, in large skillet, cook bacon over medium heat until crisp. Drain bacon on paper towels; set aside. Drain all but 1 tablespoon bacon drippings from skillet.

3. Stir in onion and bell pepper; cook until crisp-tender. Add cooked spaghetti, bacon, tomatoes and 1½ cups of the cheese; mix well. Place in ungreased 2-quart casserole.

4. Bake at 325° F. for 45 to 60 minutes or until hot and bubbly. Top with remaining ½ cup cheese. Bake an additional 5 minutes or until cheese is melted.

Nutrition Information Per Serving: Serving Size: 1½ Cups • Calories 460 • Calories from Fat 220 • % Daily Value • Total Fat 24 g 37% • Saturated 12 g 60% • Cholesterol 55 mg 18% • Sodium 1090 mg 45% • Total Carbohydrate 39 g 13% • Dietary Fiber 3 g 12% • Sugars 6 g • Protein 21 g • Vitamin A 30% • Vitamin C 40% • Calcium 35% • Iron 15%
Dietary Exchanges: 2½ Starch, 1 Vegetable, 1½ High-Fat Meat, 2 Fat OR 2½ Carbohydrate, 1 Vegetable, 1½ High-Fat Meat, 2 Fat

Pepperoni Pizza Pasta

Prep Time: 25 minutes (Ready in 1 hour)

Yield: 4 servings

8   oz. (2 cups) uncooked ziti (long tubular pasta)
1   (14-oz.) jar pizza sauce
2   oz. sliced pepperoni, halved (about ¾ cup)
¼   cup finely chopped green bell pepper
¼   cup grated Parmesan cheese
½   teaspoon dried oregano leaves
1   garlic clove, minced
4   oz. (1 cup) shredded mozzarella cheese

1. Heat oven to 375°F. Spray 8-inch square (2-quart) baking dish with nonstick cooking spray.

2. Cook ziti to desired doneness as directed on package. Drain.

3. In large bowl, combine cooked ziti, pizza sauce, pepperoni, bell pepper, Parmesan cheese, oregano and garlic; mix well. Spoon into sprayed baking dish; sprinkle with mozzarella cheese. Cover with foil.

4. Bake at 375°F. for 30 to 35 minutes or until mixture is thoroughly heated and cheese is melted.

✳ **Make-Ahead Directions:** Prepare recipe as directed above except omit mozzarella cheese; do not bake. Cover with foil; freeze. When ready to use, do not thaw; bake, covered, at 375°F. for 1 hour. Uncover; sprinkle with mozzarella cheese. Bake an additional 10 minutes or until cheese is melted and mixture is bubbly.

Nutrition Information Per Serving: Serving Size: ¼ of Recipe • Calories 440 • Calories from Fat 140 • % Daily Value • Total Fat 16 g 25% • Saturated 8 g 40% • Cholesterol 30 mg 10% • Sodium 1180 mg 49% • Total Carbohydrate 51 g 17% • Dietary Fiber 2 g 8% • Sugars 8 g • Protein 22 g • Vitamin A 15% • Vitamin C 10% • Calcium 30% • Iron 20%
Dietary Exchanges: 3½ Starch, 1½ High-Fat Meat, ½ Fat OR 3½ Carbohydrate, 1½ High-Fat Meat, ½ Fat

Make-Ahead Spaghetti and Meatball Casserole

Prep Time: 15 minutes (Ready in 9 hours)

Yield: 6 servings

1   (7-oz.) pkg. uncooked ready-cut spaghetti or elbow macaroni (short curved pasta)
1   cup water
1   (28-oz.) jar spaghetti sauce
12 frozen precooked Italian meatballs
2   tablespoons shredded fresh Parmesan cheese
2   tablespoons finely chopped fresh parsley

1. Grease 12x8-inch (2-quart) baking dish. In greased baking dish, combine uncooked spaghetti, water and spaghetti sauce; mix well. Add meatballs; turn to coat with sauce. (Cover spaghetti completely with sauce.) Cover tightly with foil; refrigerate at least 8 hours or overnight.

2. Heat oven to 350°F. Bake covered for 45 minutes. Uncover; sprinkle with cheese. Bake uncovered for an additional 5 to 10 minutes or until casserole is bubbly and cheese is melted. Sprinkle with parsley.

Nutrition Information Per Serving: Serving Size: ⅙ of Recipe • Calories 290 • Calories from Fat 90 • % Daily Value • Total Fat 10 g 15% • Saturated 4 g 20% • Cholesterol 15 mg 5% • Sodium 720 mg 30% • Total Carbohydrate 38 g 13% • Dietary Fiber 4 g 16% • Sugars 1 g • Protein 11 g • Vitamin A 10% • Vitamin C 15% • Calcium 8% • Iron 15%
Dietary Exchanges: 2½ Starch, ½ Medium-Fat Meat, 1 Fat OR 2½ Carbohydrate, ½ Medium-Fat Meat, 1 Fat

Prosciutto Basil Pasta Shells

Prep Time: 30 minutes (Ready in 1 hour 10 minutes)

Yield: 4 servings

12	jumbo shell pasta
1	tablespoon olive oil or vegetable oil
2	garlic cloves, minced
¾	cup chopped prosciutto or cooked ham
1	cup ricotta cheese
⅓	cup grated Parmesan cheese
1	tablespoon chopped fresh basil or ½ teaspoon dried basil leaves
1	egg
1	(14-oz.) jar spaghetti sauce

1. Heat oven to 375° F. Spray 8-inch square (2-quart) baking dish with nonstick cooking spray.

2. Cook pasta to desired doneness as directed on package. Drain; rinse with cold water to cool.

3. Meanwhile, heat oil in medium skillet over medium heat until hot. Add garlic and prosciutto; cook 2 to 3 minutes or until garlic is light golden brown.

4. In medium bowl, combine ½ the prosciutto mixture with ricotta cheese, Parmesan cheese, basil and egg; mix well. Stir spaghetti sauce into prosciutto mixture remaining in skillet.

5. Spoon ricotta mixture into cooked shells; place in sprayed baking dish. Spoon spaghetti sauce mixture over shells. Cover with foil.

6. Bake at 375° F. for 35 to 40 minutes or until mixture is thoroughly heated.

Nutrition Information Per Serving: Serving Size: ¼ of Recipe • Calories 360 • Calories from Fat 140 • % Daily Value • Total Fat 16 g 25% • Saturated 6 g 30% • Cholesterol 90 mg 30% • Sodium 1030 mg 43% • Total Carbohydrate 32 g 11% • Dietary Fiber 2 g 8% • Sugars 2 g • Protein 22 g • Vitamin A 15% • Vitamin C 10% • Calcium 30% • Iron 15%
Dietary Exchanges: 2 Starch, 2½ Lean Meat, 1½ Fat OR 2 Carbohydrate, 2½ Lean Meat, 1½ Fat

Calcium Booster

Dairy products are a good source of calcium, an important mineral for strong bones and teeth. To pack even more calcium into casseroles made with milk- or cream-based sauces, dissolve about ½ cup of nonfat instant milk powder into the milk before adding it to the other ingredients. The enrichment won't change the texture or flavor of the recipe.

Mediterranean Baked Chicken, page 55; Prosciutto Basil Pasta Shells

focus on lasagna

asagna is an all-around favorite for family meals, entertaining or sharing at a potluck. Although most people picture broad noodles layered with tomato sauce (with or without meat), mozzarella and ricotta cheese, the layers can include other sauces and fillings.

Lazy-Day Overnight Lasagna

Prep Time: 35 minutes (Ready in 13 hours 35 minutes)

Yield: 12 servings

1	lb. ground beef or mild Italian sausage
1	(28-oz.) jar spaghetti sauce
1	cup water
1	(15-oz.) container ricotta cheese
2	tablespoons chopped fresh chives
½	teaspoon dried oregano leaves
1	egg
8	oz. uncooked lasagna noodles
1	(16-oz.) pkg. sliced mozzarella cheese
2	tablespoons grated Parmesan cheese

1. In large skillet, cook ground beef over medium heat for 8 to 10 minutes or until thoroughly cooked, stirring frequently. Drain well. Add spaghetti sauce and water; blend well.

2. In medium bowl, combine ricotta cheese, chives, oregano and egg; mix well.

3. In ungreased 13 x 9-inch (3-quart) baking dish or lasagna pan, spread 1½ cups of the meat sauce. Top with ½ each of the uncooked noodles, ricotta cheese mixture and mozzarella cheese. Repeat with 1½ cups meat sauce and remaining noodles, ricotta cheese mixture and mozzarella cheese. Top with remaining meat sauce. Sprinkle with Parmesan cheese. Cover; refrigerate 12 hours or overnight.

4. Heat oven to 350° F. Uncover; bake 50 to 60 minutes or until noodles are tender and casserole is bubbly. Cover; let stand 15 minutes before serving.

Nutrition Information Per Serving: Serving Size: ¹⁄₁₂ of Recipe • Calories 350 • Calories from Fat 150 • % Daily Value • Total Fat 17 g 26% • Saturated 9 g 45% • Cholesterol 75 mg 25% • Sodium 580 mg 24% • Total Carbohydrate 23 g 8% • Dietary Fiber 2 g 8% • Sugars 1 g • Protein 25 g • Vitamin A 15% • Vitamin C 6% • Calcium 40% • Iron 10%
Dietary Exchanges: 1½ Starch, 3 Medium-Fat Meat OR 1½ Carbohydrate, 3 Medium-Fat Meat

Light Italian Classic Lasagna

Prep Time: 45 minutes (Ready in 2 hours 15 minutes)
Yield: 8 servings

NOODLES
6 uncooked lasagna noodles

MEAT SAUCE
½ lb. lean ground turkey or extra-lean ground beef
½ lb. turkey Italian sausage, casings removed
1 cup chopped fresh mushrooms
¾ cup chopped green bell pepper
¾ cup chopped onions
1 (28-oz.) can Italian plum tomatoes, undrained, cut up
1 (6-oz.) can tomato paste
1 teaspoon dried basil leaves
½ teaspoon dried oregano leaves
½ teaspoon sugar
¼ teaspoon garlic powder
¼ teaspoon salt

CHEESE MIXTURE
1 (15-oz.) container light ricotta cheese
1 cup nonfat cottage cheese
2 egg whites, beaten
¼ cup grated Parmesan cheese
¼ cup chopped fresh parsley
8 oz. (2 cups) shredded mozzarella cheese

1. Cook lasagna noodles to desired doneness as directed on package. Drain; place in cold water.

2. Meanwhile, in large saucepan or Dutch oven, combine ground turkey, sausage, mushrooms, bell pepper and onions. Cook over medium heat until ground turkey and sausage are no longer pink. Drain. Add remaining meat sauce ingredients. Bring to a boil. Reduce heat to low; simmer uncovered 30 to 45 minutes or until very thick, stirring occasionally.

3. In medium bowl, combine all cheese mixture ingredients except mozzarella cheese; blend well.

4. Heat oven to 350°F. Spread about ½ cup of the meat sauce in bottom of ungreased 13x9-inch (3-quart) baking dish. Drain noodles. Top meat sauce with 3 noodles, ½ the ricotta cheese mixture and ½ the remaining meat sauce. Repeat layers. Top with mozzarella cheese.

5. Bake at 350°F. for 35 to 45 minutes or until bubbly. Let stand covered for 10 to 15 minutes before serving.

Nutrition Information Per Serving: Serving Size: ⅛ of Recipe • Calories 380 • Calories from Fat 140 • % Daily Value • Total Fat 15 g 23% • Saturated 8 g 40% • Cholesterol 65 mg 22% • Sodium 950 mg 40% • Total Carbohydrate 28 g 9% • Dietary Fiber 3 g 12% • Sugars 7 g • Protein 33 g • Vitamin A 35% • Vitamin C 40% • Calcium 50% • Iron 15%
Dietary Exchanges: 1½ Starch, 1 Vegetable, 4 Lean Meat, ½ Fat OR 1½ Carbohydrate, 1 Vegetable, 4 Lean Meat, ½ Fat

Petite Lasagna

Lasagna traditionally serves 8 to 12 people, which makes it a difficult choice when serving a small family or when cooking for two. Here is a terrific recipe that's easy to make and serves 2 to 3 people.

STEP 1

Thaw the frozen noodles and lay them on a clean, flat surface. Using a kitchen shears or sharp knife, cut one of the noodles in half lengthwise to fit the 9 x 5-inch loaf baking dish.

STEP 2

Spoon ¼ cup meat mixture into the bottom of the baking dish. Place 1½ noodles in the dish lengthwise with the ruffled portion of the noodles to the outside edge of the dish. If necessary, overlap the noodles slightly. Layer half of the ricotta mixture, meat mixture and mozzarella; repeat layers starting with the noodles.

Three 12-inch cooked and drained lasagna noodles can be substituted for the frozen precooked noodles. Cut each noodle to a 9-inch length. Use two of the noodles for the first layer. For the second noodle layer, place one 9-inch noodle lengthwise in the dish; use two cut ends for the remaining noodle.

Precooked Lasagna Noodles

Precooked or ready-to-use noodles make lasagna recipes easier than ever. The noodles are fully cooked, then frozen. Look for them in the frozen food section of the supermarket. They come in strips that look like traditional lasagna noodles or in sheets that can be broken into strips. The noodles can be used frozen or thawed, with no boiling required in either case. To thaw, let them stand at room temperature for 10 to 20 minutes.

Petite Lasagna

Prep Time: 20 minutes (Ready in 55 minutes)
Yield: 3 servings

½ lb. lean ground beef or bulk mild Italian sausage
¼ cup chopped onion
¼ cup chopped green bell pepper
¼ cup chopped fresh mushrooms
1 (14-oz.) jar spaghetti sauce
¾ cup low-fat ricotta cheese
2 tablespoons grated Parmesan cheese
2 tablespoons chopped fresh parsley
1 egg, beaten
3 frozen precooked lasagna noodles (1 sheet), thawed
4 oz. (1 cup) shredded mozzarella cheese

1. Heat oven to 350° F. Spray medium nonstick skillet with nonstick cooking spray. Add ground beef, onion and bell pepper. Cook and stir until browned; drain. Reduce heat to low; stir in mushrooms and spaghetti sauce. Simmer 5 minutes, stirring occasionally.

2. In small bowl, combine ricotta cheese, Parmesan cheese, parsley and egg; mix well. If lasagna noodles are in perforated sheet, separate at perforations. Cut 1 of the lasagna noodles in half lengthwise.

3. Spread ¼ cup meat mixture in bottom of ungreased 9 x 5-inch (2-quart) loaf baking dish. Top with 1½ lasagna noodles, ½ the ricotta mixture, ½ the remaining meat mixture and ½ the mozzarella cheese. Repeat layers, starting with noodles and ending with mozzarella cheese.

4. Bake at 350° F. for 30 to 35 minutes or until thoroughly heated and bubbly.

Nutrition Information Per Serving: Serving Size: ⅓ of Recipe • Calories 460 • Calories from Fat 150 • % Daily Value • Total Fat 17 g 26% • Saturated 6 g 30% • Cholesterol 85 mg 28% • Sodium 980 mg 41% • Total Carbohydrate 34 g 11% • Dietary Fiber 3 g 12% • Sugars 2 g • Protein 42 g • Vitamin A 30% • Vitamin C 25% • Calcium 50% • Iron 20%
Dietary Exchanges: 2 Starch, 1 Vegetable, 5 Lean Meat OR 2 Carbohydrate, 1 Vegetable, 5 Lean Meat

Petite Lasagna

Southwest Lasagna

Prep Time: 35 minutes (Ready in 1 hour 25 minutes)

Yield: 12 servings

9	uncooked lasagna noodles
1	lb. extra-lean ground beef
1	(1¼-oz.) pkg. 40% less sodium taco seasoning mix
¾	cup water
1	(15-oz.) container ricotta cheese
1	(4½-oz.) can chopped green chiles
2	eggs
1	(30-oz.) jar spaghetti sauce
2	teaspoons cumin
1	(9-oz.) pkg. frozen whole kernel corn in a pouch, thawed, drained*
1	(15-oz.) can black beans, drained, rinsed
12	oz. (3 cups) shredded Monterey Jack cheese

1. Heat oven to 375° F. Spray 13 x 9-inch (3-quart) baking dish with nonstick cooking spray. Cook lasagna noodles to desired doneness as directed on package. Drain; rinse with cold water to cool. Drain well.

2. Meanwhile, in large skillet, brown ground beef over medium-high heat until thoroughly cooked. Drain. Add taco seasoning mix and water; simmer 5 minutes or until thickened.

3. In small bowl, combine ricotta cheese, green chiles and eggs; mix well. In medium bowl, combine spaghetti sauce and cumin; blend well.

4. To assemble, place 3 lasagna noodles over bottom of sprayed baking dish. Spoon and spread ⅓ the ricotta mixture over noodles; top with ⅓ each of beef mixture, corn, beans, sauce and cheese. Repeat layers 2 more times.

5. Bake at 375° F. for 40 to 50 minutes or until thoroughly heated. Place cookie sheet or foil on rack below lasagna to catch any spills. Let stand 10 minutes before serving.

☀ **Make-Ahead Directions:** Prepare recipe as directed above except omit Monterey Jack cheese; do not bake. Cover with foil; freeze. When ready to use, do not thaw; bake, covered, at 350° F. for 1 hour 40 minutes. Uncover; sprinkle with Monterey Jack cheese. Bake an additional 20 minutes or until mixture is thoroughly heated.

Tip: *To quickly thaw corn, remove corn from pouch; place in colander or strainer. Rinse with warm water until thawed; drain well. Or cut small slit in center of pouch; microwave on HIGH for 2 to 3 minutes or until thawed. Remove corn from pouch; drain well.

Nutrition Information Per Serving: Serving Size: 1/12 of Recipe • Calories 390 • Calories from Fat 170 • % Daily Value • Total Fat 19 g 29% • Saturated 9 g 45% • Cholesterol 95 mg 32% • Sodium 840 mg 35% • Total Carbohydrate 30 g 10% • Dietary Fiber 4 g 16% • Sugars 3 g • Protein 25 g • Vitamin A 15% • Vitamin C 10% • Calcium 35% • Iron 20%
Dietary Exchanges: 2 Starch, 2½ Lean Meat, 2 Fat OR 2 Carbohydrate, 2½ Lean Meat, 2 Fat

Chicken, Spinach and Mushroom Lasagna

Prep Time: 50 minutes (Ready in 1 hour 45 minutes)

Yield: 8 servings

9	uncooked lasagna noodles
3	cups milk
2	teaspoons dried Italian seasoning
1	teaspoon garlic salt
1	cup chicken broth
3	tablespoons cornstarch
¼	cup grated Parmesan cheese
1	(1-lb.) pkg. frozen cut leaf spinach, thawed, squeezed to drain*
½	cup chopped green onions
4	oz. (1 cup) shredded mozzarella cheese
2	cups sliced fresh mushrooms
2	cups cubed cooked chicken

1. Cook lasagna noodles to desired doneness as directed on package. Drain; place in cold water.

2. Meanwhile, heat oven to 350° F. In large saucepan, combine milk, Italian seasoning and garlic salt. Bring to a boil. In small bowl, combine broth and cornstarch; blend well. Slowly add cornstarch mixture to hot milk mixture, stirring constantly. Cook over medium heat for 5 minutes or until bubbly and thickened, stirring constantly. Stir in Parmesan cheese.

3. Drain noodles. Spread ½ cup white sauce in bottom of ungreased 13 x 9-inch (3-quart) baking dish. Top with 3 noodles. In medium bowl, combine 1 cup white sauce, all the spinach, green onions and ½ the mozzarella cheese; spread evenly over noodles. Arrange 3 noodles over spinach mixture.

4. In same medium bowl, combine 1 cup white sauce, mushrooms and chicken; spread over noodles. Arrange 3 noodles over chicken mixture. Top with remaining white sauce. Cover tightly with foil.

5. Bake at 350° F. for 50 to 55 minutes or until hot and bubbly. Uncover; sprinkle with remaining mozzarella cheese. Let stand 15 minutes. If desired, garnish with fresh Italian parsley.

Tip: *To quickly thaw spinach, place in colander or strainer; rinse with warm water until thawed. Squeeze dry with paper towels.

Nutrition Information Per Serving: Serving Size: ⅛ of Recipe • Calories 280 • Calories from Fat 60 • % Daily Value • Total Fat 7 g 11% • Saturated 3 g 15% • Cholesterol 45 mg 15% • Sodium 590 mg 25% • Total Carbohydrate 29 g 10% • Dietary Fiber 3 g 12% • Sugars 6 g • Protein 25 g • Vitamin A 60% • Vitamin C 15% • Calcium 35% • Iron 15%

Dietary Exchanges: 1½ Starch, 1 Vegetable, 2½ Lean Meat OR 1½ Carbohydrate, 1 Vegetable, 2½ Lean Meat

Lasagna with Golden Flaky Topping

Prep Time: 35 minutes (Ready in 1 hour 5 minutes)

Yield: 6 servings

Photo below and page 5

1   lb. ground beef
¼   cup chopped onion or
        1 tablespoon instant
        minced onion
1   (8-oz.) can tomato sauce
1   (6-oz.) can tomato paste
1   (4-oz.) can mushroom pieces
        and stems, drained
1   teaspoon dried basil leaves
1   teaspoon dried parsley flakes
½   teaspoon dried oregano leaves
¼   teaspoon salt, if desired
¼   teaspoon garlic salt
¼   teaspoon pepper
1   cup cottage cheese
1   cup chopped fresh spinach
4   oz. (1 cup) shredded
        mozzarella cheese
1   (12-oz.) can refrigerated
        flaky biscuits
1   tablespoon dried parsley
        flakes

1. Heat oven to 375° F. In large skillet, brown ground beef and onion until thoroughly cooked. Drain. Add tomato sauce, tomato paste, mushrooms, basil, 1 teaspoon parsley flakes, oregano, salt, garlic salt and pepper; mix well. Reduce heat; simmer 15 minutes.

2. In small bowl, combine cottage cheese and spinach; mix well. In ungreased 12x8-inch (2-quart) baking dish, layer ½ each of meat mixture, cottage cheese mixture and mozzarella cheese; repeat layers.

3. Separate biscuit dough into 10 biscuits. Separate each biscuit into 3 layers; arrange biscuits over cheese layer, overlapping slightly. Sprinkle with 1 tablespoon parsley flakes.

4. Bake at 375° F. for 25 to 30 minutes or until golden brown. Let stand 5 minutes before serving.

Nutrition Information Per Serving: Serving Size: ⅙ of Recipe • Calories 470 • Calories from Fat 220 • % Daily Value • Total Fat 24 g 37% • Saturated 9 g 45% • Cholesterol 60 mg 20% • Sodium 1600 mg 67% • Total Carbohydrate 35 g 12% • Dietary Fiber 3 g 12% • Sugars 6 g • Protein 28 g • Vitamin A 40% • Vitamin C 25% • Calcium 20% • Iron 25%
Dietary Exchanges: 2 Starch, 1 Vegetable, 3 Medium-Fat Meat, 1½ Fat OR 2 Carbohydrate, 1 Vegetable, 3 Medium-Fat Meat, 1½ Fat

Lasagna with
Golden Flaky Topping

Mexi-Lasagna

Mexi-Lasagna

Prep Time: 25 minutes (Ready in 45 minutes)

Yield: 6 servings

4 oz. (2 cups) uncooked mini-lasagna noodles (mafalda)
½ lb. ground beef
1 (15½- or 15-oz.) can kidney beans, drained
1 (14½-oz.) can chili-style tomatoes, undrained
1 (8-oz.) can tomato sauce
8 oz. (2 cups) shredded Monterey Jack cheese
1 (4½-oz.) can chopped green chiles

1. Heat oven to 350°F. Spray 12x8-inch (2-quart) baking dish with nonstick cooking spray. Cook noodles to desired doneness as directed on package. Drain.

2. Meanwhile, in large skillet, cook ground beef over medium-high heat until thoroughly cooked. Drain. Add kidney beans, tomatoes and tomato sauce; cook until thoroughly heated, stirring occasionally.

3. Spoon cooked noodles evenly into sprayed baking dish. Sprinkle with 1 cup of the cheese, all of the beef mixture, green chiles and remaining 1 cup cheese.

4. Bake at 350°F. for 20 minutes or until edges are bubbly and mixture is thoroughly heated.

✳ **Make-Ahead Directions:** Prepare recipe as directed above except omit Monterey Jack cheese; do not bake. Cover with foil; freeze. When ready to use, do not thaw; bake, covered, at 350°F. for 1 hour 15 minutes. Uncover; sprinkle with Monterey Jack cheese. Bake an additional 20 minutes or until mixture is thoroughly heated.

Nutrition Information Per Serving: Serving Size: ⅙ of Recipe • Calories 370 • Calories from Fat 150 • % Daily Value • Total Fat 17 g 26% • Saturated 9 g 45% • Cholesterol 55 mg 18% • Sodium 770 mg 32% • Total Carbohydrate 32 g 11% • Dietary Fiber 5 g 20% • Sugars 4 g • Protein 22 g • Vitamin A 20% • Vitamin C 20% • Calcium 35% • Iron 20%
Dietary Exchanges: 2 Starch, 1 Vegetable, 2 High-Fat Meat OR 2 Carbohydrate, 1 Vegetable, 2 High-Fat Meat

Italian Classic Lasagna

Prep Time: 45 minutes (Ready in 2 hours 15 minutes)
Yield: 8 servings

NOODLES
6 uncooked lasagna noodles

MEAT SAUCE
1 lb. ground beef
½ lb. bulk mild Italian sausage
¾ cup chopped onions
1 (28-oz.) can Italian-style plum tomatoes, undrained, cut up
1 (6-oz.) can tomato paste
1 teaspoon dried basil leaves
½ teaspoon dried oregano leaves
½ teaspoon sugar
¼ teaspoon garlic powder
¼ teaspoon salt

CHEESE MIXTURE
1 (15-oz.) container ricotta cheese
1 cup cottage cheese
2 eggs, beaten
½ cup grated Parmesan cheese
¼ cup chopped fresh parsley
1 lb. (4 cups) shredded mozzarella cheese

1. Cook lasagna noodles to desired doneness as directed on package. Drain; place in cold water.

2. Meanwhile, in large saucepan or Dutch oven, combine ground beef, sausage and onions. Cook over medium heat for 8 to 10 minutes or until thoroughly cooked, stirring frequently. Drain. Add remaining meat sauce ingredients. Bring to a boil. Reduce heat to low; simmer uncovered 30 to 45 minutes or until very thick, stirring occasionally.

3. In medium bowl, combine all cheese mixture ingredients except mozzarella cheese; blend well.

4. Heat oven to 350°F. Spread about ½ cup meat sauce over bottom of ungreased 13x9-inch (3-quart) baking dish. Drain noodles. Top meat sauce with 3 noodles, ½ the ricotta cheese mixture, ½ the remaining meat sauce and ½ the mozzarella cheese. Repeat layers, ending with mozzarella cheese.

5. Bake at 350°F. for 35 to 45 minutes or until bubbly. Let stand covered for 10 to 15 minutes before serving.

✳ **Make-Ahead Directions:** Prepare recipe as directed above except omit top layer mozzarella cheese; do not bake. Cover with foil; freeze. When ready to use, do not thaw; bake, covered, at 350°F. for 1 hour 50 minutes. Uncover; add top layer mozzarella cheese. Bake an additional 25 minutes or until mixture is thoroughly heated and bubbly. Let stand 10 to 15 minutes before serving.

Nutrition Information Per Serving: Serving Size: ⅛ of Recipe • Calories 590 • Calories from Fat 290 • % Daily Value • Total Fat 32 g 49% • Saturated 16 g 80% • Cholesterol 160 mg 53% • Sodium 1220 mg 51% • Total Carbohydrate 28 g 9% • Dietary Fiber 3 g 12% • Sugars 6 g • Protein 47 g • Vitamin A 40% • Vitamin C 30% • Calcium 70% • Iron 20%
Dietary Exchanges: 1½ Starch, 1 Vegetable, 6 Medium-Fat Meat OR 1½ Carbohydrate, 1 Vegetable, 6 Medium-Fat Meat

Lean Lasagna

Prep Time: 45 minutes (Ready in 1 hour 25 minutes)
Yield: 8 servings

10	uncooked lasagna noodles
1	lb. extra-lean ground beef
1	cup chopped onions
2	garlic cloves, minced
3	teaspoons dried parsley flakes
1	teaspoon salt
1	teaspoon dried basil leaves
1	teaspoon dried oregano leaves
½	teaspoon fennel seed
3	(8-oz.) cans no-salt-added tomato sauce
1	cup light ricotta or cottage cheese
2	egg whites
4	oz. (1 cup) shredded mozzarella cheese
2	tablespoons grated Parmesan cheese

1. Cook lasagna noodles to desired doneness as directed on package. Drain; cover to keep warm.

2. Meanwhile, heat oven to 350° F. In large skillet, brown ground beef, onions and garlic until beef is thoroughly cooked. Drain well. Stir in parsley, salt, basil, oregano, fennel seed and tomato sauce. Reduce heat to low; simmer 10 minutes, stirring occasionally.

3. In small bowl, combine ricotta cheese and egg whites; blend well.

4. Spoon and spread ¼ cup beef mixture into ungreased 13 x 9-inch (3-quart) baking dish. Top with ½ each of the cooked noodles, beef mixture and ricotta cheese mixture. Repeat layers. Sprinkle with mozzarella and Parmesan cheeses.

5. Bake at 350° F. for 35 to 40 minutes or until hot and bubbly. Let stand 10 minutes before serving.

✳ **Make-Ahead Directions:** Prepare recipe as directed above except omit mozzarella and Parmesan cheese; do not bake. Cover with foil; freeze. When ready to use, do not thaw; bake, covered, at 350° F. for 1 hour 35 minutes. Uncover; sprinkle with mozzarella and Parmesan cheese. Bake an additional 30 minutes or until mixture is bubbly. Let stand 10 minutes before serving.

Nutrition Information Per Serving: Serving Size: ⅛ of Recipe • Calories 320 • Calories from Fat 120 • % Daily Value • Total Fat 13 g 20% • Saturated 6 g 30% • Cholesterol 55 mg 18% • Sodium 460 mg 19% • Total Carbohydrate 27 g 9% • Dietary Fiber 1 g 4% • Sugars 5 g • Protein 24 g • Vitamin A 6% • Vitamin C 20% • Calcium 20% • Iron 15%
Dietary Exchanges: 1½ Starch, 1 Vegetable, 2½ Lean Meat, 1 Fat OR 1½ Carbohydrate, 1 Vegetable, 2½ Lean Meat, 1 Fat

Lasagna-Making Tips

◆ When you boil the pasta, add about 1 tablespoon of oil to the water to prevent the noodles from sticking together.

◆ Since the noodles will cook further in the oven for most lasagna recipes, drain the pot while the noodles are still slightly underdone.

◆ Use cooked noodles immediately. They can become hopelessly sticky if they stand too long. If noodles stick, rinse them in cold water.

◆ Under the bottom layer of noodles, ladle a generous coating of sauce to prevent the noodles from sticking to the pan or spray with nonstick cooking oil.

◆ Cover the pan with foil and set the lasagna in a preheated oven; 10 or 15 minutes before it should be done, remove the foil to let the top brown.

Broccoli-Shrimp Lasagna

Prep Time: 40 minutes (Ready in 1 hour 10 minutes)

Yield: 8 servings

6	uncooked lasagna noodles
1	(1-lb.) pkg. frozen cut broccoli
3	tablespoons margarine or butter
¼	cup all-purpose flour
¼	cup sliced green onions
¼	teaspoon salt
¼	teaspoon dry mustard
¼	teaspoon dried thyme leaves
⅛	teaspoon ground red pepper (cayenne)
2½	cups milk
4	oz. (1 cup) shredded Monterey Jack cheese
10	oz. (2½ cups) shredded Cheddar cheese
1	lb. shelled, deveined, cooked medium shrimp

1. Cook lasagna noodles to desired doneness as directed on package. Drain; place in cold water. Cook frozen broccoli until crisp-tender as directed on package. Drain.

2. Meanwhile, melt margarine in medium saucepan over medium heat. Stir in flour, green onions, salt, dry mustard, thyme and ground red pepper. Gradually add milk, stirring constantly. Cook and stir until mixture is bubbly and thickened. Remove from heat. Add Monterey Jack cheese; stir until melted.

3. Heat oven to 350°F. Drain noodles. In ungreased 13x9-inch (3-quart) baking dish, layer ½ cup sauce, 3 noodles, all of the cooked broccoli, ½ cup of the Cheddar cheese and 1 cup sauce. Top with remaining 3 noodles, all of the shrimp, 1 cup of the Cheddar cheese, the remaining sauce and the remaining 1 cup cheese.

4. Bake at 350°F. for 30 minutes or until hot and bubbly. Let stand 10 minutes before serving.

Nutrition Information Per Serving: Serving Size: ⅛ of Recipe • Calories 420 • Calories from Fat 210 • % Daily Value • Total Fat 23 g 35% • Saturated 12 g 60% • Cholesterol 165 mg 55% • Sodium 600 mg 25% • Total Carbohydrate 22 g 7% • Dietary Fiber 2 g 8% • Sugars 6 g • Protein 31 g • Vitamin A 25% • Vitamin C 35% • Calcium 50% • Iron 20%
Dietary Exchanges: 1½ Starch, 4 Lean Meat, 2 Fat OR 1½ Carbohydrate, 4 Lean Meat, 2 Fat

Broccoli-Shrimp Lasagna

Creamy Mushroom Lasagna with Fresh Tomatoes

Prep Time: 1 hour (Ready in 1 hour 30 minutes)
Yield: 8 servings

LASAGNA

1	oz. (1 cup) dried porcini mushrooms
8	uncooked lasagna noodles
1	(15-oz.) container light ricotta cheese
2	eggs
½	cup grated Parmesan cheese
2	tablespoons chopped fresh parsley or 2 teaspoons dried parsley flakes
½	teaspoon salt
⅛	teaspoon pepper
2	teaspoons olive oil or vegetable oil
5	oz. (1⅔ cups) sliced fresh cremini or white mushrooms
1	large garlic clove, minced
2	tablespoons dry sherry
¼	cup whipping cream
8	oz. (2 cups) shredded provolone cheese

TOMATOES

2	teaspoons olive oil or vegetable oil
2	tablespoons finely chopped shallots
1	garlic clove, minced
2	tablespoons chopped fresh basil or 2 teaspoons dried basil leaves
6	large Italian plum tomatoes, chopped (2 cups)

1. Rehydrate dried mushrooms as directed on package. Drain mushrooms; coarsely chop. Set aside.

2. Meanwhile, cook lasagna noodles to desired doneness as directed on package. Drain.

3. Heat oven to 350° F. Spray 13x9-inch (3-quart) baking dish with nonstick cooking spray.

4. In large bowl, combine ricotta cheese, eggs, Parmesan cheese, parsley, salt and pepper; mix well. Set aside.

5. In large skillet, heat 2 teaspoons oil over medium heat until hot. Add rehydrated mushrooms, cremini mushrooms and minced large garlic clove; cook and stir 2 to 3 minutes or until mushrooms are tender. Add sherry; cook until most of the liquid has evaporated. Stir in cream; bring to a boil. Remove skillet from heat.

6. To assemble lasagna, arrange 4 cooked noodles in bottom of sprayed dish. Spoon and spread ½ the cheese mixture over noodles. Evenly spoon ½ the mushroom mixture over cheese. Sprinkle with ½ the provolone cheese. Repeat layers. Cover with foil.

7. Bake at 350° F. for 20 to 30 minutes or until filling is set and edges are bubbly.

8. While lasagna is baking, prepare tomatoes. In same large skillet, heat 2 teaspoons oil over medium heat until hot. Add shallots and 1 minced garlic clove; cook and stir until tender. Stir in basil and tomatoes; cook just until thoroughly heated. Spoon tomatoes over individual servings of lasagna.

Nutrition Information Per Serving: Serving Size: ⅛ of Recipe • Calories 380 • Calories from Fat 190 • % Daily Value • Total Fat 21 g 32% • Saturated 11 g 55% • Cholesterol 105 mg 35% • Sodium 590 mg 25% • Total Carbohydrate 26 g 9% • Dietary Fiber 2 g 8% • Sugars 4 g • Protein 22 g • Vitamin A 20% • Vitamin C 15% • Calcium 45% • Iron 10%
Dietary Exchanges: 1½ Starch, 1 Vegetable, 2 High-Fat Meat, 1 Fat OR 1½ Carbohydrate, 1 Vegetable, 2 High-Fat Meat, 1 Fat

Green and White Lasagna

Prep Time: 40 minutes (Ready in 1 hour 25 minutes)

Yield: 12 servings

9   uncooked lasagna noodles
2   eggs, slightly beaten
1   (24-oz.) container (3 cups)
     cottage cheese
2   (9-oz.) pkg. frozen spinach
     in a pouch, thawed,
     squeezed to drain*
½   cup finely chopped onion
¼   cup chopped fresh parsley or
     3 teaspoons dried parsley
     flakes
½   teaspoon garlic powder
½   teaspoon salt
¼   teaspoon pepper
12   oz. (3 cups) shredded
     mozzarella cheese
½   cup grated Parmesan cheese

1. Cook lasagna noodles to desired doneness as directed on package. Drain.

2. Heat oven to 350°F. In medium bowl, combine eggs, cottage cheese, spinach, onion, parsley, garlic powder, salt and pepper; mix well.

3. In ungreased 13x9-inch pan, layer ⅓ each of the cooked noodles, spinach mixture and mozzarella cheese; repeat layers twice. Sprinkle with Parmesan cheese. ✳

4. Bake at 350°F. for 35 to 45 minutes or until hot and bubbly. Let stand 10 minutes before serving.

✳ **Make-Ahead Directions:** Prepare recipe as directed; do not bake. Cover with foil; freeze. When ready to use, do not thaw; bake, covered, at 350°F. for 1½ hours. Uncover; bake an additional 15 minutes or until mixture is thoroughly heated. Or cover; refrigerate up to 24 hours before baking. Uncover; bake at 350°F. for 45 to 50 minutes.

Tips: *To quickly thaw spinach, cut small slit in center of pouch; microwave on HIGH for 2 to 3 minutes or until thawed. Remove spinach from pouch; squeeze dry with paper towels.

Nutrition Information Per Serving: Serving Size: 1/12 of Recipe • Calories 240 • Calories from Fat 90 • % Daily Value • Total Fat 10 g 15% • Saturated 6 g 30% • Cholesterol 60 mg 20% • Sodium 660 mg 28% • Total Carbohydrate 16 g 5% • Dietary Fiber 1 g 4% • Sugars 2 g • Protein 21 g • Vitamin A 35% • Vitamin C 15% • Calcium 35% • Iron 8%
Dietary Exchanges: 1 Starch, 2½ Lean Meat, ½ Fat OR 1 Carbohydrate, 2½ Lean Meat, ½ Fat

Baked Ravioli and Meatballs

Prep Time: 25 minutes (Ready in 1 hour)

Yield: 6 servings

1   (25-oz.) pkg. frozen cheese-
     filled ravioli
1   (20-oz.) pkg. frozen cooked
     meatballs, thawed
1   (28-oz.) jar low-sodium
     spaghetti sauce
6   oz. (1½ cups) shredded
     mozzarella cheese

1. Heat oven to 375° F. Spray 13 x 9-inch (3-quart) baking dish with nonstick cooking spray.

2. Cook ravioli to desired doneness as directed on package.

3. Drain ravioli; place in sprayed baking dish. Top with meatballs and sauce; sprinkle with cheese.

4. Bake at 375° F. for 30 to 35 minutes or until thoroughly heated and cheese is melted.

Nutrition Information Per Serving: Serving Size: ⅙ of Recipe • Calories 840 • Calories from Fat 400 • % Daily Value • Total Fat 44 g 68% • Saturated 20 g 100% • Cholesterol 165 mg 55% • Sodium 1060 mg 44% • Total Carbohydrate 68 g 23% • Dietary Fiber 8 g 32% • Sugars 12 g • Protein 43 g • Vitamin A 35% • Vitamin C 4% • Calcium 60% • Iron 30%
Dietary Exchanges: 4½ Starch, 4 High-Fat Meat, 2 Fat OR 4½ Carbohydrate, 4 High-Fat Meat, 2 Fat

Baked Ravioli and Meatballs

Saucy Manicotti

Prep Time: 40 minutes (Ready in 1 hour 20 minutes)

Yield: 8 servings

MANICOTTI
- 8 uncooked manicotti

FILLING
- ½ lb. bulk mild Italian sausage
- ½ cup chopped onion
- 1 (4-oz.) can mushroom pieces and stems, drained
- 1½ cups finely chopped cooked turkey or chicken
- 2 egg yolks
- 1 (9-oz.) pkg. frozen spinach in a pouch, thawed, squeezed to drain*
- 4 oz. (1 cup) shredded mozzarella cheese
- ½ cup grated Parmesan cheese
- 1 (14-oz.) jar spaghetti sauce

WHITE SAUCE
- 2 tablespoons margarine or butter
- 2 tablespoons all-purpose flour
- 1½ cups whipping cream
- ⅓ cup grated Parmesan cheese
- Dash garlic powder
- Dash nutmeg

1. Cook manicotti to desired doneness as directed on package. Drain; place in cold water.

2. Meanwhile, heat oven to 350°F. In large skillet, brown sausage, onion and mushrooms. Remove from skillet; drain on paper towels. In large bowl, combine sausage mixture, turkey, egg yolks, spinach, mozzarella and ½ cup Parmesan cheese; mix well.**

3. Drain manicotti; fill each with sausage mixture. Pour ½ the spaghetti sauce into ungreased 13 x 9-inch (3-quart) baking dish. Place filled manicotti side by side over sauce in dish.

4. Melt margarine in medium saucepan over medium heat. Stir in flour; cook until smooth and bubbly, stirring constantly. Gradually stir in cream; cook until slightly thickened, stirring constantly. Stir in ⅓ cup Parmesan cheese, garlic powder and nutmeg; blend well. Pour white sauce over manicotti in baking dish. Pour remaining spaghetti sauce over top.

5. Bake at 350°F. for 35 to 40 minutes or until bubbly.

✳ **Make-Ahead Directions:** Prepare recipe as directed; do not bake. Cover with foil; freeze. When ready to use, do not thaw; bake, covered, at 350°F. for 1 hour 25 minutes. Uncover; bake an additional 15 minutes or until mixture is thoroughly heated.

Tips: *To quickly thaw spinach, cut small slit in center of pouch; microwave on HIGH for 2 to 3 minutes or until thawed. Remove spinach from pouch; squeeze dry with paper towels.

**For a more evenly chopped filling, place cooked sausage, onion, mushrooms, turkey and spinach in food processor. Cover; process with on/off pulses until of desired consistency.

Nutrition Information Per Serving: Serving Size: ⅛ of Recipe • Calories 490 • Calories from Fat 300 • % Daily Value • Total Fat 33 g 51% • Saturated 17 g 85% • Cholesterol 170 mg 57% • Sodium 880 mg 37% • Total Carbohydrate 23 g 8% • Dietary Fiber 2 g 8% • Sugars 3 g • Protein 26 g • Vitamin A 45% • Vitamin C 15% • Calcium 35% • Iron 15%
Dietary Exchanges: 1½ Starch, 3 Lean Meat, 4½ Fat OR 1½ Carbohydrate, 3 Lean Meat, 4½ Fat

Chicken Puff Pie

Prep Time: 30 minutes

Yield: 4 servings

2 cups frozen mixed vegetables

2 (10¾-oz.) cans condensed 98% fat-free cream of chicken soup with 30% less sodium

½ cup chicken broth

2 cups cubed cooked chicken or turkey

2 tablespoons chopped fresh parsley or 1 teaspoon dried parsley flakes

½ teaspoon poultry seasoning

⅛ teaspoon white pepper

1 (4-oz.) can mushroom pieces and stems, drained

1 (8-oz.) can refrigerated crescent dinner rolls

Additional chopped fresh parsley or dried parsley flakes

1. Heat oven to 375° F. Cook frozen vegetables as directed on package. Drain.

2. In large saucepan, combine cooked vegetables and all remaining ingredients except crescent rolls and additional parsley. Cook over medium heat until mixture is bubbly and thoroughly heated, stirring occasionally.

3. Meanwhile, separate dough into 8 triangles. Place 2 triangles together, stacking one on top of the other; press together slightly. (If necessary, gently press triangles until 6 inches long.) Repeat with remaining dough. Place triangles on ungreased cookie sheet. Bake triangles at 375° F. for 9 to 12 minutes.

4. To serve, spoon hot chicken mixture into ungreased 12x8-inch (2-quart) baking dish. Arrange warm triangles, side by side, on top of chicken mixture, alternating short sides of triangles. Sprinkle with additional parsley.

Nutrition Information Per Serving: Serving Size: ¼ of Recipe • Calories 490 • Calories from Fat 180 • % Daily Value • Total Fat 20 g 31% • Saturated 5 g 25% • Cholesterol 70 mg 23% • Sodium 1310 mg 55% • Total Carbohydrate 47 g 16% • Dietary Fiber 3 g 12% • Sugars 6 g • Protein 30 g • Vitamin A 35% • Vitamin C 10% • Calcium 8% • Iron 20%

Dietary Exchanges: 3 Starch, 1 Vegetable, 2½ Lean Meat, 2 Fat OR 3 Carbohydrate, 1 Vegetable, 2½ Lean Meat, 2 Fat

Convenient alternatives to homemade crusts include:

♦ Refrigerated pie crusts, ready to unfold, fill and bake

♦ Frozen pie crusts, in a pan and ready to fill and bake

♦ Prepared crusts in the baking aisle, ready to fill and bake

Chicken Pot Pies

Prep Time: 15 minutes (Ready in 1 hour 5 minutes)
Yield: 2 servings

1 refrigerated pie crust (from 15-oz. pkg.)
1 teaspoon all-purpose flour
2 tablespoons margarine or butter
2 tablespoons all-purpose flour
1/8 teaspoon poultry seasoning
   Dash pepper
1/2 cup chicken broth
1/3 cup milk
1 cup cubed cooked chicken
1 cup frozen mixed vegetables, thawed*

1. Let pie crust pouch stand at room temperature for 15 to 20 minutes.

2. Heat oven to 400° F. Unfold pie crust; peel off top plastic sheet. Press out fold lines; sprinkle 1 teaspoon flour over crust. Turn crust, flour side down, onto ungreased cookie sheet; peel off remaining plastic sheet.

3. Invert two 10-oz. ovenproof bowls or custard cups over crust. With sharp knife, cut round 1/2 inch larger than rims of bowls; remove bowls from crust. Line each bowl with crust, flour side down. Using remaining crust, cut desired shapes with cookie cutter or sharp knife.

4. Melt margarine in small saucepan over medium heat. Stir in 2 tablespoons flour, poultry seasoning and pepper; cook until mixture is smooth and bubbly. Gradually add broth and milk. Cook until mixture boils and thickens, stirring constantly.

5. Stir in chicken and mixed vegetables; cook until thoroughly heated. Divide mixture evenly into crust-lined bowls; top with pastry cutouts. Place bowls on cookie sheet to catch any spills.

6. Bake at 400° F. for 20 to 30 minutes or until crust is golden brown.

Tip: *To quickly thaw mixed vegetables, place in colander or strainer; rinse with warm water until thawed. Drain well.

Nutrition Information Per Serving: Serving Size: 1/2 of Recipe • Calories 790 • Calories from Fat 410 • % Daily Value • Total Fat 45 g 69% • Saturated 15 g 75% • Cholesterol 90 mg 30% • Sodium 840 mg 35% • Total Carbohydrate 68 g 23% • Dietary Fiber 3 g 12% • Sugars 6 g • Protein 28 g • Vitamin A 35% • Vitamin C 6% • Calcium 10% • Iron 15%
Dietary Exchanges: 4 Starch, 1 Vegetable, 2 Lean Meat, 7 1/2 Fat OR 4 Carbohydrate, 1 Vegetable, 2 Lean Meat, 7 1/2 Fat

Chicken Paprikash Pot Pie

Prep Time: 35 minutes (Ready in 1 hour 20 minutes)

Yield: 6 servings

1 (15-oz.) pkg. refrigerated pie crusts
4 slices bacon, cut into ½-inch pieces
¾ lb. boneless, skinless chicken breast halves, cut into ½-inch pieces
1 cup coarsely chopped onions
1 cup coarsely chopped red or green bell pepper
1 cup sliced fresh carrots
1 cup frozen sweet peas
½ cup sour cream
1 (12-oz.) jar home-style chicken gravy
3 tablespoons cornstarch
3 teaspoons paprika

1. Heat oven to 425°F. Prepare pie crusts as directed on package for *two-crust pie* using 9-inch pie pan.

2. Cook bacon in large skillet over medium heat until crisp. Reserve 1 tablespoon drippings with bacon in skillet.

3. Add chicken to skillet; cook and stir until no longer pink. Add onions, bell pepper and carrots; cook and stir until vegetables are tender. Stir in peas.

4. In small bowl, combine all remaining ingredients; mix well. Stir into chicken mixture in skillet. Spoon into crust-lined pan. Top with second crust and flute edges; cut slits or small designs in several places on top of crust.

5. Bake at 425°F. for 30 to 35 minutes or until crust is golden brown. Cover edge of crust with strips of foil after 10 to 15 minutes of baking to prevent excessive browning. Let stand 10 minutes before serving.

Nutrition Information Per Serving: Serving Size: ⅙ of Recipe • Calories 550 • Calories from Fat 270 • % Daily Value • Total Fat 30 g 46% • Saturated 12 g 60% • Cholesterol 65 mg 22% • Sodium 750 mg 31% • Total Carbohydrate 52 g 17% • Dietary Fiber 3 g 12% • Sugars 7 g • Protein 19 g • Vitamin A 160% • Vitamin C 45% • Calcium 8% • Iron 10%
Dietary Exchanges: 3 Starch, 1 Vegetable, 1 Very Lean Meat, 5½ Fat OR 3 Carbohydrate, 1 Vegetable, 1 Very Lean Meat, 5½ Fat

Pot Pie Trivia

A pot pie is simply a savory filling with a top crust, a bottom crust or both. The crust may be a traditional flaky pastry or baking powder biscuit dough, noodles, phyllo dough, puff pastry or whipped potatoes. In the days of hearth cooking, cooks lined a kettle with pastry and filled it with potatoes and leftover bits of meat and vegetables, then sealed the mixture with a top crust of pastry.

Chicken Paprikash Pot Pie

Overnight Chicken Bake

Prep Time: 15 minutes (Ready in 9 hours 10 minutes)

Yield: 6 servings

CASSEROLE

- 2 cups cubed cooked chicken
- 1 (9-oz.) pkg. frozen mixed vegetables in a pouch, slightly thawed, drained*
- 1 (7-oz.) pkg. (1⅔ cups) uncooked elbow macaroni
- 4 oz. (1 cup) shredded American cheese
- 1 (10¾-oz.) can condensed cream of celery soup
- 2 cups water

TOPPING

- ½ cup unseasoned dry bread crumbs
- 2 tablespoons margarine or butter, melted

1. In large bowl, combine all casserole ingredients; mix well. Pour into ungreased 8-inch square (2-quart) baking dish. Cover tightly with foil; refrigerate at least 8 hours or overnight.

2. Heat oven to 350° F. In small bowl, combine topping ingredients; mix well. Uncover; stir casserole. Sprinkle with topping. Bake uncovered for 45 to 55 minutes or until bubbly and golden brown.

Tip: *To quickly thaw mixed vegetables, remove vegetables from pouch; place in colander or strainer. Rinse with warm water until slightly thawed; drain well.

Nutrition Information Per Serving: Serving Size: ⅙ of Recipe • Calories 410 • Calories from Fat 150 • % Daily Value • Total Fat 17 g 26% • Saturated 6 g 30% • Cholesterol 65 mg 22% • Sodium 880 mg 37% • Total Carbohydrate 40 g 13% • Dietary Fiber 3 g 12% • Sugars 4 g • Protein 25 g • Vitamin A 25% • Vitamin C 2% • Calcium 20% • Iron 15%
Dietary Exchanges: 2½ Starch, 1 Vegetable, 2 Lean Meat, 2 Fat OR 2½ Carbohydrate, 1 Vegetable, 2 Lean Meat, 2 Fat

Swiss Chicken and Green Bean Bake

Prep Time: 30 minutes (Ready in 1 hour 25 minutes)

Yield: 4 servings

BASE

- 1½ cups uncooked instant rice
- ¾ cup skim milk
- 1 (14½-oz.) can french-style green beans, undrained
- 1 (10¾-oz.) can condensed 98% fat-free cream of mushroom soup with 30% less sodium

CHICKEN ROLLS

- 4 boneless, skinless chicken breast halves
- 4 oz. (1 cup) shredded reduced-fat Swiss cheese

TOPPING

- ½ cup canned french-fried onions

1. Heat oven to 350° F. Spray 12x8-inch or 8-inch square (2-quart) baking dish with nonstick cooking spray. In large bowl, combine all base ingredients; blend well. Pour into sprayed baking dish.

2. Place 1 chicken breast half between 2 pieces of plastic wrap. Working from center, lightly pound chicken with flat side of meat mallet or rolling pin until about ¼ inch thick; remove wrap. Repeat with remaining chicken breast halves.

3. Place ¼ cup of the Swiss cheese on each chicken breast half. Roll up jelly-roll fashion; place over rice mixture in baking dish. Cover with foil.

4. Bake at 350° F. for 55 minutes or until chicken is tender and no longer pink. Uncover; sprinkle with onions. Bake uncovered for an additional 5 minutes.

Nutrition Information Per Serving: Serving Size: ¼ of Recipe • Calories 460 • Calories from Fat 110 • % Daily Value • Total Fat 12 g 18% • Saturated 5 g 25% • Cholesterol 95 mg 32% • Sodium 820 mg 34% • Total Carbohydrate 45 g 15% • Dietary Fiber 2 g 8% • Sugars 5 g • Protein 42 g • Vitamin A 20% • Vitamin C 2% • Calcium 40% • Iron 15%
Dietary Exchanges: 2½ Starch, 1 Vegetable, 4½ Meat OR 2½ Carbohydrate, 1 Vegetable, 4½ Meat

Mediterranean Baked Chicken

Prep Time: 40 minutes (Ready in 1 hour 10 minutes)

Yield: 6 (1⅓-cup) servings

Photo page 32

6	oz. (2 cups) uncooked rotini (spiral pasta)
¼	cup butter
3	large shallots, minced
¼	cup all-purpose flour
1	(14½-oz.) can ready-to-serve chicken broth with ⅓ less sodium
1	(8-oz.) pkg. (3 cups) sliced fresh mushrooms
4	oz. (1 cup) shredded Swiss cheese
3	cups chopped cooked chicken
1	(6-oz.) jar marinated artichoke hearts, drained
½	cup oil-packed sun-dried tomatoes, drained, chopped
2	tablespoons chopped fresh parsley

1. Heat oven to 375° F. Spray 2-quart casserole with nonstick cooking spray. Cook rotini to desired doneness as directed on package. Drain.

2. Meanwhile, melt butter in large saucepan over medium-high heat. Add shallots; cook and stir 1 minute. Stir in flour; cook 30 seconds. With wire whisk, stir in broth. Add mushrooms. Bring to a boil. Cook 3 to 4 minutes or until thickened, stirring occasionally. Remove from heat; stir in cheese until melted.

3. Add cooked rotini, chicken, artichoke hearts, tomatoes and parsley to mushroom mixture; mix gently. Spoon into sprayed casserole.

4. Bake at 375° F. for 25 to 30 minutes or until thoroughly heated and bubbly. If desired, garnish with additional fresh parsley.

Nutrition Information Per Serving: Serving Size: 1⅓ Cups • Calories 460 • Calories from Fat 210 • % Daily Value • Total Fat 23 g 35% • Saturated 10 g 50% • Cholesterol 100 mg 33% • Sodium 270 mg 11% • Total Carbohydrate 32 g 11% • Dietary Fiber 2 g 8% • Sugars 4 g • Protein 32 g • Vitamin A 15% • Vitamin C 15% • Calcium 20% • Iron 15%
Dietary Exchanges: 2 Starch, 1 Vegetable, 3½ Medium-Fat Meat, ½ Fat OR 2 Carbohydrate, 1 Vegetable, 3½ Medium-Fat Meat, ½ Fat

Chicken and Rice Bake

Prep Time: 20 minutes (Ready in 1 hour 50 minutes)

Yield: 6 servings

1	(6-oz.) pkg. long-grain and wild rice
3	to 3½ lb. cut-up frying chicken, skinned if desired
1	cup sliced celery
1	(4½-oz.) jar whole mushrooms, drained
2	cups water
1	(10¾-oz.) can condensed cream of chicken or cream of celery soup
	Paprika

1. Heat oven to 350° F. Grease 13x9-inch (3-quart) baking dish. Pour uncooked rice over bottom of greased dish. Sprinkle evenly with seasoning mix packet. Arrange chicken pieces over rice. Spoon celery and mushrooms around chicken.

2. In medium saucepan, combine water and soup; mix well. Bring to a boil. Pour evenly over chicken and vegetables. Sprinkle chicken with paprika. Cover with foil.

3. Bake at 350° F. for 1 hour. Uncover; bake an additional 20 to 30 minutes or until chicken is fork-tender and juices run clear. Let stand 5 minutes before serving.

Nutrition Information Per Serving: Serving Size: ⅙ of Recipe • Calories 390 • Calories from Fat 150 • % Daily Value • Total Fat 17 g 26% • Saturated 5 g 25% • Cholesterol 95 mg 32% • Sodium 910 mg 38% • Total Carbohydrate 26 g 9% • Dietary Fiber 1 g 4% • Sugars 1 g • Protein 33 g • Vitamin A 8% • Vitamin C 0% • Calcium 4% • Iron 15%
Dietary Exchanges: 1½ Starch, 4 Lean Meat, 1 Fat OR 1½ Carbohydrate, 4 Lean Meat, 1 Fat

Chicken Tetrazzini Bake

Chicken Tetrazzini Bake

Prep Time: 25 minutes (Ready in 55 minutes)
Yield: 8 servings

1	(7-oz.) pkg. uncooked spaghetti
½	cup sliced onion
¼	cup margarine or butter
¼	cup all-purpose flour
½	teaspoon salt
½	teaspoon ground sage
¼	teaspoon pepper
2	cups chicken broth
1	cup milk
1	(4½-oz.) jar sliced mushrooms, drained
3	cups cubed cooked chicken or turkey
½	cup chopped fresh parsley
⅓	cup grated Parmesan cheese
1	(2-oz.) jar diced pimientos, drained
2	oz. (½ cup) shredded Swiss cheese

1. Cook spaghetti to desired doneness as directed on package. Drain.

2. Meanwhile, heat oven to 350°F. In large saucepan, cook onion in margarine over medium heat until tender. Stir in flour, salt, sage and pepper; cook until bubbly. Stir in broth, milk and mushrooms. Cook and stir until mixture boils and is slightly thickened.

3. Stir in cooked spaghetti and all remaining ingredients except Swiss cheese. Spoon into ungreased 12x8-inch (2-quart) baking dish; sprinkle with Swiss cheese.

4. Bake at 350°F. for 20 to 30 minutes until hot and bubbly. If desired, sprinkle with additional chopped fresh parsley.

Nutrition Information Per Serving: Serving Size: ⅛ of Recipe • Calories 330 • Calories from Fat 130 • % Daily Value • Total Fat 14 g 22% • Saturated 5 g 25% • Cholesterol 60 mg 20% • Sodium 600 mg 25% • Total Carbohydrate 26 g 9% • Dietary Fiber 2 g 8% • Sugars 3 g • Protein 26 g • Vitamin A 15% • Vitamin C 20% • Calcium 20% • Iron 15%
Dietary Exchanges: 1½ Starch, 3 Lean Meat, 1 Fat OR 1½ Carbohydrate, 3 Lean Meat, 1 Fat

Chicken and Cashew Bake

Prep Time: 20 minutes (Ready in 55 minutes)

Yield: 5 (1-cup) servings

CASSEROLE

- 2 tablespoons margarine or butter
- 1 cup sliced celery
- ¼ cup chopped onion
- 3 cups cubed cooked chicken
- ½ cup chopped salted cashews
- ¼ cup water or chicken broth
- 1 (10¾-oz.) can condensed cream of chicken soup
- 1½ cups frozen sweet peas
- 1 (2-oz.) jar sliced pimientos, drained

TOPPING

- ½ cup crisp chow mein noodles
- ¼ cup coarsely chopped salted cashews

1. Heat oven to 350° F. Melt margarine in large saucepan over medium heat. Add celery and onion; cook and stir 3 minutes or until crisp-tender.

2. Stir in all remaining casserole ingredients. Pour into ungreased 1½- or 2-quart casserole.

3. Bake at 350° F. for 30 to 35 minutes or until thoroughly heated. Sprinkle topping ingredients evenly over casserole. Bake an additional 5 minutes or until topping is warm.

✳ **Make-Ahead Directions:** Prepare recipe as directed above except omit topping; do not bake. Cover with foil; freeze. When ready to use, do not thaw; bake, covered, at 350° F. for 1 hour 40 minutes. Uncover; sprinkle with topping. Bake an additional 5 minutes until topping is warm.

Nutrition Information Per Serving: Serving Size: 1 Cup • Calories 450 • Calories from Fat 230 • % Daily Value • Total Fat 26 g 40% • Saturated 6 g 30% • Cholesterol 80 mg 27% • Sodium 850 mg 35% • Total Carbohydrate 22 g 7% • Dietary Fiber 3 g 12% • Sugars 3 g • Protein 32 g • Vitamin A 20% • Vitamin C 15% • Calcium 6% • Iron 20%
Dietary Exchanges: 1½ Starch, 4 Lean Meat, 2½ Fat OR 1½ Carbohydrate, 4 Lean Meat, 2½ Fat

Chicken and Cashew Bake

Chicken, Artichoke and Rice Casserole

Prep Time: 1 hour (Ready in 2 hours)

Yield: 12 servings

½	cup uncooked regular long-grain white rice
1	cup water
½	cup uncooked wild rice
1¼	cups water
2	slices bacon
1	tablespoon margarine or butter
2	cups julienne-cut (2x¼x¼-inch) carrots
½	cup chopped green bell pepper
⅓	cup chopped green onions
2	(10¾-oz.) cans condensed cream of chicken soup
½	cup milk
¼	cup dry sherry
2½	cups cubed cooked chicken
8	oz. (2 cups) shredded mozzarella cheese
1	to 2 (14-oz.) cans artichoke hearts, drained, quartered
¼	cup grated Parmesan cheese
2	teaspoons dried parsley flakes

1. Cook white rice in 1 cup water and wild rice in 1¼ cups water as directed on packages.

2. Meanwhile, heat oven to 350° F. Grease 13 x 9-inch (3-quart) baking dish. Cook bacon until crisp. Drain on paper towel. Crumble; set aside.

3. Melt margarine in large skillet over medium-high heat. Add carrots, bell pepper and green onions; cook and stir until crisp-tender. Stir in soup, milk, sherry, chicken, mozzarella cheese and bacon; blend well. Remove from heat.

4. Combine white and wild rice; spread evenly over bottom of greased baking dish. Arrange artichokes over rice. Spoon chicken mixture evenly over artichokes.* Sprinkle with Parmesan cheese and parsley flakes. Cover tightly with foil.

5. Bake at 350° F. for 40 minutes. Uncover; bake an additional 15 to 20 minutes or until casserole is thoroughly heated.

✳ **Make-Ahead Directions:** Prepare recipe as directed; do not bake. Cover with foil; freeze. When ready to use, do not thaw; bake, covered, at 350° F. for 1 hour 35 minutes. Uncover; bake an additional 15 minutes or until mixture is thoroughly heated. Or cover; refrigerate up to 24 hours before baking. Sprinkle casserole with Parmesan cheese and parsley flakes; cover tightly with foil. Bake at 350° F. for 1 hour. Uncover; bake an additional 15 to 20 minutes.

Nutrition Information Per Serving: Serving Size: ¹⁄₁₂ of Recipe • Calories 280 • Calories from Fat 100 • % Daily Value • Total Fat 11 g 17% • Saturated 4 g 20% • Cholesterol 45 mg 15% • Sodium 650 mg 27% • Total Carbohydrate 24 g 8% • Dietary Fiber 4 g 16% • Sugars 3 g • Protein 20 g • Vitamin A 130% • Vitamin C 15% • Calcium 25% • Iron 10%
Dietary Exchanges: 1½ Starch, 2 Lean Meat, 1 Fat OR 1½ Carbohydrate, 2 Lean Meat, 1 Fat

Quick-Topped Vegetable Chicken Casserole

Prep Time: 25 minutes (Ready in 55 minutes)
Yield: 6 servings

CASSEROLE

1	(9-oz.) pkg. frozen cut broccoli in a pouch
1	(10¾-oz.) can condensed cream of chicken soup
1	(3-oz.) pkg. cream cheese, softened
½	cup milk
½	cup chopped celery
½	cup chopped onion
¼	cup grated Parmesan cheese
¼	cup chopped green bell pepper
¼	cup shredded carrot
2	to 3 cups cubed cooked chicken

TOPPING

1	cup complete or buttermilk pancake mix
¼	cup slivered almonds
4	oz. (1 cup) shredded Cheddar cheese
¼	cup milk
1	tablespoon oil
1	egg, slightly beaten

1. Heat oven to 375°F. Cook frozen broccoli in a pouch as directed on package. Drain.

2. Meanwhile, in large saucepan, combine soup, cream cheese, ½ cup milk, celery, onion, Parmesan cheese, bell pepper and carrot; mix well. Cook over medium heat until mixture is hot and cream cheese is melted, stirring frequently. Stir in chicken and cooked broccoli. Pour into ungreased 2-quart casserole or 12x8-inch (2-quart) baking dish.

3. In medium bowl, combine all topping ingredients; blend well. Spoon tablespoonfuls of topping over hot chicken mixture.

4. Bake at 375°F. for 20 to 30 minutes or until topping is golden brown and chicken mixture bubbles around edges.

High Altitude (above 3,500 feet): No change.

Nutrition Information Per Serving: Serving Size: ⅙ of Recipe • Calories 500 • Calories from Fat 250 • % Daily Value • Total Fat 28 g 43% • Saturated 12 g 60% • Cholesterol 145 mg 48% • Sodium 1070 mg 45% • Total Carbohydrate 26 g 9% • Dietary Fiber 3 g 12% • Sugars 8 g • Protein 35 g • Vitamin A 50% • Vitamin C 30% • Calcium 35% • Iron 15%
Dietary Exchanges: 1½ Starch, 1 Vegetable, 4 Lean Meat, 3 Fat OR 1½ Carbohydrate, 1 Vegetable, 4 Lean Meat, 3 Fat

Potluck, Then and Now

"Potluck" circa 1950 meant low-ceilinged social halls and church basements. Casseroles dotting long buffet tables held lots of cream of mushroom soup, onion, green pepper, rice, egg noodles, ground beef and tuna. Today, casseroles remain a popular potluck food. Many use lighter, lower-fat ingredients and borrow from international cuisines. They are easier than ever to make and their ingredients are less predictable.

Quick Cubed Chicken

When you need cubed cooked chicken for a recipe, place four boneless, skinless chicken breast halves (1½ to 2 pounds) in a 2-quart microwave-safe dish; cover. Microwave on high power for 8 to 10 minutes or until chicken is no longer pink, turning the dish one-half turn and rearranging chicken halfway through cooking. Cool; cut into cubes. Yields 2½ to 3 cups.

Chicken-Broccoli Bake

Prep Time: 35 minutes (Ready in 5 hours 40 minutes)

Yield: 12 servings

12	slices white bread
8	oz. (8 slices) American cheese
2	cups cubed cooked chicken
¼	cup chopped onion
1	(9-oz.) pkg. frozen cut broccoli in a pouch, thawed, drained*
1	(2-oz.) jar sliced pimientos, drained
6	eggs
3	cups milk
½	teaspoon salt
¼	teaspoon dry mustard
	Paprika

1. Grease 13x9-inch (3-quart) baking dish. Using doughnut cutter, cut rings from each slice of bread; set bread rings aside. Tear remaining bread into pieces; place in greased baking dish. Arrange cheese slices over bread. Layer chicken, onion, broccoli and pimientos over cheese. Arrange bread rings over top.

2. In medium bowl, combine eggs, milk, salt and mustard; blend well. Pour egg mixture evenly over mixture in baking dish; sprinkle with paprika. Cover; refrigerate at least 4 hours or overnight.

3. Heat oven to 325°F. Uncover; bake 55 to 65 minutes or until knife inserted in center comes out clean. Let stand 10 minutes before serving.

Tip: *To quickly thaw broccoli, remove broccoli from pouch; place in colander or strainer. Rinse with warm water until thawed; drain well. Or cut small slit in center of pouch; microwave on HIGH for 2 to 3 minutes or until thawed. Remove broccoli from pouch; drain well.

Nutrition Information Per Serving: Serving Size: ½₂ of Recipe • Calories 250 • Calories from Fat 110 • % Daily Value • Total Fat 12 g 18% • Saturated 6 g 30% • Cholesterol 150 mg 50% • Sodium 610 mg 25% • Total Carbohydrate 17 g 6% • Dietary Fiber 1 g 4% • Sugars 5 g • Protein 19 g • Vitamin A 15% • Vitamin C 20% • Calcium 25% • Iron 10%
Dietary Exchanges: 1 Starch, 2½ Lean Meat, 1 Fat OR 1 Carbohydrate, 2½ Lean Meat, 1 Fat

Chicken-Broccoli Bake

Mexican Casserole

Prep Time: 20 minutes (Ready in 1 hour 15 minutes)

Yield: 8 servings

3	cups coarsely crushed tortilla chips
3	cups diced cooked chicken
¾	cup finely chopped onions
2	(11-oz.) cans tomatillos, drained, chopped
2	(4½-oz.) cans chopped green chiles
½	teaspoon cumin
1	garlic clove, minced
1	cup sour cream
8	oz. (2 cups) shredded colby–Monterey Jack cheese blend
½	cup chunky-style salsa or picante sauce, if desired

1. Heat oven to 350° F. Spray 13x9-inch (3-quart) baking dish with nonstick cooking spray. Place 2 cups of the tortilla chips in bottom of sprayed baking dish. Layer chicken over chips.

2. In medium bowl, combine onions, tomatillos, green chiles, cumin and garlic; mix well. Spread onion mixture over chicken. Drop teaspoons of sour cream over onion mixture. Sprinkle with cheese. Cover with foil.

3. Bake at 350° F. for 30 minutes. Uncover; sprinkle with remaining 1 cup tortilla chips. Bake uncovered for an additional 20 to 25 minutes or until thoroughly heated. Serve with salsa if desired.

Nutrition Information Per Serving: Serving Size: ⅛ of Recipe • Calories 420 • Calories from Fat 220 • % Daily Value • Total Fat 24 g 37% • Saturated 12 g 60% • Cholesterol 85 mg 28% • Sodium 1160 mg 48% • Total Carbohydrate 26 g 9% • Dietary Fiber 4 g 16% • Sugars 5 g • Protein 26 g • Vitamin A 15% • Vitamin C 10% • Calcium 35% • Iron 20%
Dietary Exchanges: 1½ Starch, 1 Vegetable, 3 Medium-Fat Meat, 1½ Fat OR 1½ Carbohydrate, 1 Vegetable, 3 Medium-Fat Meat, 1½ Fat

Chicken Divan

Prep Time: 20 minutes (Ready in 50 minutes)

Yield: 6 servings

Photo page xiv

2	tablespoons margarine or butter
3	tablespoons all-purpose flour
2	teaspoons chicken-flavor instant bouillon
2	cups milk
½	cup mayonnaise or salad dressing
1	tablespoon Dijon mustard
1	(1-lb.) pkg. frozen broccoli spears, thawed, drained
3	cups cubed cooked chicken or turkey
2	oz. (½ cup) shredded Cheddar cheese
⅓	cup unseasoned dry bread crumbs
1	tablespoon margarine or butter, melted

1. Heat oven to 350° F. Melt 2 tablespoons margarine in medium saucepan. Stir in flour and bouillon. Gradually stir in milk; cook until mixture boils and thickens, stirring constantly with wire whisk. Stir in mayonnaise and mustard until well blended.

2. Arrange broccoli spears in ungreased 12x8-inch (2-quart) baking dish. Top with chicken. Spoon sauce over chicken. Sprinkle with cheese.

3. In small bowl, combine bread crumbs and 1 tablespoon melted margarine; mix well. Sprinkle over top.

4. Bake at 350° F. for 30 minutes or until thoroughly heated.

Nutrition Information Per Serving: Serving Size: ⅙ of Recipe • Calories 460 • Calories from Fat 280 • % Daily Value • Total Fat 31 g 48% • Saturated 8 g 40% • Cholesterol 90 mg 30% • Sodium 790 mg 33% • Total Carbohydrate 16 g 5% • Dietary Fiber 2 g 8% • Sugars 6 g • Protein 29 g • Vitamin A 20% • Vitamin C 35% • Calcium 20% • Iron 10%
Dietary Exchanges: 1 Starch, 3½ Lean Meat, 4 Fat OR 1 Carbohydrate, 3½ Lean Meat, 4 Fat

Swiss Party Chicken

Prep Time: 25 minutes (Ready in 1 hour 15 minutes)

Yield: 6 servings

6   boneless, skinless chicken breast halves

1   (4½-oz.) jar whole mushrooms, drained

8   oz. (2 cups) shredded Swiss cheese

1   (10¾-oz.) can condensed cream of mushroom soup

¼   cup sour cream

¼   cup dry sherry or chicken broth

¼   cup grated Parmesan cheese

1. Heat oven to 350° F. Place chicken breasts in ungreased 12 x 8-inch (2-quart) baking dish. Add mushrooms; sprinkle with Swiss cheese.

2. In small bowl, combine soup, sour cream and sherry; blend well. Pour over chicken.*

3. Bake at 350° F. for 50 minutes. Sprinkle with Parmesan cheese; bake an additional 5 to 10 minutes or until chicken is fork-tender and juices run clear. Place chicken on serving plate. Stir sauce if necessary to blend; serve with chicken.

Make-Ahead Directions: Prepare recipe as directed; do not bake. Cover with foil; freeze. When ready to use, do not thaw; bake, covered, at 350° F. for 1½ hours. Uncover; bake an additional 10 minutes or until chicken is fork tender and juices run clear.

Tip: *To make ahead, prepare as directed to this point. Cover; refrigerate up to 24 hours before baking. Uncover; bake as directed above.

Nutrition Information Per Serving: Serving Size: ⅙ of Recipe • Calories 390 • Calories from Fat 180 • % Daily Value • Total Fat 20 g 31% • Saturated 11 g 55% • Cholesterol 120 mg 40% • Sodium 730 mg 30% • Total Carbohydrate 8 g 3% • Dietary Fiber 1 g 2% • Sugars 2 g • Protein 41 g • Vitamin A 15% • Vitamin C 0% • Calcium 45% • Iron 8%
Dietary Exchanges: ½ Starch, 5½ Lean Meat, 1 Fat OR ½ Carbohydrate, 5½ Lean Meat, 1 Fat

Roasted Chicken and Vegetables

Prep Time: 15 minutes (Ready in 1 hour 20 minutes)

Yield: 4 servings

CHICKEN AND VEGETABLES

3   to 3½ lb. cut-up frying chicken, skin removed

6   to 8 small new red potatoes, unpeeled, quartered

1   large red onion, cut into 8 wedges

4   oz. (1⅓ cups) fresh whole mushrooms

SAUCE

¼   cup creamy mustard-mayonnaise sauce

1   tablespoon oil

¼   teaspoon peppered seasoned salt

1. Heat oven to 375° F. Arrange chicken, meaty side up, in ungreased 15 x 10 x 1-inch baking pan. Arrange vegetables around chicken.

2. In small bowl, combine all sauce ingredients; mix well. Brush sauce over chicken and vegetables. Bake at 375° F. for 45 minutes.

3. Baste chicken and vegetables with pan juices. Bake an additional 15 to 20 minutes or until chicken is fork-tender, its juices run clear and vegetables are tender. Serve pan juices with chicken and vegetables. If desired, sprinkle with 2 tablespoons chopped fresh parsley.

Nutrition Information Per Serving: Serving Size: ¼ of Recipe • Calories 480 • Calories from Fat 140 • % Daily Value • Total Fat 16 g 25% • Saturated 4 g 20% • Cholesterol 115 mg 38% • Sodium 320 mg 13% • Total Carbohydrate 43 g 14% • Dietary Fiber 5 g 20% • Sugars 4 g • Protein 41 g • Vitamin A 0% • Vitamin C 25% • Calcium 4% • Iron 20%
Dietary Exchanges: 2½ Starch, 1 Vegetable, 4½ Lean Meat OR 2½ Carbohydrate, 1 Vegetable, 4½ Lean Meat

Crescent Chicken Newburg

Prep Time: 25 minutes (Ready in 55 minutes)

Yield: 6 servings

Photo at right and page v

1	(1-lb.) pkg. frozen broccoli florets, carrots and water chestnuts
2	tablespoons margarine or butter
6	boneless, skinless chicken breast halves, cut into ½-inch pieces
¼	cup all-purpose flour
¼	to ½ teaspoon salt
¼	teaspoon white pepper
1½	cups half-and-half
3	tablespoons dry sherry
2	tablespoons grated Parmesan cheese
1	(8-oz.) can refrigerated crescent dinner rolls
1	tablespoon margarine or butter, melted
1	tablespoon grated Parmesan cheese
¼	teaspoon paprika

1. Cook frozen vegetables as directed on package. Drain.

2. Meanwhile, heat oven to 350° F. Melt 2 tablespoons margarine in large skillet over medium-high heat. Add chicken; cook and stir until browned and no longer pink. Reduce heat to medium; stir in flour, salt, pepper, half-and-half and sherry. Cook until mixture boils and thickens, stirring constantly.

3. Stir in cooked vegetables and 2 tablespoons Parmesan cheese. Cook an additional 4 to 6 minutes or until thoroughly heated. Spoon hot mixture into ungreased 12 x 8-inch (2-quart) baking dish.

4. Remove crescent roll dough from can in rolled section; do not unroll. Cut roll into 12 slices; cut each slice in half. Arrange half-slices, curved side up, around outside of chicken mixture. Brush with 1 tablespoon melted margarine; sprinkle with 1 tablespoon Parmesan cheese. Sprinkle entire casserole with paprika.

5. Bake at 350° F. for 23 to 27 minutes or until rolls are deep golden brown.

Nutrition Information Per Serving: Serving Size: ⅙ of Recipe • Calories 460 • Calories from Fat 220 • % Daily Value • Total Fat 24 g 37% • Saturated 8 g 40% • Cholesterol 90 mg 30% • Sodium 700 mg 29% • Total Carbohydrate 28 g 9% • Dietary Fiber 2 g 8% • Sugars 8 g • Protein 32 g • Vitamin A 50% • Vitamin C 20% • Calcium 15% • Iron 10%
Dietary Exchanges: 1½ Starch, 1 Vegetable, 3½ Very Lean Meat, 4 Fat OR 1½ Carbohydrate, 1 Vegetable, 3½ Very Lean Meat, 4 Fat

Three Great Gadgets

- Apple corer-slicer: Although designed for apples, this inexpensive metal tool works well for pears and even potatoes (either peeled or simply scrubbed). With a simple downward press of two hands, the core is out and the fruit sliced into equal wedges. For potatoes, the round central core can cook along with the wedges.

- Serrated grapefruit spoon: Designed to allow easy removal of sections from halved grapefruit, the serrated teaspoon is also handy for scraping the last morsels out of avocados and melons or for seeding cucumbers, fresh tomatoes or winter squashes.

- Citrus zester: A zester resembles a vegetable peeler, but its small blade has about four tiny, sharp holes instead of one lengthwise blade. The tool works well for its intended use of peeling off thin shreds of the outer skin of citrus fruit, but can also be used to peel shreds of Parmesan or other grating cheese, blocks of chocolate or even carrot or parsnip.

Turkey Pot Roast with Vegetables

Prep Time: 30 minutes (Ready in 2 hours 30 minutes)

Yield: 8 servings

1 (2- to 3-lb.) fresh boneless turkey breast roast or 3- to 4-lb. fresh bone-in turkey breast roast
2 medium sweet potatoes, peeled, cubed
2 medium russet potatoes, peeled, cubed
1 (8-oz.) pkg. frozen cut green beans, slightly thawed, drained*
1 (4½-oz.) jar whole mushrooms, drained
½ cup chicken broth
1 tablespoon margarine or butter, melted
½ teaspoon dried thyme leaves
½ teaspoon dried rosemary leaves, crushed
¼ teaspoon salt
⅛ teaspoon pepper

1. Heat oven to 350°F. Place turkey breast roast, skin side up, in ungreased 13x9-inch (3-quart) baking dish. Arrange sweet potatoes, potatoes, green beans and mushrooms around turkey.

2. In small bowl, combine broth and remaining ingredients; drizzle over turkey and vegetables. Insert meat thermometer into turkey breast roast. Cover tightly with foil.

3. Bake at 350°F. for 1½ to 2 hours or until meat thermometer reaches 170°F. and vegetables are fork-tender, basting once with pan juices.

Tip: *To quickly thaw green beans, remove green beans from pouch; place in colander or strainer. Rinse with warm water until slightly thawed; drain well. Or cut small slit in center of pouch; microwave on HIGH for 1 to 2 minutes or until slightly thawed. Remove green beans from pouch; drain well.

Nutrition Information Per Serving: Serving Size: ⅛ of Recipe • Calories 260 • Calories from Fat 25 • % Daily Value • Total Fat 3 g 5% • Saturated 1 g 5% • Cholesterol 105 mg 35% • Sodium 310 mg 13% • Total Carbohydrate 18 g 6% • Dietary Fiber 3 g 12% • Sugars 3 g • Protein 41 g • Vitamin A 130% • Vitamin C 20% • Calcium 4% • Iron 15%
Dietary Exchanges: 1 Starch, ½ Vegetable, 5 Very Lean Meat OR 1 Carbohydrate, ½ Vegetable, 5 Very Lean Meat

Turkey Stuffing Casserole

Prep Time: 15 minutes (Ready in 35 minutes)

Yield: 6 (1⅓-cup) servings

2   cups water

1   (8-oz.) pkg. one-step chicken-flavor stuffing mix

¾   lb. turkey tenderloin, cut into ½-inch cubes

2   (10-oz.) pkg. frozen peas and carrots, thawed*

1   (10¾-oz.) can condensed 98% fat-free cream of chicken soup with 30% less sodium

1   (8-oz.) container nonfat sour cream

1   (4½-oz.) jar sliced mushrooms, drained

⅔   cup skim milk

1. Heat oven to 450° F. Spray 13x9-inch (3-quart) baking dish with nonstick cooking spray.

2. In medium saucepan, bring water to a boil. Stir in stuffing mix. Remove from heat; cover and let stand 5 minutes.

3. Meanwhile, in large nonstick skillet, cook turkey over medium-high heat until no longer pink. Add peas and carrots, soup, sour cream, mushrooms and milk; mix well. Heat until bubbly.

4. Spoon ⅔ of stuffing evenly into sprayed dish. Top with turkey mixture and remaining ⅓ of stuffing.

5. Bake at 450° F. for 10 to 15 minutes or until bubbly and browned. Let stand 5 minutes before serving.

✳ **Make-Ahead Directions:** Prepare recipe as directed; do not bake. Cover with foil; freeze. When ready to use, do not thaw; bake, covered, at 400° F. for 1 hour 20 minutes. Uncover; bake an additional 15 minutes or until mixture is bubbly and browned.

Tip: *To quickly thaw peas and carrots, place in colander or strainer; rinse with warm water until thawed. Drain well.

Nutrition Information Per Serving: Serving Size: 1⅓ Cups • Calories 340 • Calories from Fat 50 • % Daily Value • Total Fat 6 g 9% • Saturated 1 g 5% • Cholesterol 40 mg 13% • Sodium 1080 mg 45% • Total Carbohydrate 47 g 16% • Dietary Fiber 5 g 20% • Sugars 12 g • Protein 25 g • Vitamin A 190% • Vitamin C 15% • Calcium 15% • Iron 20%
Dietary Exchanges: 3 Starch, 1 Vegetable, 2 Very Lean Meat OR 3 Carbohydrate, 1 Vegetable, 2 Very Lean Meat

Layered Turkey Noodle Bake

Prep Time: 35 minutes (Ready in 1 hour 15 minutes)
Yield: 8 servings

4	oz. (2½ cups) uncooked medium egg noodles
1	lb. ground turkey
1	(15-oz.) can tomato sauce
1	(6-oz.) can tomato paste
1	teaspoon sugar
1	teaspoon dried basil leaves
½	teaspoon garlic powder
½	teaspoon dried oregano leaves
⅛	teaspoon pepper
1	(8-oz.) pkg. ⅓-less-fat cream cheese (Neufchâtel), softened
½	cup light sour cream
3	tablespoons skim milk
2	tablespoons finely chopped onion
1	(9-oz.) pkg. frozen spinach in a pouch, thawed, squeezed to drain*

1. Cook noodles to desired doneness as directed on package. Drain; rinse with hot water.

2. Meanwhile, heat oven to 350°F. In large skillet, cook ground turkey until no longer pink. Stir in tomato sauce, tomato paste, sugar, basil, garlic powder, oregano and pepper. Stir in cooked noodles.

3. In medium bowl, combine cheese, sour cream, milk and onion; beat until smooth.

4. Spoon ½ the noodle mixture into ungreased 12x8-inch (2-quart) baking dish. Top evenly with cheese mixture. Spoon spinach evenly over cheese mixture; top with remaining noodle mixture.

5. Bake at 350°F. for 35 to 40 minutes or until thoroughly heated.

Tip: *To quickly thaw spinach, cut small slit in center of pouch; microwave on HIGH for 2 to 3 minutes or until thawed. Remove spinach from pouch; squeeze dry with paper towels.

Nutrition Information Per Serving: Serving Size: ⅛ of Recipe • Calories 290 • Calories from Fat 130 • % Daily Value • Total Fat 14 g 22% • Saturated 6 g 30% • Cholesterol 80 mg 27% • Sodium 740 mg 31% • Total Carbohydrate 23 g 8% • Dietary Fiber 3 g 12% • Sugars 5 g • Protein 19 g • Vitamin A 50% • Vitamin C 25% • Calcium 10% • Iron 15%
Dietary Exchanges: 1 Starch, 1 Vegetable, 2 Lean Meat, 1½ Fat OR 1 Carbohydrate, 1 Vegetable, 2 Lean Meat, 1½ Fat

Green Bean and Turkey Casserole

Prep Time: 30 minutes

Yield: 6 servings

6 servings instant mashed potatoes

1½ to 2 cups cubed cooked turkey or chicken

1 (14½-oz.) can cut green beans, drained

1 (10¾-oz.) can condensed cream of mushroom soup

⅓ cup milk

4 oz. (1 cup) shredded Cheddar cheese

½ (2.8-oz.) can french-fried onions

1. Prepare instant mashed potatoes as directed on package. Set aside.

2. Heat oven to 375° F. In medium saucepan, combine turkey, green beans, soup and milk; mix well. Cook over medium heat until mixture is hot, stirring occasionally. Remove from heat. Add cheese; stir until melted. Pour into ungreased 2-quart casserole. Top with prepared mashed potatoes.

3. Bake at 375° F. for 10 minutes. Sprinkle with onions. Bake an additional 3 to 5 minutes or until mixture is bubbly and onions are warm.

Nutrition Information Per Serving: Serving Size: ⅙ of Recipe • Calories 430 • Calories from Fat 220 • % Daily Value • Total Fat 24 g 37% • Saturated 9 g 45% • Cholesterol 65 mg 22% • Sodium 1090 mg 45% • Total Carbohydrate 30 g 10% • Dietary Fiber 2 g 8% • Sugars 5 g • Protein 23 g • Vitamin A 15% • Vitamin C 4% • Calcium 25% • Iron 10%
Dietary Exchanges: 2 Starch, 2½ Lean Meat, 3 Fat OR 2 Carbohydrate, 2½ Lean Meat, 3 Fat

Keeping a Lid on It

Some casserole dishes now come with plastic lids or insulated carrying cases. If your casserole is not equipped with a snug cover, improvise:

♦ Cover a round casserole with a dinner plate, a pie pan or a saucepan; tape it on securely.

♦ Cover the casserole with foil or a double layer of plastic wrap and secure it with a large rubber band.

Quick Side Dishes and Desserts

Most casseroles need little else to make a complete meal. Here are some easy ideas:

SUPER SIDE SALADS

- Toss purchased coleslaw blend with bottled Italian dressing.
- Serve baby carrots, prewashed and peeled, with purchased dip.
- Toss cucumber slices and chopped onion with a sprinkle of balsamic or regular vinegar; sprinkle with minced fresh chives or shredded fresh mint leaves, if available.
- Drizzle cooked beet slices (leftover or canned) with olive oil, red wine vinegar and a sprinkling of dill seed.
- Make a quick Greek salad from a bag of purchased prewashed greens tossed with vinaigrette. Sprinkle with crumbled feta and black olives.

DRESSED-UP BREADS

- Unroll an 11-ounce can of refrigerated breadsticks and separate the dough into eight strips. Twist each strip and place on a cookie sheet, pressing the ends down firmly. Brush the top with olive oil and sprinkle with salt, pepper and dried herbs before baking.
- Top bread-style pizza crust with shredded mozzarella; heat in the oven until the cheese melts.
- Split a loaf of Italian bread lengthwise and drizzle the cut surfaces with olive oil. Top with fresh tomato slices and chopped fresh basil.
- Spread slices of white bread with butter, sprinkle with sesame seeds and toast under the broiler until the seeds are just golden brown.
- Roll up shredded cheese in flour tortillas and microwave them briefly on MEDIUM (about 30 seconds for one roll-up) to melt the cheese. Cut the roll-up into segments.

COLORFUL VEGETABLE DISHES

- Sprinkle tarragon over steamed or boiled carrots.
- Sauté washed, fresh spinach with olive oil and garlic.
- Sprinkle cooked green beans with toasted almond slivers.
- Toss steamed snow peas with sliced water chestnuts and a dash of stir-fry sauce.
- Squeeze a wedge of fresh lemon over buttered asparagus spears or zucchini slices.

FAST FRUIT FINALES

- Splash fresh orange sections or canned mandarin orange segments with a touch of orange liqueur and some grated orange zest.
- Drizzle fresh cantaloupe or papaya slices with lime juice.
- Stir frozen raspberries and/or canned pineapple chunks together with sliced bananas.

Bread Crumbs

Bread crumbs can help bind or thicken casserole mixtures or contribute to a pleasingly crisp topping. In addition to boxes or cans of plain and seasoned bread crumbs, a newly popular ingredient is Japanese bread crumbs, or panko. Panko has a lighter texture and yields an even crisper coating or topping. To make homemade bread crumbs, use the pulse setting on a food processor or blender to make crumbs out of croutons, toast or stale bread.

Creamy Potato and Sausage Casserole

Prep Time: 30 minutes (Ready in 50 minutes)

Yield: 4 servings

½ lb. bulk light turkey and pork sausage
2 cups frozen peas and carrots, thawed*
⅔ cup milk
2 (10¾-oz.) cans condensed 98% fat-free cream of mushroom soup
3 cups frozen potatoes O'Brien with onions and peppers
¼ cup unseasoned dry bread crumbs
2 teaspoons margarine or butter, melted

1. Heat oven to 375° F. Spray four 2- to 2½-cup individual casseroles with nonstick cooking spray. In small nonstick skillet, cook sausage over medium-high heat until no longer pink, breaking apart sausage with spoon. Drain.

2. Stir in peas and carrots, milk and soup. In each sprayed casserole, layer ½ the potatoes and ½ the sausage mixture.

3. In small bowl, combine bread crumbs and margarine; mix well. Sprinkle evenly over casseroles.

4. Bake at 375° F. for 15 to 20 minutes or until bubbly and lightly browned.

Tip: *To quickly thaw peas and carrots, place in colander or strainer; rinse with warm water until thawed. Drain well.

Nutrition Information Per Serving: Serving Size: ¼ of Recipe • Calories 390 • Calories from Fat 150 • % Daily Value • Total Fat 17 g 26% • Saturated 3 g 15% • Cholesterol 50 mg 17% • Sodium 1610 mg 67% • Total Carbohydrate 41 g 14% • Dietary Fiber 4 g 16% • Sugars 8 g • Protein 17 g • Vitamin A 140% • Vitamin C 20% • Calcium 10% • Iron 15%
Dietary Exchanges: 2½ Starch, 1½ Medium-Fat Meat, 2 Fat OR 2½ Carbohydrate, 1½ Medium-Fat Meat, 2 Fat

Creamy Potato and Sausage Casserole

Turkey Sausage Strata

Prep Time: 35 minutes (Ready in 7 hours 45 minutes)
Yield: 12 servings

1	lb. bulk turkey breakfast sausage
12	slices white bread, cubed (8 cups)
4	oz. (1 cup) shredded mozzarella cheese
½	cup chopped onion
1	(9-oz.) pkg. frozen cut broccoli in a pouch, thawed, drained*
1	(2-oz.) jar sliced pimientos, drained
1½	cups refrigerated or frozen fat-free egg product, thawed
3	cups skim milk
½	teaspoon salt
¼	teaspoon dry mustard
½	cup grated fresh Parmesan cheese

1. Spray 13x9-inch (3-quart) baking dish with nonstick cooking spray. Cook sausage as directed on package. Layer bread, mozzarella cheese, sausage, onion, broccoli and pimientos in sprayed baking dish.

2. In medium bowl, combine egg product, milk, salt and mustard; blend well. Pour egg product mixture evenly over sausage mixture; sprinkle with Parmesan cheese. Cover with foil; refrigerate at least 6 hours or overnight.

3. Heat oven to 325°F. Uncover; bake 55 to 70 minutes or until knife inserted in center comes out clean. Let stand 10 minutes before serving.

Tip: *To quickly thaw broccoli, remove broccoli from pouch; place in colander or strainer. Rinse with warm water until thawed; drain well. Or cut small slit in center of pouch; microwave on HIGH for 2 to 3 minutes or until thawed. Remove broccoli from pouch; drain well.

Nutrition Information Per Serving: Serving Size: ¹⁄₁₂ of Recipe • Calories 240 • Calories from Fat 100 • % Daily Value • Total Fat 11 g 17% • Saturated 4 g 20% • Cholesterol 40 mg 13% • Sodium 710 mg 30% • Total Carbohydrate 19 g 6% • Dietary Fiber 1 g 4% • Sugars 5 g • Protein 17 g • Vitamin A 10% • Vitamin C 20% • Calcium 25% • Iron 10%
Dietary Exchanges: 1½ Starch, 2 Medium-Fat Meat OR 1½ Carbohydrate, 2 Medium-Fat Meat

Confetti Egg Bake

Prep Time: 20 minutes (Ready in 1 hour)

Yield: 6 servings

½ lb. bulk turkey mild Italian sausage

2 oz. (½ cup) shredded reduced-fat Cheddar cheese

1 (9-oz.) pkg. frozen spinach in a pouch, thawed, squeezed to drain*

1 cup sliced fresh mushrooms

½ cup chopped green onions

1 (2-oz.) jar sliced pimientos, drained

6 eggs

1 cup half-and-half

2 oz. (½ cup) shredded Swiss cheese

½ teaspoon paprika

1. Heat oven to 350° F. Spray 8-inch square (2-quart) baking dish with nonstick cooking spray. In medium skillet, cook sausage until no longer pink. Drain.

2. Layer Cheddar cheese, spinach, cooked sausage, mushrooms, green onions and pimientos in sprayed baking dish.

3. In medium bowl, combine eggs and half-and-half; blend well. Pour egg mixture evenly over layered mixture. Sprinkle with Swiss cheese and paprika.**

4. Bake at 350° F. for 30 to 40 minutes or until knife inserted in center comes out clean. Let stand 5 minutes before serving.

Tips: *To quickly thaw spinach, cut small slit in center of pouch; microwave on HIGH for 2 to 3 minutes or until thawed. Remove spinach from pouch; squeeze dry with paper towels.

**To make ahead, prepare as directed to this point. Cover; refrigerate up to 1 day before baking. Uncover; bake at 350° F. for 40 to 50 minutes.

Nutrition Information Per Serving: Serving Size: ⅙ of Recipe • Calories 280 • Calories from Fat 170 • % Daily Value • Total Fat 19 g 29% • Saturated 9 g 45% • Cholesterol 260 mg 87% • Sodium 530 mg 22% • Total Carbohydrate 7 g 2% • Dietary Fiber 1 g 4% • Sugars 3 g • Protein 21 g • Vitamin A 50% • Vitamin C 30% • Calcium 30% • Iron 15%

Dietary Exchanges: 1 Vegetable, 2½ Medium-Fat Meat, 1½ Fat

Cheesy Noodle Turkey Casserole

Cheesy Noodle Turkey Casserole

Prep Time: 30 minutes (Ready in 1 hour 10 minutes)

Yield: 10 servings

Photo above and page 4

8	oz. (5 cups) uncooked dumpling egg noodles
1½	lb. lean ground turkey
1	medium onion, chopped
1	(14-oz.) jar spaghetti sauce
1	(10¾-oz.) can condensed Cheddar cheese soup
1	(8-oz.) can tomato sauce
1	(4-oz.) can mushroom pieces and stems, drained
¼	teaspoon garlic powder
¼	teaspoon dried thyme leaves
¼	teaspoon pepper
8	oz. (2 cups) shredded colby–Monterey Jack cheese blend or Cheddar cheese

1. Heat oven to 350° F. Cook noodles to desired doneness as directed on package. Drain; rinse with hot water. Place in large bowl.

2. Meanwhile, in large skillet over medium-high heat, brown ground turkey and onion until turkey is thoroughly cooked. Drain, if necessary. Stir in all remaining ingredients except cheese and noodles; simmer 3 to 4 minutes.

3. Pour turkey mixture over noodles; mix well. Spoon into ungreased 13x9-inch (3-quart) baking dish. Cover with foil.

4. Bake at 350° F. for 35 to 40 minutes or until hot and bubbly. Uncover; sprinkle with cheese. Bake uncovered for an additional 5 minutes or until cheese is melted.

Nutrition Information Per Serving: Serving Size: ⅒ of Recipe • Calories 370 • Calories from Fat 160 • % Daily Value • Total Fat 18 g 28% • Saturated 8 g 40% • Cholesterol 100 mg 33% • Sodium 760 mg 32% • Total Carbohydrate 26 g 9% • Dietary Fiber 2 g 8% • Sugars 3 g • Protein 25 g • Vitamin A 20% • Vitamin C 8% • Calcium 25% • Iron 15%
Dietary Exchanges: 1½ Starch, 3 Medium-Fat Meat, ½ Fat OR 1½ Carbohydrate, 3 Medium-Fat Meat, ½ Fat

Three-Bean Turkey Burger Bake

Prep Time: 25 minutes (Ready in 1 hour)

Yield: 6 (1-cup) servings

1	lb. ground turkey
1	cup chopped onions
1	(9-oz.) pkg. frozen baby lima beans in a pouch
1	(16-oz.) can baked beans, undrained
1	(15½- or 15-oz.) can kidney beans, drained
¼	cup firmly packed brown sugar
1	teaspoon salt
1	teaspoon prepared mustard
⅛	teaspoon pepper
½	cup ketchup
2	tablespoons molasses
1	tablespoon vinegar

1. Heat oven to 350°F. In large skillet, brown ground turkey and onions. Drain.

2. Add lima beans; cook and stir until beans are thoroughly heated. Add all remaining ingredients; mix well. Spoon into ungreased 2-quart casserole.

3. Bake at 350°F. for 35 minutes or until hot and bubbly.

✳ **Make-Ahead Directions:** These make-ahead directions work best if you substitute an 8-inch square (2-quart) baking dish for the 2-quart casserole. Prepare recipe as directed; do not bake. Cover with foil; freeze. When ready to use, do not thaw; bake, covered, at 350°F. for 1½ hours. Uncover; bake an additional 35 minutes or until mixture is thoroughly heated.

Nutrition Information Per Serving: Serving Size: 1 Cup • Calories 380 • Calories from Fat 70 • % Daily Value • Total Fat 8 g 12% • Saturated 2 g 10% • Cholesterol 55 mg 18% • Sodium 1160 mg 48% • Total Carbohydrate 52 g 17% • Dietary Fiber 9 g 36% • Sugars 22 g • Protein 24 g • Vitamin A 6% • Vitamin C 10% • Calcium 10% • Iron 20%

Dietary Exchanges: 2 Starch, 1½ Fruit, 2½ Very Lean Meat, 1 Fat OR 3½ Carbohydrate, 2½ Very Lean Meat, 1 Fat

Three-Bean Turkey Burger Bake

Tuna Casserole

Prep Time: 20 minutes (Ready in 55 minutes)

Yield: 6 (1¼-cup) servings

1   (7-oz.) pkg. (1⅔ cups)
        uncooked elbow macaroni
1   cup milk
4   oz. (1 cup) shredded
        Cheddar cheese
1   (10¾-oz.) can condensed
        cream of mushroom soup
1   (6-oz.) can water-packed
        tuna, drained, flaked
1   (4-oz.) can mushroom pieces
        and stems, drained
2   tablespoons chopped
        pimientos, if desired
2   teaspoons instant minced
        onion
½   teaspoon dry mustard
½   cup crushed potato chips

1. Heat oven to 350° F. Grease 2-quart casserole. Cook macaroni in large saucepan or Dutch oven to desired doneness as directed on package. Drain; return to saucepan.

2. Add all remaining ingredients except potato chips to cooked macaroni; stir to combine. Pour mixture into greased casserole. Sprinkle with potato chips.

3. Bake at 350° F. for 25 to 35 minutes or until thoroughly heated.

Nutrition Information Per Serving: Serving Size: 1¼ Cups • Calories 330 • Calories from Fat 120 • % Daily Value • Total Fat 13 g 20% • Saturated 6 g 30% • Cholesterol 30 mg 10% • Sodium 660 mg 28% • Total Carbohydrate 35 g 12% • Dietary Fiber 2 g 8% • Sugars 5 g • Protein 18 g • Vitamin A 10% • Vitamin C 20% • Calcium 20% • Iron 10%
Dietary Exchanges: 2½ Starch, 1½ Very Lean Meat, 2 Fat OR 2½ Carbohydrate, 1½ Very Lean Meat, 2 Fat

Overnight Tuna Casserole

Prep Time: 40 minutes (Ready in 9 hours 50 minutes)

Yield: 7 (1-cup) servings

2   eggs
1   (7-oz.) pkg. (1⅔ cups)
        uncooked elbow macaroni
2   (6-oz.) cans water-packed
        tuna, drained, flaked
½   cup finely chopped green
        bell pepper
½   cup finely chopped onion
1   tablespoon chopped
        pimientos
2   (10¾-oz.) cans condensed
        cream of mushroom soup
2   cups milk
4   oz. (1 cup) shredded
        Cheddar cheese

1. Place eggs in small saucepan; cover with cold water. Bring to a boil. Reduce heat; simmer about 15 minutes. Immediately drain; run cold water over eggs to stop cooking. Peel eggs; chop.

2. Grease 3-quart casserole. In large bowl, combine chopped eggs, uncooked macaroni and all remaining ingredients; mix well. Spoon into greased casserole. Cover; refrigerate at least 8 hours or overnight.

3. Heat oven to 375° F. Let casserole stand at room temperature for 15 minutes. Uncover; bake at 375° F. for 60 to 70 minutes or until thoroughly heated and bubbly.

Nutrition Information Per Serving: Serving Size: 1 Cup • Calories 360 • Calories from Fat 140 • % Daily Value • Total Fat 15 g 23% • Saturated 7 g 35% • Cholesterol 95 mg 32% • Sodium 880 mg 37% • Total Carbohydrate 33 g 11% • Dietary Fiber 1 g 4% • Sugars 7 g • Protein 24 g • Vitamin A 10% • Vitamin C 10% • Calcium 25% • Iron 15%
Dietary Exchanges: 2 Starch, 2½ Very Lean Meat, 2½ Fat OR 2 Carbohydrate, 2½ Very Lean Meat, 2½ Fat

Casseroles for New Parents

The arrival of a baby can put the best-organized home into disarray. New parents often appreciate the kindness of friends who deliver a home-cooked meal. Casseroles are ideal for these occasions.

- Ask before you cook. Find out about any food allergies or aversions, and whether the last six friends have all brought lasagna. Nursing mothers may be avoiding certain foods, such as beans or cabbage.

- Choose foods whose ingredients are already cut up (for instance, cubed chicken rather than bone-in pieces). New parents are learning to do everything with one hand.

- Package foods in disposable containers so the parents need not keep track of your dishes.

- Tape a written description of the contents plus instructions for reheating or serving on each casserole.

- Include super-simple side dishes such as chips and dip, washed salad greens and bottled dressing, cookies or precut brownies.

- To make the meal special, you could include a few extras such as decorative napkins, a few cut flowers already in a vase or jar and beverages.

- If the family includes other young children, set aside some of the noodles, rice, cooked chicken or other "plain" ingredients for skeptical young eaters. Include something special for the siblings, such as an individual plate of cookies or a small wrapped gift.

- Visitors are tiring for new parents. Put the food away in the refrigerator, chat for no more than five minutes, then leave.

Selecting Canned Tuna

Canned tuna comes packed in either water or vegetable oil. Water-packed tuna has fewer calories and fresher flavor than oil-packed tuna. Albacore tuna is the only species that can be labeled "white meat." It has the mildest flavor and lightest flesh. Tuna from other species is identified as "light."

Canned tuna comes in three grades:

1. Solid or fancy tuna contains three or four large pieces and is best for recipes where appearance is important.
2. Chunk tuna contains smaller pieces.
3. Flaked tuna contains the smallest bits and pieces. Chunk and flaked tuna are fine for casseroles and sandwich fillings in which the fish will be broken up anyway.

Old-Time Tuna Bake

Prep Time: 30 minutes (Ready in 1 hour)

Yield: 6 (1⅓-cup) servings

7	oz. (4 cups) uncooked wide egg noodles
1	(10¾-oz.) can condensed cream of celery soup
1	(12-oz.) can evaporated milk or 1½ cups half-and-half
1	tablespoon instant minced onion
1	teaspoon seasoned salt
2	(6-oz.) cans water-packed tuna, drained, flaked
1	(9-oz.) pkg. frozen sweet peas in a pouch, thawed, drained
1	(2.8-oz.) can french-fried onions

1. Cook noodles to desired doneness as directed on package. Drain; rinse with hot water.

2. Meanwhile, heat oven to 350° F. In ungreased 2-quart casserole, combine soup, milk, onion and salt. Add cooked noodles, tuna and peas; mix well. Cover.

3. Bake at 350° F. for 30 minutes. Remove from oven; stir well. Sprinkle with french-fried onions. Bake uncovered for an additional 5 minutes.

✳ **Make-Ahead Directions:** These make-ahead directions work best if you substitute an 8-inch square (2-quart) baking dish for the 2-quart casserole. Prepare recipe as directed above except omit french-fried onions; do not bake. Cover with foil; freeze. When ready to use, do not thaw; bake, covered, at 350° F. for 1½ hours. Uncover; bake an additional 25 minutes or until mixture is thoroughly heated. Sprinkle with french-fried onions; bake an additional 5 minutes.

Nutrition Information Per Serving: Serving Size: 1⅓ Cups • Calories 400 • Calories from Fat 140 • % Daily Value • Total Fat 15 g 23% • Saturated 6 g 30% • Cholesterol 65 mg 22% • Sodium 1040 mg 43% • Total Carbohydrate 42 g 14% • Dietary Fiber 3 g 12% • Sugars 11 g • Protein 23 g • Vitamin A 10% • Vitamin C 6% • Calcium 20% • Iron 15%
Dietary Exchanges: 3 Starch, 2 Very Lean Meat, 2 Fat OR 3 Carbohydrate, 2 Very Lean Meat, 2 Fat

Old-Time Tuna Bake

Tuna-Broccoli Spaghetti Pie

Prep Time: 30 minutes (Ready in 1 hour 15 minutes)

Yield: 6 servings

6	oz. uncooked spaghetti
2	tablespoons margarine or butter
½	cup grated Parmesan cheese
2	eggs, slightly beaten
3	cups frozen cut broccoli, thawed, drained
2	tablespoons all-purpose flour
1	(10-oz.) container refrigerated Alfredo sauce
1	(9-oz.) can water-packed tuna, drained, flaked
¼	cup Italian-style dry bread crumbs
1	teaspoon margarine or butter, melted

1. In large saucepan or Dutch oven, cook spaghetti to desired doneness as directed on package. Drain; return to saucepan.

2. Meanwhile, heat oven to 350° F. Grease 10- or 9-inch deep-dish pie pan or quiche dish.

3. To cooked spaghetti, add 2 tablespoons margarine, Parmesan cheese and eggs; stir gently. Spread over bottom and up sides of greased pie pan.

4. In large bowl, combine broccoli, flour, Alfredo sauce and tuna; mix well. Spoon into spaghetti crust. In small bowl, combine bread crumbs and 1 teaspoon melted margarine; mix well. Sprinkle over tuna mixture.

5. Bake at 350° F. for 40 to 45 minutes or until spaghetti is light golden brown. Let stand 5 minutes before serving.

Nutrition Information Per Serving: Serving Size: ⅙ of Recipe • Calories 450 • Calories from Fat 230 • % Daily Value • Total Fat 25 g 38% • Saturated 11 g 55% • Cholesterol 120 mg 40% • Sodium 700 mg 29% • Total Carbohydrate 32 g 11% • Dietary Fiber 2 g 8% • Sugars 3 g • Protein 23 g • Vitamin A 10% • Vitamin C 20% • Calcium 25% • Iron 15%
Dietary Exchanges: 2 Starch, 1 Vegetable, 2 Very Lean Meat, 4½ Fat OR 2 Carbohydrate, 1 Vegetable, 2 Very Lean Meat, 4½ Fat

Citrus-Plum Orange Roughy

Prep Time: 10 minutes (Ready in 35 minutes)

Yield: 4 servings

1⅓	cups uncooked regular long-grain white rice
2⅔	cups water
4	(4- to 5-oz.) orange roughy fillets
1	(8½-oz.) jar (¾ cup) Chinese plum sauce
¼	teaspoon coarsely grated lemon peel
2	cups thinly sliced bok choy
1	(8-oz.) can sliced bamboo shoots, drained
4	lemon wedges

1. Cook rice in water as directed on package.

2. Meanwhile, heat oven to 350° F. Arrange orange roughy fillets in single layer in ungreased 13 x 9-inch (3-quart) baking dish. Spoon plum sauce evenly over top; sprinkle with lemon peel. Arrange bok choy and bamboo shoots around sides of fish. Cover with foil.

3. Bake at 350° F. for 20 to 25 minutes or until fish flakes easily with fork. Serve fish over rice with lemon wedges.

Nutrition Information Per Serving: Serving Size: ¼ of Recipe • Calories 460 • Calories from Fat 20 • % Daily Value • Total Fat 2 g 3% • Saturated 0 g 0% • Cholesterol 30 mg 10% • Sodium 890 mg 37% • Total Carbohydrate 85 g 28% • Dietary Fiber 3 g 12% • Sugars 32 g • Protein 26 g • Vitamin A 4% • Vitamin C 20% • Calcium 8% • Iron 20%
Dietary Exchanges: 1½ Starch, 4 Fruit, 1 Vegetable, 2½ Very Lean Meat OR 5½ Carbohydrate, 1 Vegetable, 2½ Very Lean Meat

Tuna-Broccoli Rolls

Prep Time: 40 minutes (Ready in 1 hour 20 minutes)
Yield: 12 rolls; 6 servings

TUNA ROLLS
12 uncooked lasagna noodles
1 (9-oz.) pkg. frozen cut
   broccoli in a pouch,
   thawed, drained*
1 (6-oz.) can water-packed
   tuna, drained, flaked
1 (4½-oz.) jar sliced
   mushrooms, drained

SAUCE
2 tablespoons margarine or
   butter
¼ cup all-purpose flour
1½ cups skim milk
1 cup chicken broth
2 teaspoons chopped fresh
   thyme or ½ teaspoon dried
   thyme leaves
¼ teaspoon salt
⅛ teaspoon pepper
½ cup shredded reduced-fat
   Cheddar cheese

1. Cook lasagna noodles to desired doneness as directed on package. Drain; rinse with hot water. Meanwhile, in medium bowl, combine broccoli, tuna and mushrooms; mix well.

2. Heat oven to 350° F. Melt margarine in medium saucepan over low heat. Stir in flour; cook until mixture is smooth and bubbly, stirring constantly. Stir in all remaining sauce ingredients except cheese. Cook over medium heat for 5 to 8 minutes or until sauce is thickened, stirring constantly. Stir ½ the sauce (1 cup) into broccoli mixture; mix well.

3. Spread each cooked lasagna noodle with about 2 heaping tablespoons broccoli mixture. Roll up each noodle; place in ungreased 13 x 9-inch (3-quart) baking dish. Spoon remaining sauce over rolls. Cover with foil.

4. Bake at 350° F. for 25 to 35 minutes or until thoroughly heated. Uncover; sprinkle with cheese. Bake uncovered for an additional 5 minutes or until cheese is melted.

Tip: *To quickly thaw broccoli, remove broccoli from pouch; place in colander or strainer. Rinse with warm water until thawed; drain well. Or cut small slit in center of pouch; microwave on HIGH for 2 to 3 minutes or until thawed. Remove broccoli from pouch; drain well.

Nutrition Information Per Serving: Serving Size: ⅙ of Recipe • Calories 170 • Calories from Fat 45 • % Daily Value • Total Fat 5 g 8% • Saturated 1 g 5% • Cholesterol 10 mg 3% • Sodium 310 mg 13% • Total Carbohydrate 21 g 7% • Dietary Fiber 1 g 4% • Sugars 2 g • Protein 10 g • Vitamin A 8% • Vitamin C 10% • Calcium 8% • Iron 8%
Dietary Exchanges: 1½ Starch, 1 Very Lean Meat, ½ Fat OR 1½ Carbohydrate, 1 Very Lean Meat, ½ Fat

De-lightful Tuna Casserole

Prep Time: 25 minutes (Ready in 1 hour)
Yield: 6 (1¹⁄₄-cup) servings
Photo below and page 5

1   (7-oz.) pkg. (1²⁄₃ cups)
     uncooked elbow macaroni
1   cup skim milk
4   oz. (1 cup) shredded
     reduced-fat Cheddar
     cheese
1   (10³⁄₄-oz.) can condensed
     98% fat-free cream of
     mushroom soup with
     30% less sodium
1   (6-oz.) can water-packed
     tuna, drained, flaked
1   (4-oz.) can mushroom pieces
     and stems, drained
2   tablespoons chopped
     pimientos, if desired
1   tablespoon instant minced
     onion
1   teaspoon dry mustard
¹⁄₃   cup cornflake crumbs

1. Cook macaroni to desired doneness as directed on package. Drain.

2. Heat oven to 350° F. Spray 2-quart casserole with nonstick cooking spray. In large bowl, combine cooked macaroni and all remaining ingredients except cornflake crumbs; stir to combine. Pour mixture into sprayed casserole; sprinkle with cornflake crumbs.

3. Bake at 350° F. for 25 to 35 minutes or until thoroughly heated.

Nutrition Information Per Serving: Serving Size: 1¹⁄₄ cups • Calories 280 • Calories from Fat 60 • % Daily Value • Total Fat 7 g 11% • Saturated 3 g 15% • Cholesterol 20 mg 7% • Sodium 730 mg 30% • Total Carbohydrate 37 g 12% • Dietary Fiber 2 g 8% • Sugars 4 g • Protein 18 g • Vitamin A 10% • Vitamin C 10% • Calcium 20% • Iron 20%
Dietary Exchanges: 1½ Starch, 1½ Lean Meat OR 1½ Carbohydrate, 1½ Lean Meat

De-lightful Tuna Casserole

Hot Tuna Salad

Hot Tuna Salad

Prep Time: 20 minutes (Ready in 40 minutes)
Yield: 8 (1¼-cup) servings

1 (10¾-oz.) can condensed
   98% fat-free cream of
   celery soup
1 (8-oz.) can crushed
   pineapple in unsweetened
   juice, undrained
1 (8-oz.) can sliced water
   chestnuts, drained
1 (4-oz.) jar sliced pimientos,
   drained
1½ cups uncooked instant white
   or brown rice
1½ cups sliced celery
⅔ cup raisins
1 tablespoon salt-free lemon-
   pepper seasoning
1½ cups water
1 (12-oz.) can water-packed
   chunk light tuna, drained,
   flaked
1 cup fat-free mayonnaise or
   salad dressing
½ cup sliced almonds

1. Heat oven to 400°F. Spray 13x9-inch (3-quart) baking dish with nonstick cooking spray.

2. In large nonstick saucepan, combine soup, pineapple, water chestnuts, pimientos, rice, celery, raisins, lemon-pepper seasoning and water; mix well. Bring to a boil. Remove from heat. Stir in tuna and mayonnaise; mix well. Spoon into sprayed baking dish. Top with almonds.

3. Bake at 400°F. for 15 to 20 minutes or until thoroughly heated.

Nutrition Information Per Serving: Serving Size: 1¼ Cups • Calories 270 • Calories from Fat 45 • % Daily Value • Total Fat 5 g 8% • Saturated 1 g 5% • Cholesterol 10 mg 3% • Sodium 670 mg 28% • Total Carbohydrate 44 g 15% • Dietary Fiber 4 g 16% • Sugars 15 g • Protein 13 g • Vitamin A 10% • Vitamin C 30% • Calcium 4% • Iron 10%
Dietary Exchanges: 2 Starch, 1 Fruit, 1 Very Lean Meat, ½ Fat OR 3 Carbohydrate, 1 Very Lean Meat, ½ Fat

Broccoli-Shrimp Fettuccine

Prep Time: 45 minutes (Ready in 1 hour 20 minutes)

Yield: 6 servings

1	(12-oz.) pkg. frozen ready-to-cook shrimp
4	cups fresh broccoli florets
1	(10-oz.) container refrigerated Alfredo sauce
1	(9-oz.) pkg. refrigerated fettuccine
1	tablespoon olive oil or vegetable oil
1	large shallot, minced
1	(14½-oz.) can diced tomatoes, undrained
1	tablespoon tomato paste
½	teaspoon fennel seed, crushed
2	oz. (½ cup) shredded fresh Parmesan cheese

1. Heat oven to 375° F. Spray 12x8-inch (2-quart) baking dish with nonstick cooking spray.

2. In large saucepan, bring 6 cups water to a boil. Add shrimp and broccoli; cook 2 to 3 minutes or until shrimp turn pink. Drain. In medium bowl, combine shrimp, broccoli and Alfredo sauce; mix gently. Set aside.

3. Cook fettuccine to desired doneness as directed on package. Drain.

4. Meanwhile, in medium saucepan, heat oil until hot. Add shallot; cook 1 minute. Stir in tomatoes, tomato paste and fennel seed; simmer 10 minutes.

5. Arrange ⅓ of cooked fettuccine in sprayed baking dish. Cover with ½ of tomato mixture. Top with ⅓ of fettuccine and all the shrimp-broccoli mixture. Top with remaining fettuccine and remaining tomato mixture. Sprinkle with cheese.

6. Bake at 375° F. for 25 to 35 minutes or until mixture is thoroughly heated and cheese is melted. Let stand 10 minutes before serving.

✳ **Make-Ahead Directions:** Prepare recipe as directed above; do not bake. Cover with foil; freeze. When ready to use, do not thaw; bake, covered, at 375° F. for 1 hour 15 minutes. Uncover; bake an additional 20 minutes or until mixture is thoroughly heated and bubbly. Let stand 10 minutes before serving.

Nutrition Information Per Serving: Serving Size: ⅙ of Recipe • Calories 360 • Calories from Fat 190 • % Daily Value • Total Fat 21 g 32% • Saturated 10 g 50% • Cholesterol 120 mg 40% • Sodium 590 mg 25% • Total Carbohydrate 22 g 7% • Dietary Fiber 3 g 12% • Sugars 4 g • Protein 20 g • Vitamin A 45% • Vitamin C 70% • Calcium 25% • Iron 15%
Dietary Exchanges: 1 Starch, 1 Vegetable, 2 Very Lean Meat, 4 Fat OR 1 Carbohydrate, 1 Vegetable, 2 Very Lean Meat, 4 Fat

Turning Up the Heat

You can spike practically any casserole recipe with one of the following. If someone at the table may prefer mild to wild, pass the hot stuff at the table rather than adding it to the recipe.

Hot pepper flakes or dried red peppers

Cayenne pepper

Chopped jalapeños

Hot ground chile peppers or hot paprika

Hot chili powder

Bottled hot sauce

Shrimp and Pasta Bake

Prep Time: 30 minutes (Ready in 50 minutes)

Yield: 6 servings

1 (16-oz.) pkg. uncooked bow tie pasta (farfalle)
1 (14½-oz.) can diced tomatoes, undrained
1 (12-oz.) pkg. frozen shelled, deveined, cooked small shrimp, thawed
1 (8-oz.) can tomato sauce
1 (4½-oz.) jar sliced mushrooms, drained
1 teaspoon dried oregano leaves
¼ teaspoon crushed red pepper flakes
¼ cup grated Parmesan cheese

1. Heat oven to 350° F. Cook pasta to desired doneness as directed on package. Drain.

2. Place cooked pasta in ungreased 13 x 9-inch (3-quart) baking dish. Stir in tomatoes, shrimp, tomato sauce, mushrooms, oregano and red pepper flakes. Sprinkle with cheese. Cover with foil.

3. Bake at 350° F. for 15 to 20 minutes or until thoroughly heated.

Nutrition Information Per Serving: Serving Size: ⅙ of Recipe • Calories 380 • Calories from Fat 25 • % Daily Value • Total Fat 3 g 5% • Saturated 1 g 5% • Cholesterol 115 mg 38% • Sodium 600 mg 25% • Total Carbohydrate 64 g 21% • Dietary Fiber 4 g 16% • Sugars 6 g • Protein 25 g • Vitamin A 20% • Vitamin C 20% • Calcium 10% • Iron 30%
Dietary Exchanges: 4 Starch, 1 Vegetable, 1½ Very Lean Meat OR 4 Carbohydrate, 1 Vegetable, 1½ Very Lean Meat

Overnight Salmon Bake

Prep Time: 15 minutes (Ready in 9 hours 10 minutes)
Yield: 5 servings

EASY WHITE SAUCE*
- 3 tablespoons margarine or butter
- 3 tablespoons all-purpose flour
- ¼ teaspoon salt
- ⅛ teaspoon pepper
- ¾ cup chicken broth
- ½ cup milk

CASSEROLE
- 3½ oz. (2 cups) uncooked mini-lasagna noodles (mafalda)
- 1 (14¾-oz.) can salmon, drained, flaked
- 1 (9-oz.) pkg. frozen cut broccoli in a pouch, thawed, drained**
- ½ teaspoon onion powder
- ¼ to ½ teaspoon dried tarragon leaves
- 1 cup milk

TOPPING
- ½ cup unseasoned dry bread crumbs
- 2 tablespoons grated Parmesan cheese
- 2 tablespoons margarine or butter, melted

1. Melt 3 tablespoons margarine in medium saucepan over medium heat. Stir in flour, salt and pepper. Cook until mixture is smooth and bubbly, stirring constantly. Gradually stir in broth and milk. Cook until mixture boils and thickens, stirring constantly. Set aside.

2. In ungreased 8-inch square (2-quart) baking dish, combine all casserole ingredients; mix well. Stir in white sauce; blend well. Cover tightly with foil; refrigerate at least 8 hours or overnight.

3. Heat oven to 350°F. In small bowl, combine topping ingredients; mix well. Uncover casserole; sprinkle with topping. Bake uncovered for 45 to 55 minutes or until bubbly and golden brown.

Tips: *One 10¾-oz. can condensed cream of mushroom soup (undiluted) can be substituted for the white sauce.

**To quickly thaw broccoli, remove broccoli from pouch; place in colander or strainer. Rinse with warm water until thawed; drain well. Or cut small slit in center of pouch; microwave on HIGH for 2 to 3 minutes or until thawed. Remove broccoli from pouch; drain well.

Nutrition Information Per Serving: Serving Size: ⅕ of Recipe • Calories 410 • Calories from Fat 180 • % Daily Value • Total Fat 20 g 31% • Saturated 5 g 25% • Cholesterol 40 mg 13% • Sodium 980 mg 41% • Total Carbohydrate 33 g 11% • Dietary Fiber 2 g 8% • Sugars 5 g • Protein 24 g • Vitamin A 20% • Vitamin C 30% • Calcium 15% • Iron 15%
Dietary Exchanges: 2 Starch, 1 Vegetable, 2½ Lean Meat, 2 Fat OR 2 Carbohydrate, 1 Vegetable, 2½ Lean Meat, 2 Fat

Overnight Salmon Bake

Seafood Almond Casserole

Prep Time: 30 minutes (Ready in 1 hour 15 minutes)

Yield: 7 (1-cup) servings

CASSEROLE

⅔ cup uncooked regular long-grain white rice

1⅓ cups water

2 (6-oz.) cans shrimp, drained, rinsed

1 cup shredded imitation crabmeat (surimi)

1 (8-oz.) can sliced water chestnuts, drained

½ cup chopped green bell pepper

½ cup chopped celery

½ cup chopped onion

1 cup mayonnaise

1 cup tomato juice

¼ teaspoon pepper

TOPPING

4 oz. (1 cup) shredded Cheddar cheese

½ cup slivered almonds, toasted*

1. Cook rice in water as directed on package.

2. Heat oven to 350° F. In ungreased 2-quart casserole, combine cooked rice and all remaining casserole ingredients; mix well. Sprinkle cheese and almonds over top.

3. Bake at 350° F. for 35 to 45 minutes or until hot and bubbly.

Tip: *To toast almonds, spread on cookie sheet; bake at 350° F. for 5 to 7 minutes or until light golden brown, stirring occasionally. Or spread in thin layer in microwave-safe pie pan. Microwave on HIGH for 4 to 6 minutes or until light golden brown, stirring frequently.

Nutrition Information Per Serving: Serving Size: 1 Cup • Calories 510 • Calories from Fat 320 • % Daily Value • Total Fat 36 g 55% • Saturated 8 g 40% • Cholesterol 105 mg 35% • Sodium 680 mg 28% • Total Carbohydrate 27 g 9% • Dietary Fiber 2 g 8% • Sugars 6 g • Protein 19 g • Vitamin A 10% • Vitamin C 20% • Calcium 20% • Iron 15%
Dietary Exchanges: 1½ Starch, 1 Vegetable, 2 Very Lean Meat, 6½ Fat OR 1½ Carbohydrate, 1 Vegetable, 2 Very Lean Meat, 6½ Fat

Kinds of Rice

To give your rice casserole a slightly different character, try:

♦ Jasmine rice, a fragrant variety available in Asian markets and specialty food shops

♦ Basmati (or Texmati) rice, sold in supermarkets, Indian groceries and gourmet food stores

♦ Arborio rice, a short-grained Italian rice used for risotto, available in Italian markets and specialty food shops

Light Crab Linguine

Prep Time: 20 minutes (Ready in 1 hour 10 minutes)

Yield: 8 servings

CASSEROLE

12   oz. uncooked linguine

2   (10¾-oz.) cans condensed cream of asparagus soup

1   (12-oz.) can light evaporated skim milk

1   cup fat-free half-and-half

6   oz. (1½ cups) shredded reduced-fat Monterey Jack cheese

1   (10½-oz.) can cut asparagus spears, drained

1   (6-oz.) can crabmeat, drained, flaked

¼   cup white wine

TOPPING

1   cup unseasoned dry bread crumbs

2   tablespoons margarine or butter, melted

½   cup fat-free half-and-half

1. Heat oven to 350°F. Spray 13x9-inch (3-quart) baking dish with nonstick cooking spray. Cook linguine to desired doneness as directed on package. Drain.

2. Meanwhile, in large bowl, combine soup, milk, 1 cup half-and-half and cheese; mix well. Add asparagus, crabmeat and wine; mix gently. Add cooked linguine; toss gently to mix. Pour into sprayed baking dish.

3. In small bowl, combine bread crumbs and margarine; mix well. Stir in ½ cup half-and-half until well combined. Sprinkle evenly over linguine mixture. Spray topping with nonstick cooking spray to coat well.

4. Bake at 350°F. for 45 to 50 minutes or until top is golden brown and edges are bubbly.

Nutrition Information Per Serving: Serving Size: ⅛ of Recipe • Calories 450 • Calories from Fat 120 • % Daily Value • Total Fat 13 g 20% • Saturated 4 g 20% • Cholesterol 35 mg 12% • Sodium 1140 mg 48% • Total Carbohydrate 59 g 20% • Dietary Fiber 2 g 8% • Sugars 10 g • Protein 24 g • Vitamin A 20% • Vitamin C 6% • Calcium 45% • Iron 20%
Dietary Exchanges: 3½ Starch, 1 Vegetable, 1½ Very Lean Meat, 2 Fat OR 3½ Carbohydrate, 1 Vegetable, 1½ Very Lean Meat, 2 Fat

Sole Fillets with Broccoli Stuffing

Prep Time: 30 minutes (Ready in 1 hour)

Yield: 4 servings

STUFFING

1 (7-oz.) pkg. seasoned cube-style stuffing mix (4 cups)
¼ cup margarine or butter
Water
1 (9-oz.) pkg. frozen cut broccoli in a pouch, thawed, drained*

FILLETS

1 lb. sole or flounder fillets
1 tablespoon margarine or butter, melted
2 teaspoons lemon juice
½ teaspoon onion powder
Paprika

1. Heat oven to 375°F. Lightly grease 12x8-inch (2-quart) baking dish. Prepare stuffing mix as directed on package using ¼ cup margarine and water. Stir in broccoli. Spoon evenly into greased baking dish. Place fillets evenly over stuffing mixture.

2. In small bowl, combine 1 tablespoon margarine, lemon juice and onion powder. Brush over fish. Sprinkle with paprika. Cover with foil.

3. Bake at 375°F. for 30 minutes. Uncover; bake an additional 10 minutes or until fish flakes easily with fork.

Tip: *To quickly thaw broccoli, remove broccoli from pouch; place in colander or strainer. Rinse with warm water until thawed; drain well. Or cut small slit in center of pouch; microwave on HIGH for 2 to 3 minutes or until thawed. Remove broccoli from pouch; drain well.

Nutrition Information Per Serving: Serving Size: ¼ of Recipe • Calories 440 • Calories from Fat 150 • % Daily Value • Total Fat 17 g 26% • Saturated 3 g 15% • Cholesterol 60 mg 20% • Sodium 1060 mg 44% • Total Carbohydrate 42 g 14% • Dietary Fiber 5 g 20% • Sugars 3 g • Protein 29 g • Vitamin A 20% • Vitamin C 35% • Calcium 8% • Iron 15%
Dietary Exchanges: 2½ Starch, 1 Vegetable, 3 Very Lean Meat, 2½ Fat OR 2½ Carbohydrate, 1 Vegetable, 3 Very Lean Meat, 2½ Fat

Sole Fillets with Broccoli Stuffing

Stuffed Pasta Shells

Prep Time: 45 minutes (Ready in 1 hour 20 minutes)

Yield: 4 servings

12	uncooked jumbo pasta shells
1	(14-oz.) jar spaghetti sauce
1	cup light ricotta cheese
4	oz. nonfat cream cheese, softened
2	oz. (½ cup) shredded 6-cheese Italian recipe blend cheese
½	cup frozen cut leaf spinach, thawed, squeezed to drain*
½	teaspoon garlic salt
2	tablespoons shredded 6-cheese Italian recipe blend cheese

1. Cook pasta shells to desired doneness as directed on package. Drain.

2. Heat oven to 350° F. Spread 1 cup of the spaghetti sauce in bottom of ungreased 12 x 8-inch (2-quart) baking dish.

3. In medium bowl, combine ricotta cheese, cream cheese, ½ cup shredded cheese, spinach and garlic salt; mix well. Fill each cooked shell with about 2 rounded tablespoonfuls ricotta mixture. Place shells in baking dish. Spoon remaining spaghetti sauce over shells; sprinkle with 2 tablespoons shredded cheese. Cover with sprayed foil.

4. Bake at 350° F. for 25 to 35 minutes or until thoroughly heated.

Tip: *To quickly thaw spinach, place in colander or strainer; rinse with warm water until thawed. Squeeze dry with paper towels.

Nutrition Information Per Serving: Serving Size: ¼ of Recipe • Calories 330 • Calories from Fat 110 • % Daily Value • Total Fat 12 g 18% • Saturated 6 g 30% • Cholesterol 35 mg 12% • Sodium 1060 mg 44% • Total Carbohydrate 34 g 11% • Dietary Fiber 3 g 12% • Sugars 4 g • Protein 21 g • Vitamin A 35% • Vitamin C 10% • Calcium 45% • Iron 15%
Dietary Exchanges: 2 Starch, 2 Lean Meat, 1 Fat OR 2 Carbohydrate, 2 Lean Meat, 1 Fat

Celebration Brunch Strata

Prep Time: 45 minutes (Ready in 1 hour 35 minutes)

Yield: 12 servings

Photo page 4

½ cup margarine or butter, softened
12 slices white bread
8 oz. (2 cups) shredded Cheddar cheese
1 (9-oz.) pkg. frozen asparagus cuts in a pouch, thawed, drained*
6 oz. flaked cooked crabmeat
8 eggs
2½ cups milk
3 tablespoons chopped fresh parsley or chervil
1 teaspoon salt
1 teaspoon paprika
¼ teaspoon pepper

1. Heat oven to 325°F. Spread margarine on one side of each slice of bread. Arrange 6 slices, margarine side down, in ungreased 13x9-inch (3-quart) baking dish. Layer cheese, asparagus and crabmeat over bread. Place remaining bread slices, margarine side up, over crabmeat.
2. In large bowl, combine all remaining ingredients; blend well. Pour egg mixture evenly over bread. Let stand 10 to 15 minutes.
3. Bake at 325°F. for 55 to 65 minutes or until knife inserted in center comes out clean.

Tip: *To quickly thaw asparagus, remove asparagus from pouch; place in colander or strainer. Rinse with warm water until thawed; drain well.

Nutrition Information Per Serving: Serving Size: ¹⁄₁₂ of Recipe • Calories 300 • Calories from Fat 170 • % Daily Value • Total Fat 19 g 29% • Saturated 7 g 35% • Cholesterol 175 mg 58% • Sodium 760 mg 32% • Total Carbohydrate 17 g 6% • Dietary Fiber 1 g 4% • Sugars 4 g • Protein 16 g • Vitamin A 20% • Vitamin C 8% • Calcium 25% • Iron 10%
Dietary Exchanges: 1 Starch, 2 Medium-Fat Meat, 1½ Fat OR 1 Carbohydrate, 2 Medium-Fat Meat, 1½ Fat

Three-Color Macaroni and Cheese

Prep Time: 40 minutes (Ready in 1 hour)

Yield: 4 (1½-cup) servings

9 oz. (3 cups) uncooked tricolor rotini (spiral pasta)
¼ cup margarine or butter
¼ cup all-purpose flour
½ teaspoon salt
⅛ teaspoon pepper
2½ cups milk
1 tablespoon prepared mustard
⅛ to ¼ teaspoon hot pepper sauce
4 oz. (1 cup) shredded Cheddar cheese
4 oz. (1 cup) shredded natural Swiss cheese
1 medium tomato, chopped, drained
¼ cup unseasoned dry bread crumbs
1 tablespoon margarine or butter, melted

1. Heat oven to 375°F. In large saucepan, cook macaroni to desired doneness as directed on package. Drain; rinse with hot water. Set aside.
2. In same saucepan, melt ¼ cup margarine. Stir in flour, salt and pepper; cook until mixture is smooth and bubbly. Gradually add milk; stir in mustard and hot pepper sauce. Cook until mixture boils and thickens, stirring constantly.
3. Add cheeses, stirring until melted. Carefully stir in tomato and cooked macaroni. Spoon into ungreased 2-quart casserole. Combine bread crumbs and 1 tablespoon melted margarine; mix well. Sprinkle evenly over top.
4. Bake at 375°F. for 20 minutes or until bubbly.

Nutrition Information Per Serving: Serving Size: 1½ Cups • Calories 720 • Calories from Fat 320 • % Daily Value • Total Fat 36 g 55% • Saturated 16 g 80% • Cholesterol 65 mg 22% • Sodium 870 mg 36% • Total Carbohydrate 69 g 23% • Dietary Fiber 2 g 8% • Sugars 11 g • Protein 30 g • Vitamin A 35% • Vitamin C 8% • Calcium 70% • Iron 20%
Dietary Exchanges: 4½ Starch, 2½ High-Fat Meat, 2½ Fat OR 4½ Carbohydrate, 2½ High-Fat Meat, 2½ Fat

Grown-Up Mac and Cheese

Prep Time: 30 minutes (Ready in 55 minutes)

Yield: 4 (1½-cup) servings

8   oz. (2½ cups) uncooked mostaccioli or penne (tube-shaped pasta)
2   tablespoons margarine or butter
2   tablespoons all-purpose flour
¼   teaspoon salt
⅛   teaspoon white pepper
    Dash nutmeg
1¼ cups fat-free half-and-half
2   oz. (½ cup) shredded fontina cheese
2   oz. (½ cup) shredded Swiss cheese
2   oz. (½ cup) shredded fresh Parmesan cheese
2   tablespoons dry white wine
2   Italian plum tomatoes, thinly sliced
1   teaspoon olive oil or vegetable oil
2   tablespoons sliced green onions

1. Heat oven to 350° F. Spray 1½-quart casserole with nonstick cooking spray. Cook mostaccioli to desired doneness as directed on package. Drain.

2. Meanwhile, melt margarine in large saucepan over medium heat. Stir in flour, salt, pepper and nutmeg; cook and stir until bubbly. Gradually add half-and-half, stirring constantly. Cook until mixture boils and thickens, stirring frequently. Remove from heat. Stir in fontina, Swiss and Parmesan cheeses until melted. (Cheeses will be stringy.) Stir in wine.

3. Add cooked mostaccioli to cheese sauce; stir gently to coat. Pour into sprayed dish. Arrange sliced tomatoes around outside edge of dish. Brush tomatoes with oil; sprinkle with green onions.

4. Bake at 350° F. for 20 to 25 minutes or until edges are bubbly and mixture is thoroughly heated.

Nutrition Information Per Serving: Serving Size: 1½ Cups • Calories 520 • Calories from Fat 200 • % Daily Value • Total Fat 22 g 34% • Saturated 11 g 55% • Cholesterol 40 mg 13% • Sodium 700 mg 29% • Total Carbohydrate 56 g 19% • Dietary Fiber 2 g 8% • Sugars 5 g • Protein 24 g • Vitamin A 25% • Vitamin C 6% • Calcium 50% • Iron 15%
Dietary Exchanges: 3½ Starch, 2 High-Fat Meat, 1 Fat OR 3½ Carbohydrate, 2 High-Fat Meat, 1 Fat

Planning a Buffet

- If guests will be balancing plates on their laps rather than gathering around a table, serve foods that are already in bite-sized pieces or can be easily managed with just a fork.
- Choose foods with a variety of textures, flavors and colors.
- Keep hot casseroles hot (at least 140° F.) throughout the meal by using chafing dishes, electric food warming trays or food warming pots.
- Refrigerate leftovers promptly.

Grown-Up Mac and Cheese

Basil Ravioli with Red and White Sauce

Prep Time: 25 minutes (Ready in 45 minutes)

Yield: 6 servings

1   (25-oz.) pkg. frozen cheese-filled ravioli
1⅓ oz. (⅓ cup) shredded fresh Parmesan cheese
2   tablespoons chopped fresh basil or 2 teaspoons dried basil leaves
1   (28-oz.) jar spaghetti sauce
⅓ cup refrigerated, purchased Alfredo sauce

1. Heat oven to 400° F. Spray 12 x 8-inch (2-quart) baking dish with nonstick cooking spray.

2. Cook ravioli to desired doneness as directed on package. Drain ravioli; place in sprayed baking dish.

3. Sprinkle with cheese and basil. Pour spaghetti sauce over ravioli; spread evenly. Place Alfredo sauce in squeeze bottle or small resealable plastic bag with one corner cut off. Squeeze sauce in thin strips across spaghetti sauce. Draw knife through sauce to form pattern.

4. Bake at 400° F. for 15 to 20 minutes or until thoroughly heated.

Nutrition Information Per Serving: Serving Size: ⅙ of Recipe • Calories 530 • Calories from Fat 200 • % Daily Value • Total Fat 22 g 34% • Saturated 10 g 50% • Cholesterol 115 mg 38% • Sodium 1120 mg 47% • Total Carbohydrate 59 g 20% • Dietary Fiber 5 g 20% • Sugars 3 g • Protein 23 g • Vitamin A 15% • Vitamin C 15% • Calcium 40% • Iron 15%
Dietary Exchanges: 4 Starch, 1½ High-Fat Meat, 1½ Fat OR 4 Carbohydrate, 1½ High-Fat Meat, 1½ Fat

Penne and Spinach Bake

Prep Time: 30 minutes (Ready in 50 minutes)

Yield: 6 servings

6   oz. (1½ cups) uncooked penne or mostaccioli (tube-shaped pasta)
1   (26- to 28-oz.) jar spaghetti sauce
1   (1-lb.) pkg. frozen cut leaf spinach, thawed, squeezed to drain
½ cup low-fat cottage cheese
2   tablespoons grated Parmesan cheese
¼ teaspoon salt
1   (19-oz.) can white kidney or cannellini beans, drained, rinsed
1⅓ oz. (⅓ cup) shredded mozzarella cheese

1. Cook penne to desired doneness as directed on package. Drain.

2. Meanwhile, heat oven to 400° F. Spray 8-inch square (2-quart) baking dish with nonstick cooking spray. In medium saucepan, heat spaghetti sauce over low heat.

3. In large bowl, combine cooked penne, spinach, cottage cheese, Parmesan cheese and salt; mix well. Add beans; toss gently to mix.

4. Spoon ½ the mixture into sprayed dish. Spread with 1 cup warm spaghetti sauce. Top with remaining penne mixture and remaining sauce. Sprinkle with mozzarella cheese.

5. Bake at 400° F. for 20 minutes or until thoroughly heated.

✳ **Make-Ahead Directions:** Prepare recipe as directed above except omit mozzarella cheese; do not bake. Cover with foil; freeze. When ready to use, do not thaw; bake, covered, at 400° F. for 1 hour 20 minutes. Uncover; sprinkle with mozzarella cheese. Bake an additional 10 minutes or until thoroughly heated.

Nutrition Information Per Serving: Serving Size: ⅙ of Recipe • Calories 320 • Calories from Fat 50 • % Daily Value • Total Fat 6 g 9% • Saturated 2 g 10% • Cholesterol 5 mg 2% • Sodium 940 mg 39% • Total Carbohydrate 49 g 16% • Dietary Fiber 9 g 36% • Sugars 4 g • Protein 17 g • Vitamin A 80% • Vitamin C 25% • Calcium 25% • Iron 25%
Dietary Exchanges: 3 Starch, 1 Vegetable, 1 Lean Meat OR 3 Carbohydrate, 1 Vegetable, 1 Lean Meat

Artichoke Cheese 'n Rice Casserole

Prep Time: 25 minutes (Ready in 1 hour)

Yield: 6 (1-cup) servings

1   (6.2-oz.) pkg. fast-cooking long-grain and wild rice mix
2   cups water
1   tablespoon margarine or butter
8   oz. (2 cups) shredded Monterey Jack cheese
2   tablespoons unseasoned dry bread crumbs
1   large tomato, seeded and chopped, reserving ¼ cup for garnish
1   (14-oz.) can artichoke hearts, drained, quartered
½   cup mayonnaise or salad dressing
½   cup sour cream
2   green onions, thinly sliced
3   tablespoons chopped fresh parsley

1. Heat oven to 350°F. In 2-quart saucepan, combine rice, seasoning packet, water and margarine. Bring to a boil over high heat. Reduce heat to low; cover and simmer 5 minutes or until water is absorbed.

2. Spread cooked rice in bottom of ungreased 8-inch square (2-quart) baking dish or 1½-quart casserole; sprinkle with ½ the cheese. Sprinkle bread crumbs over cheese; top with tomato and artichokes.

3. In small bowl, combine mayonnaise, sour cream, green onions and 1 tablespoon of the parsley; spoon evenly over artichokes. Top with remaining cheese.*

4. Bake at 350°F. for 25 to 35 minutes or until casserole is thoroughly heated and cheese is melted and bubbly. Garnish with remaining 2 tablespoons parsley and reserved tomato.

Tip: *To make ahead, prepare as directed to this point. Cover; refrigerate several hours or overnight before baking. Uncover; bake at 350°F. for 30 to 40 minutes.

Nutrition Information Per Serving: Serving Size: 1 Cup • Calories 540 • Calories from Fat 360 • % Daily Value • Total Fat 40 g 62% • Saturated 13 g 65% • Cholesterol 55 mg 18% • Sodium 870 mg 36% • Total Carbohydrate 30 g 10% • Dietary Fiber 1 g 4% • Sugars 3 g • Protein 15 g • Vitamin A 20% • Vitamin C 15% • Calcium 35% • Iron 10%
Dietary Exchanges: 2 Starch, 1½ High-Fat Meat, 5 Fat OR 2 Carbohydrate, 1½ High-Fat Meat, 5 Fat

Mediterranean Pasta Torte

Prep Time: 40 minutes (Ready in 1 hour 25 minutes)

Yield: 6 servings

12	oz. (3 cups) uncooked ziti (long tubular pasta)
2½	cups cubed (½-inch) peeled eggplant (8 oz.)
1	medium onion, chopped
1	(15-oz.) can chunky tomato sauce with onions, celery and green bell peppers, undrained
½	teaspoon cinnamon
½	teaspoon dried oregano leaves, crushed
2	cups milk
2	tablespoons all-purpose flour
¼	teaspoon salt
⅛	teaspoon pepper
2	eggs
½	cup grated Parmesan cheese
3	tablespoons unseasoned dry bread crumbs
2	teaspoons margarine or butter, melted

1. Heat oven to 350° F. Spray 12 x 8-inch (2-quart) baking dish and 14 x 12-inch sheet of foil with nonstick cooking spray. Set aside.

2. In Dutch oven or large saucepan, cook ziti to desired doneness as directed on package. Drain; return to Dutch oven. Cover to keep warm.

3. Meanwhile, in medium saucepan, combine eggplant, onion, tomato sauce, cinnamon and oregano; mix well. Bring to a boil. Reduce heat; simmer 10 to 15 minutes or until onion and eggplant are crisp-tender, stirring frequently.

4. In another medium saucepan, combine ½ cup of the milk, flour, salt and pepper; mix with wire whisk until smooth. Stir in remaining 1½ cups milk. Cook over medium heat until mixture boils and thickens, stirring constantly. Boil and stir 1 minute. Remove from heat.

5. In medium bowl, beat eggs; gradually add ½ the hot milk mixture to beaten eggs, stirring constantly. Stir egg mixture back into mixture in saucepan. Add cheese; mix well. Add to cooked ziti; toss gently to coat evenly.

6. Place ½ the ziti mixture in sprayed baking dish. Spoon tomato sauce over ziti. Top with remaining ziti mixture. Cover tightly with sprayed foil.

7. Bake at 350° F. for 35 to 45 minutes or until casserole is bubbly. In small bowl, combine bread crumbs and margarine; mix well. Uncover; sprinkle over top. Bake uncovered for an additional 5 minutes. Let stand 5 minutes before serving.

Nutrition Information Per Serving: Serving Size: ⅙ of Recipe • Calories 390 • Calories from Fat 80 • % Daily Value • Total Fat 9 g 14% • Saturated 4 g 20% • Cholesterol 85 mg 28% • Sodium 740 mg 31% • Total Carbohydrate 61 g 20% • Dietary Fiber 4 g 16% • Sugars 11 g • Protein 17 g • Vitamin A 20% • Vitamin C 15% • Calcium 25% • Iron 20%
Dietary Exchanges: 3½ Starch, 2 Vegetable, 1½ Fat OR 3½ Carbohydrate, 2 Vegetable, 1½ Fat

Mediterranean Pasta Torte

Broccoli Fanfare Pie

Prep Time: 45 minutes (Ready in 1 hour 10 minutes)
Yield: 6 servings

CRUST
½ cup uncooked regular long-grain white rice
1 cup water
3 oz. (¾ cup) shredded Cheddar cheese
1 egg, beaten

FILLING
1 (1-lb.) pkg. frozen broccoli florets, carrots and cauliflower, thawed, drained*
1 (2½-oz.) jar sliced mushrooms, drained
4 oz. (1 cup) shredded Cheddar cheese
2 eggs, beaten
2 tablespoons all-purpose flour
½ teaspoon salt
⅓ cup coarsely crushed canned french-fried onions, if desired

1. Cook rice in water as directed on package.

2. Heat oven to 350° F. Lightly grease 9-inch pie pan. In small bowl, combine cooked rice, ¾ cup cheese and 1 egg; mix well. Press over bottom and up sides of greased pan to form crust. Bake at 350° F. for 10 minutes.

3. Meanwhile, in large bowl, combine all filling ingredients except onions; mix well. Spoon into baked crust.

4. Bake at 350° F. for 20 to 25 minutes or until center is set. Sprinkle with french-fried onions if desired. Bake an additional 1 to 2 minutes or until onions are warm. Let stand 5 minutes before serving.

✳ **Make-Ahead Directions:** Prepare recipe as directed above except omit french-fried onions; do not bake. Cover with foil; freeze. When ready to use, do not thaw; bake, covered, at 350° F. for 1 hour 15 minutes. Uncover; bake an additional 15 minutes or until mixture is thoroughly heated. Sprinkle with french-fried onions; bake an additional 1 to 2 minutes.

Tip: *To quickly thaw vegetables, place in colander or strainer; rinse with warm water until thawed. Drain well.

Nutrition Information Per Serving: Serving Size: ⅙ of Recipe • Calories 280 • Calories from Fat 140 • % Daily Value • Total Fat 15 g 23% • Saturated 8 g 40% • Cholesterol 140 mg 47% • Sodium 500 mg 21% • Total Carbohydrate 21 g 7% • Dietary Fiber 3 g 12% • Sugars 3 g • Protein 15 g • Vitamin A 70% • Vitamin C 20% • Calcium 30% • Iron 8%
Dietary Exchanges: 1 Starch, 1 Vegetable, 1½ High-Fat Meat, ½ Fat OR 1 Carbohydrate, 1 Vegetable, 1½ High-Fat Meat, ½ Fat

Summer Squash–Bulgur Casserole

Prep Time: 45 minutes (Ready in 1 hour 20 minutes)

Yield: 6 servings

1	(14½-oz.) can ready-to-serve vegetable or chicken broth
1	cup uncooked bulgur
1	tablespoon margarine or butter
½	cup chopped onion
5	to 6 medium summer squash, sliced (6 cups)
½	cup chopped red bell pepper
½	cup water
½	teaspoon garlic salt
⅛	teaspoon pepper
1	egg
½	cup milk
½	teaspoon dry mustard
1	cup dry cornbread stuffing mix

1. In small saucepan, bring broth to a boil. Place bulgur in medium bowl; pour boiling broth over bulgur. Let stand 20 minutes.

2. Meanwhile, heat oven to 350°F. Grease 12x8-inch (2-quart) baking dish. Melt margarine in large skillet over medium-high heat. Add onion; cook and stir 2 to 3 minutes or until onion is tender.

3. Reduce heat to medium; add squash, bell pepper, water, garlic salt and pepper. Cover; simmer 9 to 12 minutes or until squash is tender, stirring occasionally. Remove from heat; mash squash slightly. Stir in bulgur.

4. In small bowl, beat egg, milk and mustard until well blended; stir into squash mixture in skillet. Add ½ cup of the cornbread stuffing mix; mix well. Spoon mixture into greased baking dish; sprinkle with remaining ½ cup stuffing mix.

5. Bake at 350°F. for 30 to 35 minutes or until set.

Nutrition Information Per Serving: Serving Size: ⅙ of Recipe • Calories 220 • Calories from Fat 45 • % Daily Value • Total Fat 5 g 8% • Saturated 1 g 5% • Cholesterol 35 mg 12% • Sodium 670 mg 28% • Total Carbohydrate 36 g 12% • Dietary Fiber 9 g 36% • Sugars 8 g • Protein 8 g • Vitamin A 30% • Vitamin C 40% • Calcium 8% • Iron 10%
Dietary Exchanges: 2 Starch, 1 Vegetable, 1 Fat OR 2 Carbohydrate, 1 Vegetable, 1 Fat

Broccoli-Rice Quiche

Prep Time: 15 minutes (Ready in 50 minutes)
Yield: 6 servings

1½   cups milk
3   eggs
1   tablespoon Dijon mustard
¼   cup finely chopped onion
3   oz. (¾ cup) shredded Swiss
     cheese
1   (2-oz.) jar diced pimientos,
     drained
1½   cups chopped fresh broccoli
¾   cup uncooked instant brown
     or white rice

1. Heat oven to 350° F. Spray 9-inch pie pan with nonstick cooking spray. In large saucepan, heat milk until very hot but not boiling.

2. Meanwhile, in small bowl, beat eggs and mustard until well blended. Add onion, cheese and pimientos; mix well.

3. Stir broccoli and rice into hot milk. Slowly add egg mixture, stirring constantly. Pour into sprayed pan.

4. Bake at 350° F. for 30 to 35 minutes or until knife inserted in center comes out clean. Let stand 5 minutes before serving.

Nutrition Information Per Serving: Serving Size: ⅙ of Recipe • Calories 170 • Calories from Fat 70 • % Daily Value • Total Fat 8 g 12% • Saturated 4 g 20% • Cholesterol 125 mg 42% • Sodium 170 mg 7% • Total Carbohydrate 14 g 5% • Dietary Fiber 1 g 4% • Sugars 4 g • Protein 11 g • Vitamin A 20% • Vitamin C 40% • Calcium 25% • Iron 4%
Dietary Exchanges: 1 Starch, 1 Medium-Fat Meat, ½ Fat OR 1 Carbohydrate, 1 Medium-Fat Meat, ½ Fat

Overnight Southwestern Egg Bake

Prep Time: 15 minutes (Ready in 8 hours 50 minutes)
Yield: 15 servings

12   eggs
½   cup half-and-half or milk
1   (11-oz.) can vacuum-packed
     whole kernel corn with red
     and green peppers,
     drained
10   (6-inch) soft corn tortillas,
     cut into quarters
4   oz. (1 cup) shredded
     Cheddar cheese or
     Monterey Jack cheese (or
     a combination of both)
2   cups salsa
1   cup sour cream
1   cup guacamole

1. Generously grease 13 x 9-inch (3-quart) baking dish. In large bowl, combine eggs and half-and-half; beat slightly. Stir in corn.

2. Place tortillas in bottom of greased baking dish. Pour egg mixture over tortillas. Sprinkle with cheese. Cover with foil; refrigerate at least 8 hours or overnight.

3. Heat oven to 375° F. Bake covered for 25 to 30 minutes or until eggs are just set. Let stand covered 5 minutes. Uncover; spoon salsa over eggs. Serve with sour cream and guacamole.

Nutrition Information Per Serving: Serving Size: 1⁄15 of Recipe • Calories 230 • Calories from Fat 120 • % Daily Value • Total Fat 13 g 20% • Saturated 7 g 35% • Cholesterol 190 mg 63% • Sodium 620 mg 26% • Total Carbohydrate 17 g 6% • Dietary Fiber 2 g 8% • Sugars 4 g • Protein 10 g • Vitamin A 15% • Vitamin C 0% • Calcium 15% • Iron 6%
Dietary Exchanges: 1 Starch, 1 High-Fat Meat, 1 Fat OR 1 Carbohydrate, 1 High-Fat Meat, 1 Fat

Broccoli-Rice Quiche

Spinach and Tofu Manicotti

Prep Time: 30 minutes (Ready in 1 hour 10 minutes)

Yield: 4 servings

8	uncooked manicotti
2	cups spaghetti sauce
1	(8-oz.) pkg. fat-free cream cheese
1	teaspoon dried basil leaves
1/8	teaspoon garlic powder
2	cups frozen cut leaf spinach, thawed, squeezed to drain*
1/4	cup grated Parmesan cheese
1	(12.3-oz.) pkg. firm tofu, drained, cut into cubes
2	oz. (1/2 cup) shredded mozzarella cheese

1. Cook manicotti to desired doneness as directed on package. Drain; cover to keep warm.

2. Meanwhile, heat oven to 350° F. Spread 1 cup of the spaghetti sauce in bottom of ungreased 12 x 8-inch (2-quart) baking dish.

3. In large bowl, combine cream cheese, basil and garlic powder; mix well. Add spinach, Parmesan cheese and tofu; mix with fork until texture resembles cottage cheese.

4. Stuff tofu mixture into cooked manicotti; arrange in baking dish over sauce. Top with remaining 1 cup sauce. Cover tightly with foil.

5. Bake at 350° F. for 25 to 35 minutes or until thoroughly heated. Uncover; sprinkle with mozzarella cheese. Let stand 5 minutes before serving.

Tip: *To quickly thaw spinach, place in colander or strainer; rinse with warm water until thawed. Squeeze dry with paper towels.

Nutrition Information Per Serving: Serving Size: 1/4 of Recipe • Calories 400 • Calories from Fat 100 • % Daily Value • Total Fat 11 g 17% • Saturated 4 g 20% • Cholesterol 20 mg 7% • Sodium 1100 mg 46% • Total Carbohydrate 45 g 15% • Dietary Fiber 5 g 20% • Sugars 5 g • Protein 30 g • Vitamin A 70% • Vitamin C 20% • Calcium 70% • Iron 25%
Dietary Exchanges: 2½ Starch, 1 Vegetable, 3 Lean Meat OR 2½ Carbohydrate, 1 Vegetable, 3 Lean Meat

Mexican Torta

Prep Time: 25 minutes (Ready in 40 minutes)

Yield: 6 servings

3   ancho chiles (dried chiles)
1   (15-oz.) can tomato sauce
½   cup water
2   garlic cloves, minced
10 (6-inch) soft corn tortillas
1   (15-oz.) can black beans,
       drained, rinsed
12 oz. (3 cups) shredded
       Mexican cheese blend

1. Heat oven to 400° F. Spray 12-inch round pizza pan with nonstick cooking spray.

2. Place chiles in small nonstick skillet. Heat over medium–high heat until lightly toasted and slightly puffed up, turning occasionally. Cool slightly. Remove and discard stem and seeds from chiles; coarsely chop chiles. Place chiles, tomato sauce, water and garlic in blender container; blend on high speed until well combined.

3. Place 5 tortillas in circle, overlapping slightly, in sprayed pan to form 12-inch round. Top with ½ each of the tomato sauce mixture, beans and cheese. Place remaining 5 tortillas over cheese. Spoon remaining tomato sauce mixture over tortillas to within 1 inch of edge. Sprinkle with remaining ½ of beans and cheese.

4. Bake at 400° F. for 10 to 15 minutes or until thoroughly heated. Let stand 5 minutes. To serve, cut into wedges.

Nutrition Information Per Serving: Serving Size: ⅙ of Recipe • Calories 420 • Calories from Fat 180 • % Daily Value • Total Fat 20 g 31% • Saturated 12 g 60% • Cholesterol 50 mg 17% • Sodium 1060 mg 44% • Total Carbohydrate 39 g 13% • Dietary Fiber 6 g 24% • Sugars 4 g • Protein 20 g • Vitamin A 100% • Vitamin C 10% • Calcium 50% • Iron 10%
Dietary Exchanges: 2½ Starch, 2 High-Fat Meat, ½ Fat OR 2½ Carbohydrate, 2 High-Fat Meat, ½ Fat

Creamy Spinach Enchiladas

Prep Time: 40 minutes (Ready in 1 hour)

Yield: 6 servings

Photo on back jacket

1   tablespoon margarine or
      butter
½   cup sliced green onions
1   (9-oz.) pkg. frozen spinach
      in a pouch, thawed,
      squeezed to drain*
1   cup low-fat (1%) small-curd
      cottage cheese or ricotta
      cheese
½   cup light sour cream
6   oz. (1½ cups) shredded
      Monterey Jack cheese
12   (6-inch) corn tortillas,
      heated
1   (10-oz.) can mild enchilada
      sauce
      Sliced green onions, if
      desired

1. Heat oven to 375° F. Melt margarine in large skillet over medium-high heat. Add ½ cup green onions; cook and stir 2 minutes or until crisp-tender. Add spinach; cook 1 minute or until spinach is warm, stirring occasionally. Remove from heat. Stir in cottage cheese, sour cream and 1 cup of the cheese.

2. Spoon ¼ cup filling down center of each tortilla; roll up. Place, seam side down, in ungreased 13 x 9-inch (3-quart) baking dish. Pour enchilada sauce evenly over tortillas; sprinkle with remaining cheese.

3. Bake at 375° F. for 15 to 20 minutes or until bubbly and thoroughly heated. Sprinkle with sliced green onions if desired.

Tip: *To quickly thaw spinach, cut small slit in center of pouch; microwave on HIGH for 2 to 3 minutes or until thawed. Remove spinach from pouch; squeeze dry with paper towels.

Nutrition Information Per Serving: Serving Size: ⅙ of Recipe • Calories 330 • Calories from Fat 140 • % Daily Value • Total Fat 15 g 23% • Saturated 7 g 35% • Cholesterol 35 mg 12% • Sodium 680 mg 28% • Total Carbohydrate 32 g 11% • Dietary Fiber 3 g 12% • Sugars 4 g • Protein 17 g • Vitamin A 50% • Vitamin C 10% • Calcium 40% • Iron 8%
Dietary Exchanges: 2 Starch, 1½ Medium-Fat Meat, 1½ Fat OR 2 Carbohydrate, 1½ Medium-Fat Meat, 1½ Fat

Creamy Spinach Enchiladas

Red and white kidney beans, black-eyed peas, black beans, pintos and garbanzos all contribute slightly different character to a recipe, but differences in color and texture are greater than those of flavor. Feel free to use them interchangeably. For a more colorful dish, combine two or more varieties.

Black Bean and Corn Enchilada Egg Bake

Prep Time: 30 minutes (Ready in 5 hours 30 minutes)
Yield: 12 servings

10	(6-inch) corn tortillas
1	(15-oz.) can black beans, drained, rinsed
1	(11-oz.) can vacuum-packed whole kernel corn with red and green peppers, drained
1	(10¾-oz.) can condensed nacho cheese soup
6	eggs
2	cups milk
1	teaspoon cumin
2	oz. (½ cup) shredded Cheddar cheese
½	red bell pepper, if desired
3	sprigs fresh cilantro, if desired

1. Grease 13x9-inch (3-quart) baking dish. Arrange 6 tortillas on bottom of greased baking dish, overlapping. Spoon beans and corn evenly over tortillas. Spoon cheese soup evenly over vegetables. Cut remaining 4 tortillas into 1-inch strips; arrange over top.

2. In large bowl, combine eggs, milk and cumin; beat until well blended. Pour over tortilla strips. Cover tightly; refrigerate 4 hours or overnight.

3. Heat oven to 325°F. Uncover dish; sprinkle with cheese. Bake uncovered for 55 to 60 minutes or until eggs are set. Let stand 5 minutes before serving.

4. To garnish, cut five 1-inch-long poinsettia-petal shapes from bell pepper; arrange in center of dish to resemble poinsettia flower. Tuck 2 or 3 sprigs of cilantro between petals. Or, chop bell pepper and cilantro; sprinkle over top.

5. To serve, cut into squares. If desired, top with salsa and sour cream.

Nutrition Information Per Serving: Serving Size: ½₂ of Recipe • Calories 190 • Calories from Fat 60 • % Daily Value • Total Fat 7 g 11% • Saturated 3 g 15% • Cholesterol 115 mg 38% • Sodium 420 mg 18% • Total Carbohydrate 22 g 7% • Dietary Fiber 3 g 12% • Sugars 5 g • Protein 10 g • Vitamin A 15% • Vitamin C 8% • Calcium 15% • Iron 8%
Dietary Exchanges: 1½ Starch, 1 Lean Meat, ½ Fat OR 1½ Carbohydrate, 1 Lean Meat, ½ Fat

Harvest Vegetable Casserole

Prep Time: 40 minutes (Ready in 1 hour 20 minutes)

Yield: 6 servings

2 cups coarsely chopped fresh
    cauliflower
4 eggs
½ cup milk
1 cup all-purpose flour
1½ teaspoons baking powder
½ teaspoon salt
½ teaspoon dry mustard
¼ teaspoon dried thyme leaves
¼ teaspoon pepper
2 cups shredded carrots
⅓ cup finely chopped green
    bell pepper
4 oz. (1 cup) shredded
    Cheddar cheese
4 oz. (1 cup) shredded
    Monterey Jack cheese

1. Heat oven to 350° F. Grease 8-inch square (2-quart) baking dish. Cook cauliflower in small amount of boiling water for 8 to 12 minutes or until crisp-tender. Drain; set aside.

2. In large bowl, beat eggs until foamy; add milk. Add flour, baking powder, salt, dry mustard, thyme and pepper; beat well. Fold in cooked cauliflower and all remaining ingredients. Spoon into greased baking dish.

3. Bake at 350° F. for 35 to 40 minutes or until set.

High Altitude (above 3,500 feet): No change.

✳ **Make-Ahead Directions:** Prepare recipe as directed; do not bake. Cover with foil; freeze. When ready to use, do not thaw; bake, covered, at 350° F. for 1 hour 45 minutes. Uncover; bake an additional 15 minutes or until top is golden brown and center is set.

Nutrition Information Per Serving: Serving Size: ⅙ of Recipe • Calories 310 • Calories from Fat 140 • % Daily Value • Total Fat 16 g 25% • Saturated 9 g 45% • Cholesterol 180 mg 60% • Sodium 590 mg 25% • Total Carbohydrate 24 g 8% • Dietary Fiber 3 g 12% • Sugars 5 g • Protein 18 g • Vitamin A 220% • Vitamin C 30% • Calcium 40% • Iron 15%
Dietary Exchanges: 1 Starch, 1 Vegetable, 2 High-Fat Meat OR 1 Carbohydrate, 1 Vegetable, 2 High-Fat Meat

Vegetable and Bean Polenta Pie

Prep Time: 40 minutes (Ready in 1 hour 15 minutes)

Yield: 6 servings

POLENTA

1½	cups yellow cornmeal
2½	cups chicken broth
2	tablespoons margarine or butter
1	egg, slightly beaten
¼	cup grated Parmesan cheese

FILLING

1	tablespoon olive oil or vegetable oil
1	cup coarsely chopped onions
1	cup coarsely chopped green bell pepper
1	small zucchini, cut into ½-inch cubes
1	(15½- or 15-oz.) can dark red kidney beans, drained
1	(14½-oz.) can diced tomatoes with garlic, oregano and basil, undrained
1	(6-oz.) can tomato paste
4	oz. (1 cup) shredded mozzarella cheese

1. Heat oven to 375°F. Grease 9- or 10-inch deep-dish glass pie pan. In medium saucepan, combine cornmeal and broth. Cook over medium heat until mixture begins to boil, stirring constantly. Continue to boil 2 to 3 minutes or until mixture is thickened. Remove from heat; stir in margarine, egg and Parmesan cheese. Set aside.

2. Heat oil in large skillet over medium-high heat until hot. Add onions and bell pepper; cook and stir until tender. Stir in zucchini, beans, tomatoes and tomato paste. Bring to a boil. Reduce heat to medium-low; cook 5 minutes.

3. Spread cornmeal mixture in bottom and up sides of greased pie pan. Spoon vegetable mixture over top. Sprinkle with mozzarella cheese.

4. Bake at 375°F. for 30 to 35 minutes or until set. Let stand 5 minutes before serving.

✳ **Make-Ahead Directions:** Prepare recipe as directed above except omit mozzarella cheese; do not bake. Cover with foil; freeze. When ready to use, do not thaw; bake, covered, at 350°F. for 1 hour 10 minutes. Uncover; sprinkle with mozzarella cheese. Bake an additional 30 minutes or until mixture is set.

Nutrition Information Per Serving: Serving Size: ⅙ of Recipe • Calories 390 • Calories from Fat 130 • % Daily Value • Total Fat 14 g 22% • Saturated 5 g 25% • Cholesterol 50 mg 17% • Sodium 1030 mg 43% • Total Carbohydrate 48 g 16% • Dietary Fiber 8 g 32% • Sugars 6 g • Protein 18 g • Vitamin A 35% • Vitamin C 45% • Calcium 30% • Iron 20%
Dietary Exchanges: 3 Starch, 1 Vegetable, 1 Very Lean Meat, 2 Fat OR 3 Carbohydrate, 1 Vegetable, 1 Very Lean Meat, 2 Fat

Vegetable and Bean Polenta Pie

Italian Zucchini Crescent Pie

Prep Time: 30 minutes (Ready in 55 minutes)

Yield: 6 servings

2	tablespoons margarine or butter
4	cups thinly sliced zucchini
1	cup chopped onions
2	tablespoons dried parsley flakes
½	teaspoon salt
½	teaspoon pepper
¼	teaspoon garlic powder
¼	teaspoon dried basil leaves
¼	teaspoon dried oregano leaves
2	eggs, well beaten
8	oz. (2 cups) shredded Muenster or mozzarella cheese
1	(8-oz.) can refrigerated crescent dinner rolls
2	teaspoons prepared mustard

1. Heat oven to 375° F. Melt margarine in 12-inch skillet over medium-high heat. Add zucchini and onions; cook and stir 6 to 8 minutes or until tender. Stir in parsley flakes, salt, pepper, garlic powder, basil and oregano.

2. In large bowl, combine eggs and cheese; mix well. Stir in cooked vegetable mixture.

3. Separate dough into 8 triangles. Place in ungreased 10-inch pie pan, 12x8-inch (2-quart) baking dish or 11-inch quiche pan; press over bottom and up sides to form crust. Firmly press perforations to seal. Spread crust with mustard. Pour egg mixture evenly into crust-lined pan.

4. Bake at 375° F. for 18 to 22 minutes or until knife inserted near center comes out clean. Cover edge of crust with strips of foil during last 10 minutes of baking if necessary to prevent excessive browning. Let stand 10 minutes before serving.

Nutrition Information Per Serving: Serving Size: ⅙ of Recipe • Calories 370 • Calories from Fat 230 • % Daily Value • Total Fat 25 g 38% • Saturated 10 g 50% • Cholesterol 105 mg 35% • Sodium 790 mg 33% • Total Carbohydrate 21 g 7% • Dietary Fiber 2 g 8% • Sugars 7 g • Protein 15 g • Vitamin A 20% • Vitamin C 10% • Calcium 30% • Iron 10%
Dietary Exchanges: 1 Starch, 1 Vegetable, 1½ High-Fat Meat, 2½ Fat OR 1 Carbohydrate, 1 Vegetable, 1½ High-Fat Meat, 2½ Fat

Cornbread-Topped Ratatouille Casserole

Prep Time: 45 minutes (Ready in 1 hour 10 minutes)

Yield: 6 servings

1	tablespoon olive oil or vegetable oil
1	small eggplant (1¼ lb.), cut into ¾-inch cubes (4 cups)
1	medium zucchini, sliced
1	medium onion, sliced
1	medium green bell pepper, cut into 1-inch pieces
1	garlic clove, minced
1	(14½-oz.) can diced tomatoes, undrained
½	teaspoon dried basil leaves
¼	teaspoon dried Italian seasoning
⅛	teaspoon coarsely ground black pepper
1	(15½- or 15-oz.) can dark red kidney beans, drained, rinsed
1	(6½- to 8½-oz.) pkg. cornbread mix
	Milk
	Egg, if required by mix
1½	oz. (⅓ cup) shredded mozzarella cheese

1. Heat oil in large skillet over medium-high heat until hot. Add eggplant, zucchini, onion, bell pepper and garlic; cook and stir 4 to 6 minutes or until vegetables are lightly browned.

2. Reduce heat; stir in tomatoes, basil, Italian seasoning and pepper. Cover; simmer 12 to 15 minutes or until vegetables are crisp-tender.

3. Meanwhile, heat oven to 400°F. Spray 12x8-inch (2-quart) baking dish with nonstick cooking spray.

4. Remove skillet from heat; stir in kidney beans. Spoon eggplant mixture into sprayed baking dish.

5. In medium bowl, prepare cornbread mix as directed on package using milk and, if required by mix, egg. Stir in cheese; mix just until blended. Drop by spoonfuls over hot eggplant mixture.

6. Bake at 400°F. for 18 to 22 minutes or until cornbread is deep golden brown.

Nutrition Information Per Serving: Serving Size: ⅙ of Recipe • Calories 340 • Calories from Fat 90 • % Daily Value • Total Fat 10 g 15% • Saturated 3 g 15% • Cholesterol 40 mg 13% • Sodium 690 mg 29% • Total Carbohydrate 50 g 17% • Dietary Fiber 9 g 36% • Sugars 9 g • Protein 12 g • Vitamin A 15% • Vitamin C 30% • Calcium 15% • Iron 15%
Dietary Exchanges: 2½ Starch, 2 Vegetable, 2 Fat OR 2½ Carbohydrate, 2 Vegetable, 2 Fat

2

skillet dishes

Stove-top meals offer an enticing blend of ingredients, flavors and textures, with the convenience of one-pot cooking and cleanup. Most are ready in less time than their oven-baked counterparts, making them a sensible choice for weeknight suppers and last-minute entertaining.

Chicken and Vegetable Skillet Supper, page 191

Skillet Meals Cookware

One of the joys of pan cooking is fast and easy meal preparation. The following information will help you select the right pans for your style of cooking. The cookware called for most frequently in this chapter includes: a large (10-inch or 12-inch) skillet, a wok, and a dutch oven (large, deep cooking pot). In addition, you'll find it handy to have saucepans in a few sizes plus some large mixing bowls.

Stove-Top Cookware

MATERIAL	TYPICAL USES	CHARACTERISTICS
1. Cast iron	Skillets	Traditional, economical and virtually indestructible. Color gradually deepens from dark silver-gray to pitch black. Properly seasoned cast iron requires very little added fat for cooking. Browns foods nicely and heats very evenly. Not recommended for dishes made with tomatoes or other acidic ingredients; the reaction between acid and iron can create a metallic taste. Can be used on stove top and in oven.
2. Aluminum / Anodized aluminum	Skillets, saucepans	Aluminum conducts heat very well—sometimes too well in thin, inexpensive skillets that can scorch foods quickly. Aluminum can react with acidic ingredients (citrus, tomatoes, vinegar), yielding an off taste. Heavier aluminum pots are usually more satisfactory (and more expensive). Anodized aluminum has a fused-on coating, so the surface does not react to acids.

MATERIAL	TYPICAL USES	CHARACTERISTICS
3. Nonstick surface	Skillets, saucepans, Dutch ovens, woks	These allow cooking with little or no added fat. Today's nonstick pans work better than early versions, but still may not brown ingredients as well as cast iron or metal surfaces. Easy to clean. Most nonstick materials are coatings applied to the surface of a metal pan and can become scratched or worn away over time. Most can be used only with plastic or wooden utensils, not metal. Protect the surface during storage. On some nonstick pans, the nonstick quality is impregnated into the metal itself rather than applied just to the surface, enhancing durability and permitting the use of metal utensils.
4. Stainless steel	Skillets, saucepans, Dutch ovens	Can be scoured to shine beautifully. Not the best heat conductor. Typically requires more added fat than nonstick or cast-iron cookware to prevent sticking. Browns foods nicely. Suitable for induction (magnetic field) cooktops.
5. Enameled steel or cast iron	Dutch ovens, saucepans	Flameproof-ovenproof character gives versatility. Many are attractive enough to go straight to the table instead of transferring the food to a serving dish. Enameled cast iron offers excellent heat conduction without reacting to acidic foods. Enamel may chip over time.
6. Rolled steel	Woks	The traditional wok material darkens with use and conducts heat well for high-heat stir-frying. Rolled steel should be heated with a smear of oil after each use to seal pores and prevent rusting while maintaining a virtually nonstick cooking surface.
7. Clad metals	Skillets, saucepans, roasting pans, Dutch ovens	These combine the benefits of two metals—for example, aluminum for heat conductivity and stainless steel for a sturdy, rust-free pan that won't react to acidic ingredients; copper bottoms on stainless steel pans help conduct heat. Some pans with heavy bottoms "sandwich" metals to improve conductivity and give the density needed to help prevent scorching.

Kids' Favorites

**Children love basic flavors
and classic combinations:**

Scalloped Potatoes and Ham Skillet, page 133

Easy Entertaining

**Spices and flavors from around the world
dress up quick meals for guests:**

Parmesan Pork and Penne in Tomato Sauce, page 141

Tried and True Family Favorites

We've updated ingredients and streamlined preparation, but these will bring back memories for many:

Quick Hungarian Goulash, page 125

Chuck Wagon Skillet Dinner

Prep Time: 25 minutes

Yield: 6 (1-cup) servings

Photo on front jacket

1 lb. ground beef or ground turkey
½ cup chopped onion
1 (1¼-oz.) pkg. taco seasoning mix
1½ cups water
1½ cups thinly sliced zucchini
1 cup frozen whole kernel corn
1 (14½-oz.) can stewed tomatoes, undrained
1½ cups uncooked instant rice
4 oz. (1 cup) shredded Cheddar cheese

1. In large skillet, brown ground beef and onion until beef is thoroughly cooked. Drain. Stir in seasoning mix, water, zucchini, corn and tomatoes. Bring to a boil. Stir in rice. Reduce heat to low; cover and simmer 5 to 7 minutes or until liquid is absorbed, stirring occasionally.

2. Remove from heat. Fluff mixture with fork; sprinkle with cheese. Cover; let stand 3 minutes or until cheese is melted. If desired, garnish with diced red bell pepper and jalapeño chiles.

Nutrition Information Per Serving: Serving Size: 1 Cup • Calories 390 • Calories from Fat 150 • % Daily Value • Total Fat 17 g 26% • Saturated 8 g 40% • Cholesterol 65 mg 22% • Sodium 850 mg 35% • Total Carbohydrate 37 g 12% • Dietary Fiber 2 g 8% • Sugars 4 g • Protein 21 g • Vitamin A 20% • Vitamin C 15% • Calcium 20% • Iron 15%
Dietary Exchanges: 2 Starch, 1 Vegetable, 2 Medium-Fat Meat, 1 Fat OR 2 Carbohydrate, 1 Vegetable, 2 Medium-Fat Meat, 1 Fat

Easy Tex-Mex Hash

Prep Time: 30 minutes

Yield: 4 (1-cup) servings

1 lb. lean ground beef
1 tablespoon oil
3 cups frozen potatoes O'Brien with onions and peppers (from 24-oz. pkg.)
1 cup chunky-style salsa
2 teaspoons chili powder, if desired
4 oz. (1 cup) shredded colby–Monterey Jack cheese blend

1. In large nonstick skillet, brown ground beef until thoroughly cooked. Remove ground beef from skillet; cover to keep warm. Discard drippings.

2. In same skillet, heat oil over medium heat until hot. Add potatoes; cook and stir 8 to 10 minutes or until browned.

3. Stir in salsa, chili powder if desired and ground beef. Cook 5 to 8 minutes or until thoroughly heated, stirring occasionally.

4. Sprinkle with cheese. Cover; cook 2 to 4 minutes or until cheese is melted.

Nutrition Information Per Serving: Serving Size: 1 Cup • Calories 440 • Calories from Fat 240 • % Daily Value • Total Fat 27 g 42% • Saturated 12 g 60% • Cholesterol 95 mg 32% • Sodium 730 mg 30% • Total Carbohydrate 20 g 7% • Dietary Fiber 2 g 8% • Sugars 3 g • Protein 28 g • Vitamin A 20% • Vitamin C 10% • Calcium 25% • Iron 15%
Dietary Exchanges: 1½ Starch, 3½ Medium-Fat Meat, 1½ Fat OR 1½ Carbohydrate, 3½ Medium-Fat Meat, 1½ Fat

Elbow Macaroni and Beef

Prep Time: 25 minutes

Yield: 8 (1-cup) servings

8 cups water
6 oz. (1½ cups) uncooked
   elbow macaroni
1 (1-lb.) pkg. frozen broccoli
   florets, carrots and
   cauliflower
1 lb. ground beef
1 (14-oz.) jar spaghetti sauce
4 slices (3 oz.) American
   cheese, halved diagonally

1. Bring water to a boil in Dutch oven or large saucepan. Add macaroni and vegetables; cook 8 to 10 minutes or until macaroni and vegetables are tender. Drain.

2. Meanwhile, in 12-inch skillet, brown ground beef over medium-high heat until thoroughly cooked. Drain.

3. Reduce heat to low. Add spaghetti sauce and cooked macaroni and vegetables; mix well. Place cheese around edge of skillet with longest side of each triangle touching skillet. Cover; let stand 1 to 2 minutes or until cheese is melted.

Nutrition Information Per Serving: Serving Size: 1 Cup • Calories 280 • Calories from Fat 130 • % Daily Value • Total Fat 14 g 22% • Saturated 6 g 30% • Cholesterol 45 mg 15% • Sodium 410 mg 17% • Total Carbohydrate 23 g 8% • Dietary Fiber 3 g 12% • Sugars 2 g • Protein 16 g • Vitamin A 35% • Vitamin C 20% • Calcium 10% • Iron 15%
Dietary Exchanges: 1½ Starch, 1½ Medium-Fat Meat, 1 Fat OR 1½ Carbohydrate, 1½ Medium-Fat Meat, 1 Fat

Chili Macaroni

Prep Time: 40 minutes

Yield: 7 (1-cup) servings

4   oz. (1 cup) uncooked elbow
    macaroni
1   lb. ground beef
½   cup chopped onion
¼   cup chopped green bell
    pepper
1   garlic clove, minced
1   (14½- or 16-oz.) can whole
    tomatoes, undrained, cut
    up
1   (15½- or 15-oz.) can dark
    red kidney beans, drained
1   (6-oz.) can tomato paste
½   cup water
1   to 2 teaspoons chili powder
½   teaspoon salt
½   teaspoon pepper
4   oz. (1 cup) shredded
    Cheddar cheese, if desired

1. Cook macaroni to desired doneness as directed on package. Drain; rinse with hot water.

2. Meanwhile, in large skillet or saucepan, brown ground beef, onion, bell pepper and garlic until beef is thoroughly cooked. Drain. Stir in all remaining ingredients except cheese; blend well.

3. Stir in cooked macaroni. Cover; simmer 15 to 20 minutes or until slightly thickened and thoroughly heated, stirring occasionally. Serve in bowls; sprinkle with cheese if desired.

Nutrition Information Per Serving: Serving Size: 1 Cup • Calories 340 • Calories from Fat 140 • % Daily Value • Total Fat 15 g 23% • Saturated 7 g 35% • Cholesterol 55 mg 18% • Sodium 660 mg 28% • Total Carbohydrate 31 g 10% • Dietary Fiber 5 g 20% • Sugars 4 g • Protein 21 g • Vitamin A 30% • Vitamin C 30% • Calcium 20% • Iron 20%
Dietary Exchanges: 1½ Starch, 1 Vegetable, 2 Medium-Fat Meat, 1 Fat OR 1½ Carbohydrate, 1 Vegetable, 2 Medium-Fat Meat, 1 Fat

Quick Hungarian Goulash

Prep Time: 30 minutes

Yield: 4 (1¼-cup) servings

Photo at left and page 121

1	tablespoon oil
1	lb. boneless beef sirloin steak, cut into thin strips
1	medium onion, coarsely chopped
1	medium green bell pepper, coarsely chopped
1½	cups water
1	(14½-oz.) can diced tomatoes, undrained
1	(8-oz.) can tomato sauce
1	teaspoon sugar
3	teaspoons paprika
½	teaspoon salt
½	teaspoon caraway seed
¼	teaspoon pepper
4	oz. (1⅓ cups) uncooked rotini (spiral pasta)

1. Heat oil in 12-inch skillet or Dutch oven over medium-high heat until hot. Add beef strips; cook and stir 3 to 5 minutes or until browned.

2. Add all remaining ingredients except rotini; mix well. Bring to a boil. Add rotini. Reduce heat to medium; cook 10 to 15 minutes or until rotini is tender, stirring occasionally.

Nutrition Information Per Serving: Serving Size: 1¼ Cups • Calories 330 • Calories from Fat 80 • % Daily Value • Total Fat 9 g 14% • Saturated 2 g 10% • Cholesterol 60 mg 20% • Sodium 830 mg 35% • Total Carbohydrate 36 g 12% • Dietary Fiber 4 g 16% • Sugars 8 g • Protein 27 g • Vitamin A 45% • Vitamin C 50% • Calcium 6% • Iron 30%
Dietary Exchanges: 2 Starch, 1 Vegetable, 2½ Lean Meat OR 2 Carbohydrate, 1 Vegetable, 2½ Lean Meat

Mom's Skillet Goulash

Prep Time: 35 minutes

Yield: 6 (1⅓-cup) servings

8	oz. (2⅔ cups) uncooked rotini (spiral pasta)
1	lb. ground beef
1½	cups chopped celery
1	cup chopped onions
2	(14½- or 16-oz.) cans whole tomatoes, undrained, cut up
1	(10¾-oz.) can condensed tomato soup
1	teaspoon dried basil leaves
½	teaspoon salt
¼	teaspoon pepper

1. Cook rotini to desired doneness as directed on package. Drain.

2. Meanwhile, in large saucepan or Dutch oven, combine ground beef, celery and onions. Cook over medium heat for 8 to 10 minutes or until beef is thoroughly cooked, stirring frequently. Drain.

3. Add cooked rotini and all remaining ingredients; mix well. Cook 10 to 15 minutes or until thoroughly heated, stirring occasionally.

Nutrition Information Per Serving: Serving Size: 1⅓ Cups • Calories 370 • Calories from Fat 110 • % Daily Value • Total Fat 12 g 18% • Saturated 4 g 20% • Cholesterol 45 mg 15% • Sodium 750 mg 31% • Total Carbohydrate 45 g 15% • Dietary Fiber 4 g 16% • Sugars 9 g • Protein 20 g • Vitamin A 25% • Vitamin C 60% • Calcium 8% • Iron 25%
Dietary Exchanges: 2½ Starch, 1 Vegetable, 1½ Medium-Fat Meat, ½ Fat OR 2½ Carbohydrate, 1 Vegetable, 1½ Medium-Fat Meat, ½ Fat

Quick Hungarian Goulash

Beef with Mushrooms and Noodles

Prep Time: 20 minutes

Yield: 4 (1¼-cup) servings

6 oz. (3½ cups) uncooked medium egg noodles
½ lb. boneless beef sirloin steak, cut into thin strips
¼ teaspoon peppered seasoned salt
1 (15-oz.) can Italian-style chunky tomato sauce
1 (8-oz.) pkg. (3 cups) sliced fresh mushrooms
6 small green onions, cut into ½-inch pieces

1. Cook noodles to desired doneness as directed on package. Drain; place on serving platter or in serving bowl. Cover to keep warm.

2. Meanwhile, sprinkle beef with seasoned salt. Spray large nonstick skillet with nonstick cooking spray. Heat over medium-high heat until hot. Add beef; cook and stir 2 minutes or until browned.

3. Stir in tomato sauce, mushrooms and green onions. (If necessary, break up larger pieces of tomatoes with spoon.) Bring to a boil. Reduce heat; simmer 3 to 5 minutes or until vegetables are tender, stirring occasionally. Pour beef mixture over noodles; toss gently to mix.

Nutrition Information Per Serving: Serving Size: 1¼ Cups • Calories 290 • Calories from Fat 50 • % Daily Value • Total Fat 6 g 9% • Saturated 1 g 5% • Cholesterol 70 mg 23% • Sodium 620 mg 26% • Total Carbohydrate 41 g 14% • Dietary Fiber 4 g 16% • Sugars 9 g • Protein 18 g • Vitamin A 8% • Vitamin C 8% • Calcium 10% • Iron 25%
Dietary Exchanges: 2½ Starch, 1 Vegetable, 1 Lean Meat, ½ Fat OR 2½ Carbohydrate, 1 Vegetable, 1 Lean Meat, ½ Fat

Meatballs with Orzo and Italian Vegetables

Prep Time: 25 minutes

Yield: 4 (1¼-cup) servings

1 (14½-oz.) can ready-to-serve beef broth
7 oz. (1 cup) uncooked orzo or rosamarina (rice-shaped pasta)
1 lb. frozen cooked Italian meatballs
4 Italian plum tomatoes, sliced
1 medium zucchini, cut into cubes
1 to 2 oz. (¼ to ½ cup) shredded fresh Parmesan cheese

1. In large skillet, bring broth to a boil. Add orzo and meatballs; return to a boil. Reduce heat to medium-low; cover and simmer 5 to 8 minutes or until liquid is almost absorbed, stirring occasionally.

2. Stir in tomatoes and zucchini. Cook 6 to 10 minutes or until vegetables and orzo are tender, stirring occasionally. Sprinkle with cheese.

Nutrition Information Per Serving: Serving Size: 1¼ Cups • Calories 590 • Calories from Fat 270 • % Daily Value • Total Fat 30 g 46% • Saturated 15 g 75% • Cholesterol 85 mg 28% • Sodium 1400 mg 58% • Total Carbohydrate 48 g 16% • Dietary Fiber 6 g 24% • Sugars 5 g • Protein 32 g • Vitamin A 10% • Vitamin C 15% • Calcium 25% • Iron 30%
Dietary Exchanges: 3 Starch, 3½ Medium-Fat Meat, 2 Fat OR 3 Carbohydrate, 3½ Medium-Fat Meat, 2 Fat

Cabbage and Bratwurst

Prep Time: 25 minutes (Ready in 1 hour 10 minutes)

Yield: 8 servings

4 slices bacon, cut into 1-inch pieces
2 medium onions, thinly sliced
2 garlic cloves, minced
2 cups thickly sliced carrots
1 medium head cabbage or savoy cabbage (about 2 lb.), cut into 1-inch chunks
2 whole cloves
1 bay leaf
1 to 1½ lb. cooked bratwurst, cut into 2-inch pieces
1 cup beef broth
½ cup dry white wine, water or beef broth
   Dash salt and pepper

1. In 12-inch skillet or Dutch oven, cook bacon, onions and garlic over medium heat until bacon is crisp, stirring occasionally. Stir in carrots and cabbage.

2. Tie cloves and bay leaf in piece of cheesecloth or, if desired, place in tea ball. Add to cabbage mixture. Add bratwurst; partially cover with cabbage mixture. Pour broth and wine over cabbage mixture. Bring to a boil. Reduce heat; cover and simmer 30 to 45 minutes or until vegetables are tender.

3. Remove spices. Stir in salt and pepper. If desired, serve with German-style or Dijon mustard and dark bread.

Nutrition Information Per Serving: Serving Size: ⅛ of Recipe • Calories 390 • Calories from Fat 260 • % Daily Value • Total Fat 29 g 45% • Saturated 10 g 50% • Cholesterol 60 mg 20% • Sodium 770 mg 32% • Total Carbohydrate 14 g 5% • Dietary Fiber 4 g 16% • Sugars 8 g • Protein 17 g • Vitamin A 170% • Vitamin C 50% • Calcium 10% • Iron 10%
Dietary Exchanges: 2 Vegetable, 2 High-Fat Meat, 3 Fat

Cheesy Wieners and Pasta

Prep Time: 25 minutes

Yield: 6 (¾-cup) servings

6 oz. (3 cups) uncooked wagon wheel pasta
1 lb. pasteurized processed cheese spread, cubed
½ cup milk
5 wieners, sliced

1. Cook pasta to desired doneness as directed on package. Drain.

2. Meanwhile, in medium saucepan, combine cheese spread and milk. Cook over low heat until smooth, stirring occasionally.

3. Add cooked pasta and wieners; cook until thoroughly heated.

Nutrition Information Per Serving: Serving Size: ¾ Cup • Calories 490 • Calories from Fat 280 • % Daily Value • Total Fat 31 g 48% • Saturated 16 g 80% • Cholesterol 65 mg 22% • Sodium 1560 mg 65% • Total Carbohydrate 30 g 10% • Dietary Fiber 1 g 3% • Sugars 9 g • Protein 22 g • Vitamin A 15% • Vitamin C 0% • Calcium 45% • Iron 10%
Dietary Exchanges: 2 Starch, 2½ High-Fat Meat, 2 Fat OR 2 Carbohydrate, 2½ High-Fat Meat, 2 Fat

Beef 'n Noodle Skillet

Beef 'n Noodle Skillet

Prep Time: 30 minutes

Yield: 4 (1½-cup) servings

1	lb. extra-lean ground beef
4	oz. (2 cups) uncooked medium egg noodles
1	cup frozen whole kernel corn
1	cup sliced green onions
1	cup water
½	cup salsa
2	(8-oz.) cans no-salt-added tomato sauce
1	oz. (¼ cup) shredded Cheddar cheese

1. In large skillet, brown ground beef until thoroughly cooked. Drain.

2. Add all remaining ingredients except cheese; mix well. Bring to a boil. Reduce heat to low; cover and simmer 10 to 12 minutes or until noodles are of desired doneness, stirring occasionally. Sprinkle with cheese.

Nutrition Information Per Serving: Serving Size: 1½ Cups • Calories 290 • Calories from Fat 110 • % Daily Value • Total Fat 12 g 18% • Saturated 5 g 25% • Cholesterol 70 mg 23% • Sodium 240 mg 10% • Total Carbohydrate 25 g 8% • Dietary Fiber 2 g 8% • Sugars 5 g • Protein 20 g • Vitamin A 6% • Vitamin C 20% • Calcium 6% • Iron 15%
Dietary Exchanges: 1½ Starch, 1 Vegetable, 2 Lean Meat, 1 Fat OR 1½ Carbohydrate, 1 Vegetable, 2 Lean Meat, 1 Fat

Hearty Beef and Macaroni Dinner

Prep Time: 40 minutes

Yield: 4 (1½-cup) servings

¾ lb. lean ground beef round
2   cups chopped onions
½   cup chopped green bell
    pepper
1   (14½-oz.) can diced
    tomatoes, undrained
4   oz. (1 cup) uncooked elbow
    macaroni
1   cup hot water
½   cup ketchup
½   teaspoon salt
½   teaspoon dried Italian
    seasoning

1. Spray nonstick Dutch oven with nonstick cooking spray. Heat over medium-high heat until hot. Add ground beef round, onions and bell pepper; cook 4 to 6 minutes or until beef is thoroughly cooked and onions are tender. Remove beef mixture from skillet; drain on paper towels.

2. Wipe Dutch oven dry with paper towels. Return beef mixture to Dutch oven. Stir in all remaining ingredients. Bring to a boil. Reduce heat; cover tightly and simmer 10 to 15 minutes to blend flavors.

Nutrition Information Per Serving: Serving Size: 1½ Cups • Calories 360 • Calories from Fat 110 • % Daily Value • Total Fat 12 g 18% • Saturated 5 g 25% • Cholesterol 55 mg 18% • Sodium 830 mg 35% • Total Carbohydrate 42 g 14% • Dietary Fiber 4 g 16% • Sugars 11 g • Protein 21 g • Vitamin A 20% • Vitamin C 40% • Calcium 6% • Iron 20%
Dietary Exchanges: 2 Starch, 2 Vegetable, 2 Medium-Fat Meat OR 2 Carbohydrate, 2 Vegetable, 2 Medium-Fat Meat

Creamy Beef Mostaccioli

Prep Time: 30 minutes

Yield: 4 (1½-cup) servings

5   oz. (1½ cups) uncooked
    mostaccioli or penne
    (tube-shaped pasta)
¾   cup low-fat plain yogurt
1   tablespoon cornstarch
1   tablespoon olive oil
¾   lb. boneless beef round
    steak, cut into very thin
    strips
1   onion, cut into thin wedges
2   tablespoons all-purpose flour
½   cup beef broth
2   medium tomatoes, cut into
    bite-sized pieces
1   green bell pepper, cut into
    1-inch squares
1   cup quartered fresh
    mushrooms
1   teaspoon dried basil leaves
½   teaspoon dried thyme leaves
½   teaspoon salt
½   teaspoon brown sugar

1. Cook mostaccioli to desired doneness as directed on package. Drain; cover to keep warm.

2. Meanwhile, in medium bowl, combine yogurt and cornstarch; mix well. Set aside.

3. Heat oil in large skillet or Dutch oven over medium-high heat until hot. Add beef and onion; cook and stir until beef is browned. Add flour; stir until well blended. Add all remaining ingredients except mostaccioli and yogurt mixture. Cover; cook over medium heat for 5 to 8 minutes or until vegetables are crisp-tender, stirring occasionally.

4. Remove skillet from heat. Gradually stir 2 cups beef mixture into yogurt mixture, stirring constantly. Return beef and yogurt mixture to skillet; cook and stir over medium heat until bubbly. Add cooked mostaccioli to beef mixture; toss to combine.

Nutrition Information Per Serving: Serving Size: 1½ Cups • Calories 350 • Calories from Fat 80 • % Daily Value • Total Fat 9 g 14% • Saturated 3 g 15% • Cholesterol 50 mg 17% • Sodium 440 mg 18% • Total Carbohydrate 42 g 14% • Dietary Fiber 3 g 12% • Sugars 8 g • Protein 26 g • Vitamin A 10% • Vitamin C 35% • Calcium 10% • Iron 20%
Dietary Exchanges: 2½ Starch, 1 Vegetable, 2½ Lean Meat OR 2½ Carbohydrate, 1 Vegetable, 2½ Lean Meat

Pork Chop Dinner with Bacon and Cider Gravy

Prep Time: 30 minutes

Yield: 4 servings

4	oz. (2½ cups) uncooked extra-wide egg noodles
2	cups frozen cut green beans
3	slices bacon, cut into small pieces
4	(4-oz.) boneless pork loin chops
¼	cup chopped onion
1	cup apple cider or apple juice
1	teaspoon honey mustard
¼	teaspoon salt
¼	teaspoon dried thyme leaves
⅛	teaspoon pepper
1	tablespoon water
1	tablespoon cornstarch

1. Cook noodles to desired doneness as directed on package, adding green beans during last 4 minutes of cooking time. Drain; cover to keep warm.

2. Meanwhile, in large skillet, cook bacon over medium heat until brown and crisp. With slotted spoon, remove bacon from skillet; drain on paper towels. Set aside. Drain and discard all drippings from skillet.

3. Place pork chops in skillet near center. Sprinkle onion around pork chops. Cook 3 to 5 minutes or until pork chops are golden brown, turning once. In small bowl, combine cider, mustard, salt, thyme and pepper; mix well. Pour over chops. Reduce heat to low; cover and cook 10 to 15 minutes or until pork is no longer pink in center.

4. Arrange cooked noodles and green beans on serving platter. Place pork chops on top of noodle mixture; cover to keep warm.

5. In small bowl, combine water and cornstarch; blend until smooth. Add to juices in skillet; mix well. Cook and stir over medium-low heat until bubbly and thickened; boil 1 minute. (If desired, gravy can be strained.)

6. To serve, pour gravy over pork chops and noodles. Sprinkle with bacon.

Nutrition Information Per Serving: Serving Size: ¼ of Recipe • Calories 380 • Calories from Fat 120 • % Daily Value • Total Fat 13 g 20% • Saturated 4 g 20% • Cholesterol 100 mg 33% • Sodium 320 mg 13% • Total Carbohydrate 34 g 11% • Dietary Fiber 2 g 8% • Sugars 9 g • Protein 31 g • Vitamin A 4% • Vitamin C 6% • Calcium 4% • Iron 15%
Dietary Exchanges: 1½ Starch, ½ Fruit, 1 Vegetable, 3½ Lean Meat, ½ Fat OR 2 Carbohydrate, 1 Vegetable, 3½ Lean Meat, ½ Fat

Kitchen Safety

Because skillet suppers and stir-frying keep the cook close to hot burners, cooking safety takes on more importance.

◆ Tie back long hair and roll up loose sleeves.

◆ Keep a fire extinguisher in the kitchen; make sure it is charged and that you know how to use it. Store it across the kitchen from the stove.

◆ Cooking oils are flammable. Do not store them beside the stove.

◆ Use your stove's ventilation system to remove heat, steam and grease from the air. Clean the filter screens periodically to prevent buildup of grease.

◆ Be aware that ingredients, especially those with moisture, can spit and sputter when added to a hot wok or skillet.

◆ Don't use wet potholders; they can steam-burn your hands.

◆ Turn pot handles to the back of the stove (but make sure they're not directly over another hot burner) and keep toddlers and pets out of the cooking area.

◆ Have a "landing spot" for hot pots with a trivet or other protection for the counter.

Smoked Sausage and Chunky Vegetables

Prep Time: 20 minutes

Yield: 4 servings

2	cups uncooked instant rice
2	cups water
¾	lb. 97% fat-free smoked sausage, sliced
1	medium onion, cut into 1-inch pieces
1	medium green bell pepper, cut into 1-inch pieces
1	medium zucchini, sliced
⅓	cup water
½	teaspoon dried thyme leaves, if desired
1½	teaspoons Worcestershire sauce

1. Cook rice in 2 cups water as directed on package, omitting margarine and salt.

2. Meanwhile, spray nonstick Dutch oven or 12-inch skillet with nonstick cooking spray. Heat over high heat until hot. Add sausage; cook and stir 2 minutes. Reduce heat to medium–high; add onion and bell pepper. Cook an additional 2 minutes.

3. Add all remaining ingredients; mix well. Bring to a boil. Reduce heat to medium; cover tightly and cook 4 to 6 minutes or until vegetables are crisp–tender. Serve over rice.

Nutrition Information Per Serving: Serving Size: ¼ of Recipe • Calories 290 • Calories from Fat 25 • % Daily Value • Total Fat 3 g 5% • Saturated 2 g 10% • Cholesterol 30 mg 10% • Sodium 1120 mg 47% • Total Carbohydrate 45 g 15% • Dietary Fiber 2 g 8% • Sugars 6 g • Protein 20 g • Vitamin A 6% • Vitamin C 35% • Calcium 4% • Iron 15%
Dietary Exchanges: 2½ Starch, 1 Vegetable, 1½ Very Lean Meat OR 2½ Carbohydrate, 1 Vegetable, 1½ Very Lean Meat

Risotto with Vegetables and Ham

Prep Time: 30 minutes

Yield: 4 (1½-cup) servings

1 tablespoon margarine or
   butter
½ cup chopped onion
1 (12-oz.) pkg. (1⅔ cups)
   short-grain Arborio rice
2 (14½-oz.) cans ready-to-
   serve fat-free chicken
   broth with ⅓ less sodium
1 (8-oz.) pkg. frozen broccoli,
   cauliflower and carrots in
   a pouch, thawed, drained*
⅓ cup cooked ham strips
   (1 x ¼ inch)
½ teaspoon dried marjoram
   leaves
⅓ cup shredded fresh
   Parmesan cheese

1. Melt margarine in large nonstick skillet over medium–high heat. Add onion; cook and stir until tender. Add rice; stir to coat. Add broth; bring to a boil. Reduce heat to low; cover and cook 10 minutes.

2. Stir in vegetables, ham and marjoram. Bring to a boil. Cover; simmer 8 to 10 minutes or until liquid is absorbed and rice is tender, stirring occasionally. Stir in cheese until melted.

Tip: *To quickly thaw vegetables, remove vegetables from pouch; place in colander or strainer. Rinse with warm water until thawed; drain well. Or cut small slit in center of pouch; microwave on HIGH for 2 to 3 minutes or until thawed. Remove vegetables from pouch; drain well.

Nutrition Information Per Serving: Serving Size: 1½ Cups • Calories 400 • Calories from Fat 45 • % Daily Value • Total Fat 5 g 8% • Saturated 2 g 10% • Cholesterol 10 mg 3% • Sodium 870 mg 36% • Total Carbohydrate 74 g 25% • Dietary Fiber 2 g 8% • Sugars 3 g • Protein 14 g • Vitamin A 30% • Vitamin C 15% • Calcium 10% • Iron 30%
Dietary Exchanges: 4½ Starch, 1 Vegetable, ½ Fat OR 4½ Carbohydrate, 1 Vegetable, ½ Fat

Risotto with Vegetables
and Ham

Scalloped Potatoes and Ham Skillet

Scalloped Potatoes and Ham Skillet

Prep Time: 30 minutes

Yield: 4 (1½-cup) servings

Photo above and page 120

2   cups cubed cooked ham
1   lb. small new red potatoes,
       thinly sliced (about
       1½ cups)
1   cup thinly sliced celery
1   cup thinly sliced carrots
½   cup chopped onion
⅓   cup water
3   cups skim milk
¼   cup all-purpose flour
⅛   teaspoon pepper

1. Spray large nonstick skillet with nonstick cooking spray. Heat over medium heat until hot. Add ham, potatoes, celery, carrot, onion and water. Cook until bubbly. Reduce heat to medium-low; cover and cook 5 to 8 minutes or until vegetables are tender, stirring once.

2. Meanwhile, in medium bowl, combine milk, flour and pepper; blend well. Add to skillet; cook and stir over medium heat until bubbly and thickened.

Nutrition Information Per Serving: Serving Size: 1½ Cups • Calories 300 • Calories from Fat 35 • % Daily Value • Total Fat 4 g 6% • Saturated 1 g 5% • Cholesterol 35 mg 12% • Sodium 1140 mg 48% • Total Carbohydrate 42 g 14% • Dietary Fiber 4 g 16% • Sugars 12 g • Protein 23 g • Vitamin A 180% • Vitamin C 20% • Calcium 25% • Iron 15%
Dietary Exchanges: 3 Starch, 2 Very Lean Meat OR 3 Carbohydrate, 2 Very Lean Meat

Rotini with Zucchini and Ham

Prep Time: 30 minutes

Yield: 4 (1½-cup) servings

6	oz. (2 cups) uncooked rotini (spiral pasta) or short fusilli (curly spaghetti)
2	tablespoons olive oil
1	cup sliced carrots
½	cup chopped onion
2	cups sliced zucchini
½	lb. cooked ham, cut into 2 x ½ x ¼-inch strips
¼	teaspoon fennel seed

1. Cook rotini to desired doneness as directed on package. Drain.
2. Meanwhile, heat oil in large skillet over medium heat until hot. Add carrots and onion; cook and stir 2 to 3 minutes or until crisp-tender. Add zucchini; cook 1 to 2 minutes or until crisp-tender.
3. Stir in ham and fennel seed; cook 1 to 2 minutes or until thoroughly heated.
4. Add cooked rotini to ham mixture; toss gently to combine.

Nutrition Information Per Serving: Serving Size: 1½ Cups • Calories 320 • Calories from Fat 90 • % Daily Value • Total Fat 10 g 15% • Saturated 2 g 10% • Cholesterol 25 mg 8% • Sodium 830 mg 35% • Total Carbohydrate 39 g 13% • Dietary Fiber 3 g 12% • Sugars 5 g • Protein 18 g • Vitamin A 180% • Vitamin C 10% • Calcium 4% • Iron 15%
Dietary Exchanges: 2 Starch, 2 Vegetable, 1 Lean Meat, 1 Fat OR 2 Carbohydrate, 2 Vegetable, 1 Lean Meat, 1 Fat

Pork Diane Skillet Supper

Prep Time: 20 minutes (Ready in 35 minutes)

Yield: 4 servings

2	tablespoons margarine or butter
1	lb. pork tenderloin, cut crosswise into ¼-inch slices
1	(14½-oz.) can ready-to-serve chicken broth
2	teaspoons Worcestershire sauce
¼	teaspoon salt
⅛	teaspoon pepper
8	small new red potatoes, quartered
1	cup sliced fresh mushrooms
½	cup sliced green onions
2	tablespoons all-purpose flour

1. Melt margarine in 12-inch skillet or Dutch oven over medium-high heat. Add pork slices; cook 3 to 5 minutes or until browned on both sides. Remove pork from skillet; set aside.
2. Reserve ¼ cup of the broth. Add remaining broth, Worcestershire sauce, salt, pepper and potatoes to skillet. Bring to a boil. Reduce heat to low; cover and simmer 15 minutes or until potatoes are tender.
3. Stir in mushrooms, green onions and pork slices. Cover; simmer an additional 5 minutes or until pork is no longer pink in center.
4. In small bowl, combine reserved ¼ cup broth and flour; blend until smooth. Gradually stir into pork mixture. Cook and stir over medium-high heat until mixture is bubbly and thickened.

Nutrition Information Per Serving: Serving Size: ¼ of Recipe • Calories 430 • Calories from Fat 100 • % Daily Value • Total Fat 11 g 17% • Saturated 3 g 15% • Cholesterol 65 mg 22% • Sodium 620 mg 26% • Total Carbohydrate 52 g 17% • Dietary Fiber 5 g 20% • Sugars 3 g • Protein 31 g • Vitamin A 6% • Vitamin C 30% • Calcium 4% • Iron 25%
Dietary Exchanges: 3½ Starch, 3 Lean Meat OR 3½ Carbohydrate, 3 Lean Meat

Harvest Pasta

Prep Time: 35 minutes

Yield: 6 (1⅓-cup) servings

8 oz. (2⅔ cups) uncooked gemelli or rotini (spiral pasta)

¾ lb. fresh small Brussels sprouts, trimmed, halved

1 cup (about 5 oz.) fresh baby carrots, halved lengthwise

¾ lb. pork tenderloin, cut into thin bite-sized strips

2 garlic cloves, minced

1 (10-oz.) container refrigerated light Alfredo sauce

1. In Dutch oven, cook gemelli in boiling water for 4 minutes. Add Brussels sprouts and carrots; cook an additional 9 to 11 minutes or until gemelli and vegetables are of desired doneness. Drain; return to Dutch oven. Cover to keep warm.

2. Meanwhile, spray large nonstick skillet with nonstick cooking spray. Heat over medium-high heat until hot. Add pork and garlic; cook and stir 4 to 5 minutes or until pork is lightly browned and no longer pink. Stir in Alfredo sauce.

3. Add pork mixture to cooked gemelli and vegetables in Dutch oven; toss gently to mix. Cook over low heat until thoroughly heated.

Nutrition Information Per Serving: Serving Size: 1⅓ Cups • Calories 320 • Calories from Fat 70 • % Daily Value • Total Fat 8 g 12% • Saturated 4 g 20% • Cholesterol 50 mg 17% • Sodium 270 mg 11% • Total Carbohydrate 39 g 13% • Dietary Fiber 4 g 16% • Sugars 6 g • Protein 22 g • Vitamin A 140% • Vitamin C 50% • Calcium 15% • Iron 15%
Dietary Exchanges: 2 Starch, 2 Vegetable, 2 Lean Meat OR 2 Carbohydrate, 2 Vegetable, 2 Lean Meat

Browning in the Skillet

One of the best things about skillet suppers is the nice way that ingredients turn golden brown. For best browning:

♦ Make sure the pan is hot before ingredients are added.

♦ Allow enough space between ingredients, especially meat and poultry. If the pan is crowded, ingredients will steam rather than brown.

♦ Allow the ingredients to develop a nicely browned side before turning or even moving them.

♦ Do not cover the pan before ingredients have browned. Covering holds in steam, which helps keep ingredients moist but interferes with browning.

Spicy Ham and Cheese Pasta

Prep Time: 30 minutes

Yield: 4 (1½-cup) servings

1   (10-oz.) pkg. frozen cut
    broccoli with cheese-
    flavored sauce in a pouch
7   oz. (about 2 cups) uncooked
    medium shell pasta
1   teaspoon oil
¼   teaspoon crushed red pepper
    flakes
1   medium red bell pepper,
    chopped
6   oz. cooked ham, cut into
    thin strips (1 cup)

1. Bring large saucepan of water to a boil. Add unopened pouch of broccoli with cheese-flavored sauce; cook 5 minutes. Add pasta to water; return to a boil. Cook an additional 10 to 11 minutes or until pasta is tender. Drain.

2. Meanwhile, in medium nonstick skillet, heat oil and red pepper flakes over medium-high heat until hot. Add bell pepper and ham; cook and stir 3 to 4 minutes or until bell pepper is crisp-tender.

3. Return cooked pasta to large saucepan. Open broccoli pouch; add to pasta. Add ham mixture; toss gently to mix.

Nutrition Information Per Serving: Serving Size: 1½ Cups • Calories 300 • Calories from Fat 50 • % Daily Value • Total Fat 6 g 9% • Saturated 2 g 10% • Cholesterol 25 mg 8% • Sodium 970 mg 40% • Total Carbohydrate 44 g 15% • Dietary Fiber 3 g 12% • Sugars 6 g • Protein 17 g • Vitamin A 30% • Vitamin C 60% • Calcium 6% • Iron 15%
Dietary Exchanges: 3 Starch, 1 Lean Meat OR 3 Carbohydrate, 1 Lean Meat

Ham from the Deli

You may not have a leftover baked ham on hand, ready to provide that cup and a half or so of cooked ham needed for many one-dish recipes. At the deli, ask the counter assistant to cut you a chunk of baked ham rather than slicing the meat for sandwiches.

Spicy Ham and Cheese Pasta

Pork Chops with Creamy Gravy and Vegetables

Prep Time: 30 minutes

Yield: 4 servings

4	bone-in pork loin chops (½ inch thick)
¼ to ½	teaspoon seasoned salt
½	cup sour cream
1	(10¾-oz.) can condensed cream of celery soup
¼ to ½	teaspoon dried sage leaves
3	cups frozen cut green beans
1½	cups frozen potatoes O'Brien with onions and peppers (from 24-oz. pkg.)

1. Spray large nonstick skillet with nonstick cooking spray. Heat over medium-high heat until hot. Sprinkle pork chops with seasoned salt; place in skillet. Cook 5 to 6 minutes or until browned on both sides. Remove chops from skillet; cover to keep warm.

2. In medium bowl, combine sour cream, soup and sage; mix well. Add to skillet; stir in frozen vegetables. Arrange chops over vegetable mixture; press gently into mixture. Bring to a boil. Reduce heat to medium-low; cover and cook 10 to 15 minutes or until pork chops are no longer pink in center and vegetables are tender, stirring occasionally.

Nutrition Information Per Serving: Serving Size: ¼ of Recipe • Calories 360 • Calories from Fat 160 • % Daily Value • Total Fat 18 g 28% • Saturated 8 g 40% • Cholesterol 85 mg 28% • Sodium 850 mg 35% • Total Carbohydrate 22 g 7% • Dietary Fiber 4 g 16% • Sugars 5 g • Protein 27 g • Vitamin A 15% • Vitamin C 15% • Calcium 10% • Iron 15%
Dietary Exchanges: 1 Starch, 1 Vegetable, 3 Lean Meat, 2 Fat OR 1 Carbohydrate, 1 Vegetable, 3 Lean Meat, 2 Fat

Linguine with Pork and Garden Vegetables

Prep Time: 35 minutes

Yield: 4 (1½-cup) servings

1	(9-oz.) pkg. refrigerated linguine
1	tablespoon olive oil or vegetable oil
¾	lb. boneless pork loin chops, cut into thin strips
1	large onion, sliced
3	large garlic cloves, minced
2	cups fresh broccoli florets
6	Italian plum tomatoes, chopped
1	yellow or red bell pepper, cut into 1-inch pieces
¼	cup chopped fresh basil or 1 tablespoon dried basil leaves
¼	cup halved pitted kalamata olives

1. In large saucepan, cook linguine to desired doneness as directed on package. Drain; return to saucepan or place in serving bowl.

2. Meanwhile, heat oil in large skillet over medium-high heat until hot. If desired, sprinkle pork with salt and pepper. Add pork to skillet; cook and stir 3 to 4 minutes or until browned.

3. Add onion and garlic; cook and stir 2 to 3 minutes. Add broccoli, tomatoes and bell pepper; cook and stir 2 to 3 minutes or until vegetables are crisp-tender and pork is no longer pink. Stir in basil and olives.

4. Add pork and vegetable mixture to cooked linguine; toss gently to mix.

Nutrition Information Per Serving: Serving Size: 1½ Cups • Calories 330 • Calories from Fat 120 • % Daily Value • Total Fat 13 g 20% • Saturated 3 g 15% • Cholesterol 50 mg 17% • Sodium 190 mg 8% • Total Carbohydrate 30 g 10% • Dietary Fiber 4 g 16% • Sugars 6 g • Protein 24 g • Vitamin A 35% • Vitamin C 110% • Calcium 6% • Iron 15%
Dietary Exchanges: 1½ Starch, 1 Vegetable, 2½ Lean Meat, 1 Fat OR 1½ Carbohydrate, 1 Vegetable, 2½ Lean Meat, 1 Fat

Teriyaki Pork and Sweet Potatoes

Prep Time: 30 minutes

Yield: 4 (1¼-cup) servings

2   medium sweet potatoes, peeled, cut into ¾-inch cubes (3 cups)
½   cup water
1   tablespoon oil
1   lb. boneless pork loin, cut into ¾-inch cubes
2   cups frozen cut green beans, thawed, drained*
½   cup purchased teriyaki baste and glaze
1   teaspoon grated orange peel

1. In large skillet, combine sweet potatoes and water. Bring to a boil. Reduce heat to medium-low; cover and cook 8 to 10 minutes or until potatoes are tender. Drain and remove potatoes from skillet; cover to keep warm.

2. Wipe skillet dry with paper towels. Heat oil in same skillet over medium-high heat until hot. Add pork; cook and stir until browned.

3. Add green beans and teriyaki baste and glaze; mix well. Reduce heat to medium; cover and cook 8 to 10 minutes or until pork is no longer pink, stirring occasionally.

4. Stir in cooked potatoes and orange peel; cook an additional 1 to 2 minutes or until thoroughly heated.

Tip: *To quickly thaw green beans, place in colander or strainer; rinse with warm water until thawed. Drain well.

Nutrition Information Per Serving: Serving Size: 1¼ Cups • Calories 320 • Calories from Fat 110 • % Daily Value • Total Fat 12 g 18% • Saturated 3 g 15% • Cholesterol 70 mg 23% • Sodium 1440 mg 60% • Total Carbohydrate 25 g 8% • Dietary Fiber 3 g 12% • Sugars 9 g • Protein 28 g • Vitamin A 260% • Vitamin C 25% • Calcium 6% • Iron 15%
Dietary Exchanges: 1½ Starch, 1 Vegetable, 3 Lean Meat OR 1½ Carbohydrate, 1 Vegetable, 3 Lean Meat

Parmesan Pork and Penne in Tomato Sauce

Prep Time: 25 minutes

Yield: 4 servings

Photo at left and page 120

8 oz. (2½ cups) uncooked penne or mostaccioli (tube-shaped pasta)

2 tablespoons unseasoned dry bread crumbs

2 tablespoons grated Parmesan cheese

¾ lb. pork tenderloin, thinly sliced

2 teaspoons olive oil

1 (14½-oz.) can diced tomatoes with garlic, oregano and basil, undrained

1 (8-oz.) can no-salt-added tomato sauce

½ cup sliced green onions

1 (2¼-oz.) can sliced ripe olives, drained

1. Cook penne to desired doneness as directed on package. Drain; cover to keep warm.

2. Meanwhile, combine bread crumbs and cheese in plastic bag. Add pork slices; shake to coat. In large nonstick skillet, heat oil over medium-high heat until hot. Add pork; cook 4 to 6 minutes or until browned on each side, turning occasionally.

3. Add tomatoes, tomato sauce, green onions and olives to pork; stir gently to mix. Bring to a boil. Reduce heat to low; cover and simmer 5 to 10 minutes or until pork is tender and sauce is of desired consistency, stirring occasionally. Serve pork mixture over penne.

Nutrition Information Per Serving: Serving Size: ¼ of Recipe • Calories 420 • Calories from Fat 80 • % Daily Value • Total Fat 9 g 14% • Saturated 2 g 10% • Cholesterol 50 mg 17% • Sodium 490 mg 20% • Total Carbohydrate 56 g 19% • Dietary Fiber 3 g 12% • Sugars 7 g • Protein 29 g • Vitamin A 15% • Vitamin C 30% • Calcium 10% • Iron 30%
Dietary Exchanges: 3½ Starch, 1 Vegetable, 2 Lean Meat OR 3½ Carbohydrate, 1 Vegetable, 2 Lean Meat

Grate Ideas for Parmesan

Parmesan purchased already grated is convenient, but many recipes specify "freshly grated" cheese for best flavor. Purchase a chunk of Parmesan (Romano works well, too) at the grocery store, and keep it tightly wrapped in plastic between uses. Slice off a little piece and taste it straight: it's usually quite salty and tangy, which is why it's the perfect finishing touch for so many recipes.

Grate Parmesan manually with a box grater, flat grater or small table grater. A citrus zester will produce tiny shreds; a vegetable peeler can shave off thin curls that give an entirely different appearance and flavor.

To speed up grating for larger quantities, an electric food processor or blender can be used.

Parmesan Pork and Penne in Tomato Sauce

Golden Pork Chow Mein

Prep Time: 30 minutes

Yield: 6 servings

1	tablespoon oil
1½	lb. lean pork steak, cut into ¼-inch slices
1	cup sliced carrots
½	cup diagonally sliced celery
1	cup water
2	tablespoons soy sauce
2	teaspoons sugar
1	teaspoon beef-flavor instant bouillon
½	teaspoon garlic powder
½	teaspoon grated gingerroot or ⅛ teaspoon ground ginger
8	to 9 oz. (4 cups) fresh bean sprouts
½	cup diagonally sliced green onions
1	(2-oz.) jar sliced pimientos, drained
¼	cup cold water
2	tablespoons cornstarch
	Chow mein noodles

1. Heat oil in large skillet or wok over medium-high heat until hot. Add pork; cook and stir until browned. Remove pork from skillet; cover to keep warm.

2. To liquid in skillet, add carrots, celery, 1 cup water, soy sauce, sugar, bouillon, garlic powder and gingerroot; mix well. Reduce heat to medium-low; cover and simmer 4 to 5 minutes or until vegetables are crisp-tender. Stir in cooked pork, bean sprouts, green onions and pimientos; cook until thoroughly heated.

3. In small bowl, combine ¼ cup water and cornstarch; blend until smooth. Gradually stir into mixture in skillet. Cook and stir over medium-high heat until sauce is bubbly and thickened. Serve over chow mein noodles.

Nutrition Information Per Serving: Serving Size: ⅙ of Recipe • Calories 320 • Calories from Fat 140 • % Daily Value • Total Fat 15 g 23% • Saturated 3 g 15% • Cholesterol 50 mg 17% • Sodium 650 mg 27% • Total Carbohydrate 23 g 8% • Dietary Fiber 3 g 12% • Sugars 4 g • Protein 22 g • Vitamin A 60% • Vitamin C 25% • Calcium 4% • Iron 15%
Dietary Exchanges: 1 Starch, 1 Vegetable, 2½ Lean Meat, 1½ Fat OR 1 Carbohydrate, 1 Vegetable, 2½ Lean Meat, 1½ Fat

Cutting on the Bias

Chinese recipes often call for cutting vegetables on the bias, or diagonally. This technique exposes more surface area to the heat, encouraging quicker cooking.

Chinese Sweet-and-Sour Pork

Prep Time: 40 minutes

Yield: 4 servings

1⅓ cups uncooked regular long-grain white rice

2⅔ cups water

¼ cup cornstarch

2 tablespoons all-purpose flour

1 teaspoon sugar

¼ teaspoon baking soda

3 tablespoons water

1 egg, beaten

½ lb. boneless pork loin, cut into 2 x ½ x ¼-inch pieces

Oil for frying

3 tablespoons brown sugar

2 tablespoons cornstarch

½ teaspoon chicken-flavor instant bouillon

½ cup water

3 tablespoons rice vinegar

2 tablespoons ketchup

2 teaspoons soy sauce

1 (20-oz.) can pineapple chunks in unsweetened juice, drained, reserving 3 tablespoons liquid

1 garlic clove, minced

1 green bell pepper, cut into ¾-inch pieces

1. Cook rice in 2⅔ cups water as directed on package.

2. Meanwhile, in medium bowl, combine ¼ cup cornstarch, flour, sugar, baking soda, 3 tablespoons water and egg; mix well. Add pork; stir until well coated.

3. In deep fryer, heavy saucepan or wok, heat 2 to 3 inches oil to 375° F. Fry coated pork pieces, ¼ of total amount at a time, for 2 to 3 minutes or until golden brown and no longer pink in center, turning once. Drain on paper towels. Reserve 1 tablespoon of the oil from deep fryer.

4. In small saucepan, combine brown sugar, 2 tablespoons cornstarch, bouillon, ½ cup water, vinegar, ketchup, soy sauce and reserved 3 tablespoons pineapple liquid; blend well. Cook over medium-high heat until bubbly and thickened, stirring constantly. Keep warm.

5. Heat reserved 1 tablespoon oil in large skillet or wok until hot. Add garlic and bell pepper; cook and stir 2 to 3 minutes or until bell pepper is crisp-tender. Stir in pineapple chunks, pork and sauce. Cook until thoroughly heated. Serve over rice.

Nutrition Information Per Serving: Serving Size: ¼ of Recipe • Calories 680 • Calories from Fat 230 • % Daily Value • Total Fat 26 g 40% • Saturated 5 g 25% • Cholesterol 90 mg 30% • Sodium 510 mg 21% • Total Carbohydrate 92 g 31% • Dietary Fiber 3 g 12% • Sugars 26 g • Protein 20 g • Vitamin A 6% • Vitamin C 35% • Calcium 8% • Iron 25%
Dietary Exchanges: 3 Starch, 3 Fruit, 1½ Medium-Fat Meat, 3½ Fat OR 6 Carbohydrate, 1½ Medium-Fat Meat, 3½ Fat

Barley, Bacon, Lentils and Tomatoes

Prep Time: 25 minutes (Ready in 1 hour)

Yield: 4 (1½-cup) servings

3	slices bacon
1	small onion, thinly sliced
1	cup dried lentils, rinsed
1	cup uncooked quick-cooking barley
2	teaspoons beef-flavor instant bouillon
1	teaspoon cumin
⅛	teaspoon allspice
3½	cups water
1	(14½-oz.) can stewed tomatoes, undrained
2	tablespoons chopped fresh parsley

1. In 12-inch skillet, cook bacon over medium heat until crisp. Remove bacon from skillet; drain on paper towel. Set aside.

2. Add onion and lentils to bacon drippings in skillet. Cook over medium heat for 3 to 5 minutes or until onion is tender and lentils are lightly browned.

3. Add barley, bouillon, cumin, allspice and water. Bring to a boil. Reduce heat to medium–low; cover and simmer 15 minutes or until lentils are soft.

4. Add tomatoes. Cook uncovered for an additional 15 to 20 minutes or until lentils and barley are tender and liquid is absorbed.

5. Just before serving, stir in parsley. Crumble bacon over top.

Nutrition Information Per Serving: Serving Size: 1½ Cups • Calories 440 • Calories from Fat 110 • % Daily Value • Total Fat 12 g 18% • Saturated 4 g 20% • Cholesterol 10 mg 3% • Sodium 810 mg 34% • Total Carbohydrate 64 g 21% • Dietary Fiber 20 g 80% • Sugars 5 g • Protein 20 g • Vitamin A 15% • Vitamin C 20% • Calcium 8% • Iron 35%
Dietary Exchanges: 4 Starch, 1 Vegetable, 1 Very Lean Meat, 1½ Fat OR 4 Carbohydrate, 1 Vegetable, 1 Very Lean Meat, 1½ Fat

Cinnamon Pork Chops and Sweet Potatoes

Prep Time: 30 minutes (Ready in 55 minutes)

Yield: 4 servings

1	tablespoon oil
4	pork loin chops (½ inch thick)
1	(20-oz.) can pineapple chunks in unsweetened juice, drained, reserving liquid
2	tablespoons brown sugar
¼	teaspoon salt
¼	teaspoon cinnamon
2	medium sweet potatoes, peeled, cut into 1-inch pieces
1	medium green bell pepper, cut into 1-inch pieces
1	tablespoon cornstarch

1. Heat oil in 12-inch skillet or Dutch oven over medium-high heat until hot. Add pork chops; cook 2 to 3 minutes on each side or until browned. Remove pork chops from skillet.

2. Add ½ cup of the pineapple liquid, brown sugar, salt and cinnamon to same skillet; blend well. Reserve remaining pineapple liquid. Add sweet potatoes to skillet; turn to coat with liquid. Add pork chops. Bring to a boil. Reduce heat to low; cover and simmer 15 to 25 minutes or until potatoes are tender.

3. Stir in bell pepper and pineapple chunks. Cover; simmer an additional 5 minutes. Transfer pork chops to warm platter.

4. In small bowl, stir cornstarch into remaining pineapple liquid until dissolved. Gradually stir into mixture in skillet. Cook and stir over medium-high heat until sauce is bubbly and thickened. Spoon over pork chops.

Nutrition Information Per Serving: Serving Size: ¼ of Recipe • Calories 400 • Calories from Fat 110 • % Daily Value • Total Fat 12 g 18% • Saturated 3 g 15% • Cholesterol 65 mg 22% • Sodium 190 mg 8% • Total Carbohydrate 48 g 16% • Dietary Fiber 4 g 16% • Sugars 31 g • Protein 25 g • Vitamin A 260% • Vitamin C 50% • Calcium 6% • Iron 10%
Dietary Exchanges: 1 Starch, 2 Fruit, 3 Lean Meat, ½ Fat OR 3 Carbohydrate, 3 Lean Meat, ½ Fat

Making Chicken Stock

Canned broth is quick and convenient, but making homemade chicken stock is easy, too. It's an economical way to use up chicken backs, wing tips, necks and bones. Exact proportions are not required, as long as you have enough ingredients to make the mixture flavorful rather than watery.

In a large stockpot, combine some chicken, one or two cut-up carrots, a stalk of celery, one or two chopped onions, a handful of parsley and salt and pepper. Other optional ingredients include parsnips, other fresh or dried herbs, leftover vegetables, garlic and fresh gingerroot.

Cover ingredients with water, bring to a boil, then reduce heat to a simmer and cook an hour or more, until the chicken is cooked and the soup has taken on a nice color, flavor and aroma. Strain the broth and reduce the mixture (boil until volume is decreased) for more intense flavor. Store in the refrigerator or freezer until needed.

Lamb and Couscous Skillet

Prep Time: 35 minutes

Yield: 4 (1⅓-cup) servings

¾ lb. ground lamb
1 medium onion, chopped (½ cup)
1 medium carrot, thinly sliced
2 garlic cloves, minced
1½ teaspoons dried oregano leaves
½ teaspoon lemon-pepper seasoning
½ cup finely chopped green bell pepper
1 (14½-oz.) can ready-to-serve fat-free chicken broth with ⅓ less sodium
½ cup water
1 (10-oz.) pkg. (about 1⅓ cups) uncooked couscous

1. Heat large nonstick skillet over medium-high heat until hot. Add ground lamb, onion, carrot, garlic, oregano and lemon-pepper seasoning; cook until lamb is no longer pink and onion is tender. Remove lamb mixture from skillet; drain on paper towels.

2. Wipe skillet dry with paper towels. Return lamb mixture to skillet. Add all remaining ingredients; mix thoroughly. Bring to a boil. Reduce heat; cover and simmer 5 to 10 minutes or until couscous is tender and most of liquid is absorbed. Fluff with fork before serving.

Nutrition Information Per Serving: Serving Size: 1⅓ Cups • Calories 460 • Calories from Fat 110 • % Daily Value • Total Fat 12 g 18% • Saturated 5 g 25% • Cholesterol 55 mg 18% • Sodium 350 mg 15% • Total Carbohydrate 61 g 20% • Dietary Fiber 5 g 20% • Sugars 5 g • Protein 26 g • Vitamin A 100% • Vitamin C 20% • Calcium 4% • Iron 10%
Dietary Exchanges: 4 Starch, 2 Medium-Fat Meat OR 4 Carbohydrate, 2 Medium-Fat Mea

focus on stir-fry

Stir-frying originated in China as a way to produce hot meals quickly while conserving scarce cooking fuel. It is a simple technique with delicious results. Fresh vegetables retain their vibrant color, texture and vitamins, while meat and poultry stay juicy and flavorful.

How to Stir-Fry

STEP STEP 1
Spray a large nonstick skillet or wok with cooking spray. Heat the skillet or wok over medium-high heat until hot. Add the firmest vegetables, quickly lifting and turning for 2 minutes. Cover and steam vegetables until almost crisp-tender.

STEP 2
Add the tender vegetables that require little cooking and any seasonings. Stir-fry until vegetables are crisp-tender and any liquid accumulated during cooking has evaporated. Serve as soon as possible for crisp, bright-colored delicious vegetables.

Note: To reduce the preparation time for stir-fry dishes, purchase your favorite frozen blend. Frozen vegetables work equally well as fresh because they thaw as they cook to crisp-tender perfection.

Tip: Check the international aisle of your grocery store or a local Asian market to choose from the many stir-fry sauces now on the market. They range from sweet to fiery. Read the label to compare sodium, sugar and fat content, and to get an idea of the heat level of the product. With a shake of the sauce, a quick skillet supper gains the cachet of a far more elaborate recipe.

Stir-Fry Basics

♦ Preparation can be time-consuming, but actual stir-frying goes quickly. Cut ingredients into uniformly sized pieces for even cooking, and have them all ready to go before you heat the wok.

♦ If the recipe is a two-step stir-fry in which, for instance, meat and vegetables are cooked separately, have a covered dish nearby to keep the first batch of ingredients warm while the second batch cooks.

♦ Preheat the wok (a large skillet can also be used) before adding ingredients.

♦ Add ingredients in the order specified. If you're improvising, toss in firmer, longer-cooking ingredients (such as carrots) before quicker-cooking items such as bean sprouts.

♦ If you're using a wok, add ingredients to the center of the wok, where the heat is most intense, then stir them up the side of the wok to continue cooking while the next items are added to the wok.

Szechuan Beef Lo Mein, page 150

Spicy Szechuan Beef and Vegetables

Prep Time: 25 minutes

Yield: 4 servings

2	cups uncooked instant rice
2	cups water
¾	lb. extra-lean ground beef
1	(1-lb.) pkg. frozen broccoli florets, carrots and water chestnuts
4	oz. (1 cup) fresh snow pea pods, trimmed
½	cup purchased Szechuan spicy stir-fry sauce
3	tablespoons dry-roasted salted peanuts

1. Cook rice in water as directed on package.

2. Meanwhile, in large skillet or wok, brown ground beef over medium-high heat until thoroughly cooked. Remove from skillet; drain on paper towels.

3. In same skillet, combine frozen vegetables, pea pods and stir-fry sauce; mix well. Reduce heat to medium; cover and cook 7 to 10 minutes or until vegetables are crisp-tender, stirring occasionally.

4. Return beef to skillet; mix well. Cook until thoroughly heated. Stir in peanuts. Serve over rice.

Nutrition Information Per Serving: Serving Size: ¼ of Recipe • Calories 450 • Calories from Fat 140 • % Daily Value • Total Fat 16 g 25% • Saturated 6 g 30% • Cholesterol 55 mg 18% • Sodium 960 mg 40% • Total Carbohydrate 50 g 17% • Dietary Fiber 7 g 28% • Sugars 7 g • Protein 26 g • Vitamin A 60% • Vitamin C 45% • Calcium 6% • Iron 20%
Dietary Exchanges: 2½ Starch, 2 Vegetable, 2 Medium-Fat Meat, 1 Fat OR 2½ Carbohydrate, 2 Vegetable, 2 Medium-Fat Meat, 1 Fat

Szechuan Beef Lo Mein

Prep Time: 35 minutes

Yield: 4 (1½-cup) servings

Photo page 149

1	lb. boneless beef sirloin steak, cut into thin strips
1	medium onion, cut into thin wedges
1½	cups fresh baby carrots, halved lengthwise
1	(14½-oz.) can ready-to-serve beef broth
½	cup purchased Szechuan stir-fry sauce
2	tablespoons honey
4	oz. (1½ cups) uncooked fine egg noodles
1½	cups fresh snow pea pods, trimmed, cut in half crosswise
¼	cup chopped salted cashews, if desired

1. Spray large nonstick skillet with nonstick cooking spray. Heat over medium-high heat until hot. Add beef; cook and stir until browned. Remove beef from skillet; cover to keep warm.

2. In same skillet, combine onion and carrots; cook and stir 2 minutes. Stir in broth, stir-fry sauce and honey. Bring to a boil. Reduce heat to medium-low; cover and cook 5 to 10 minutes or until vegetables are crisp-tender.

3. Stir in egg noodles; cover and cook 5 to 10 minutes or until noodles are tender, stirring occasionally. Add beef and pea pods; cover and cook 3 to 4 minutes or until pea pods are crisp-tender. Sprinkle with cashews if desired.

Nutrition Information Per Serving: Serving Size: 1½ Cups • Calories 420 • Calories from Fat 110 • % Daily Value • Total Fat 12 g 18% • Saturated 4 g 20% • Cholesterol 85 mg 28% • Sodium 1280 mg 53% • Total Carbohydrate 46 g 15% • Dietary Fiber 6 g 24% • Sugars 18 g • Protein 31 g • Vitamin A 240% • Vitamin C 45% • Calcium 6% • Iron 30%
Dietary Exchanges: 2½ Starch, 1½ Vegetable, 3 Lean Meat, ½ Fat OR 2½ Carbohydrate, 1½ Vegetable, 3 Lean Meat, ½ Fat

Stir-Fry Improvisation

Once you've mastered the techniques of stir-frying, it's easy to cook up your own combo, toss with a purchased stir-fry sauce and serve over rice or noodles. Suggestions:

- Peeled shrimp, chopped garlic, grated gingerroot and broccoli florets
- Diced chicken, red bell pepper strips and canned baby corn
- Sliced boneless pork, chopped green onions and canned straw mushrooms
- Strips of beef, julienned green and yellow squash and sliced water chestnuts
- Diced lamb, chopped garlic, bean sprouts and chopped yellow bell pepper

Orange Pepper Steak

Prep Time: 25 minutes

Yield: 4 servings

2	cups uncooked instant rice
2	cups water
²⁄₃	cup orange juice
2	tablespoons soy sauce
2	teaspoons cornstarch
¼	teaspoon crushed red pepper flakes
1	tablespoon oil
1	lb. boneless beef sirloin steak, cut into thin strips
1	large garlic clove, minced
1	green bell pepper, cut into 1-inch pieces
1	yellow bell pepper, cut into 1-inch pieces
⅓	cup sliced green onions
1	orange, peeled, halved and sliced

1. Cook rice in water as directed on package.

2. Meanwhile, in small cup, combine orange juice, soy sauce, cornstarch and red pepper flakes; blend well. Set aside.

3. Heat oil in large skillet or wok over high heat until hot. Add beef and garlic; cook and stir until beef is browned. Add bell peppers; cook and stir until crisp-tender.

4. Stir orange juice mixture into beef mixture. Bring to a boil. Cook until thickened, stirring occasionally. Stir in green onions and orange; cook until thoroughly heated. Serve over rice.

Nutrition Information Per Serving: Serving Size: ¼ of Recipe • Calories 380 • Calories from Fat 80 • % Daily Value • Total Fat 9 g 14% • Saturated 2 g 10% • Cholesterol 60 mg 20% • Sodium 570 mg 24% • Total Carbohydrate 49 g 16% • Dietary Fiber 3 g 12% • Sugars 9 g • Protein 25 g • Vitamin A 6% • Vitamin C 100% • Calcium 6% • Iron 20%
Dietary Exchanges: 3 Starch, ½ Fruit, 2 Lean Meat OR 3½ Carbohydrate, 2 Lean Meat

Pepper Steak

Prep Time: 30 minutes

Yield: 4 servings

2 cups uncooked instant rice
2 cups water
1 cup beef broth
¼ cup hoisin sauce
1 tablespoon cornstarch
¼ to ½ teaspoon coarsely
   ground black pepper
3 tablespoons ketchup
1 tablespoon rice vinegar
½ teaspoon Worcestershire
   sauce
1 tablespoon oil
1 lb. beef flank or boneless top
   sirloin steak, thinly sliced
1 medium onion, cut into
   8 pieces
1 medium green bell pepper,
   cut into strips
1 medium red bell pepper, cut
   into strips
1 medium yellow bell pepper,
   cut into strips

1. Cook rice in water as directed on package.

2. Meanwhile, in small bowl, combine broth, hoisin sauce, cornstarch, pepper, ketchup, vinegar and Worcestershire sauce; blend well. Set aside.

3. Heat oil in large skillet or wok over medium-high heat until hot. Add beef and onion; cook and stir 2 to 3 minutes or until beef is no longer pink. Add bell peppers and cornstarch mixture; cook and stir 2 to 3 minutes or until vegetables are crisp-tender and sauce is bubbly and thickened. Serve over rice.

Nutrition Information Per Serving: Serving Size: ¼ of Recipe • Calories 470 • Calories from Fat 120 • % Daily Value • Total Fat 13 g 20% • Saturated 4 g 20% • Cholesterol 45 mg 15% • Sodium 690 mg 29% • Total Carbohydrate 65 g 22% • Dietary Fiber 2 g 8% • Sugars 13 g • Protein 24 g • Vitamin A 25% • Vitamin C 100% • Calcium 4% • Iron 30%
Dietary Exchanges: 3 Starch, 1 Fruit, 1 Vegetable, 2 Lean Meat, 1 Fat OR 4 Carbohydrate, 1 Vegetable, 2 Lean Meat, 1 Fat

Chill Before Slicing

To make it easier to slice meat or poultry for stir-frying, place it in the freezer for 30 minutes or so. The meat will firm up just enough to make cutting easier.

Pepper Steak

Asian Beef in Ginger Sauce

Prep Time: 20 minutes

Yield: 4 servings

2 cups uncooked instant rice
2 cups water
1 teaspoon light sesame oil or vegetable oil
½ lb. precut beef flank or sirloin steak strips for stir-frying
1 medium onion, thinly sliced
3 cups fresh broccoli florets
¼ cup purchased stir-fry sauce with ginger and garlic
¼ cup water
2 teaspoons water
2 teaspoons cornstarch

1. Cook rice in 2 cups water as directed on package, omitting margarine and salt.

2. Meanwhile, heat oil in large nonstick skillet or wok over high heat until hot. Add beef and onion; cook 3 to 5 minutes or until beef is lightly browned, stirring occasionally.

3. Stir in broccoli, stir-fry sauce and ¼ cup water. Reduce heat to medium; cover and cook 4 minutes or until broccoli is crisp-tender, stirring occasionally.

4. In measuring cup or small bowl, combine 2 teaspoons water and cornstarch; blend well. Add to skillet; cook and stir about 1 minute or until thickened. Serve over rice.

Nutrition Information Per Serving: Serving Size: ¼ of Recipe • Calories 300 • Calories from Fat 60 • % Daily Value • Total Fat 7 g 11% • Saturated 2 g 10% • Cholesterol 20 mg 7% • Sodium 360 mg 15% • Total Carbohydrate 45 g 15% • Dietary Fiber 3 g 12% • Sugars 5 g • Protein 14 g • Vitamin A 40% • Vitamin C 70% • Calcium 6% • Iron 15%
Dietary Exchanges: 2½ Starch, 1 Vegetable, ½ Lean Meat, 1 Fat OR 2½ Carbohydrate, 1 Vegetable, ½ Lean Meat, 1 Fat

Skillet Beef and Green Beans

Prep Time: 45 minutes

Yield: 4 (1½-cup) servings

1 teaspoon oil
1 lb. boneless beef top round steak, cut into thin strips
¼ cup chopped onion
3 cups sliced new red potatoes
2 cups frozen cut green beans
¾ cup beef broth
½ teaspoon dried thyme leaves
¼ teaspoon pepper
1 teaspoon Worcestershire sauce
¼ cup water
2 teaspoons cornstarch
¼ cup chopped fresh parsley

1. Heat oil in large nonstick skillet or wok over medium-high heat until hot. Add beef and onion; cook and stir 2 to 3 minutes or until beef is browned. Remove beef from skillet; cover to keep warm.

2. In same skillet, combine potatoes, green beans, broth, thyme, pepper and Worcestershire sauce. Bring to a boil. Reduce heat; cover and simmer 15 to 20 minutes or until vegetables are tender.

3. In small bowl, combine water and cornstarch; blend well. Add beef mixture, cornstarch mixture and parsley to vegetables; cook and stir until bubbly and thickened.

Nutrition Information Per Serving: Serving Size: 1½ Cups • Calories 310 • Calories from Fat 45 • % Daily Value • Total Fat 5 g 8% • Saturated 2 g 10% • Cholesterol 65 mg 22% • Sodium 170 mg 7% • Total Carbohydrate 36 g 12% • Dietary Fiber 5 g 20% • Sugars 3 g • Protein 29 g • Vitamin A 6% • Vitamin C 30% • Calcium 4% • Iron 25%
Dietary Exchanges: 2 Starch, 1 Vegetable, 3 Lean Meat OR 2 Carbohydrate, 1 Vegetable, 3 Lean Meat

Cabbage in the Skillet

Cabbage, often served raw, also works well for many skillet suppers and stir-fries. Choose from the following varieties:

- Green head cabbage: This "garden variety" is a true bargain. High in vitamins, fiber and flavor, it is almost always one of the cheapest vegetables in the market. It is also very durable and can last for weeks in the refrigerator. Red head cabbage is best saved for raw dishes as it tends to discolor unattractively when cooked. At the market, choose heads that still have the coarse, darker green outer leaves attached. Although you'll end up discarding them, they're a sign of freshness; grocers sometimes peel off wilted outer layers of old cabbages and return the inner core to the shelf.

- Savoy cabbage: This ruffle-leafed round green cabbage is more delicate in flavor and texture than the ordinary green cabbage, but can be used interchangeably in any stir-fry or skillet supper.

- Chinese cabbage: These cabbages, also variously known as celery cabbage or napa cabbage, can be slender or fat but are more elongated in shape than their American cousins. Both have edible whitish stalks and crinkled pale green leaves. The leaves are more delicate in texture but spicier in flavor than ordinary cabbage. They are excellent in stir-fries.

Beef and Pea Pod Stir-Fry

Prep Time: 40 minutes

Yield: 4 servings

8	oz. fresh Chinese noodles (from 16-oz. pkg.) or 8 oz. uncooked vermicelli
1	tablespoon oil
¾	lb. beef flank, top sirloin or round steak, cut into thin strips
1	lb. (4 cups) fresh snow pea pods, trimmed
1	(8-oz.) can sliced bamboo shoots, drained
⅔	cup purchased stir-fry sauce
2	cups thinly sliced Chinese (napa) cabbage

1. Cook noodles as directed on package. Drain; cover to keep warm.

2. Meanwhile, heat oil in large skillet or wok over medium-high heat until hot. Add beef strips; cook and stir 2 to 3 minutes or until no longer pink.

3. Add pea pods, bamboo shoots and stir-fry sauce; cook and stir 3 to 4 minutes or until vegetables are crisp-tender. Add cabbage; cook and stir 30 to 40 seconds or until mixture is thoroughly heated. Serve over noodles.

Nutrition Information Per Serving: Serving Size: ¼ of Recipe • Calories 440 • Calories from Fat 90 • % Daily Value • Total Fat 10 g 15% • Saturated 3 g 15% • Cholesterol 35 mg 12% • Sodium 1480 mg 62% • Total Carbohydrate 67 g 22% • Dietary Fiber 4 g 16% • Sugars 8 g • Protein 20 g • Vitamin A 25% • Vitamin C 90% • Calcium 10% • Iron 30%
Dietary Exchanges: 2 Starch, 2 Fruit, 1½ Vegetable, 1½ Lean Meat, 1 Fat OR 4 Carbohydrate, 1½ Vegetable, 1½ Lean Meat, 1 Fat

Skillet Beef and Vegetables

Prep Time: 25 minutes

Yield: 4 (1-cup) servings

1	tablespoon oil
1	lb. boneless beef sirloin steak, cut into 1 x ¼-inch strips
1	(1-lb.) pkg. frozen broccoli florets, carrots and cauliflower
½	cup purchased stir-fry sauce
1	teaspoon cornstarch

1. Heat oil in large skillet over medium-high heat until hot. Add beef; cook and stir 5 to 6 minutes or until no longer pink. Drain. Add vegetables.

2. In small bowl, combine stir-fry sauce and cornstarch; mix well. Pour over vegetable mixture; stir to combine. Reduce heat; cover and simmer 6 to 8 minutes or until vegetables are crisp-tender, stirring occasionally.

Nutrition Information Per Serving: Serving Size: 1 Cup • Calories 220 • Calories from Fat 70 • % Daily Value • Total Fat 8 g 12% • Saturated 2 g 10% • Cholesterol 60 mg 20% • Sodium 1150 mg 48% • Total Carbohydrate 14 g 5% • Dietary Fiber 4 g 16% • Sugars 5 g • Protein 24 g • Vitamin A 80% • Vitamin C 30% • Calcium 4% • Iron 15%
Dietary Exchanges: ½ Starch, 1½ Vegetable, 3 Very Lean Meat, 1 Fat OR ½ Carbohydrate, 1½ Vegetable, 3 Very Lean Meat, 1 Fat

Beef with Broccoli and Black Mushrooms

Prep Time: 30 minutes

Yield: 4 servings

2 cups uncooked instant rice
2 cups water
1 (1-oz.) pkg. beef and
    broccoli–flavored
    authentic oriental
    seasoning mix
¾ cup beef broth
2 tablespoons lite soy sauce
1 tablespoon oil
1 garlic clove, minced
½ lb. beef top sirloin steak, cut
    into thin strips
½ lb. fresh broccoli, cut into
    small pieces (2 cups)
1 cup diagonally sliced celery
6 dried black mushrooms
    (from .75-oz. pkg.)

1. Cook rice in water as directed on package.

2. Meanwhile, in small bowl, combine seasoning mix, broth and soy sauce; blend well. Set aside.

3. Heat oil in large skillet or wok over medium-high heat until hot. Add garlic and beef strips; cook and stir 2 to 3 minutes or until beef is no longer pink.

4. Add broccoli and celery; cover and cook 4 to 5 minutes or until crisp-tender, stirring occasionally. Add mushrooms and broth mixture; cook and stir 1 to 2 minutes or until bubbly and thickened. Serve over rice.

Nutrition Information Per Serving: Serving Size: ¼ of Recipe • Calories 330 • Calories from Fat 60 • % Daily Value • Total Fat 7 g 11% • Saturated 2 g 10% • Cholesterol 30 mg 10% • Sodium 710 mg 30% • Total Carbohydrate 50 g 17% • Dietary Fiber 4 g 16% • Sugars 3 g • Protein 17 g • Vitamin A 20% • Vitamin C 60% • Calcium 6% • Iron 15%
Dietary Exchanges: 3 Starch, 1 Vegetable, 1 Lean Meat, ½ Fat OR 3 Carbohydrate, 1 Vegetable, 1 Lean Meat, ½ Fat

Stir-Fry Shortcuts

Peeling and chopping ingredients for stir-fries can be time-consuming. Here are some quick stir-ins:

◆ Coleslaw blend (shredded cabbage and carrots)

◆ Fresh bean sprouts

◆ Broccoli or cauliflower florets and sliced carrots from the supermarket salad bar

◆ Canned baby corn, bamboo shoots, straw mushrooms or sliced water chestnuts from the Asian market or international aisle of the supermarket

◆ Frozen mixed vegetables

◆ Meat or poultry precut into stir-fry strips or cubes

Twice-Cooked Noodles with Hoisin Pork

Prep Time: 50 minutes

Yield: 4 servings

8 oz. uncooked fresh Chinese noodles or angel hair pasta, broken into 2-inch pieces

1 tablespoon soy sauce

1 tablespoon sesame oil

3 tablespoons peanut oil

¾ lb. boneless pork loin chops, thinly sliced

½ lb. fresh green beans, trimmed, halved

¼ cup water

½ cup purchased garlic and ginger stir-fry sauce

¼ cup hoisin sauce

6 green onions, cut into 1-inch pieces (½ cup)

1. Cook noodles as directed on package. Drain well. In large bowl, combine cooked noodles, soy sauce and sesame oil.

2. Heat 1 tablespoon of the peanut oil in large nonstick skillet or wok over medium-high heat until hot. Add noodle mixture, pressing to form thin pancake; cook 8 to 12 minutes or until bottom of noodle pancake is golden brown.

3. Slide pancake from skillet onto plate; invert pancake onto another plate, browned side up. Add another 1 tablespoon peanut oil to skillet. Slide noodle pancake into skillet, browned side up; cook 4 to 6 minutes or until bottom is browned. Slide onto serving plate; cover to keep warm.

4. In same skillet, heat remaining 1 tablespoon peanut oil until hot. Add pork; cook and stir 3 to 5 minutes or until pork is no longer pink. Remove from skillet; cover to keep warm.

5. In same skillet, combine green beans and water. Reduce heat to medium; cover and cook 6 to 8 minutes or until crisp-tender, stirring occasionally. Drain; stir in stir-fry sauce, hoisin sauce, green onions and pork. Cook 1 to 2 minutes or until thoroughly heated.

6. To serve, with sharp knife or kitchen scissors, cut hot noodle pancake into 4 wedges. Top pancake with pork mixture.

Nutrition Information Per Serving: Serving Size: ¼ of Recipe • Calories 550 • Calories from Fat 200 • % Daily Value • Total Fat 22 g 34% • Saturated 5 g 25% • Cholesterol 50 mg 17% • Sodium 1230 mg 51% • Total Carbohydrate 69 g 23% • Dietary Fiber 3 g 12% • Sugars 16 g • Protein 20 g • Vitamin A 8% • Vitamin C 15% • Calcium 6% • Iron 15%
Dietary Exchanges: 3 Starch, 1 Fruit, 1 Vegetable, 1½ Lean Meat, 3 Fat OR 4 Carbohydrate, 1 Vegetable, 1½ Lean Meat, 3 Fat

Pork with Orange-Glazed Onions and Pea Pods

Prep Time: 20 minutes

Yield: 4 (1-cup) servings

2	tablespoons oil
1	lb. pork tenderloin, cut crosswise into 1/4-inch slices
1/2	cup orange marmalade
2	tablespoons chili sauce
8	oz. (2 cups) fresh snow pea pods, trimmed
2	small onions, sliced, separated into rings

1. Heat oil in large skillet or wok over medium-high heat until hot. Add pork; cook and stir 3 to 4 minutes or until pork is no longer pink. Remove from skillet; cover to keep warm.

2. Reduce heat to medium. In same skillet, combine all remaining ingredients; cook and stir 3 to 5 minutes or until vegetables are crisp-tender. Return pork to skillet; cook and stir 1 to 2 minutes or until thoroughly heated.

Nutrition Information Per Serving: Serving Size: 1 Cup • Calories 340 • Calories from Fat 100 • % Daily Value • Total Fat 11 g 17% • Saturated 2 g 10% • Cholesterol 65 mg 22% • Sodium 190 mg 8% • Total Carbohydrate 35 g 12% • Dietary Fiber 2 g 8% • Sugars 25 g • Protein 26 g • Vitamin A 4% • Vitamin C 45% • Calcium 6% • Iron 15%
Dietary Exchanges: 2 Fruit, 1 Vegetable, 3 Lean Meat, 1/2 Fat OR 2 Carbohydrate, 1 Vegetable, 3 Lean Meat, 1/2 Fat

Sweet-and-Sour Chicken and Rice Stir-Fry

Prep Time: 20 minutes

Yield: 4 (1³/₄-cup) servings

1	lb. precut chicken breast strips for stir-frying
1	(1-lb.) pkg. frozen broccoli florets, carrots and water chestnuts, thawed, drained*
1	(8-oz.) can pineapple chunks in unsweetened juice, undrained
	Water
1 1/2	cups uncooked instant white rice
3/4	cup purchased sweet-and-sour sauce

1. Spray large nonstick skillet with nonstick cooking spray. Heat over medium-high heat until hot. Add chicken; cook and stir 3 to 4 minutes or until lightly browned.

2. Stir in vegetables. Cover; cook 3 to 5 minutes or until vegetables are hot and chicken is no longer pink.

3. Meanwhile, drain pineapple liquid into 2-cup measuring cup; add water to make 1 1/2 cups.

4. Add pineapple liquid mixture and pineapple to skillet. Bring to a boil. Stir in rice; return to a boil. Reduce heat to low; cover and cook 5 minutes or until vegetables are crisp-tender and liquid is absorbed. Stir in sweet-and-sour sauce.

Tip: *To quickly thaw vegetables, place in colander or strainer; rinse with warm water until thawed. Drain well.

Nutrition Information Per Serving: Serving Size: 1³/₄ Cups • Calories 380 • Calories from Fat 25 • % Daily Value • Total Fat 3 g 5% • Saturated 1 g 5% • Cholesterol 65 mg 22% • Sodium 380 mg 16% • Total Carbohydrate 60 g 20% • Dietary Fiber 3 g 12% • Sugars 22 g • Protein 29 g • Vitamin A 60% • Vitamin C 30% • Calcium 4% • Iron 15%
Dietary Exchanges: 2 1/2 Starch, 1 Fruit, 1 Vegetable, 2 1/2 Very Lean Meat OR 3 1/2 Carbohydrate, 1 Vegetable, 2 1/2 Very Lean Meat

Sweet and Hot Pork and Pineapple Stir-Fry

Prep Time: 25 minutes

Yield: 4 servings

Photo at right, page vi and on back jacket

1½ cups uncooked instant rice
1½ cups water
4 tablespoons brown sugar
1½ teaspoons cornstarch
½ teaspoon ginger
¼ teaspoon crushed red pepper flakes, if desired
½ cup water
3 tablespoons soy sauce
1 (20-oz.) can pineapple chunks or 16 purchased fresh pineapple chunks, drained, reserving 2 tablespoons liquid
¾ lb. boneless lean pork, trimmed of fat, cut into thin bite-sized strips
1 (16-oz.) pkg. coleslaw blend

1. Cook rice in 1½ cups water as directed on package, omitting margarine and salt.

2. Meanwhile, in small bowl, combine 3 tablespoons of the brown sugar, cornstarch, ginger, red pepper flakes, ½ cup water, soy sauce and reserved 2 tablespoons pineapple liquid; mix well. Set aside.

3. Spray 12-inch nonstick skillet with nonstick cooking spray. Heat over medium-high heat until hot. Add drained pineapple chunks; sprinkle with remaining 1 tablespoon brown sugar. Cook 5 minutes, turning chunks occasionally.

4. Remove skillet from heat. Remove pineapple from skillet; set aside. Spray skillet again with cooking spray. Add pork; cook and stir over medium-high heat for 2 minutes.

5. Add coleslaw blend; cook and stir 3 to 6 minutes or until pork is no longer pink and cabbage is tender.

6. Add pineapple and cornstarch mixture to pork mixture; cook and stir 3 minutes or until pork is glazed and sauce is slightly thickened. Serve over rice.

Nutrition Information Per Serving: Serving Size: ¼ of Recipe • Calories 380 • Calories from Fat 50 • % Daily Value • Total Fat 6 g 9% • Saturated 2 g 10% • Cholesterol 45 mg 15% • Sodium 830 mg 35% • Total Carbohydrate 61 g 20% • Dietary Fiber 2 g 8% • Sugars 32 g • Protein 21 g • Vitamin A 70% • Vitamin C 50% • Calcium 10% • Iron 15%
Dietary Exchanges: 2 Starch, 1½ Fruit, 1 Vegetable, 2 Lean Meat OR 3½ Carbohydrate, 1 Vegetable, 2 Lean Meat

Sweet and Hot Pork and
Pineapple Stir-Fry

Honey-Orange Chicken Stir-Fry

Prep Time: 25 minutes

Yield: 4 servings

1 cup uncooked regular long-grain white rice

2 cups water

4 boneless, skinless chicken breast halves (about ½ lb.), cut into thin strips

½ teaspoon salt

¼ teaspoon pepper

1 cup orange juice

2 tablespoons honey

1 tablespoon cornstarch

1 teaspoon grated orange peel

2 cups frozen sweet peas, thawed*

⅔ cup salted cashews

1. Cook rice in water as directed on package.

2. Meanwhile, spray large nonstick skillet or wok with nonstick cooking spray. Heat over medium-high heat until hot. Add chicken, salt and pepper; cook and stir 3 to 4 minutes or until chicken is no longer pink.

3. In small bowl, combine orange juice, honey, cornstarch and orange peel; blend well. Add peas and orange juice mixture to chicken in skillet; cook and stir until mixture thickens and peas are hot. Stir in cashews. Serve over rice.

Tip: *To quickly thaw peas, place in colander or strainer; rinse with warm water until thawed. Drain well.

Nutrition Information Per Serving: Serving Size: ¼ of Recipe • Calories 580 • Calories from Fat 150 • % Daily Value • Total Fat 17 g 26% • Saturated 4 g 20% • Cholesterol 75 mg 25% • Sodium 660 mg 28% • Total Carbohydrate 69 g 23% • Dietary Fiber 5 g 20% • Sugars 21 g • Protein 38 g • Vitamin A 6% • Vitamin C 35% • Calcium 6% • Iron 30%

Dietary Exchanges: 4½ Starch, 3½ Very Lean Meat, 2 Fat OR 4½ Carbohydrate, 3½ Very Lean Meat, 2 Fat

Chinese Chicken, Vegetables and Pasta

Prep Time: 25 minutes

Yield: 4 servings

3 boneless, skinless chicken breast halves, cut into thin narrow strips

1 cup julienne-cut (2 x ⅛ x ⅛-inch) carrots

6 to 8 green onions, cut into ½-inch pieces (1 cup)

2 cups thinly sliced Chinese (napa) cabbage

½ cup purchased stir-fry sauce

2 to 3 tablespoons brown sugar

1 (9-oz.) pkg. refrigerated angel hair pasta

2 to 3 tablespoons chopped fresh cilantro

1. Spray large nonstick skillet with nonstick cooking spray. Heat over medium-high heat until hot. Add chicken; cook and stir 3 minutes. Add carrots and green onions; cook and stir 3 minutes or until chicken is no longer pink and vegetables are crisp-tender.

2. Add cabbage, stir-fry sauce and brown sugar; cook and stir until well blended. Cover; cook 2 to 3 minutes or until cabbage is crisp-tender.

3. Meanwhile, cook pasta to desired doneness as directed on package. Drain. Serve chicken mixture over pasta; sprinkle with cilantro.

Nutrition Information Per Serving: Serving Size: ¼ of Recipe • Calories 390 • Calories from Fat 35 • % Daily Value • Total Fat 4 g 6% • Saturated 1 g 5% • Cholesterol 100 mg 33% • Sodium 1170 mg 49% • Total Carbohydrate 57 g 19% • Dietary Fiber 4 g 16% • Sugars 16 g • Protein 31 g • Vitamin A 200% • Vitamin C 30% • Calcium 10% • Iron 20%

Dietary Exchanges: 3½ Starch, 1 Vegetable, 2½ Very Lean Meat OR 3½ Carbohydrate, 1 Vegetable, 2½ Very Lean Meat

Peanut Chicken Stir-Fry

Prep Time: 20 minutes
Yield: 4 (1¼-cup) servings

1 tablespoon oil
4 boneless, skinless chicken breast halves, cut into 1-inch pieces
2 garlic cloves, minced
1 (1-lb.) pkg. frozen broccoli florets, carrots and water chestnuts
½ cup chicken broth
¼ cup smooth or crunchy peanut butter
1 tablespoon brown sugar
3 tablespoons soy sauce
2 teaspoons cornstarch
¾ teaspoon ginger
5 to 6 drops hot pepper sauce
3 cups purchased coleslaw blend
¼ cup chopped salted peanuts

1. Heat oil in large skillet over medium–high heat until hot. Add chicken and garlic; cook and stir 3 minutes. Add frozen vegetables; cook and stir 5 to 7 minutes or until vegetables are crisp-tender and chicken is no longer pink.

2. Add all remaining ingredients except coleslaw blend and peanuts; cook 2 minutes or until mixture comes to a boil. Stir in coleslaw blend; cook and stir 2 minutes. Sprinkle with peanuts.

Nutrition Information Per Serving: Serving Size: 1¼ Cups • Calories 420 • Calories from Fat 180 • % Daily Value • Total Fat 20 g 31% • Saturated 4 g 20% • Cholesterol 75 mg 25% • Sodium 1100 mg 46% • Total Carbohydrate 22 g 7% • Dietary Fiber 5 g 20% • Sugars 12 g • Protein 37 g • Vitamin A 90% • Vitamin C 45% • Calcium 8% • Iron 15%
Dietary Exchanges: 1 Starch, 2 Vegetable, 4 Very Lean Meat, 3½ Fat OR 1 Carbohydrate, 2 Vegetable, 4 Very Lean Meat, 3½ Fat

Chicken and Rotini Primavera

Prep Time: 30 minutes
Yield: 6 (1⅓-cup) servings

6 oz. (2 cups) uncooked rotini (spiral pasta)
10 oz. (2 cups) fresh baby carrots
½ lb. fresh asparagus spears, trimmed, cut into 1-inch pieces
1 cup skim milk
2 tablespoons all-purpose flour
1½ teaspoons chicken-flavor instant bouillon
Dash pepper
4 boneless, skinless chicken breast halves, cut into bite-sized pieces
⅓ cup finely shredded fresh Parmesan cheese

1. Cook rotini and carrots in boiling water for 8 to 10 minutes or until of desired doneness, adding asparagus during last minute of cooking time. Drain.

2. Meanwhile, in small bowl, combine milk, flour, bouillon and pepper; blend well. Set aside.

3. Spray large nonstick skillet with nonstick cooking spray. Heat over medium–high heat until hot. Add chicken; cook and stir 4 to 6 minutes or until chicken is lightly browned and no longer pink.

4. Add milk mixture to skillet; cook and stir 2 to 3 minutes or until bubbly and thickened. Stir in Parmesan cheese; cook over medium-low heat until cheese is melted, stirring constantly.

5. Add cooked rotini and vegetables to chicken mixture; toss gently.

Nutrition Information Per Serving: Serving Size: 1⅓ Cups • Calories 270 • Calories from Fat 35 • % Daily Value • Total Fat 4 g 6% • Saturated 2 g 10% • Cholesterol 55 mg 18% • Sodium 400 mg 17% • Total Carbohydrate 32 g 11% • Dietary Fiber 3 g 12% • Sugars 7 g • Protein 26 g • Vitamin A 270% • Vitamin C 10% • Calcium 15% • Iron 15%
Dietary Exchanges: 2 Starch, 1 Vegetable, 2½ Very Lean Meat OR 2 Carbohydrate, 1 Vegetable, 2½ Very Lean Meat

Orange Chicken Stir-Fry

Prep Time: 15 minutes
Yield: 4 servings

- 2 cups uncooked instant rice
- 2 cups water
- 3 tablespoons frozen orange juice concentrate, thawed
- 2 tablespoons soy sauce
- ½ teaspoon cornstarch
- ¼ teaspoon garlic powder
- 1 lb. precut chicken breast strips for stir-frying
- 1 (1-lb.) pkg. frozen broccoli florets, carrots and water chestnuts, thawed, drained*

1. Cook rice in water as directed on package, omitting margarine and salt.

2. Meanwhile, in small bowl, combine orange juice concentrate, soy sauce, cornstarch and garlic powder; blend well.

3. Spray large nonstick skillet with nonstick cooking spray. Heat over medium-high heat until hot. Add chicken; cook 5 to 8 minutes or until chicken is no longer pink.

4. Stir in juice concentrate mixture and vegetables. Cover; cook over medium heat for 6 to 8 minutes or until vegetables are crisp-tender, stirring occasionally. Serve over rice. If desired, garnish with chopped green onions.

Tip: *To quickly thaw vegetables, place in colander or strainer; rinse with warm water until thawed. Drain well.

Nutrition Information Per Serving: Serving Size: ¼ of Recipe • Calories 350 • Calories from Fat 35 • % Daily Value • Total Fat 4 g 6% • Saturated 1 g 5% • Cholesterol 65 mg 22% • Sodium 620 mg 26% • Total Carbohydrate 48 g 16% • Dietary Fiber 4 g 16% • Sugars 8 g • Protein 31 g • Vitamin A 60% • Vitamin C 45% • Calcium 6% • Iron 15%
Dietary Exchanges: 3 Starch, 3 Very Lean Meat OR 3 Carbohydrate, 3 Very Lean Meat

Orange Chicken Stir-Fry

Glazed Mandarin Chicken

Prep Time: 25 minutes

Yield: 4 servings

1	cup water
1	cup uncooked instant white rice
½	cup frozen sweet peas
¼	cup barbecue sauce
¼	cup frozen orange juice concentrate, thawed
¼	teaspoon salt
3	boneless, skinless chicken breast halves, cut into 1-inch pieces
1	tablespoon oil
¼	cup water

1. In medium saucepan, bring 1 cup water to a boil. Add rice and peas; return to a boil. Cover; remove from heat. Set aside.

2. In medium bowl, combine barbecue sauce, orange juice concentrate and salt; blend well. Add chicken; stir to coat thoroughly.

3. Heat oil in large nonstick skillet over high heat for 1 minute. Add chicken; cook and stir about 4 minutes or until chicken is no longer pink. Remove skillet from heat. Remove chicken from skillet; set aside.

4. Add ¼ cup water to skillet. Cook and stir over high heat, scraping sides and bottom of skillet to remove cooked-on marinade. Cook about 30 seconds or until slightly thickened. Return chicken to skillet; toss to coat. Cook 1 minute or until chicken is glazed.

5. Serve over rice.

Nutrition Information Per Serving: Serving Size: ¼ of Recipe • Calories 270 • Calories from Fat 50 • % Daily Value • Total Fat 6 g 9% • Saturated 1 g 5% • Cholesterol 55 mg 18% • Sodium 340 mg 14% • Total Carbohydrate 31 g 10% • Dietary Fiber 1 g 4% • Sugars 6 g • Protein 23 g • Vitamin A 6% • Vitamin C 30% • Calcium 2% • Iron 10%
Dietary Exchanges: 2 Starch, 2 Very Lean Meat, 1 Fat OR 2 Carbohydrate, 2 Very Lean Meat, 1 Fat

Curry-Spiced Chicken and Peach Sauté

Prep Time: 20 minutes

Yield: 4 servings

1⅓	cups uncooked couscous
¼	cup orange juice
¼	cup honey
2	teaspoons cornstarch
½	teaspoon ginger
½	teaspoon curry powder
¼	teaspoon paprika
¼	teaspoon coarsely ground black pepper
2	tablespoons oil
1	lb. chicken breast tenders
1	medium green bell pepper, thinly sliced
1	small onion, cut into thin wedges
2	peaches, peeled, thinly sliced

1. Cook couscous as directed on package. Set aside.

2. In small bowl, combine orange juice, honey, cornstarch, ginger, curry powder, paprika and pepper; blend well. Set aside.

3. Heat oil in large skillet or wok over medium-high heat until hot. Add chicken; cook 4 to 6 minutes or until browned, stir occasionally.

4. Add bell pepper and onion; cook and stir 4 to 5 minutes or until chicken is no longer pink and vegetables are crisp-tender.

5. Stir orange juice mixture until smooth. Add orange juice mixture and peaches to skillet; cook and stir 2 to 3 minutes or until sauce is bubbly and thickened. Serve over couscous.

Nutrition Information Per Serving: Serving Size: ¼ of Recipe • Calories 530 • Calories from Fat 90 • % Daily Value • Total Fat 10 g 15% • Saturated 2 g 10% • Cholesterol 65 mg 22% • Sodium 65 mg 3% • Total Carbohydrate 76 g 25% • Dietary Fiber 5 g 20% • Sugars 25 g • Protein 33 g • Vitamin A 10% • Vitamin C 30% • Calcium 4% • Iron 10%
Dietary Exchanges: 4 Starch, 1 Fruit, 3 Very Lean Meat, 1 Fat OR 5 Carbohydrate, 3 Very Lean Meat, 1 Fat

Chicken and Vegetable Curry

Prep Time: 30 minutes

Yield: 4 servings

1½ cups uncooked instant rice
1½ cups water
1 cup chicken broth
3 teaspoons curry powder
1 tablespoon cornstarch
2 tablespoons dark brown sugar
⅛ teaspoon ground red pepper (cayenne), if desired
3 boneless, skinless chicken breast halves, cut into bite-sized pieces
1 (1-lb.) pkg. frozen broccoli florets, carrots and water chestnuts, thawed, drained*
2 tablespoons water
2 tablespoons soy sauce

1. Cook rice in 1½ cups water as directed on package, omitting margarine and salt.

2. Meanwhile, in small bowl, combine broth, curry powder, cornstarch, brown sugar and ground red pepper; blend with wire whisk until smooth. Set aside.

3. Spray large nonstick skillet with nonstick cooking spray. Heat over high heat until hot. Add chicken; cook and stir 3 to 4 minutes or until lightly browned. Remove chicken from skillet; set aside.

4. Reduce heat to medium-high; add vegetables and 2 tablespoons water to skillet. Cover; cook 3 to 4 minutes or until vegetables are crisp-tender. Return chicken to skillet. Stir broth mixture; add to skillet, stirring to blend. Cook about 1 minute or until sauce is thickened and chicken is no longer pink.

5. To serve, fluff rice with fork; spoon onto serving platter. Top with chicken mixture. Sprinkle with soy sauce.

Tip: *To quickly thaw vegetables, place in colander or strainer; rinse with warm water until thawed. Drain well.

Nutrition Information Per Serving: Serving Size: ¼ of Recipe • Calories 310 • Calories from Fat 25 • % Daily Value • Total Fat 3 g 5% • Saturated 1 g 5% • Cholesterol 55 mg 18% • Sodium 800 mg 33% • Total Carbohydrate 44 g 15% • Dietary Fiber 4 g 16% • Sugars 10 g • Protein 27 g • Vitamin A 60% • Vitamin C 25% • Calcium 6% • Iron 15%
Dietary Exchanges: 2½ Starch, 1 Vegetable, 2½ Meat OR 2½ Carbohydrate, 1 Vegetable, 2½ Meat

Chicken Almond Ding

Prep Time: 25 minutes

Yield: 4 servings

1⅓ cups uncooked regular long-
      grain white rice
2⅔ cups water
1 cup chicken broth
2 tablespoons cornstarch
2 tablespoons soy sauce
1 tablespoon rice vinegar
1 teaspoon sugar
¼ teaspoon salt, if desired
1 tablespoon oil
2 garlic cloves, minced
½ cup slivered almonds
4 boneless, skinless chicken
      breast halves, cut into
      ½-inch pieces
1 medium red bell pepper, cut
      into ¾-inch pieces
1 cup fresh snow pea pods,
      trimmed, cut diagonally in
      half
1 (8-oz.) can sliced water
      chestnuts, drained
2 cups chopped Chinese
      (napa) cabbage

1. Cook rice in water as directed on package.

2. Meanwhile, in small bowl, combine broth, cornstarch, soy sauce, vinegar, sugar and salt if desired; mix well. Set aside.

3. Heat oil in large skillet or wok over medium-high heat until hot. Add garlic, almonds and chicken; cook and stir 3 to 4 minutes or until chicken is no longer pink and almonds are golden brown.

4. Add bell pepper; cook and stir 2 to 3 minutes. Add pea pods and water chestnuts; cook and stir 3 to 4 minutes or until vegetables are crisp-tender. Add cabbage and cornstarch mixture; cook and stir until sauce is bubbly and thickened. Serve over rice.

Nutrition Information Per Serving: Serving Size: ¼ of Recipe • Calories 580 • Calories from Fat 140 • % Daily Value • Total Fat 15 g 23% • Saturated 2 g 10% • Cholesterol 75 mg 25% • Sodium 940 mg 39% • Total Carbohydrate 72 g 24% • Dietary Fiber 5 g 20% • Sugars 7 g • Protein 38 g • Vitamin A 45% • Vitamin C 90% • Calcium 15% • Iron 30%
Dietary Exchanges: 4½ Starch, 1 Vegetable, 3 Very Lean Meat, 2 Fat OR 4½ Carbohydrate, 1 Vegetable, 3 Very Lean Meat, 2 Fat

Herbal Basics

Oregano and similar flavorings are herbs, not spices. Herbs are the leaves of a plant; spices are made from seeds or, in the case of ginger, from the root.

In most cases, the leaves are trimmed or stripped from the stalk for cooking; the stems are usually discarded but can be used to flavor soups or sauces, then removed before serving.

In general, fresh and dried herbs can stand in for one another, particularly in cooked dishes, though to slightly different effect. One teaspoon of dried herbs is equivalent to 1 tablespoon of fresh herbs.

Rosemary Turkey and Vegetables with Parmesan Couscous

Prep Time: 30 minutes

Yield: 4 servings

1 (5.9-oz.) pkg. uncooked Parmesan-flavored couscous
½ cup dry white wine or chicken broth
2 teaspoons cornstarch
2 tablespoons olive oil or vegetable oil
2 garlic cloves, minced
1 lb. fresh turkey breast slices, cut into ¼-inch-thick strips
¾ teaspoon salt
⅛ teaspoon pepper
1 red bell pepper, thinly sliced
1 medium zucchini, julienne-cut (2 x ⅛ x ⅛-inch)
3 Italian plum tomatoes, thinly sliced
1 to 2 teaspoons chopped fresh rosemary or ¼ to ¾ teaspoon dried rosemary leaves, crushed

1. Cook couscous as directed on package. Cover to keep warm.
2. Meanwhile, in small bowl, combine wine and cornstarch; blend well. Set aside.
3. Heat oil in large skillet or wok over medium-high heat until hot. Add garlic; cook and stir 30 seconds. Add turkey, salt and pepper; cook and stir 5 to 7 minutes or until turkey is no longer pink.
4. Add bell pepper and zucchini; cook and stir 3 to 4 minutes or until crisp-tender.
5. Stir wine mixture until smooth. Add wine mixture, tomatoes and rosemary to skillet. Cook and stir until sauce is bubbly and thickened. Serve with couscous.

Nutrition Information Per Serving: Serving Size: ¼ of Recipe • Calories 400 • Calories from Fat 100 • % Daily Value • Total Fat 11 g 17% • Saturated 3 g 15% • Cholesterol 85 mg 28% • Sodium 850 mg 35% • Total Carbohydrate 37 g 12% • Dietary Fiber 3 g 12% • Sugars 5 g • Protein 34 g • Vitamin A 30% • Vitamin C 50% • Calcium 6% • Iron 15%
Dietary Exchanges: 2 Starch, 1 Vegetable, 4 Very Lean Meat, 1½ Fat OR 2 Carbohydrate, 1 Vegetable, 4 Very Lean Meat, 1½ Fat

Rosemary Turkey and Vegetables with Parmesan Couscous

Mediterranean Shrimp and Bow Ties

Prep Time: 25 minutes

Yield: 4 (1½-cup) servings

6   oz. (2⅔ cups) uncooked bow tie pasta (farfalle)
1   tablespoon olive oil or vegetable oil
1   lb. shelled, deveined, uncooked medium or large shrimp
½   cup green onion pieces (½ inch)
2   garlic cloves, minced
½   teaspoon dried oregano leaves
¼   teaspoon salt
2   tablespoons lemon juice
½   cup sliced kalamata or ripe olives

1. Cook pasta to desired doneness as directed on package. Drain.

2. Meanwhile, heat oil in large skillet over medium-high heat until hot. Add shrimp, green onions and garlic; cook and stir 3 to 5 minutes or until shrimp turn pink. Remove skillet from heat.

3. Add cooked pasta and all remaining ingredients; toss gently to mix. Return to heat; cook 1 to 2 minutes or until thoroughly heated.

Nutrition Information Per Serving: Serving Size: 1½ Cups • Calories 320 • Calories from Fat 90 • % Daily Value • Total Fat 10 g 15% • Saturated 1 g 5% • Cholesterol 160 mg 53% • Sodium 600 mg 25% • Total Carbohydrate 35 g 12% • Dietary Fiber 1 g 4% • Sugars 2 g • Protein 23 g • Vitamin A 4% • Vitamin C 8% • Calcium 6% • Iron 25%
Dietary Exchanges: 2½ Starch, 2 Very Lean Meat, 1½ Fat OR 2½ Carbohydrate, 2 Very Lean Meat, 1½ Fat

Coral and Jade Shrimp

Prep Time: 30 minutes

Yield: 4 servings

1⅓   cups uncooked regular long-grain white rice
2⅔   cups water
2   tablespoons water
8   oz. (2 cups) fresh snow pea pods, trimmed, cut diagonally in half
1   tablespoon oil
1   garlic clove, minced
¾   lb. shelled, deveined, uncooked large or medium shrimp
½   to ¾ cup purchased sweet-and-sour sauce

1. Cook rice in 2⅔ cups water as directed on package.

2. Meanwhile, in large skillet or wok, combine 2 tablespoons water and pea pods. Bring to a boil. Reduce heat; cover and cook 3 to 4 minutes or until crisp-tender. Drain pea pods; wipe skillet clean with paper towel.

3. Heat oil in same skillet over medium-high heat until hot. Add garlic and shrimp; cook and stir 2 to 3 minutes or until shrimp turn pink. Add sauce and pea pods; cook and stir 1 to 2 minutes or until thoroughly heated. Serve over rice.

Nutrition Information Per Serving: Serving Size: ¼ of Recipe • Calories 370 • Calories from Fat 45 • % Daily Value • Total Fat 5 g 8% • Saturated 1 g 5% • Cholesterol 120 mg 40% • Sodium 430 mg 18% • Total Carbohydrate 62 g 21% • Dietary Fiber 2 g 8% • Sugars 13 g • Protein 19 g • Vitamin A 4% • Vitamin C 40% • Calcium 6% • Iron 25%
Dietary Exchanges: 3 Starch, 1 Fruit, 1½ Very Lean Meat, ½ Fat OR 4 Carbohydrate, 1½ Very Lean Meat, ½ Fat

Shrimp and Vegetables in Black Bean Sauce

Prep Time: 30 minutes

Yield: 4 servings

1⅓   cups uncooked regular long-grain white rice
2⅔   cups water
2   tablespoons fermented black beans, drained, rinsed and finely chopped
1   tablespoon soy sauce
2   teaspoons dry sherry
1   teaspoon grated gingerroot
½   teaspoon sugar
1   garlic clove, minced
1   cup chicken broth
2   tablespoons cornstarch
2   tablespoons water
1   (1-lb.) pkg. frozen broccoli florets, carrots and water chestnuts
1   tablespoon oil
½   lb. shelled, deveined, uncooked medium shrimp

1. Cook rice in 2⅔ cups water as directed on package.

2. Meanwhile, in small bowl, combine beans, soy sauce, sherry, gingerroot, sugar and garlic; mix well. In another small bowl, combine broth and cornstarch; blend well. Set aside.

3. In large skillet or wok, combine 2 tablespoons water and frozen vegetables. Bring to a boil. Reduce heat to medium; cover and cook 7 to 9 minutes or until crisp-tender. Drain vegetables in colander.

4. Wipe skillet dry with paper towel. Heat oil in same skillet over medium-high heat until hot. Add shrimp; cook and stir 2 to 3 minutes or until shrimp turn pink.

5. Add bean mixture; cook and stir 1 minute. Add cornstarch mixture and cooked vegetables; cook and stir 2 to 3 minutes or until sauce is bubbly and thickened. Serve over rice.

Nutrition Information Per Serving: Serving Size: ¼ of Recipe • Calories 350 • Calories from Fat 45 • % Daily Value • Total Fat 5 g 8% • Saturated 1 g 5% • Cholesterol 80 mg 27% • Sodium 610 mg 25% • Total Carbohydrate 58 g 19% • Dietary Fiber 3 g 12% • Sugars 4 g • Protein 17 g • Vitamin A 60% • Vitamin C 25% • Calcium 6% • Iron 20%
Dietary Exchanges: 3 Starch, 2 Vegetable, 1 Very Lean Meat, ½ Fat OR 3 Carbohydrate, 2 Vegetable, 1 Very Lean Meat, ½ Fat

Kung Pao Shrimp

Prep Time: 20 minutes

Yield: 4 servings

3   tablespoons hoisin sauce
1   tablespoon dry sherry
1   teaspoon sugar
½   to 1 teaspoon chili paste
1   egg white
1   tablespoon cornstarch
¾   lb. shelled, deveined, uncooked medium shrimp
1   tablespoon oil
½   teaspoon grated gingerroot
1   garlic clove, minced
¼   cup dry-roasted salted peanuts

1. In small bowl, combine hoisin sauce, sherry, sugar and chili paste; mix well. Set aside.

2. In medium bowl, combine egg white and cornstarch; beat well. Add shrimp; mix well to coat.

3. Heat oil in large skillet or wok over medium-high heat until hot. Add shrimp mixture, gingerroot and garlic; cook and stir 2 to 3 minutes or until shrimp turn pink. Add sauce mixture; cook and stir 1 to 2 minutes or until shrimp are well coated. Stir in peanuts.

Nutrition Information Per Serving: Serving Size: ¼ of Recipe • Calories 190 • Calories from Fat 80 • % Daily Value • Total Fat 9 g 14% • Saturated 1 g 5% • Cholesterol 120 mg 40% • Sodium 530 mg 22% • Total Carbohydrate 12 g 4% • Dietary Fiber 1 g 4% • Sugars 8 g • Protein 16 g • Vitamin A 4% • Vitamin C 2% • Calcium 4% • Iron 15%
Dietary Exchanges: 1 Starch, 2 Lean Meat OR 1 Carbohydrate, 2 Lean Meat

Tarragon Shrimp and Vegetable Stir-Fry

Prep Time: 20 minutes

Yield: 3 (1⅓-cup) servings

SAUCE
- ½ cup water
- 3 tablespoons dry white wine or water
- 1 teaspoon lemon juice
- 1 tablespoon cornstarch
- 1 teaspoon chicken-flavor instant bouillon
- 1 teaspoon dried tarragon leaves, crushed

STIR-FRY
- 2 tablespoons oil
- 1½ cups frozen cut green beans
- 1½ cups frozen cauliflower florets
- 1 cup julienne-cut (2 x ⅛ x ⅛-inch) carrots
- 1 (12-oz.) pkg. frozen uncooked medium shrimp, thawed
- 3 green onions, cut into 1-inch pieces

1. In small bowl, combine all sauce ingredients; blend well. Set aside.

2. Heat oil in large skillet or wok over medium-high heat until hot. Gradually add green beans, cauliflower and carrots; cook and stir 5 minutes.

3. Add shrimp; cook and stir 3 to 4 minutes or until shrimp turn pink and vegetables are crisp-tender.

4. Stir in green onions and sauce; cook until thickened and bubbly, stirring constantly.

Nutrition Information Per Serving: Serving Size: 1⅓ Cups • Calories 260 • Calories from Fat 100 • % Daily Value • Total Fat 11 g 17% • Saturated 2 g 10% • Cholesterol 160 mg 53% • Sodium 550 mg 23% • Total Carbohydrate 16 g 5% • Dietary Fiber 5 g 20% • Sugars 5 g • Protein 21 g • Vitamin A 240% • Vitamin C 60% • Calcium 10% • Iron 20%
Dietary Exchanges: ½ Fruit, 2 Vegetable, 2½ Very Lean Meat, 2 Fat OR ½ Carbohydrate, 2 Vegetable, 2½ Very Lean Meat, 2 Fat

Instant Bouillon

Instant bouillon is a quick and easy way to add flavor to soups and stews. Beef, chicken and vegetable bouillons are available as granules or cubes and are found in the soup section of supermarkets. To substitute instant bouillon for canned or homemade broth, dissolve 1 teaspoon of granules or 1 cube in each cup of hot water used.

Tarragon Shrimp and Vegetable Stir-Fry

Seafood Broccoli Stir-Fry

Prep Time: 30 minutes

Yield: 4 servings

1 tablespoon oil
¾ lb. shelled, deveined, uncooked medium shrimp
2 garlic cloves, minced
¼ cup water
1 (14-oz.) pkg. frozen broccoli florets
1 small onion, chopped
1 teaspoon grated gingerroot
1 tablespoon cornstarch
2 tablespoons soy sauce

1. Heat oil in large skillet or wok over medium-high heat until hot. Add shrimp and garlic; cook and stir 5 to 6 minutes or until shrimp turn pink, stirring constantly. Remove shrimp from skillet; cover to keep warm.

2. In same skillet, bring water to a boil over medium-high heat. Stir in frozen broccoli, onion and gingerroot. Cook and stir 6 to 8 minutes or until vegetables are crisp-tender. Add warm shrimp.

3. In small bowl, combine cornstarch and soy sauce; blend well. Stir into hot shrimp mixture. Cook, stirring constantly, 1 to 2 minutes or until glaze has slightly thickened and covers all ingredients. If desired, serve with hot cooked rice or pasta.

Nutrition Information Per Serving: Serving Size: ¼ of Recipe • Calories 150 • Calories from Fat 45 • % Daily Value • Total Fat 5 g 8% • Saturated 1 g 5% • Cholesterol 120 mg 40% • Sodium 680 mg 28% • Total Carbohydrate 9 g 3% • Dietary Fiber 3 g 12% • Sugars 2 g • Protein 17 g • Vitamin A 15% • Vitamin C 50% • Calcium 6% • Iron 15%
Dietary Exchanges: 2 Vegetable, 2 Very Lean Meat, ½ Fat

Teriyaki Salmon and Vegetables

Prep Time: 25 minutes

Yield: 4 (1-cup) servings

1 tablespoon oil
1 lb. salmon fillets, cut into 1-inch pieces
1 teaspoon purchased chopped garlic and ginger stir-fry blend
2 cups fresh broccoli florets
1½ cups thinly sliced carrots
1 cup thinly sliced celery
3 tablespoons water
½ cup purchased teriyaki baste and glaze

1. Heat oil in large skillet or wok over medium heat until hot. Add salmon and stir-fry blend; cook and stir 3 to 5 minutes or until fish flakes easily with fork. Remove fish from skillet; cover to keep warm.

2. In same skillet, combine broccoli, carrots and celery; cook and stir 3 minutes. Add water; cover and cook 3 to 4 minutes or until vegetables are crisp-tender, stirring occasionally.

3. Gently stir in cooked fish and teriyaki baste and glaze; cook until thoroughly heated.

Nutrition Information Per Serving: Serving Size: 1 Cup • Calories 320 • Calories from Fat 130 • % Daily Value • Total Fat 14 g 22% • Saturated 2 g 10% • Cholesterol 85 mg 28% • Sodium 920 mg 38% • Total Carbohydrate 19 g 6% • Dietary Fiber 3 g 12% • Sugars 13 g • Protein 29 g • Vitamin A 290% • Vitamin C 50% • Calcium 10% • Iron 15%
Dietary Exchanges: ½ Fruit, 2 Vegetable, 3½ Lean Meat, 1 Fat OR ½ Carbohydrate, 2 Vegetable, 3½ Lean Meat, 1 Fat

Tangy Scallops with Chinese Noodles

Prep Time: 30 minutes

Yield: 4 servings

8   oz. fresh Chinese noodles (from 16-oz. pkg.) or 8 oz. uncooked vermicelli
1   cup chicken broth
⅓   cup dry sherry
¼   cup oyster sauce
2   tablespoons cornstarch
2   tablespoons honey
1   tablespoon soy sauce
⅛   to ¼ teaspoon crushed red pepper flakes
¾   lb. scallops, cut in half if large, rinsed and drained
2   tablespoons water
2   (9-oz.) pkg. (7 cups) fresh stir-fry vegetables (broccoli, green cabbage, carrots and snow pea pods)

1. Cut noodles into 4-inch pieces. Cook noodles as directed on package. Drain; cover to keep warm.

2. Meanwhile, in small bowl, combine broth, sherry, oyster sauce, cornstarch, honey, soy sauce and red pepper flakes; blend well. Add scallops; stir until coated. Set aside.

3. In large skillet or wok, combine water and vegetables. Cover; cook over medium-high heat for 5 to 7 minutes or until crisp-tender.

4. Add scallop mixture; cook and stir 1 to 2 minutes or until scallops are opaque and sauce is bubbly and thickened. Stir in cooked noodles; mix well. Cook until thoroughly heated.

Nutrition Information Per Serving: Serving Size: ¼ of Recipe • Calories 390 • Calories from Fat 20 • % Daily Value • Total Fat 2 g 3% • Saturated 0 g 0% • Cholesterol 30 mg 10% • Sodium 1520 mg 63% • Total Carbohydrate 69 g 23% • Dietary Fiber 5 g 20% • Sugars 16 g • Protein 23 g • Vitamin A 150% • Vitamin C 45% • Calcium 10% • Iron 25%
Dietary Exchanges: 2 Starch, 2 Fruit, 1½ Vegetable, 2 Very Lean Meat OR 4 Carbohydrate, 1½ Vegetable, 2 Very Lean Meat

Imperial Beef and Scallops

Prep Time: 30 minutes

Yield: 4 servings

1⅓ cups uncooked regular long-
grain white rice
2⅔ cups water
½ lb. scallops, cut in half if
large
¼ cup dry sherry
2 tablespoons soy sauce
1 tablespoon oyster sauce
1 tablespoon cornstarch
2 teaspoons sugar
1 tablespoon oil
¾ teaspoon grated gingerroot
1 garlic clove, minced
½ lb. beef top sirloin or round
steak, cut into 2 x ½ x ¼-
inch strips
½ cup beef broth
2 cups frozen cut broccoli
1 (8-oz.) can sliced water
chestnuts, drained

1. Cook rice in water as directed on package.

2. Meanwhile, rinse scallops; drain. In small bowl, combine sherry, soy sauce, oyster sauce, cornstarch and sugar; blend well. Add scallops; stir gently to coat. Set aside.

3. Heat oil in large skillet or wok over medium-high heat until hot. Add gingerroot, garlic and beef strips; cook and stir 2 to 3 minutes or until beef is browned. Add broth, broccoli and water chestnuts. Cover; cook 5 to 7 minutes or until broccoli is crisp-tender, stirring occasionally.

4. Add scallop mixture; cook 1 to 2 minutes or until scallops are opaque and sauce is thickened, stirring constantly. Serve over rice.

Nutrition Information Per Serving: Serving Size: ¼ of Recipe • Calories 420 • Calories from Fat 60 • % Daily Value • Total Fat 7 g 11% • Saturated 2 g 10% • Cholesterol 50 mg 17% • Sodium 1020 mg 43% • Total Carbohydrate 63 g 21% • Dietary Fiber 3 g 12% • Sugars 7 g • Protein 26 g • Vitamin A 6% • Vitamin C 25% • Calcium 6% • Iron 20%
Dietary Exchanges: 4 Starch, 1 Vegetable, 1½ Very Lean Meat, ½ Fat OR 4 Carbohydrate, 1 Vegetable, 1½ Very Lean Meat, ½ Fat

Ginger

Fresh ginger is a key ingredient in many stir-fry recipes. Its flavor, at once spicy, sweet and hot, is irreplaceable. At the market, choose a section of fresh gingerroot that looks firm, with taut (though bumpy) skin; avoid any pieces that look shriveled or moldy. Store the root unpeeled at room temperature or peeled and submersed in sherry in the refrigerator.

At cooking time, peel away the outer tan skin; a sharp paring knife will work better than a vegetable peeler on the gnarled surface.

For most recipes, grating with a fine-holed grater will be best; this will evenly distribute the flavor and spare diners the shock of biting into a chunk of intensely flavored ginger.

Imperial Beef and Scallops

Fish and Fresh Vegetable Stir-Fry

Prep Time: 40 minutes

Yield: 4 servings

½ cup chicken broth
2 tablespoons dry sherry
2 tablespoons oyster sauce
1 teaspoon sugar
1 lb. firm white fish fillets (such as cod, pollack or haddock), cut crosswise into 2 x 1-inch strips
1 tablespoon cornstarch
3 tablespoons oil
1 teaspoon grated gingerroot
1 garlic clove, minced
1 medium onion, halved crosswise, each half cut into 6 wedges
8 oz. (2 cups) fresh snow pea pods, trimmed, cut diagonally in half
1 medium tomato, cut into 8 wedges

1. In medium bowl, combine broth, sherry, oyster sauce and sugar; mix well. Add fish; stir gently to coat. Cover; refrigerate 15 to 30 minutes to marinate.

2. Drain fish, reserving marinade in small bowl. Add cornstarch to marinade; mix well. Set aside.

3. Heat oil in large skillet or wok over medium heat until hot. Add gingerroot, garlic and fish; cook and stir 3 to 5 minutes or until fish turns white. Remove fish from skillet.

4. Add onion to skillet; cook and stir 2 minutes. Add pea pods; cook and stir 4 to 5 minutes or until vegetables are crisp-tender. Add marinade mixture; cook and stir 1 to 2 minutes or until sauce is bubbly and thickened.

5. Gently stir in fish; cook until thoroughly heated. Place mixture on serving platter. Arrange tomato wedges around mixture.

Nutrition Information Per Serving: Serving Size: ¼ of Recipe • Calories 250 • Calories from Fat 100 • % Daily Value • Total Fat 11 g 17% • Saturated 2 g 10% • Cholesterol 50 mg 17% • Sodium 590 mg 25% • Total Carbohydrate 14 g 5% • Dietary Fiber 2 g 8% • Sugars 8 g • Protein 23 g • Vitamin A 6% • Vitamin C 45% • Calcium 4% • Iron 15%
Dietary Exchanges: ½ Starch, 1 Vegetable, 3 Very Lean Meat, 1½ Fat OR ½ Carbohydrate, 1 Vegetable, 3 Very Lean Meat, 1½ Fat

Spicy Vegetable Stir-Fry

Prep Time: 30 minutes

Yield: 4 servings

1½ cups uncooked instant rice
1½ cups water
1 cup water
1 tablespoon soy sauce
1 tablespoon cornstarch
½ teaspoon crushed red pepper flakes
1 teaspoon oil
¼ cup chopped onion
1 medium green bell pepper, cut into thin strips
2 tablespoons water
3 medium zucchini, halved lengthwise, thinly sliced
4 frozen breaded chicken substitute patties, thawed, cut into bite-sized pieces
3 tomatoes, cut into thin wedges

1. Cook rice in 1½ cups water as directed on package, omitting margarine and salt.

2. Meanwhile, in small bowl, combine 1 cup water, soy sauce, cornstarch and red pepper flakes; blend well. Set aside.

3. Heat oil in large nonstick skillet or wok over medium heat until hot. Add onion and bell pepper; cook 3 to 4 minutes or until onion is tender. Add 2 tablespoons water and zucchini; cover and cook until all vegetables are tender.

4. Add chicken substitute pieces and tomatoes; cook until thoroughly heated. Stir cornstarch mixture; add to skillet. Cook and stir until thickened. Serve mixture over rice.

Nutrition Information Per Serving: Serving Size: ¼ of Recipe • Calories 380 • Calories from Fat 110 • % Daily Value • Total Fat 12 g 18% • Saturated 2 g 10% • Cholesterol 0 mg 0% • Sodium 840 mg 35% • Total Carbohydrate 54 g 18% • Dietary Fiber 6 g 24% • Sugars 8 g • Protein 13 g • Vitamin A 25% • Vitamin C 60% • Calcium 4% • Iron 15%
Dietary Exchanges: 3 Starch, 2 Vegetable OR 3 Carbohydrate, 2 Vegetable

Five-Spice Mushroom and Broccoli Stir-Fry

Prep Time: 35 minutes

Yield: 4 servings

1 (7-oz.) pkg. uncooked vermicelli
½ cup orange juice
1 tablespoon cornstarch
¾ teaspoon Chinese five-spice powder
⅛ to ¼ teaspoon crushed red pepper flakes
2 tablespoons soy sauce
2 teaspoons honey
8 large mushrooms (12 oz.), cut into ¼-inch-thick slices
1 cup fresh baby carrots, quartered lengthwise
1 medium onion, cut into thin wedges
1 garlic clove, minced
3 cups small fresh broccoli florets (about 6 oz.)

1. Cook vermicelli to desired doneness as directed on package. Drain; cover to keep warm.

2. Meanwhile, in small bowl, combine orange juice, cornstarch, five-spice powder, red pepper flakes, soy sauce and honey; stir until well blended. Set aside.

3. Spray large nonstick skillet with nonstick cooking spray. Heat over medium-high heat until hot. Add mushrooms, carrots, onion and garlic; cook and stir 4 minutes.

4. Add broccoli; cover and cook 2 to 4 minutes or until vegetables are crisp-tender, stirring occasionally. Add orange juice mixture; cook and stir 2 to 3 minutes or until bubbly and thickened. Serve over vermicelli.

Nutrition Information Per Serving: Serving Size: ¼ of Recipe • Calories 300 • Calories from Fat 20 • % Daily Value • Total Fat 2 g 3% • Saturated 0 g 0% • Cholesterol 0 mg 0% • Sodium 550 mg 23% • Total Carbohydrate 59 g 20% • Dietary Fiber 6 g 24% • Sugars 13 g • Protein 11 g • Vitamin A 180% • Vitamin C 90% • Calcium 6% • Iron 25%
Dietary Exchanges: 3½ Starch, 1 Vegetable OR 3½ Carbohydrate, 1 Vegetable

Fish and Vegetable Stir-Fry

Prep Time: 30 minutes

Yield: 4 servings

⅔   cup uncooked regular long-
      grain white rice
1⅓ cups water
¼   cup water
2   tablespoons lite soy sauce
2   teaspoons cornstarch
¼   teaspoon ginger
⅛   to ¼ teaspoon pepper
⅛   teaspoon crushed red pepper
      flakes
1   garlic clove, minced
1   lb. cod or haddock fillets,
      cut into 1½-inch squares
2   tablespoons water
1   (1-lb.) pkg. frozen broccoli
      florets, carrots and water
      chestnuts

1. Cook rice in 1⅓ cups water as directed on package.

2. Meanwhile, in small bowl, combine ¼ cup water, soy sauce, corn-starch, ginger, pepper, red pepper flakes and garlic; blend well. Set aside.

3. Spray large nonstick skillet or wok with nonstick cooking spray. Heat over high heat until hot. Add cod; cook and stir 2 to 4 minutes or until fish is opaque and flakes easily with fork. Remove from skillet; cover to keep warm.

4. Remove skillet from heat; spray with nonstick cooking spray. Add 2 tablespoons water and frozen vegetables; cover and cook 6 to 7 minutes or until vegetables are crisp-tender.

5. Stir cornstarch mixture until smooth. Add to skillet; cook and stir until thickened. Return fish to skillet; toss gently to heat thoroughly. Serve over rice.

Nutrition Information Per Serving: Serving Size: ¼ of Recipe • Calories 230 • Calories from Fat 10 • % Daily Value • Total Fat 1 g 2% • Saturated 0 g 0% • Cholesterol 50 mg 17% • Sodium 430 mg 18% • Total Carbohydrate 31 g 10% • Dietary Fiber 3 g 12% • Sugars 3 g • Protein 25 g • Vitamin A 60% • Vitamin C 30% • Calcium 4% • Iron 10%
Dietary Exchanges: 1½ Starch, 1 Vegetable, 2½ Very Lean Meat OR 1½ Carbohydrate, 1 Vegetable, 2½ Very Lean Meat

New Potato, Pasta
and Vegetable
Stir-Fry

New Potato, Pasta and Vegetable Stir-Fry

Prep Time: 30 minutes

Yield: 4 (1³/₄-cup) servings

8 oz. (3½ cups) uncooked bow
tie pasta (farfalle)

2 tablespoons olive oil or
vegetable oil

1 medium onion, cut into 8
wedges

4 new red potatoes, unpeeled,
sliced

8 oz. fresh asparagus spears,
trimmed, cut into 2-inch
pieces

1 medium red or yellow bell
pepper, cut into strips

2 tablespoons chopped fresh
oregano

½ teaspoon salt

⅛ teaspoon pepper

4 oz. (1 cup) shredded Swiss
cheese

1. Cook pasta to desired doneness as directed on package. Drain.

2. Meanwhile, heat oil in large skillet over medium-high heat until
hot. Add onion; cook and stir 2 minutes. Add potatoes; cover and
cook 5 to 6 minutes or until partially cooked, stirring occasionally.

3. Stir in asparagus, bell pepper, oregano, salt and pepper. Reduce
heat to medium-low; cover and cook 5 to 8 minutes or until vegetables are tender, stirring occasionally.

4. Stir in cooked pasta; cook until thoroughly heated. Remove from
heat. Sprinkle with cheese. Cover; let stand until cheese is melted.

Nutrition Information Per Serving: Serving Size: 1¾ Cups • Calories 510 • Calories from Fat 140 •
% Daily Value • Total Fat 16 g 25% • Saturated 6 g 30% • Cholesterol 25 mg 8% • Sodium 350 mg 15% • Total
Carbohydrate 72 g 24% • Dietary Fiber 6 g 24% • Sugars 7 g • Protein 19 g • Vitamin A 35% • Vitamin C 70% •
Calcium 30% • Iron 25%
Dietary Exchanges: 4½ Starch, 1 Vegetable, ½ High-Fat Meat, 2 Fat OR 4½ Carbohydrate, 1 Vegetable, ½ High-
Fat Meat, 2 Fat

Linguine with Fresh Vegetables and Herbs

Prep Time: 30 minutes

Yield: 4 (1½-cup) servings

8	oz. uncooked linguine
4	tablespoons olive oil or vegetable oil
1	cup thinly sliced carrots
1	medium zucchini, halved lengthwise, thinly sliced
3	tomatoes, seeded, finely chopped
1	tablespoon chopped fresh basil
2	teaspoons chopped fresh oregano
2	teaspoons chopped fresh marjoram
1	teaspoon chopped fresh thyme
½	teaspoon salt
¼	teaspoon pepper
4	oz. fresh mozzarella cheese, diced

1. In large saucepan, cook linguine to desired doneness as directed on package. Drain; return to saucepan.

2. Meanwhile, heat 3 tablespoons of the oil in large skillet or wok over medium-high heat until hot. Add carrots; cook and stir 2 minutes.

3. Add zucchini; cook and stir 2 to 3 minutes or until vegetables are crisp-tender. Add all remaining ingredients except cheese; cook and stir until thoroughly heated.

4. Add remaining 1 tablespoon oil to cooked linguine; toss to coat. Add linguine and cheese to vegetable mixture; toss gently to combine.

Nutrition Information Per Serving: Serving Size: 1½ Cups • Calories 460 • Calories from Fat 180 • % Daily Value • Total Fat 20 g 31% • Saturated 5 g 25% • Cholesterol 15 mg 5% • Sodium 440 mg 18% • Total Carbohydrate 53 g 18% • Dietary Fiber 4 g 16% • Sugars 7 g • Protein 17 g • Vitamin A 190% • Vitamin C 30% • Calcium 25% • Iron 20%
Dietary Exchanges: 3 Starch, 1 Vegetable, 1 Medium-Fat Meat, 2½ Fat OR 3 Carbohydrate, 1 Vegetable, 1 Medium-Fat Meat, 2½ Fat

Sesame Broccoli Stir-Fry with Noodles

Prep Time: 25 minutes

Yield: 4 (1½-cup) servings

4	oz. (2½ cups) uncooked egg noodles
1	tablespoon sesame seed
1	tablespoon peanut oil
2	garlic cloves, minced
4	cups fresh broccoli florets
1	(8-oz.) can sliced water chestnuts, drained
1	(4½-oz.) jar whole mushrooms, drained
½	cup chicken broth
2	tablespoons dry white wine or chicken broth
2	tablespoons soy sauce
2	teaspoons cornstarch

1. Cook noodles to desired doneness as directed on package. Drain.

2. Meanwhile, in large skillet or wok, cook and stir sesame seed over medium-high heat for 2 to 3 minutes or until golden brown. Remove from skillet; set aside.

3. In same skillet, heat oil over medium-high heat until hot. Add garlic; cook and stir 30 seconds. Add broccoli, water chestnuts and mushrooms; cook and stir 6 to 7 minutes or until broccoli is crisp-tender.

4. In small bowl, combine broth, wine, soy sauce and cornstarch; blend well. Add cooked noodles and cornstarch mixture to skillet; cook and stir until bubbly and thickened. Sprinkle with sesame seed.

Nutrition Information Per Serving: Serving Size: 1½ Cups • Calories 250 • Calories from Fat 50 • % Daily Value • Total Fat 6 g 9% • Saturated 1 g 5% • Cholesterol 25 mg 8% • Sodium 740 mg 31% • Total Carbohydrate 38 g 13% • Dietary Fiber 5 g 20% • Sugars 5 g • Protein 10 g • Vitamin A 50% • Vitamin C 90% • Calcium 6% • Iron 15%
Dietary Exchanges: 2 Starch, 2 Vegetable, 1 Fat OR 2 Carbohydrate, 2 Vegetable, 1 Fat

Cooking Oil Comparison

For stove-top meals, oil plays an important role by promoting browning, keeping food from sticking to the pan and contributing to the flavor.

TYPE OF OIL	DESCRIPTION	SUGGESTED USES
Virgin or Extra-Virgin Olive Oil	Strong, distinctive flavor; made from the first cold pressing of the olives; color ranges from green to golden.	Since cooking destroys the subtleties of flavor, and since virgin olive oil is much more expensive than pure, reserve the virgin olive oil for uncooked uses such as salad dressing or a drizzle over an already cooked dish for flavor. Often used in Mediterranean recipes.
Pure Olive Oil	Less pronounced olive flavor; more golden color; made from subsequent pressings of the olives.	Pure olive oil imparts great flavor to stove-top meals. Since it burns more easily than other oils, use it for gentle stove-top cooking rather than stir-frying or deep-frying.
Corn Oil, Safflower Oil, Sunflower Oil	Very neutral-tasting oils that stand up well even over high cooking heat. Pale golden color.	Good all-purpose cooking oils.
Canola Oil	Almost clear color; almost no flavor.	Good for stove-top cooking; does not mask the flavors of other ingredients.
Peanut Oil	Slight peanutty flavor; golden color.	Fine for salads and cooking; it doesn't burn easily so makes a good choice for stir-frying. Often used in Asian recipes.
Nonstick Cooking Spray	Vegetable oil that can be sprayed in a very fine layer. You can purchase a re-fillable dispenser and use your own oil.	Excellent for stove-top cooking, including stir-frying.
Walnut Oil	Nice nutty flavor; expensive.	Good for salad dressings.
Sesame Oil (two types: one is light in color and the other is darker)	Light sesame oil has a deliciously nutty flavor. The darker, Asian sesame oil has a much stronger flavor.	Light sesame oil is excellent for everything from salad dressing to sautéing. The darker sesame oil is often used to accent Asian dishes.

Vegetarian Fried Rice

Prep Time: 45 minutes

Yield: 3 (1⅓-cup) servings

1½ cups uncooked instant brown
    rice
1½ cups water
½ cup sliced fresh mushrooms
½ cup shredded carrot
¼ cup sliced green onions
¼ cup chopped green bell
    pepper
¼ teaspoon ginger
1 garlic clove, minced
2 tablespoons lite soy sauce
2 eggs, beaten
⅛ teaspoon pepper
¾ cup frozen sweet peas,
    thawed, drained*

1. Cook rice in water as directed on package.

2. Meanwhile, spray large nonstick skillet or wok with nonstick cooking spray. Heat over medium heat until hot. Add mushrooms, carrot, green onions, bell pepper, ginger and garlic; cook and stir 1 minute.

3. Reduce heat to low. Stir in cooked rice and soy sauce; cook 5 minutes, stirring occasionally.

4. Push rice mixture to side of skillet; add eggs and pepper to other side. Cook over low heat for 3 to 4 minutes, stirring constantly until eggs are cooked.

5. Add peas to rice and egg mixture; stir gently to combine. Cook until thoroughly heated. If desired, serve with additional soy sauce.

Tip: *To quickly thaw peas, place in colander or strainer; rinse with warm water until thawed. Drain well.

Nutrition Information Per Serving: Serving Size: 1⅓ Cups • Calories 350 • Calories from Fat 50 • % Daily Value • Total Fat 6 g 9% • Saturated 1 g 5% • Cholesterol 140 mg 47% • Sodium 540 mg 23% • Total Carbohydrate 61 g 20% • Dietary Fiber 6 g 24% • Sugars 3 g • Protein 13 g • Vitamin A 120% • Vitamin C 20% • Calcium 4% • Iron 10%
Dietary Exchanges: 4 Starch, ½ Vegetable, ½ Fat OR 4 Carbohydrate, ½ Vegetable, ½ Fat

Vegetarian Fried Rice

Asian Sesame Noodles with Chicken

Prep Time: 35 minutes

Yield: 4 servings

8	oz. uncooked angel hair pasta (capellini)
¼	cup purchased stir-fry sauce
2	tablespoons honey
¼	teaspoon crushed red pepper flakes
1	tablespoon oil
4	boneless, skinless chicken breast halves, cut into bite-sized strips
1	red bell pepper, cut into thin strips
1	onion, cut into thin wedges
1	tablespoon chopped fresh cilantro
1	teaspoon Asian sesame oil
1	tablespoon sesame seed

1. Cook pasta to desired doneness as directed on package. Drain; cover to keep warm.

2. Meanwhile, in small bowl, combine stir-fry sauce, honey and red pepper flakes; mix well.

3. Heat oil in large skillet over medium-high heat until hot. Add chicken; cook 4 to 5 minutes or until no longer pink. Add bell pepper and onion; cook and stir 2 to 3 minutes or until crisp-tender. Stir in sauce mixture and cilantro; cook 1 minute.

4. Toss cooked pasta with sesame oil. Serve chicken mixture over pasta. Sprinkle with sesame seed.

Nutrition Information Per Serving: Serving Size: ¼ of Recipe • Calories 470 • Calories from Fat 90 • % Daily Value • Total Fat 10 g 15% • Saturated 2 g 10% • Cholesterol 75 mg 25% • Sodium 600 mg 25% • Total Carbohydrate 58 g 19% • Dietary Fiber 3 g 12% • Sugars 14 g • Protein 36 g • Vitamin A 25% • Vitamin C 45% • Calcium 4% • Iron 20%
Dietary Exchanges: 3½ Starch, ½ Fruit, 3½ Very Lean Meat, 1 Fat OR 4 Carbohydrate, 3½ Very Lean Meat, 1 Fat

Chicken and Ravioli Cacciatore

Prep Time: 30 minutes

Yield: 4 (1½-cup) servings

1	tablespoon olive oil or vegetable oil
1	lb. boneless, skinless chicken breast halves, cut into ½ to 1-inch pieces
1	medium onion, halved, sliced
½	medium green bell pepper, sliced
1	cup water
1	(14½-oz.) can diced tomatoes with garlic, oregano and basil, undrained
1	(8-oz.) can tomato sauce
1	(9-oz.) pkg. refrigerated cheese-filled ravioli

1. Heat oil in large skillet over medium-high heat until hot. Add chicken, onion and bell pepper; cook and stir until chicken is browned.

2. Stir in water, tomatoes and tomato sauce. Bring to a boil. Add ravioli; carefully stir until separated and covered with tomato mixture. Cook 12 to 15 minutes or until sauce is of desired consistency and chicken is no longer pink, stirring frequently to prevent sticking.

Nutrition Information Per Serving: Serving Size: 1½ Cups • Calories 430 • Calories from Fat 130 • % Daily Value • Total Fat 14 g 22% • Saturated 5 g 25% • Cholesterol 120 mg 40% • Sodium 890 mg 37% • Total Carbohydrate 40 g 13% • Dietary Fiber 4 g 16% • Sugars 7 g • Protein 37 g • Vitamin A 25% • Vitamin C 30% • Calcium 20% • Iron 20%
Dietary Exchanges: 2 Starch, 2 Vegetable, 4 Very Lean Meat, 2 Fat OR 2 Carbohydrate, 2 Vegetable, 4 Very Lean Meat, 2 Fat

Canned beans are usually packed in a viscous, salty liquid. For most recipes, it's best to rinse the beans and drain them thoroughly in a colander set over the sink.

Chicken with Black-Eyed Peas and Rice

Prep Time: 45 minutes

Yield: 4 (1³/₄-cup) servings

1	tablespoon olive oil or vegetable oil
1	lb. boneless, skinless chicken breast halves, cut into ½- to 1-inch pieces
1	medium onion, chopped
1	garlic clove, minced
1	(14½-oz.) can ready-to-serve chicken broth
1	tablespoon Worcestershire sauce
¼	teaspoon salt
¼	teaspoon dried oregano or thyme leaves
⅛	teaspoon ground red pepper (cayenne)
¾	cup uncooked regular long-grain white rice
1	cup frozen whole kernel corn
1	(15-oz.) can black-eyed peas, drained
	Chopped fresh parsley, if desired

1. Heat oil in large skillet over medium-high heat until hot. Add chicken, onion and garlic; cook and stir until chicken is browned.

2. Stir in broth, Worcestershire sauce, salt, oregano and ground red pepper. Bring to a boil. Reduce heat to medium-low. Stir in rice; cover and cook 10 minutes.

3. Stir in corn and black-eyed peas; cover and cook an additional 10 to 15 minutes or until liquid is absorbed and chicken is no longer pink, stirring occasionally. Sprinkle with parsley if desired.

Nutrition Information Per Serving: Serving Size: 1¾ Cups • Calories 420 • Calories from Fat 70 • % Daily Value • Total Fat 8 g 12% • Saturated 2 g 10% • Cholesterol 65 mg 22% • Sodium 720 mg 30% • Total Carbohydrate 52 g 17% • Dietary Fiber 5 g 20% • Sugars 3 g • Protein 36 g • Vitamin A 2% • Vitamin C 6% • Calcium 8% • Iron 20%

Dietary Exchanges: 3½ Starch, 3½ Very Lean Meat, ½ Fat OR 3½ Carbohydrate, 3½ Very Lean Meat, ½ Fat

Tomato-Basil Linguine with Chicken

Prep Time: 20 minutes

Yield: 4 (1½-cup) servings

5	oz. refrigerated linguine
4	boneless, skinless chicken breast halves, cut into 1-inch cubes
2	teaspoons chopped garlic in water (from 4½-oz. jar)
1	(14½-oz.) can diced tomatoes with Italian-style herbs, undrained
1½	teaspoons dried basil leaves
¼	cup grated Parmesan cheese

1. Cook linguine to desired doneness as directed on package. Drain; cover to keep warm.

2. Meanwhile, spray large nonstick skillet with nonstick cooking spray. Heat over medium-high heat until hot. Add chicken and garlic; cook 5 to 8 minutes or until chicken is no longer pink.

3. Stir in tomatoes and basil. Bring to a boil. Reduce heat; cover and simmer 5 minutes, stirring occasionally.

4. Add cooked linguine; toss gently to mix. Sprinkle with cheese.

Nutrition Information Per Serving: Serving Size: 1½ Cups • Calories 310 • Calories from Fat 50 • % Daily Value • Total Fat 6 g 9% • Saturated 2 g 10% • Cholesterol 105 mg 35% • Sodium 420 mg 18% • Total Carbohydrate 28 g 9% • Dietary Fiber 2 g 8% • Sugars 3 g • Protein 35 g • Vitamin A 15% • Vitamin C 15% • Calcium 15% • Iron 20%
Dietary Exchanges: 1½ Starch, 1 Vegetable, 4 Very Lean Meat, ½ Fat OR 1½ Carbohydrate, 1 Vegetable, 4 Very Lean Meat, ½ Fat

Basil Basics

Although sweet basil is the variety most likely found in your local market, other basils include the purple-tinged opal basil used in Thai cooking and lemon basil, whose citrus flavor complements fish nicely.

Basil is easy to grow at home, asking only a sunny spot and the regular pinching off of the top leaves to prevent the plant from going to seed. If you find flowers at the top of the stalks, pinch them off and cook with them, too—they have the same flavor as the leaves. They also look nice in a salad.

If you buy basil at the market, keep it fresh by trimming the ends and placing the cut stems in a glass or jar with an inch or so of water. Cover the glass with plastic and refrigerate, and the fragrant bouquet should last for at least a week. Second best: wrap it in paper towels and refrigerate in a self-sealing plastic bag.

To use fresh basil, pinch the leaves from the fibrous stem. If basil will serve as a garnish, don't mince or chop it until just before serving, to prevent the edges from darkening.

Tomato-Basil Linguine with Chicken

Chicken Barley Dinner

Prep Time: 35 minutes (Ready in 55 minutes)

Yield: 5 (1½-cup) servings

3	boneless, skinless chicken breast halves, cut into ¾-inch pieces
2	medium onions, chopped (1 cup)
½	cup chopped celery
1	(14½-oz.) can ready-to-serve fat-free chicken broth with ⅓ less sodium
1	(10¾-oz.) can condensed 98% fat-free cream of chicken soup with 30% less sodium
½	cup water
¼	teaspoon dried thyme leaves Dash pepper
3	cups frozen mixed vegetables
1½	cups uncooked quick-cooking barley

1. Spray nonstick Dutch oven or large skillet with nonstick cooking spray. Heat over medium–high heat until hot. Add chicken; cook and stir 3 minutes or until no longer pink.

2. Add onions and celery; cover and cook 3 minutes or until celery is tender.

3. Stir in broth, soup, water, thyme and pepper until well mixed. Stir in frozen vegetables and barley. Bring to a boil. Reduce heat; cover and simmer 12 to 18 minutes or until barley is tender.

Nutrition Information Per Serving: Serving Size: 1½ Cups • Calories 370 • Calories from Fat 35 • % Daily Value • Total Fat 4 g 6% • Saturated 1 g 5% • Cholesterol 45 mg 15% • Sodium 590 mg 25% • Total Carbohydrate 58 g 19% • Dietary Fiber 9 g 36% • Sugars 5 g • Protein 26 g • Vitamin A 35% • Vitamin C 8% • Calcium 4% • Iron 10%
Dietary Exchanges: 3½ Starch, 1 Vegetable, 2 Very Lean Meat OR 3½ Carbohydrate, 1 Vegetable, 2 Very Lean Meat

Chicken and Vegetable Skillet Supper

Prep Time: 40 minutes

Yield: 4 servings

Photo page 116

2 tablespoons oil
2 lb. cut-up frying chicken, skin removed
2 small onions, thinly sliced
2 teaspoons chicken-flavor instant bouillon
1 teaspoon dried tarragon leaves
1½ cups hot water
1 (1-lb.) pkg. frozen broccoli florets, carrots and cauliflower
¼ cup water
2 tablespoons cornstarch

1. Heat oil in large skillet over medium heat until hot. Add chicken and onions; cook until chicken is browned on all sides.

2. Meanwhile, in small bowl, combine bouillon, tarragon and 1½ cups hot water; mix well. Add bouillon mixture to chicken; bring to a boil. Reduce heat to low; cover and simmer 15 to 20 minutes or until chicken is fork-tender and juices run clear.

3. Add frozen vegetables to chicken; cook 4 to 6 minutes or until vegetables are crisp-tender.

4. Meanwhile, in small bowl, combine ¼ cup water and cornstarch; blend well. Add to liquid in skillet; cook and stir until bubbly and thickened.

Nutrition Information Per Serving: Serving Size: ¼ of Recipe • Calories 260 • Calories from Fat 120 • % Daily Value • Total Fat 13 g 20% • Saturated 2 g 10% • Cholesterol 65 mg 22% • Sodium 590 mg 25% • Total Carbohydrate 12 g 4% • Dietary Fiber 3 g 12% • Sugars 4 g • Protein 24 g • Vitamin A 50% • Vitamin C 30% • Calcium 4% • Iron 8%
Dietary Exchanges: ½ Starch, 1 Vegetable, 3 Lean Meat, ½ Fat OR ½ Carbohydrate, 1 Vegetable, 3 Lean Meat, ½ Fat

Skillet Chicken and Rice

Prep Time: 15 minutes (Ready in 45 minutes)

Yield: 4 servings

4 boneless, skinless chicken breast halves
1 (8-oz.) can no-salt-added tomato sauce
½ cup water
1 (14½-oz.) can Mexican-style stewed tomatoes, undrained*
1 (15½- or 15-oz.) can dark red kidney beans, drained
1 cup uncooked instant brown rice

1. Spray large nonstick skillet with nonstick cooking spray. Heat over medium-high heat until hot. Add chicken; cook 3 to 4 minutes or until browned, turning once. Remove chicken from skillet.

2. In same skillet, combine all remaining ingredients; mix well. Top with chicken. Bring mixture to a boil. Reduce heat; cover and simmer 20 to 25 minutes or until chicken is fork-tender, its juices run clear, and almost all liquid is absorbed. Let stand 5 minutes before serving.

Tip: *For a milder flavor, substitute Italian-style stewed tomatoes.

Nutrition Information Per Serving: Serving Size: ¼ of Recipe • Calories 350 • Calories from Fat 45 • % Daily Value • Total Fat 5 g 8% • Saturated 1 g 5% • Cholesterol 75 mg 25% • Sodium 430 mg 18% • Total Carbohydrate 40 g 13% • Dietary Fiber 6 g 24% • Sugars 5 g • Protein 36 g • Vitamin A 10% • Vitamin C 25% • Calcium 8% • Iron 20%
Dietary Exchanges: 2½ Starch, 1 Vegetable, 4 Very Lean Meat OR 2½ Carbohydrate, 1 Vegetable, 4 Very Lean Meat

Spicy Chicken and Couscous

Prep Time: 25 minutes

Yield: 4 servings

¾ cup uncooked couscous
1 lb. boneless, skinless chicken breast halves, cut into ¾ to 1-inch pieces
1 (14½-oz.) can Mexican-style stewed tomatoes, undrained
1 (15-oz.) can garbanzo beans, drained, rinsed
1½ cups frozen bell pepper and onion stir-fry
1 teaspoon cumin

1. Cook couscous as directed on package.

2. Meanwhile, spray large nonstick skillet with nonstick cooking spray. Heat over medium-high heat until hot. Add chicken; cook 3 minutes, stirring occasionally.

3. Stir in all remaining ingredients. Reduce heat to medium-low; cover and simmer 8 to 10 minutes or until chicken is no longer pink, stirring occasionally.

4. Fluff couscous with fork; spoon onto serving platter. Top with chicken mixture.

Nutrition Information Per Serving: Serving Size: ¼ of Recipe • Calories 390 • Calories from Fat 45 • % Daily Value • Total Fat 5 g 8% • Saturated 1 g 5% • Cholesterol 65 mg 22% • Sodium 450 mg 19% • Total Carbohydrate 51 g 17% • Dietary Fiber 8 g 32% • Sugars 5 g • Protein 35 g • Vitamin A 15% • Vitamin C 20% • Calcium 10% • Iron 15%
Dietary Exchanges: 3 Starch, 1 Vegetable, 3½ Very Lean Meat OR 3 Carbohydrate, 1 Vegetable, 3½ Very Lean Meat

Chicken Checkup

♦ Boneless, skinless chicken breasts make short work of stove-top suppers. Purchase extra, wrap them individually and store in a resealable freezer bag. It will be easy to defrost just the amount you need.

♦ When comparison-shopping for bone-in vs. boneless chicken breasts, calculate the price per serving rather than the price per pound—and don't forget to factor in convenience. Boneless meat usually commands a higher price per pound but may in fact be more economical when you calculate the waste from discarding bones. On average, bone-in breast halves weigh 6 to 8 ounces each; without the bone, it's closer to 3 to 4 ounces.

♦ If you ask the butcher to bone the breasts to order, remember that you're paying for the bones anyway and have them wrapped to go, too. Store them in the freezer—they make great soup stock.

♦ A 3-ounce portion of boneless, skinless white meat cooked with no added fat contains about 130 calories and 3 grams of fat. If you eat the skin, the calorie count goes up to 160 and the fat increases to 7 grams per serving.

♦ Twelve ounces of boneless, skinless chicken will yield about 2 cups cubed meat.

♦ Cook white meat just until the juices run clear and the center of the breast is white rather than pink, then remove from the heat at once to prevent drying out.

Spicy Chicken and Couscous

Pineapple Chicken and Rice

Prep Time: 50 minutes

Yield: 4 servings

2 tablespoons oil
4 bone-in chicken breast halves, skin removed if desired
1 (14½-oz.) can ready-to-serve chicken broth
½ cup purchased sweet-and-sour sauce
1 (8-oz.) can pineapple tidbits in unsweetened juice, drained, reserving liquid
1 cup uncooked regular long-grain white rice
½ cup chopped red bell pepper
½ cup chopped green bell pepper
½ cup sliced green onions

1. Heat oil in large skillet over medium-high heat until hot. Add chicken breast halves; cook 2 to 3 minutes on each side or until browned. Remove chicken from skillet.

2. In same skillet, combine broth, sweet-and-sour sauce, reserved pineapple liquid and rice; blend well. Bring to a boil. Add chicken breast halves, meaty side down. Reduce heat to low; cover and simmer 25 to 30 minutes or until most of liquid is absorbed, chicken is fork-tender and juices run clear.

3. Remove chicken from skillet; cover to keep warm. Add bell peppers, green onions and pineapple tidbits to rice mixture. Cook an additional 5 minutes or until peppers are crisp-tender. Spoon rice mixture onto platter; top with chicken.

Nutrition Information Per Serving: Serving Size: ¼ of Recipe • Calories 510 • Calories from Fat 140 • % Daily Value • Total Fat 15 g 23% • Saturated 3 g 15% • Cholesterol 80 mg 27% • Sodium 590 mg 25% • Total Carbohydrate 58 g 19% • Dietary Fiber 2 g 8% • Sugars 17 g • Protein 35 g • Vitamin A 20% • Vitamin C 50% • Calcium 4% • Iron 20%
Dietary Exchanges: 3 Starch, 1 Fruit, 3½ Lean Meat, ½ Fat OR 4 Carbohydrate, 3½ Lean Meat, ½ Fat

Marinara Chicken with Pasta and Parmesan

Prep Time: 30 minutes

Yield: 4 servings

8 oz. uncooked spaghetti
4 boneless, skinless chicken breast halves
2 cups no-fat chunky vegetable spaghetti sauce
1 teaspoon dried Italian seasoning
¼ cup grated Parmesan cheese

1. Cook spaghetti to desired doneness as directed on package. Drain; cover to keep warm.

2. Meanwhile, spray large nonstick skillet with nonstick cooking spray. Heat over medium-high heat until hot. Add chicken; cook 3 minutes on each side or until browned.

3. Spoon spaghetti sauce over chicken; sprinkle with Italian seasoning. Bring to a boil. Reduce heat to medium-low; cover and cook 5 to 10 minutes or until chicken is fork-tender and juices run clear.

4. Place cooked spaghetti on large serving platter. Place chicken over spaghetti; spoon sauce over top. Sprinkle with cheese.

Nutrition Information Per Serving: Serving Size: ¼ of Recipe • Calories 420 • Calories from Fat 50 • % Daily Value • Total Fat 6 g 9% • Saturated 2 g 10% • Cholesterol 80 mg 27% • Sodium 570 mg 24% • Total Carbohydrate 52 g 17% • Dietary Fiber 2 g 8% • Sugars 11 g • Protein 39 g • Vitamin A 10% • Vitamin C 0% • Calcium 15% • Iron 20%
Dietary Exchanges: 3½ Starch, 4 Very Lean Meat OR 3½ Carbohydrate, 4 Very Lean Meat

Easy Arroz con Pollo

Prep Time: 45 minutes

Yield: 4 servings

1 tablespoon olive oil or vegetable oil

4 boneless, skinless chicken breast halves

1 large onion, coarsely chopped

1 cup uncooked converted or regular long-grain white rice

1 teaspoon cumin

1/8 teaspoon saffron threads, crushed

2 cups chicken broth

1/2 cup salsa

1 red bell pepper, coarsely chopped

1/2 cup frozen baby sweet peas

1. Heat oil in large skillet over medium-high heat until hot. Add chicken breast halves; cook 4 to 5 minutes or until browned, turning once. Remove chicken from skillet; cover to keep warm.

2. Add onion to skillet; cook and stir 3 to 4 minutes or until tender. Add rice, cumin and saffron; stir to mix well. Stir in broth and salsa. Bring to a boil. Return chicken to skillet. Reduce heat; cover and simmer 15 minutes.

3. Stir in bell pepper and peas; cook an additional 5 minutes or until liquid is absorbed, chicken is fork-tender and juices run clear.

Nutrition Information Per Serving: Serving Size: 1/4 of Recipe • Calories 400 • Calories from Fat 70 • % Daily Value • Total Fat 8 g 12% • Saturated 2 g 10% • Cholesterol 75 mg 25% • Sodium 720 mg 30% • Total Carbohydrate 47 g 16% • Dietary Fiber 3 g 12% • Sugars 6 g • Protein 34 g • Vitamin A 25% • Vitamin C 45% • Calcium 4% • Iron 20%
Dietary Exchanges: 3 Starch, 3½ Very Lean Meat, 1 Fat OR 3 Carbohydrate, 3½ Very Lean Meat, 1 Fat

Taco Chicken and Rice

Prep Time: 20 minutes

Yield: 4 servings

2 cups uncooked instant rice
2 cups water
1 (1¼-oz.) pkg. 40% less sodium taco seasoning mix
1 lb. precut chicken breast strips for stir-frying
1 (14½-oz.) can diced tomatoes, undrained
⅛ teaspoon ground red pepper (cayenne)

1. Cook rice in water as directed on package, omitting margarine and salt.

2. Meanwhile, place 2 tablespoons of the taco seasoning mix in plastic bag or medium bowl. Add chicken; seal bag and shake or stir to coat well.

3. In large nonstick skillet, combine chicken, tomatoes, ground red pepper and remaining taco seasoning mix; mix well. Bring to a boil. Reduce heat to medium-low; cover tightly and simmer 8 to 10 minutes or until chicken is no longer pink, stirring once. Serve over rice. If desired, top with nonfat sour cream and chopped fresh cilantro.

Nutrition Information Per Serving: Serving Size: ¼ of Recipe • Calories 320 • Calories from Fat 25 • % Daily Value • Total Fat 3 g 5% • Saturated 1 g 5% • Cholesterol 65 mg 22% • Sodium 700 mg 29% • Total Carbohydrate 45 g 15% • Dietary Fiber 2 g 8% • Sugars 2 g • Protein 29 g • Vitamin A 20% • Vitamin C 15% • Calcium 6% • Iron 15%
Dietary Exchanges: 2½ Starch, 1 Vegetable, 3 Very Lean Meat OR 2½ Carbohydrate, 1 Vegetable, 3 Very Lean Meat

Taco Chicken and Rice

Peas for stir-frying include:

- Green "shell" peas. These "regular" sweet peas come from inedible pods. Usually purchased frozen, they are available fresh in season and can be extremely sweet. To buy fresh peas, choose pods that look nicely green, are fairly thick-skinned and are not too bulging—overmature peas that crowd the pod can be disappointingly starchy.

- Snow pea pods. Chinese cooking makes extensive use of these flat, almost paper-thin peas, cultivated for their edible pods rather than the tiny, immature peas inside. To prepare the fresh pods, snap off the stem end and peel down the string that runs along the "seam." Frozen snow peas are convenient but not as crisp.

- Sugar snap peas. Many consider these the best of all: edible pods of thick, exceptionally sweet and crunchy flesh surround plump, juicy sweet peas. Prepare the fresh sugar snaps as for snow peas: snap off the stem end and peel the strings from the sides.

Fast and Easy Jambalaya

Prep Time: 40 minutes

Yield: 6 servings

1	cup uncooked regular long-grain white rice
2	cups water
½	teaspoon lemon-pepper seasoning
½	teaspoon garlic powder
5	boneless, skinless chicken breast halves, cut into ½-inch pieces
3	tablespoons oil
1	cup chopped onions
¾	lb. smoked Polish or kielbasa sausage, cut into ½-inch slices
1	(16-oz.) jar picante sauce or salsa
1	(14½-oz.) can Italian-style stewed tomatoes, undrained
1¼	cups frozen sweet peas

1. Cook rice in water as directed on package.

2. Meanwhile, sprinkle lemon-pepper seasoning and garlic powder over chicken pieces. Heat oil in large skillet or 3-quart saucepan over medium-high heat until hot. Add chicken; cook 5 minutes or until no longer pink, stirring frequently.

3. Add onions and sausage; cook an additional 5 minutes, stirring occasionally. Stir in picante sauce and tomatoes. Reduce heat to medium; cook 12 minutes. Add peas; cook an additional 5 to 7 minutes or until peas are tender. Serve over rice.

Nutrition Information Per Serving: Serving Size: ⅙ of Recipe • Calories 510 • Calories from Fat 230 • % Daily Value • Total Fat 25 g 38% • Saturated 7 g 35% • Cholesterol 95 mg 32% • Sodium 1430 mg 60% • Total Carbohydrate 37 g 12% • Dietary Fiber 4 g 16% • Sugars 6 g • Protein 33 g • Vitamin A 10% • Vitamin C 80% • Calcium 8% • Iron 20%
Dietary Exchanges: 2 Starch, 1 Vegetable, 3½ Lean Meat, 3 Fat OR 2 Carbohydrate, 1 Vegetable, 3½ Lean Meat, 3 Fat

Broccoli, Chicken and Stuffing Skillet

Prep Time: 30 minutes

Yield: 4 (1¼-cup) servings

2	tablespoons margarine or butter
3	cups fresh broccoli florets*
¼	cup chopped onion
1	tablespoon water
¾	cup milk
1	tablespoon white wine Worcestershire sauce
1	(10¾-oz.) can condensed cream of broccoli soup
2	cups cubed cooked chicken
1	(2-oz.) jar sliced pimientos, drained
1	cup white and whole wheat seasoned stuffing cubes mix

1. Melt margarine in large skillet over medium-high heat. Stir in broccoli, onion and water. Cover; cook 4 to 6 minutes or until vegetables are crisp-tender.

2. Add milk, Worcestershire sauce and soup; mix well. Stir in chicken, pimientos and ½ cup of the stuffing cubes. Reduce heat to low; cover and cook 8 to 10 minutes or until mixture is thoroughly heated, stirring occasionally. Top with remaining stuffing cubes.

Tip: *One 1-lb. pkg. frozen cut broccoli, thawed, can be substituted for fresh broccoli.

Nutrition Information Per Serving: Serving Size: 1¼ Cups • Calories 360 • Calories from Fat 150 • % Daily Value • Total Fat 17 g 26% • Saturated 5 g 25% • Cholesterol 70 mg 23% • Sodium 900 mg 38% • Total Carbohydrate 25 g 8% • Dietary Fiber 4 g 16% • Sugars 7 g • Protein 27 g • Vitamin A 70% • Vitamin C 100% • Calcium 15% • Iron 15%
Dietary Exchanges: 1½ Starch, 3 Lean Meat, 1½ Fat OR 1½ Carbohydrate, 3 Lean Meat, 1½ Fat

Mafalda with Chicken, Vegetables and Pesto

Prep Time: 30 minutes

Yield: 6 (1⅓-cup) servings

5 oz. (2 cups) uncooked mini-lasagna noodles (mafalda) or wide egg noodles

½ lb. new red potatoes, unpeeled, diced (2 cups)

1 (10-oz.) pkg. frozen peas and carrots

½ lb. cubed cooked chicken breast (1⅓ cups)

¼ cup purchased refrigerated reduced-fat pesto

2 tablespoons grated Parmesan cheese

1. In Dutch oven, cook noodles in boiling water for 5 minutes.

2. Add potatoes; return to a boil. Immediately add peas and carrots. Cook an additional 6 minutes or until noodles and vegetables are of desired doneness.

3. Drain noodles and vegetables; return to Dutch oven. Add chicken, pesto and cheese; toss gently to coat.

Nutrition Information Per Serving: Serving Size: 1⅓ Cups • Calories 240 • Calories from Fat 45 • % Daily Value • Total Fat 5 g 8% • Saturated 1 g 5% • Cholesterol 25 mg 8% • Sodium 190 mg 8% • Total Carbohydrate 34 g 11% • Dietary Fiber 3 g 12% • Sugars 4 g • Protein 15 g • Vitamin A 90% • Vitamin C 10% • Calcium 8% • Iron 15%
Dietary Exchanges: 2 Starch, 1 Vegetable, 1½ Very Lean Meat, ½ Fat OR 2 Carbohydrate, 1 Vegetable, 1½ Very Lean Meat, ½ Fat

Mafalda with Chicken, Vegetables and Pesto

Simple Sweet-and-Sour
Chicken

Simple Sweet-and-Sour Chicken

Prep Time: 15 minutes

Yield: 4 servings

1 (10½-oz.) pkg. frozen
    chicken nuggets
1 tablespoon oil
1 green bell pepper, cut into
    squares
1 small onion, cut into thin
    wedges
½ cup purchased sweet-and-
    sour sauce
1 (8-oz.) can pineapple chunks
    in unsweetened juice,
    undrained

1. Prepare chicken nuggets as directed on package.

2. Meanwhile, heat oil in medium skillet over medium–high heat until hot. Add bell pepper and onion; cook and stir until crisp-tender. Stir in sweet-and-sour sauce and pineapple; cook until thoroughly heated. Serve over chicken nuggets.

Nutrition Information Per Serving: Serving Size: ¼ of Recipe • Calories 320 • Calories from Fat 140 • % Daily Value • Total Fat 16 g 25% • Saturated 3 g 15% • Cholesterol 45 mg 15% • Sodium 550 mg 23% • Total Carbohydrate 31 g 10% • Dietary Fiber 1 g 4% • Sugars 16 g • Protein 13 g • Vitamin A 2% • Vitamin C 25% • Calcium 2% • Iron 6%
Dietary Exchanges: 1 Starch, 1 Fruit, 1½ Medium-Fat Meat, 1½ Fat OR 2 Carbohydrate, 1½ Medium-Fat Meat, 1½ Fat

Turkey and Penne Pasta

Prep Time: 25 minutes

Yield: 4 servings

8	oz. (2 cups) uncooked penne (tube-shaped pasta)
½	lb. lean ground turkey
2	garlic cloves, minced
½	teaspoon dried Italian seasoning
¼	teaspoon fennel seed, crushed, if desired
2	cups no-fat extra-chunky spaghetti sauce
¼	teaspoon sugar
2	oz. (½ cup) finely shredded or shredded mozzarella cheese

1. Cook penne to desired doneness as directed on package. Drain; cover to keep warm.

2. Meanwhile, spray large nonstick skillet or Dutch oven with nonstick cooking spray. Add turkey, garlic, Italian seasoning and fennel; cook over medium-high heat for 3 to 5 minutes or until turkey is no longer pink.

3. Stir in spaghetti sauce and sugar. Bring to a boil. Reduce heat; cover and simmer 10 minutes to blend flavors. Serve sauce over penne. Sprinkle with mozzarella cheese.

Nutrition Information Per Serving: Serving Size: ¼ of Recipe • Calories 380 • Calories from Fat 70 • % Daily Value • Total Fat 8 g 12% • Saturated 3 g 15% • Cholesterol 50 mg 17% • Sodium 520 mg 22% • Total Carbohydrate 53 g 18% • Dietary Fiber 2 g 8% • Sugars 11 g • Protein 23 g • Vitamin A 10% • Vitamin C 0% • Calcium 15% • Iron 20%
Dietary Exchanges: 3 Starch, ½ Fruit, 2 Very Lean Meat, 1 Fat OR 3½ Carbohydrate, 2 Very Lean Meat, 1 Fat

Cheesy Noodle Skillet Supper

Prep Time: 25 minutes

Yield: 4 (1½-cup) servings

Photo page 204

1	lb. ground turkey
½	cup chopped onion
1	(14-oz.) jar spaghetti sauce
1	(10¾-oz.) can condensed Cheddar cheese soup
1	cup water
3	oz. (2 cups) uncooked dumpling egg noodles
1	(4½-oz.) jar sliced mushrooms, drained
4	oz. (1 cup) shredded Cheddar cheese

1. In large skillet, brown ground turkey with onion. Drain. Add spaghetti sauce and soup; mix well. Stir in water. Bring to a boil. Stir in egg noodles. Return to a boil. Reduce heat to medium; cover and cook 8 to 10 minutes or until noodles are tender, stirring occasionally.

2. Uncover; stir in mushrooms. Cook uncovered for 2 to 4 minutes or until sauce is of desired consistency, stirring occasionally. Sprinkle with cheese; cover and cook 1 to 2 minutes or until cheese is melted.

Nutrition Information Per Serving: Serving Size: 1½ Cups • Calories 550 • Calories from Fat 260 • % Daily Value • Total Fat 29 g 45% • Saturated 13 g 65% • Cholesterol 150 mg 50% • Sodium 1340 mg 56% • Total Carbohydrate 33 g 11% • Dietary Fiber 4 g 16% • Sugars 3 g • Protein 39 g • Vitamin A 25% • Vitamin C 10% • Calcium 35% • Iron 25%
Dietary Exchanges: 2 Starch, 4½ Medium-Fat Meat, 1 Fat OR 2 Carbohydrate, 4½ Medium-Fat Meat, 1 Fat

Quick Turkey Tetrazzini

Prep Time: 20 minutes

Yield: 4 (1-cup) servings

4	oz. uncooked spaghetti
1	teaspoon margarine or butter
1	garlic clove, minced
1½	cups sliced fresh mushrooms
1½	cups skim milk
2	tablespoons all-purpose flour
¼	cup garlic and herbs soft spreadable cheese
¼	cup shredded fresh Parmesan cheese
2	cups chopped cooked turkey

1. In Dutch oven or large saucepan, cook spaghetti to desired doneness as directed on package. Drain; return to Dutch oven.

2. Meanwhile, melt margarine in medium nonstick saucepan over medium heat. Add garlic; cook 1 minute. Add mushrooms; cook 1 minute.

3. In small bowl, combine milk and flour; blend well.* Add to mushrooms in saucepan; cook, stirring constantly, until bubbly and thickened. Add spreadable cheese and 2 tablespoons of the Parmesan cheese; cook and stir until cheeses are melted. Stir in turkey.

4. Add sauce to cooked spaghetti; toss over low heat until well mixed. Sprinkle with remaining 2 tablespoons Parmesan cheese.

Tip: *To dress up recipe, prepare milk and flour mixture using 1¼ cups milk; add ¼ cup dry sherry with cheeses. Garnish tetrazzini with chopped fresh parsley.

Nutrition Information Per Serving: Serving Size: 1 Cup • Calories 340 • Calories from Fat 80 • % Daily Value • Total Fat 9 g 14% • Saturated 4 g 20% • Cholesterol 65 mg 22% • Sodium 320 mg 13% • Total Carbohydrate 31 g 10% • Dietary Fiber 1 g 4% • Sugars 6 g • Protein 33 g • Vitamin A 10% • Vitamin C 2% • Calcium 25% • Iron 15%
Dietary Exchanges: 2 Starch, 4 Very Lean Meat, 1 Fat OR 2 Carbohydrate, 4 Very Lean Meat, 1 Fat

Skillet Turkey with Rice and Pasta

Prep Time: 45 minutes
Yield: 4 (1¼-cup) servings

1   lb. fresh turkey tenderloins, cut into 1-inch pieces
1   tablespoon margarine or butter
1   (5.3-oz.) pkg. rice and pasta mix with oriental seasonings
2¼ cups water
⅛   teaspoon ground red pepper (cayenne)
1½ cups frozen whole kernel corn
1   cup frozen cut broccoli
2   tablespoons chopped red bell pepper, if desired

1. Spray large nonstick skillet with nonstick cooking spray. Heat over medium-high heat until hot. Add turkey; cook and stir until browned. Remove turkey from skillet; cover to keep warm.

2. Melt margarine in same skillet. Add rice and pasta from package; cook and stir 2 to 3 minutes or until light golden brown.

3. Add water, seasoning packet from rice and pasta mix, ground red pepper and turkey. Bring to a boil. Reduce heat to medium-low; cover and cook 15 minutes.

4. Add frozen vegetables; cover and cook 10 minutes. Uncover; add red bell pepper if desired. Cook an additional 5 minutes or until turkey is no longer pink and liquid is absorbed, stirring occasionally.

Nutrition Information Per Serving: Serving Size: 1¼ Cups • Calories 330 • Calories from Fat 45 • % Daily Value • Total Fat 5 g 8% • Saturated 1 g 5% • Cholesterol 75 mg 25% • Sodium 790 mg 33% • Total Carbohydrate 39 g 13% • Dietary Fiber 3 g 12% • Sugars 3 g • Protein 32 g • Vitamin A 10% • Vitamin C 20% • Calcium 4% • Iron 15%
Dietary Exchanges: 2½ Starch, 3½ Very Lean Meat OR 2½ Carbohydrate, 3½ Very Lean Meat

Top to bottom: Cheesy Noodle Skillet Supper, page 202;
Skillet Turkey with Rice and Pasta

Quick Turkey Stroganoff

Prep Time: 20 minutes

Yield: 4 servings

8 oz. (4 cups) uncooked egg
   noodles
2 cups cubed cooked turkey
1 (4½-oz.) jar sliced
   mushrooms, drained
1 (10¾-oz.) can condensed
   cream of mushroom soup
1 cup sour cream
1 (2-oz.) jar diced pimientos,
   drained

1. Cook noodles to desired doneness as directed on package. Drain.

2. Meanwhile, in large skillet, combine turkey, mushrooms and soup; mix well. Cook over medium heat until bubbly, stirring frequently. Stir in sour cream and pimientos. Cook until thoroughly heated. DO NOT BOIL. Serve turkey mixture over noodles.

Nutrition Information Per Serving: Serving Size: ¼ of Recipe • Calories 550 • Calories from Fat 220 • % Daily Value • Total Fat 24 g 37% • Saturated 11 g 55% • Cholesterol 135 mg 45% • Sodium 720 mg 30% • Total Carbohydrate 51 g 17% • Dietary Fiber 3 g 12% • Sugars 6 g • Protein 33 g • Vitamin A 20% • Vitamin C 25% • Calcium 15% • Iron 25%
Dietary Exchanges: 3½ Starch, 3 Lean Meat, 2½ Fat OR 3½ Carbohydrate, 3 Lean Meat, 2½ Fat

Home-Style Sausage, Potato and Onion Skillet

Prep Time: 40 minutes

Yield: 4 (1¼-cup) servings

½ lb. bulk light turkey and pork
   sausage
2 medium onions, chopped
   (1 cup)
2 lb. (about 12 medium) red
   potatoes, unpeeled, very
   thinly sliced
1 cup water
½ teaspoon salt
½ teaspoon paprika
¼ teaspoon dried thyme leaves
⅛ teaspoon pepper

1. Heat nonstick Dutch oven over medium-high heat until hot. Add sausage; cook 4 to 5 minutes or until no longer pink. Remove sausage from Dutch oven; drain on paper towels. Set aside.

2. Wipe Dutch oven dry with paper towels; spray with nonstick cooking spray. Add onions; cook over medium heat for about 5 minutes.

3. Add cooked sausage and all remaining ingredients; mix gently but thoroughly. Bring to a boil. Reduce heat to medium-low; cover tightly and cook 8 to 10 minutes or just until potatoes are tender, stirring occasionally.

4. Remove Dutch oven from heat; stir mixture gently. Let stand covered for 10 minutes to allow flavors to blend and light sauce to form.

Nutrition Information Per Serving: Serving Size: 1¼ Cups • Calories 360 • Calories from Fat 100 • % Daily Value • Total Fat 11 g 17% • Saturated 1 g 5% • Cholesterol 40 mg 13% • Sodium 660 mg 28% • Total Carbohydrate 51 g 17% • Dietary Fiber 5 g 20% • Sugars 5 g • Protein 14 g • Vitamin A 4% • Vitamin C 30% • Calcium 4% • Iron 20%
Dietary Exchanges: 3½ Starch, ½ High-Fat Meat, 1 Fat OR 3½ Carbohydrate, ½ High-Fat Meat, 1 Fat

Turkey and Twists in Tomato-Cream Sauce

Prep Time: 20 minutes

Yield: 4 servings

8 oz. (2⅔ cups) uncooked rotini (spiral pasta)

½ lb. fully cooked, honey-roasted turkey breast

1 (15-oz.) container refrigerated marinara sauce

½ cup light sour cream

2 tablespoons finely shredded fresh Parmesan cheese

2 tablespoons chopped fresh parsley

1. In large saucepan, cook rotini to desired doneness as directed on package. Drain; cover to keep warm.

2. Meanwhile, cut turkey into 1 x ¼ x ¼-inch strips. In medium skillet, heat marinara sauce over medium heat. Stir in sour cream until well blended. Stir in turkey; cook until thoroughly heated. Serve sauce over rotini. Sprinkle with cheese and parsley.

Nutrition Information Per Serving: Serving Size: ¼ of Recipe • Calories 410 • Calories from Fat 80 • % Daily Value • Total Fat 9 g 14% • Saturated 3 g 15% • Cholesterol 65 mg 22% • Sodium 520 mg 22% • Total Carbohydrate 53 g 18% • Dietary Fiber 3 g 12% • Sugars 10 g • Protein 28 g • Vitamin A 20% • Vitamin C 2% • Calcium 15% • Iron 25%
Dietary Exchanges: 3½ Starch, 2½ Very Lean Meat, 1 Fat OR 3½ Carbohydrate, 2½ Very Lean Meat, 1 Fat

Smoked Turkey and Pasta with Cream Sauce

Prep Time: 45 minutes

Yield: 6 servings

8 oz. (3½ cups) uncooked bow tie pasta (farfalle)

2 cups quartered fresh Brussels sprouts

1½ cups julienne-cut (2 x ¼ x ¼-inch) carrots

¼ cup finely chopped onion

¾ cup lite evaporated skimmed milk

½ cup dry white wine

2 oz. ⅓-less-fat cream cheese (Neufchâtel)

1 to 2 teaspoons creamy horseradish sauce

¾ lb. (2 cups) julienne-cut (2 x ¼ x ¼-inch) smoked turkey breast

1. In Dutch oven or large saucepan, bring 3 quarts (12 cups) water to a boil. Add pasta and Brussels sprouts; return to a boil. Boil over medium-high heat for 15 to 17 minutes or until pasta and Brussels sprouts are tender, adding carrots during last 4 minutes of cooking time.

2. Meanwhile, spray large skillet with nonstick cooking spray. Heat over medium heat until hot. Add onion; cook and stir 2 to 3 minutes or until tender. With wire whisk, stir in milk, wine, cream cheese and horseradish sauce; cook and stir until smooth and slightly thickened. Add turkey; cook 2 to 3 minutes or until thoroughly heated, stirring occasionally.

3. To serve, drain pasta, Brussels sprouts and carrots; arrange on serving platter. Top with cream sauce.

Nutrition Information Per Serving: Serving Size: ⅙ of Recipe • Calories 280 • Calories from Fat 35 • % Daily Value • Total Fat 4 g 6% • Saturated 2 g 10% • Cholesterol 30 mg 10% • Sodium 750 mg 31% • Total Carbohydrate 42 g 14% • Dietary Fiber 4 g 16% • Sugars 10 g • Protein 20 g • Vitamin A 190% • Vitamin C 60% • Calcium 15% • Iron 15%
Dietary Exchanges: 2½ Starch, 1 Vegetable, 1½ Very Lean Meat OR 2½ Carbohydrate, 1 Vegetable, 1½ Very Lean Meat

Creole-Style Skillet Dinner

Prep Time: 20 minutes

Yield: 4 (1½-cup) servings

1	medium onion, chopped
½	medium green bell pepper, chopped
½	lb. 97% fat-free smoked turkey kielbasa, quartered lengthwise, sliced
1	(14½-oz.) can diced tomatoes with olive oil, garlic and herbs, undrained
1	cup water
1½	cups uncooked instant rice

1. Spray large nonstick skillet with nonstick cooking spray. Heat over medium-high heat until hot. Add onion and bell pepper; cover and cook until vegetables are crisp-tender, stirring once.

2. Add kielbasa, tomatoes and water; mix well. Bring to a boil. Stir in rice; return to a boil. Cook over low heat for about 5 minutes or until rice is tender. Fluff with fork before serving. If desired, serve with hot pepper sauce.

Nutrition Information Per Serving: Serving Size: 1½ Cups • Calories 240 • Calories from Fat 25 • % Daily Value • Total Fat 3 g 5% • Saturated 1 g 5% • Cholesterol 15 mg 5% • Sodium 1140 mg 48% • Total Carbohydrate 39 g 13% • Dietary Fiber 2 g 8% • Sugars 8 g • Protein 14 g • Vitamin A 6% • Vitamin C 20% • Calcium 4% • Iron 15%
Dietary Exchanges: 1½ Starch, ½ Fruit, 2 Vegetable, 1 Lean Meat OR 2 Carbohydrate, 2 Vegetable, 1 Lean Meat

Choosing Onions

Onions are the starting point for countless soups and stews. Choose firm onions with papery skin that has a slight gloss; avoid those that appear soft or moldy. The ordinary yellow onion, typically the least expensive, is best for most of the recipes in this book. Store onions in a cool, dark, dry place, but not with potatoes. Use them before they begin to sprout green tops. Browning onions in oil before cooking them with liquid brings out their natural sweetness.

Creole-Style Skillet Dinner

Beer-Spiked Shrimp and Spaghetti

Prep Time: 20 minutes

Yield: 4 servings

8 oz. uncooked spaghetti
2 tablespoons olive oil
2 garlic cloves, minced
½ lb. shelled, deveined, uncooked shrimp
¾ cup beer
1 tablespoon chopped fresh thyme or ½ teaspoon dried thyme leaves

1. Cook spaghetti to desired doneness as directed on package. Drain; cover to keep warm.

2. Meanwhile, in nonstick Dutch oven or large skillet, heat oil and garlic over medium-high heat until oil is hot. Add shrimp; cook 3 to 5 minutes or until shrimp turn pink. Remove shrimp from Dutch oven; place in bowl and cover to keep warm.

3. Pour beer into same Dutch oven; cook over medium heat for 3 to 4 minutes or until reduced by about half, stirring occasionally. Stir in thyme.

4. Add cooked spaghetti; stir gently to coat with beer. Cook an additional minute, stirring frequently. Add shrimp with any accumulated liquid in bowl; toss to coat well.

Nutrition Information Per Serving: Serving Size: ¼ of Recipe • Calories 320 • Calories from Fat 70 • % Daily Value • Total Fat 8 g 12% • Saturated 1 g 5% • Cholesterol 65 mg 22% • Sodium 80 mg 3% • Total Carbohydrate 45 g 15% • Dietary Fiber 1 g 4% • Sugars 2 g • Protein 15 g • Vitamin A 0% • Vitamin C 0% • Calcium 2% • Iron 20%
Dietary Exchanges: 3 Starch, 1 Very Lean Meat, 1 Fat OR 3 Carbohydrate, 1 Very Lean Meat, 1 Fat

Lemon Pesto Capellini with Shrimp

Prep Time: 20 minutes

Yield: 4 (1¼-cup) servings

8 oz. uncooked angel hair pasta (capellini)
1 (12-oz.) pkg. frozen ready-to-cook shrimp
1 (7-oz.) container refrigerated pesto, room temperature
¼ cup whipping cream
2 teaspoons grated lemon peel
1⅓ oz. (⅓ cup) shredded fresh Parmesan cheese

1. Cook pasta to desired doneness as directed on package, adding shrimp during last 2 minutes of cooking time. Cook until shrimp turn pink. Drain.

2. Meanwhile, in large bowl, combine pesto, cream and lemon peel; mix well.

3. Add cooked pasta and shrimp to pesto mixture; toss gently to mix. Sprinkle with cheese.

Nutrition Information Per Serving: Serving Size: 1¼ Cups • Calories 580 • Calories from Fat 280 • % Daily Value • Total Fat 31 g 48% • Saturated 8 g 40% • Cholesterol 160 mg 53% • Sodium 580 mg 24% • Total Carbohydrate 47 g 16% • Dietary Fiber 1 g 4% • Sugars 5 g • Protein 28 g • Vitamin A 15% • Vitamin C 4% • Calcium 25% • Iron 25%
Dietary Exchanges: 3 Starch, 2½ Very Lean Meat, 5½ Fat OR 3 Carbohydrate, 2½ Very Lean Meat, 5½ Fat

Alfredo Shrimp and Linguine

Prep Time: 25 minutes

Yield: 4 (1½-cup) servings

8	oz. uncooked linguine, broken into thirds
1½	cups frozen sweet peas
¾	cup refrigerated light Alfredo sauce
¼	cup fat-free half-and-half or skim milk
1	lb. shelled, deveined, cooked medium shrimp
½	teaspoon dried basil leaves
⅛	teaspoon pepper

1. In large saucepan, cook linguine to desired doneness as directed on package, adding peas during last 2 to 3 minutes of cooking time. Pour into colander to drain.

2. In same saucepan over low heat, combine Alfredo sauce, half-and-half, shrimp, basil and pepper; mix well. Add cooked linguine and peas; cook 2 to 4 minutes or until thoroughly heated, stirring constantly.

Nutrition Information Per Serving: Serving Size: 1½ Cups • Calories 400 • Calories from Fat 60 • % Daily Value • Total Fat 7 g 11% • Saturated 3 g 15% • Cholesterol 175 mg 58% • Sodium 490 mg 20% • Total Carbohydrate 55 g 18% • Dietary Fiber 4 g 16% • Sugars 5 g • Protein 30 g • Vitamin A 10% • Vitamin C 10% • Calcium 15% • Iron 30%
Dietary Exchanges: 3½ Starch, 2½ Very Lean Meat, 1 Fat OR 3½ Carbohydrate, 2½ Very Lean Meat, 1 Fat

Cooking Shrimp

Cooked, peeled shrimp sometimes costs double the price of raw shrimp in the shell. The reason: it takes about two pounds of raw shrimp in the shell—and a lot of labor—to yield a pound of cooked, peeled shrimp.

Cooking shrimp yourself may save money and gives you control over the doneness, letting you remove shrimp from the heat before they become rubbery.

To cook raw shrimp, bring to a boil enough water to cover the shrimp. Add the unpeeled shrimp and reduce heat to a simmer. As soon as the shells start to turn pink, begin testing the shrimp by removing one from the pot and cutting into the center. When the center becomes white and opaque (instead of grayish and translucent), drain the pot. It takes only three to five minutes, depending on size.

Shrimp may be peeled before cooking (useful if shrimp will be served hot in a stir-fry or sauté) or after (easy if shrimp will be served cold for salad or shrimp cocktail). To peel, use your thumbnail or a small paring knife to split the shell on the belly (inner curve) of the shrimp and peel it back; it should come off in more or less a single piece. The tailfins, which are not eaten, may be removed or left on to serve as a handle.

Deveining is optional. The black vein that usually runs along the back (outer curve) is not harmful and has no flavor, but some people find it unappetizing. Slit the shrimp along the back (outer curve) to expose the black vein, which can then be removed with the tip of the knife.

Garlic Shrimp and Peas

Prep Time: 30 minutes

Yield: 4 servings

8	oz. uncooked spaghetti
2⅔	cups water
1	(10-oz.) pkg. frozen sweet peas with butter sauce in a pouch
1	cup water
1	teaspoon chicken-flavor instant bouillon
½	lb. shelled, deveined, uncooked medium shrimp
1	(4½-oz.) jar sliced mushrooms, drained
½	cup sliced onion
¼	teaspoon ginger
⅛	teaspoon salt
3	large garlic cloves, minced
2	tablespoons water
2	tablespoons cornstarch

1. Cook spaghetti to desired doneness as directed on package. Drain; cover to keep warm.

2. Meanwhile, place unopened pouch of peas in warm water for 15 to 20 minutes to thaw.

3. Meanwhile, in large skillet or wok, bring 1 cup water to a boil. Add bouillon; stir to dissolve. Add shrimp, mushrooms, onion, ginger, salt and garlic; mix well. Cook over medium–high heat for 3 to 5 minutes or until shrimp turn pink, stirring occasionally.

4. In small bowl, combine 2 tablespoons water and cornstarch; blend well. Gradually stir into shrimp mixture. Cook over medium heat until mixture boils and thickens, stirring constantly. Stir in peas; cook until thoroughly heated. Serve over spaghetti.

Nutrition Information Per Serving: Serving Size: ¼ of Recipe • Calories 360 • Calories from Fat 25 • % Daily Value • Total Fat 3 g 5% • Saturated 1 g 5% • Cholesterol 115 mg 38% • Sodium 790 mg 33% • Total Carbohydrate 60 g 20% • Dietary Fiber 5 g 20% • Sugars 6 g • Protein 23 g • Vitamin A 10% • Vitamin C 6% • Calcium 6% • Iron 20%
Dietary Exchanges: 4 Starch, 1½ Very Lean Meat OR 4 Carbohydrate, 1½ Very Lean Meat

Garlic Shrimp and Peas

Southern-Style Shrimp and Rice

Southern-Style Shrimp and Rice

Prep Time: 45 minutes

Yield: 4 (1½-cup) servings

⅔	cup uncooked regular long-grain white rice
1⅓	cups water
6	slices bacon
2	green bell peppers, cut into 1-inch pieces
2	medium onions, cut into eighths
¼	teaspoon pepper
¼	teaspoon hot pepper sauce
1	(14½-oz.) can whole tomatoes, undrained, cut up
1	(6-oz.) can tomato paste
1	lb. shelled, deveined, cooked medium shrimp

1. Cook rice in water as directed on package.

2. Meanwhile, cook bacon in large skillet until crisp. Remove bacon from skillet; drain on paper towels. Set aside.

3. Reserve 2 tablespoons drippings in skillet. Add bell peppers and onions; cook and stir until tender.

4. Stir in cooked rice, pepper, hot pepper sauce, tomatoes and tomato paste. Cover; simmer 15 minutes, stirring occasionally.

5. Crumble bacon. Add bacon and shrimp to skillet mixture; cook until thoroughly heated.

Nutrition Information Per Serving: Serving Size: 1½ Cups • Calories 410 • Calories from Fat 120 • % Daily Value • Total Fat 13 g 20% • Saturated 5 g 25% • Cholesterol 235 mg 78% • Sodium 900 mg 38% • Total Carbohydrate 42 g 14% • Dietary Fiber 5 g 20% • Sugars 7 g • Protein 32 g • Vitamin A 45% • Vitamin C 80% • Calcium 10% • Iron 35%
Dietary Exchanges: 2 Starch, 2 Vegetable, 3 Very Lean Meat, 2 Fat OR 2 Carbohydrate, 2 Vegetable, 3 Very Lean Meat, 2 Fat

Vegetable and Bean Pasta

Prep Time: 15 minutes

Yield: 4 servings

8 oz. uncooked spaghetti
1 tablespoon garlic-flavored oil or olive oil*
3 medium zucchini, halved lengthwise, sliced (3 cups)
1 (8-oz.) pkg. (3 cups) sliced fresh mushrooms
2 cups garden-style pasta or spaghetti sauce
1 (15-oz.) can garbanzo beans, drained, rinsed

1. In large saucepan, cook spaghetti to desired doneness as directed on package. Drain; cover to keep warm.

2. Meanwhile, heat oil in large nonstick skillet over medium-high heat until hot. Add zucchini and mushrooms; cover and cook 4 to 6 minutes or until vegetables are tender, stirring once.

3. Stir in pasta sauce and garbanzo beans; cook until thoroughly heated. Serve sauce over spaghetti.

Tip: *If using olive oil, add ⅛ teaspoon garlic powder.

Nutrition Information Per Serving: Serving Size: ¼ of Recipe • Calories 490 • Calories from Fat 90 • % Daily Value • Total Fat 10 g 15% • Saturated 1 g 5% • Cholesterol 0 mg 0% • Sodium 700 mg 29% • Total Carbohydrate 82 g 27% • Dietary Fiber 11 g 44% • Sugars 18 g • Protein 17 g • Vitamin A 30% • Vitamin C 20% • Calcium 15% • Iron 30%
Dietary Exchanges: 4 Starch, 1 Fruit, 2 Vegetable, 1½ Fat OR 5 Carbohydrate, 2 Vegetable, 1½ Fat

Creamy Fettuccine Primavera

Prep Time: 25 minutes

Yield: 4 (1½-cup) servings

8 oz. uncooked fettuccine
1 (1-lb.) pkg. frozen broccoli florets, carrots and cauliflower, thawed, drained*
½ (8-oz.) pkg. ⅓-less-fat cream cheese (Neufchâtel), softened
½ cup skim milk
1 teaspoon garlic salt

1. Cook fettuccine in Dutch oven or large saucepan to desired doneness as directed on package, adding vegetables during last 5 minutes of cooking time. Drain; return to Dutch oven.

2. Meanwhile, in small nonstick saucepan, combine cream cheese, milk and garlic salt; mix well. Cook over medium-low heat, stirring with wire whisk until smooth.

3. Add cream cheese mixture to cooked fettuccine and vegetables; toss gently over low heat until well combined. If desired, add salt and pepper to taste and sprinkle with grated fresh Parmesan cheese.

Tip: *To quickly thaw vegetables, place in colander or strainer; rinse with warm water until thawed. Drain well.

Nutrition Information Per Serving: Serving Size: 1½ Cups • Calories 340 • Calories from Fat 80 • % Daily Value • Total Fat 9 g 14% • Saturated 5 g 25% • Cholesterol 75 mg 25% • Sodium 650 mg 27% • Total Carbohydrate 50 g 17% • Dietary Fiber 5 g 20% • Sugars 7 g • Protein 14 g • Vitamin A 90% • Vitamin C 30% • Calcium 10% • Iron 20%
Dietary Exchanges: 3 Starch, 1 Vegetable, ½ High-Fat Meat, ½ Fat OR 3 Carbohydrate, 1 Vegetable, ½ High-Fat Meat, ½ Fat

Linguine with Seafood Sauce

Prep Time: 20 minutes

Yield: 8 servings

12	oz. uncooked linguine
4	tablespoons margarine or butter
4	green onions, sliced
1	garlic clove, minced
1	(12-oz.) pkg. frozen shelled, deveined, uncooked medium shrimp, thawed, drained
1	(6½-oz.) can minced clams, undrained
1	cup chicken broth
½	cup dry white wine
2	tablespoons lemon juice
¼	cup chopped fresh parsley
1	teaspoon dried basil leaves
1	teaspoon dried oregano leaves
¼	teaspoon pepper
2	tablespoons cold water
2	tablespoons cornstarch
¼	cup sour cream

1. Cook linguine to desired doneness as directed on package. Drain; cover to keep warm.

2. Meanwhile, melt 2 tablespoons of the margarine in large skillet over medium heat. Add green onions and garlic; cook and stir until onions are tender. Stir in shrimp, clams, broth, wine, lemon juice, parsley, basil, oregano and pepper. Bring to a boil. Reduce heat to low; simmer 5 minutes.

3. In small bowl, combine water and cornstarch; blend well. Gradually stir into seafood mixture. Cook until mixture boils and thickens, stirring constantly.

4. In large bowl, combine cooked linguine, sour cream and remaining 2 tablespoons margarine; toss to coat. Serve seafood sauce over linguine.

Nutrition Information Per Serving: Serving Size: ⅛ of Recipe • Calories 290 • Calories from Fat 90 • % Daily Value • Total Fat 10 g 15% • Saturated 3 g 15% • Cholesterol 105 mg 35% • Sodium 390 mg 16% • Total Carbohydrate 35 g 12% • Dietary Fiber 2 g 8% • Sugars 3 g • Protein 14 g • Vitamin A 10% • Vitamin C 8% • Calcium 6% • Iron 20%
Dietary Exchanges: 2½ Starch, 1 Very Lean Meat, 1½ Fat OR 2½ Carbohydrate, 1 Very Lean Meat, 1½ Fat

Spaghetti with Fish and Vegetables

Prep Time: 30 minutes

Yield: 6 servings

1 (7-oz.) pkg. uncooked
spaghetti
2 tablespoons margarine or
butter
2 tablespoons all-purpose flour
½ teaspoon dried thyme leaves
½ to 1 teaspoon salt
¼ teaspoon pepper
2 cups milk
1 lb. fish fillets, cut into
1-inch chunks
2 cups frozen mixed
vegetables, thawed,
drained*
2 tablespoons chopped fresh
parsley

1. Cook spaghetti to desired doneness as directed on package. Drain; cover to keep warm.

2. Meanwhile, melt margarine in large skillet. Stir in flour, thyme, salt and pepper; cook until mixture is smooth and bubbly. Gradually stir in milk; cook until mixture boils and thickens, stirring constantly.

3. Add fish and vegetables. Bring to a boil. Reduce heat; cover and simmer 5 to 10 minutes or until fish flakes easily with fork. Serve over spaghetti. Sprinkle with parsley.

Tip: *To quickly thaw mixed vegetables, place in colander or strainer; rinse with warm water until thawed. Drain well.

Nutrition Information Per Serving: Serving Size: ⅙ of Recipe • Calories 300 • Calories from Fat 60 • % Daily Value • Total Fat 7 g 11% • Saturated 2 g 10% • Cholesterol 45 mg 15% • Sodium 520 mg 22% • Total Carbohydrate 36 g 12% • Dietary Fiber 2 g 8% • Sugars 6 g • Protein 23 g • Vitamin A 25% • Vitamin C 6% • Calcium 15% • Iron 10%
Dietary Exchanges: 2 Starch, 1 Vegetable, 2 Very Lean Meat, 1 Fat OR 2 Carbohydrate, 1 Vegetable, 2 Very Lean Meat, 1 Fat

Cream of the Crop

Watch the heat closely when preparing a stove-top recipe that includes cream, milk or sour cream. When cooked too long or at too high a temperature, these ingredients curdle.

Macaroni and Cheese

Prep Time: 30 minutes

Yield: 4 (1¼-cup) servings

8   oz. (2 cups) uncooked elbow
      macaroni
1½   cups milk
1   lb. pasteurized processed
      cheese spread, cubed

1. In large saucepan or Dutch oven, cook macaroni to desired doneness as directed on package. Drain; rinse with hot water. Return to saucepan.

2. Add milk and cheese; cook over medium heat until cheese is melted and sauce is smooth, stirring occasionally. Let stand 3 to 5 minutes before serving.

Nutrition Information Per Serving: Serving Size: 1¼ Cups • Calories 570 • Calories from Fat 240 • % Daily Value • Total Fat 27 g 42% • Saturated 16 g 80% • Cholesterol 70 mg 23% • Sodium 1570 mg 65% • Total Carbohydrate 53 g 18% • Dietary Fiber 1 g 4% • Sugars 15 g • Protein 28 g • Vitamin A 20% • Vitamin C 0% • Calcium 80% • Iron 15%
Dietary Exchanges: 3½ Starch, 2½ Meat, 1 Fat OR 3½ Carbohydrate, 2½ Meat, 1 Fat

Rings 'n Cheese

Prep Time: 20 minutes

Yield: 6 (1-cup) servings

9   oz. (2¼ cups) uncooked
      macaroni rings
2   tablespoons margarine or
      butter
¼   cup chopped onion
1   (10¾-oz.) can condensed
      tomato soup
4   oz. (1 cup) shredded
      American cheese
½   cup water

1. Cook macaroni to desired doneness as directed on package. Drain.

2. Meanwhile, melt margarine in large saucepan. Add onion; cook and stir until crisp-tender. Reduce heat; stir in soup, cheese and water. Cook over low heat until cheese is melted, stirring occasionally.

3. Stir in cooked macaroni; cook until thoroughly heated.

Nutrition Information Per Serving: Serving Size: 1 Cup • Calories 300 • Calories from Fat 100 • % Daily Value • Total Fat 11 g 17% • Saturated 5 g 25% • Cholesterol 20 mg 7% • Sodium 600 mg 25% • Total Carbohydrate 39 g 13% • Dietary Fiber 1 g 4% • Sugars 5 g • Protein 11 g • Vitamin A 15% • Vitamin C 30% • Calcium 15% • Iron 15%
Dietary Exchanges: 2½ Starch, ½ High-Fat Meat, 1 Fat OR 2½ Carbohydrate, ½ High-Fat Meat, 1 Fat

Pesto Pasta and Vegetables

Prep Time: 30 minutes

Yield: 4 (1¾-cup) servings

3	eggs
8	oz. (3 cups) uncooked medium shell pasta
1	tablespoon olive oil or vegetable oil
2	leeks, cut in half lengthwise, sliced (3 cups)
½	cup drained marinated sun-dried tomatoes (from 8-oz. jar), chopped
¼	cup sliced ripe olives
½	cup purchased pesto
2	tablespoons shredded fresh Parmesan cheese

1. Place eggs in medium saucepan; cover with cold water. Bring to a boil. Reduce heat; simmer about 15 minutes. Immediately drain; run cold water over eggs to stop cooking. Peel eggs; chop. Set aside.

2. Cook pasta to desired doneness as directed on package. Drain.

3. Meanwhile, heat oil in large nonstick skillet over medium-high heat until hot. Add leeks; cook and stir until tender. Reduce heat to medium; stir in tomatoes and olives.

4. Add cooked pasta; cook over medium heat until thoroughly heated, stirring occasionally. Add chopped eggs and pesto; cook and stir 1 to 2 minutes or until thoroughly heated. Remove from heat; sprinkle with cheese.

Nutrition Information Per Serving: Serving Size: 1¾ Cups • Calories 550 • Calories from Fat 240 • % Daily Value • Total Fat 27 g 42% • Saturated 5 g 25% • Cholesterol 165 mg 55% • Sodium 450 mg 19% • Total Carbohydrate 58 g 19% • Dietary Fiber 4 g 16% • Sugars 8 g • Protein 18 g • Vitamin A 15% • Vitamin C 25% • Calcium 20% • Iron 30%
Dietary Exchanges: 3½ Starch, 1 Vegetable, 1 Medium-Fat Meat, 4 Fat OR 3½ Carbohydrate, 1 Vegetable, 1 Medium-Fat Meat, 4 Fat

Ratatouille Pasta

Prep Time: 30 minutes

Yield: 4 servings

6	oz. (2⅔ cups) uncooked bow tie pasta (farfalle)
2	teaspoons olive oil
2	small onions, sliced
4	large garlic cloves, minced
2	cups chopped eggplant
2	(14½-oz.) cans diced tomatoes, undrained
1	medium zucchini, halved lengthwise, sliced
⅓	cup coarsely chopped fresh basil
¼	teaspoon coarsely ground black pepper
⅛	teaspoon salt

1. Cook pasta to desired doneness as directed on package. Drain; cover to keep warm.

2. Meanwhile, heat oil in large nonstick skillet over medium heat until hot. Add onions and garlic; cook 1 to 2 minutes or until tender. Add eggplant and tomatoes. Bring to a boil. Reduce heat; cover and simmer 10 minutes.

3. Add zucchini, basil, pepper and salt; cover and cook an additional 5 minutes or until vegetables are crisp-tender. Serve over pasta. If desired, sprinkle with additional chopped fresh basil.

Nutrition Information Per Serving: Serving Size: ¼ of Recipe • Calories 280 • Calories from Fat 25 • % Daily Value • Total Fat 3 g 5% • Saturated 0 g 0% • Cholesterol 0 mg 0% • Sodium 530 mg 22% • Total Carbohydrate 53 g 18% • Dietary Fiber 5 g 20% • Sugars 10 g • Protein 9 g • Vitamin A 30% • Vitamin C 35% • Calcium 10% • Iron 20%
Dietary Exchanges: 3 Starch, 1½ Vegetable OR 3 Carbohydrate, 1½ Vegetable

Peeling Garlic

Kitchen shops stock many inexpensive gadgets designed to separate the fragrant cloves of garlic from their papery husks, but you'll do just as well with a broad-bladed kitchen knife. Press the cloves with the flat side of the knife to loosen the husks, then trim the stem end and the garlic should pretty much pop free of its skin.

"Instant" garlic products are convenient to keep on hand for times when you find you're out of fresh garlic, though the flavor won't be quite as fresh. Dehydrated choices include finely ground garlic powder or, for more texture, granulated or minced garlic. Substitute $\frac{1}{8}$ to $\frac{1}{4}$ teaspoon of the dried product for 1 clove of minced fresh garlic. Garlic salt combines dehydrated garlic powder and salt.

Minced garlic in oil or water is an option that some cooks think approaches the flavor of fresh garlic. Substitute about 1 teaspoon of minced garlic in oil or water for 1 clove of fresh. Read the label; in addition to oil or water, the product may contain added citric acid, salt or even sugar. Refrigerate the jar after opening.

Low-Fat Alfredo Sauce over Fettuccine

Prep Time: 25 minutes

Yield: 5 (1½-cup) servings

16	oz. refrigerated fettuccine or 12 oz. uncooked fettuccine
2	teaspoons margarine or butter
1	teaspoon olive oil
3	large garlic cloves, minced
¼	cup finely chopped red bell pepper
¼	cup sliced green onions
¼	cup chopped fresh parsley or 3 teaspoons dried parsley flakes
1	tablespoon all-purpose flour
1	(12-oz.) can lite evaporated skim milk
½	teaspoon dried basil leaves
¼	teaspoon dried oregano leaves
¼	cup grated Parmesan cheese

1. Cook fettuccine to desired doneness as directed on package. Drain.

2. Meanwhile, in large nonstick skillet or Dutch oven, melt margarine with oil over medium-high heat. Add garlic; cook 1 minute. Add bell pepper, green onions, parsley and flour; cook and stir 1 minute.

3. Gradually stir in milk; blend well. Bring to a boil, stirring constantly. Cook 3 to 5 minutes or until sauce boils and thickens, stirring frequently.

4. Remove skillet from heat; stir in basil and oregano. Add cooked fettuccine; toss gently to coat. Sprinkle with cheese.

Nutrition Information Per Serving: Serving Size: 1½ Cups • Calories 330 • Calories from Fat 60 • % Daily Value • Total Fat 7 g 11% • Saturated 2 g 10% • Cholesterol 85 mg 28% • Sodium 200 mg 8% • Total Carbohydrate 51 g 17% • Dietary Fiber 2 g 8% • Sugars 9 g • Protein 16 g • Vitamin A 15% • Vitamin C 15% • Calcium 25% • Iron 15%
Dietary Exchanges: 3½ Starch, ½ Medium-Fat Meat, ½ Fat OR 3½ Carbohydrate, ½ Medium-Fat Meat, ½ Fat

Low-Fat Alfredo Sauce over Fettuccine

Pasta and Vegetable Carbonara

Prep Time: 30 minutes

Yield: 4 (1½-cup) servings

6   oz. (2⅔ cups) uncooked bow tie pasta (farfalle)
8   slices bacon
1   cup coarsely chopped red bell pepper
1   (9-oz.) pkg. frozen cut broccoli in a pouch, thawed (do not drain)*
2   teaspoons all-purpose flour
¼   teaspoon salt
¼   teaspoon pepper
¾   cup half-and-half
¼   cup grated fresh Parmesan cheese

1. Cook pasta to desired doneness as directed on package. Drain.

2. Meanwhile, cook bacon in large skillet over medium heat until crisp. Remove bacon from skillet; drain on paper towels. Drain drippings, reserving 1 tablespoon drippings in skillet. Crumble bacon; set aside.

3. Add bell pepper and thawed broccoli with liquid to drippings in skillet; cook 3 to 5 minutes or until vegetables are crisp-tender, stirring frequently.

4. Stir in bacon and cooked pasta. Cook 3 to 5 minutes over medium heat or until thoroughly heated, stirring frequently.

5. In small bowl, combine flour, salt, pepper and half-and-half; stir until smooth with wire whisk. Add to mixture in skillet; cook until mixture is thickened, stirring constantly. Stir in Parmesan cheese.

Tip: *To quickly thaw broccoli, cut small slit in center of pouch; microwave on HIGH for 2 to 3 minutes or until thawed. Do not drain.

Nutrition Information Per Serving: Serving Size: 1½ Cups • Calories 390 • Calories from Fat 160 • % Daily Value • Total Fat 18 g 28% • Saturated 9 g 45% • Cholesterol 40 mg 13% • Sodium 650 mg 27% • Total Carbohydrate 40 g 13% • Dietary Fiber 3 g 12% • Sugars 6 g • Protein 17 g • Vitamin A 40% • Vitamin C 90% • Calcium 25% • Iron 15%
Dietary Exchanges: 2½ Starch, 1 Vegetable, 1 High-Fat Meat, 1½ Fat OR 2½ Carbohydrate, 1 Vegetable, 1 High-Fat Meat, 1½ Fat

Penne Pasta with Broccoli and Tomato Sauce

Prep Time: 10 minutes (Ready in 30 minutes)

Yield: 6 servings

12	oz. (3½ cups) uncooked penne (large tube-shaped pasta)
3½	cups fresh broccoli florets
1	tablespoon oil
2	to 4 garlic cloves, minced
1	(28-oz.) can crushed tomatoes with added puree, undrained
¼	cup dry red wine
1	tablespoon chopped fresh basil or 1 teaspoon dried basil leaves
1	teaspoon sugar
½	teaspoon salt

1. Cook penne to desired doneness as directed on package, adding broccoli during last 4 minutes of cooking time. Drain; cover to keep warm.

2. Meanwhile, heat oil in large skillet over medium heat until hot. Add garlic; cook and stir 2 to 3 minutes or until tender. Stir in tomatoes and all remaining ingredients; simmer 15 to 20 minutes or until thickened, stirring occasionally.

3. To serve, arrange cooked penne and broccoli on serving platter. Spoon sauce over top. If desired, sprinkle with Parmesan cheese.

Nutrition Information Per Serving: Serving Size: ⅙ of Recipe • Calories 290 • Calories from Fat 35 • % Daily Value • Total Fat 4 g 6% • Saturated 0 g 0% • Cholesterol 0 mg 0% • Sodium 390 mg 16% • Total Carbohydrate 52 g 17% • Dietary Fiber 4 g 16% • Sugars 6 g • Protein 10 g • Vitamin A 30% • Vitamin C 80% • Calcium 8% • Iron 20%
Dietary Exchanges: 3 Starch, 1 Vegetable, ½ Fat OR 3 Carbohydrate, 1 Vegetable, ½ Fat

Spicy Rigatoni, Beans and Greens

Prep Time: 30 minutes

Yield: 4 servings

8	oz. (3¼ cups) uncooked rigatoni (pasta tubes with ridges)
1	teaspoon olive oil
1	medium onion, sliced
3	garlic cloves, minced
1	(14½-oz.) can diced tomatoes with Italian-style herbs, undrained
1	(15½-oz.) can great northern beans, drained, rinsed
2	tablespoons thinly sliced fresh sage leaves or 1 teaspoon dried sage leaves
¼	teaspoon crushed red pepper flakes
6	cups thinly sliced fresh spinach leaves

1. Cook rigatoni to desired doneness as directed on package. Drain; cover to keep warm.

2. Meanwhile, spray large nonstick skillet with nonstick cooking spray. Add oil; heat over medium-high heat until hot. Add onion and garlic; cook 3 to 4 minutes or until onion begins to brown, stirring frequently.

3. Stir in tomatoes; simmer 2 minutes. Stir in beans, sage and red pepper flakes; cook until thoroughly heated. Add spinach; mix well. Serve tomato mixture over rigatoni.

Nutrition Information Per Serving: Serving Size: ¼ of Recipe • Calories 370 • Calories from Fat 25 • % Daily Value • Total Fat 3 g 5% • Saturated 0 g 0% • Cholesterol 0 mg 0% • Sodium 460 mg 19% • Total Carbohydrate 70 g 23% • Dietary Fiber 10 g 40% • Sugars 6 g • Protein 16 g • Vitamin A 120% • Vitamin C 45% • Calcium 20% • Iron 40%
Dietary Exchanges: 4 Starch, 2 Vegetable OR 4 Carbohydrate, 2 Vegetable

Fusilli with Fresh Tomatoes

Prep Time: 25 minutes

Yield: 6 (1½-cup) servings

1 (12-oz.) pkg. uncooked fusilli (curly spaghetti)
4 cups chopped seeded fresh Italian plum tomatoes (about 2 lb.)
¼ cup chopped fresh basil
2 tablespoons chopped fresh parsley
1 tablespoon olive oil
½ teaspoon salt
¼ teaspoon pepper

1. Cook fusilli to desired doneness as directed on package. Drain.
2. Meanwhile, in large bowl, combine all remaining ingredients; mix well.
3. Add cooked fusilli to tomato mixture; toss gently to mix.

Nutrition Information Per Serving: Serving Size: 1½ Cups • Calories 260 • Calories from Fat 35 • % Daily Value • Total Fat 4 g 6% • Saturated 0 g 0% • Cholesterol 0 mg 0% • Sodium 190 mg 8% • Total Carbohydrate 48 g 16% • Dietary Fiber 3 g 12% • Sugars 5 g • Protein 8 g • Vitamin A 20% • Vitamin C 30% • Calcium 2% • Iron 15%
Dietary Exchanges: 3 Starch, ½ Fat OR 3 Carbohydrate, ½ Fat

Tuscany Pasta Toss

Prep Time: 20 minutes

Yield: 4 (1½-cup) servings

1 (9-oz.) pkg. refrigerated fettuccine
2 cups chopped tomatoes
⅓ cup chopped fresh basil
1 (4½-oz.) jar sliced mushrooms, drained
3 tablespoons olive oil or vegetable oil
2 tablespoons balsamic vinegar
1 tablespoon minced garlic in water (from 4½-oz. jar)
½ teaspoon salt
¼ teaspoon cracked black pepper
4 oz. Gorgonzola or blue cheese, crumbled (1 cup)
½ cup chopped walnuts
Fresh basil leaves, if desired

1. Cook fettuccine to desired doneness as directed on package. Drain.
2. Meanwhile, in large serving bowl, combine tomatoes, chopped basil, mushrooms, oil, vinegar, garlic, salt and pepper; mix well.
3. Add cooked fettuccine; toss to coat. Add cheese and walnuts; mix gently. Garnish with basil leaves.

Nutrition Information Per Serving: Serving Size: 1½ Cups • Calories 530 • Calories from Fat 280 • % Daily Value • Total Fat 31 g 48% • Saturated 8 g 40% • Cholesterol 85 mg 28% • Sodium 790 mg 33% • Total Carbohydrate 45 g 15% • Dietary Fiber 4 g 16% • Sugars 4 g • Protein 18 g • Vitamin A 20% • Vitamin C 25% • Calcium 20% • Iron 20%
Dietary Exchanges: 3 Starch, 1 High-Fat Meat, 4 Fat OR 3 Carbohydrate, 1 High-Fat Meat, 4 Fat

Garden Risotto

Prep Time: 30 minutes

Yield: 3 (1¼-cup) servings

1	tablespoon olive oil
¼	cup chopped green onions
¼	cup chopped red bell pepper
1	cup uncooked short-grain Arborio rice, rinsed
1	(14½-oz.) can ready-to-serve vegetable broth
¾	cup water
1	cup chopped fresh broccoli
½	cup shredded carrot
1	teaspoon dried thyme leaves
2	tablespoons shredded fresh Parmesan cheese

1. In large nonstick saucepan or Dutch oven, heat oil over medium heat until hot. Add green onions and bell pepper; cook 2 minutes or until tender, stirring occasionally. Add rice; cook and stir 2 minutes.

2. Add broth and water; bring to a boil. Reduce heat to medium-low; cover and cook 10 minutes.

3. Stir in broccoli and carrot; simmer an additional 5 to 10 minutes. Remove from heat; stir in thyme. Cover; let stand 3 minutes. Sprinkle with cheese.

Nutrition Information Per Serving: Serving Size: 1¼ Cups • Calories 260 • Calories from Fat 60 • % Daily Value • Total Fat 7 g 11% • Saturated 1 g 5% • Cholesterol 3 mg 1% • Sodium 700 mg 29% • Total Carbohydrate 43 g 14% • Dietary Fiber 2 g 8% • Sugars 4 g • Protein 6 g • Vitamin A 130% • Vitamin C 50% • Calcium 8% • Iron 20%

Dietary Exchanges: 2½ Starch, 1 Vegetable, 1 Fat OR 2½ Carbohydrate, 1 Vegetable, 1 Fat

Fresh Pasta with Skinny Tomato Sauce

Prep Time: 35 minutes

Yield: 4 servings

1 medium onion, finely chopped
1 garlic clove, minced
2 tablespoons water
2 (9-oz.) pkg. refrigerated linguine
1 (28-oz.) can crushed tomatoes with Italian herbs, undrained
1 tablespoon olive oil
2 teaspoons sugar
¼ teaspoon salt
¼ teaspoon freshly ground black pepper
1 bay leaf

1. In nonstick Dutch oven or large saucepan, combine onion, garlic and water. Bring to a boil. Reduce heat to low; cover and cook 10 minutes or until onion is tender and translucent, stirring occasionally and adding additional water if necessary to prevent scorching.

2. Meanwhile, cook linguine to desired doneness as directed on package. Drain.

3. Add all remaining ingredients except linguine to onion mixture. Bring to a boil. Reduce heat; cover and simmer 10 minutes to blend flavors. Remove and discard bay leaf. Serve sauce over linguine.

Nutrition Information Per Serving: Serving Size: ¼ of Recipe • Calories 480 • Calories from Fat 60 • % Daily Value • Total Fat 7 g 11% • Saturated 1 g 5% • Cholesterol 95 mg 32% • Sodium 610 mg 25% • Total Carbohydrate 88 g 29% • Dietary Fiber 6 g 24% • Sugars 10 g • Protein 17 g • Vitamin A 25% • Vitamin C 30% • Calcium 10% • Iron 30%
Dietary Exchanges: 5½ Starch, 1 Vegetable, ½ Fat OR 5½ Carbohydrate, 1 Vegetable, ½ Fat

Ravioli with Tomatoes and Zucchini

Prep Time: 20 minutes

Yield: 3 (1½-cup) servings

1 (9-oz.) pkg. refrigerated cheese-filled ravioli
2 small zucchini, cut into 2 x ¼ x ¼-inch strips
1 small onion, cut into thin wedges
1 (14½-oz.) can diced tomatoes with Italian-style herbs, undrained
2 tablespoons sliced ripe olives
2 tablespoons shredded fresh Parmesan cheese

1. Cook ravioli to desired doneness as directed on package. Drain; cover to keep warm.

2. Meanwhile, spray large nonstick skillet with nonstick cooking spray. Heat over medium-high heat until hot. Add zucchini and onion; cook and stir 3 to 4 minutes or until vegetables are crisp-tender.

3. Add tomatoes and olives; cook and stir 2 to 3 minutes or until thoroughly heated.

4. Add cooked ravioli; stir gently to mix. Cook over medium heat for 3 to 4 minutes or until sauce is of desired consistency, stirring occasionally. Sprinkle with cheese.

Nutrition Information Per Serving: Serving Size: 1½ Cups • Calories 370 • Calories from Fat 110 • % Daily Value • Total Fat 12 g 18% • Saturated 6 g 30% • Cholesterol 75 mg 25% • Sodium 750 mg 31% • Total Carbohydrate 48 g 16% • Dietary Fiber 5 g 20% • Sugars 7 g • Protein 18 g • Vitamin A 25% • Vitamin C 30% • Calcium 30% • Iron 15%
Dietary Exchanges: 3 Starch, 1 Vegetable, 1 High-Fat Meat, ½ Fat OR 3 Carbohydrate, 1 Vegetable, 1 High-Fat Meat, ½ Fat

Ravioli with Vegetables

Prep Time: 30 minutes

Yield: 4 (1-cup) servings

1	(9-oz.) pkg. refrigerated cheese-filled ravioli
1	tablespoon olive oil or vegetable oil
2	cups frozen cut green beans, thawed, drained*
1	small onion, cut into thin wedges
½	teaspoon vegetable-flavor or chicken-flavor instant bouillon
½	teaspoon garlic salt
½	teaspoon dried marjoram leaves
⅛	teaspoon pepper
3	tablespoons water
1	cup chopped seeded Italian plum tomatoes
½	cup frozen sweet peas
2	tablespoons shredded fresh Parmesan cheese

1. Cook ravioli to desired doneness as directed on package. Drain; cover to keep warm.

2. Meanwhile, heat oil in large skillet over medium-high heat until hot. Add green beans and onion; cook and stir 3 minutes. Add bouillon, garlic salt, marjoram, pepper and water; cook an additional 3 to 5 minutes or until beans are crisp-tender.

3. Add tomatoes, peas and cooked ravioli. Reduce heat to medium-low; cook 3 to 5 minutes or until mixture is thoroughly heated and sauce is slightly thickened, stirring occasionally. Sprinkle with Parmesan cheese.

Tip: *To quickly thaw green beans, place in colander or strainer; rinse with warm water until thawed. Drain well.

Nutrition Information Per Serving: Serving Size: 1 Cup • Calories 300 • Calories from Fat 110 • % Daily Value • Total Fat 12 g 18% • Saturated 5 g 25% • Cholesterol 55 mg 18% • Sodium 710 mg 30% • Total Carbohydrate 35 g 12% • Dietary Fiber 4 g 16% • Sugars 5 g • Protein 14 g • Vitamin A 15% • Vitamin C 20% • Calcium 20% • Iron 10%
Dietary Exchanges: 2 Starch, 1 Vegetable, 1 High-Fat Meat, ½ Fat OR 2 Carbohydrate, 1 Vegetable, 1 High-Fat Meat, ½ Fat

Ratatouille with Hot Pepper Tortellini

Prep Time: 25 minutes

Yield: 3 (1¼-cup) servings

1	cup coarsely chopped onions
1	medium green bell pepper, coarsely chopped (1 cup)
2	cups coarsely chopped tomatoes (2 medium)
½	small eggplant, 1 medium yellow summer squash or 1 medium zucchini, cubed
⅓	cup tomato paste with Italian seasonings
2	tablespoons chopped fresh basil or ½ teaspoon dried basil leaves
1	(9-oz.) pkg. refrigerated hot pepper cheese–filled tortellini
2	tablespoons chopped fresh parsley

1. Spray large nonstick skillet with nonstick cooking spray. Heat over medium heat until hot. Add onions and bell pepper; cook 3 to 5 minutes or until crisp-tender, stirring occasionally.

2. Stir in tomatoes, eggplant, tomato paste and basil. Cover; cook 5 to 8 minutes or until eggplant is tender, stirring occasionally.

3. Meanwhile, cook tortellini to desired doneness as directed on package. Drain tortellini; add to tomato mixture. Cook 1 to 3 minutes or until thoroughly heated. Sprinkle with parsley.

Nutrition Information Per Serving: Serving Size: 1¼ Cups • Calories 350 • Calories from Fat 70 • % Daily Value • Total Fat 8 g 12% • Saturated 4 g 20% • Cholesterol 35 mg 12% • Sodium 540 mg 23% • Total Carbohydrate 53 g 18% • Dietary Fiber 7 g 28% • Sugars 7 g • Protein 17 g • Vitamin A 40% • Vitamin C 70% • Calcium 25% • Iron 15%
Dietary Exchanges: 3 Starch, 2 Vegetable, ½ High-Fat Meat, ½ Fat OR 3 Carbohydrate, 2 Vegetable, ½ High-Fat Meat, ½ Fat

Vegetable Fiesta Skillet Supper

Prep Time: 25 minutes

Yield: 6 (1-cup) servings

Photo at right and page v

1	cup chopped carrots
½	cup chopped onion
1	small zucchini, halved lengthwise, cut into ¼-inch-thick slices (¾ cup)
1	small yellow summer squash, halved lengthwise, cut into ¼-inch-thick slices (¾ cup)
1	(15½- or 15-oz.) can kidney beans, drained, rinsed
1	(11-oz.) can vacuum-packed whole kernel corn with red and green peppers, undrained
1	(8-oz.) can tomato sauce
½	cup medium chunky-style picante sauce
¼	cup water
4	teaspoons taco seasoning mix (half of 1¼-oz. pkg.)
4	oz. (1 cup) shredded Cheddar cheese

1. Spray large nonstick skillet with nonstick cooking spray. Heat over medium-high heat until hot. Add carrots and onion; cook and stir 8 to 10 minutes or until vegetables are crisp-tender, adding 2 to 3 tablespoons water if necessary to prevent sticking.

2. Stir in all remaining ingredients except cheese. Bring to a boil. Reduce heat to medium-low; cover and simmer 5 to 7 minutes, stirring once. Remove from heat. Sprinkle with cheese. Cover; let stand until cheese is melted.

Nutrition Information Per Serving: Serving Size: 1 Cup • Calories 230 • Calories from Fat 60 • % Daily Value • Total Fat 7 g 11% • Saturated 4 g 20% • Cholesterol 20 mg 7% • Sodium 1090 mg 45% • Total Carbohydrate 31 g 10% • Dietary Fiber 6 g 24% • Sugars 10 g • Protein 11 g • Vitamin A 130% • Vitamin C 25% • Calcium 20% • Iron 10% **Dietary Exchanges:** 1½ Starch, 1½ Vegetable, ½ High-Fat Meat, ½ Fat OR 1½ Carbohydrate, 1½ Vegetable, ½ High-Fat Meat, ½ Fat

Chili Powder

What's the difference between ground chile pepper and chili powder? Ground chile pepper is pure, dried ground peppers, which may be hot or mild. Chili powder is a blend that also may be hot or mild; the formula varies by brand and may include not only ground chile peppers but other seasonings such as cumin, salt, black pepper or even sugar. Add chili powder sparingly at first, then adjust the seasoning to your family's liking.

Vegetable Fiesta Skillet Supper

Easy Risotto with Asparagus

Prep Time: 40 minutes

Yield: 4 (1¼-cup) servings

1	tablespoon margarine or butter
¼	cup chopped red onion
1	cup uncooked short-grain Arborio rice, rinsed
2	(14½-oz.) cans ready-to-serve vegetable broth
½	cup sliced roasted red bell pepper (from 7¼-oz. jar)
1	(9-oz.) pkg. frozen asparagus cuts in a pouch, thawed, drained*
2	oz. (½ cup) shredded fresh Parmesan cheese

1. Melt margarine in large skillet over medium-high heat. Add onion; cook and stir until tender. Stir in rice and 1 can of the broth. Bring to a boil. Reduce heat to medium; cook 8 to 10 minutes or until liquid is absorbed, stirring frequently.

2. Add roasted peppers and asparagus; mix well. Cook an additional 15 to 17 minutes or until rice is tender, stirring frequently and adding remaining 1 can broth ¼ cup at a time as necessary. (There may be a small amount of broth left.) Stir in cheese.

Tip: *To quickly thaw asparagus, remove asparagus from pouch; place in colander or strainer. Rinse with warm water until thawed; drain well. Or cut small slit in center of pouch; microwave on HIGH for 2 to 3 minutes or until thawed. Remove asparagus from pouch; drain well.

Nutrition Information Per Serving: Serving Size: 1¼ Cups • Calories 250 • Calories from Fat 70 • % Daily Value • Total Fat 8 g 12% • Saturated 3 g 15% • Cholesterol 10 mg 3% • Sodium 1240 mg 52% • Total Carbohydrate 35 g 12% • Dietary Fiber 1 g 4% • Sugars 4 g • Protein 9 g • Vitamin A 30% • Vitamin C 45% • Calcium 20% • Iron 15%
Dietary Exchanges: 2 Starch, 1 Vegetable, 1½ Fat OR 2 Carbohydrate, 1 Vegetable, 1½ Fat

Vegetable Chili Skillet Supper

Prep Time: 25 minutes

Yield: 3 (1⅓-cup) servings

1	tablespoon olive oil or vegetable oil
½	cup chopped onion
1	(1-lb.) pkg. frozen broccoli florets, carrots and cauliflower
1	(8-oz.) can tomato sauce
1	teaspoon chili powder
½	teaspoon sugar
¼	teaspoon salt
⅛	to ¼ teaspoon ground red pepper (cayenne)
1	(15½-oz.) can pinto beans, drained
4	oz. (1 cup) shredded Cheddar cheese

1. Heat oil in large skillet over medium-high heat until hot. Add onion and frozen vegetables; cook and stir 7 to 10 minutes or until vegetables are crisp-tender.

2. Add tomato sauce, chili powder, sugar, salt and ground red pepper. Bring to a boil. Reduce heat to low; simmer 5 minutes.

3. Add beans; simmer an additional 5 minutes or until thoroughly heated. Sprinkle with cheese.

Nutrition Information Per Serving: Serving Size: 1⅓ Cups • Calories 390 • Calories from Fat 160 • % Daily Value • Total Fat 18 g 28% • Saturated 9 g 45% • Cholesterol 40 mg 13% • Sodium 1120 mg 47% • Total Carbohydrate 37 g 12% • Dietary Fiber 10 g 40% • Sugars 11 g • Protein 19 g • Vitamin A 100% • Vitamin C 60% • Calcium 40% • Iron 15%
Dietary Exchanges: 2 Starch, 2 Vegetable, 1½ Very Lean Meat, 3 Fat OR 2 Carbohydrate, 2 Vegetable, 1½ Very Lean Meat, 3 Fat

Cheese Choices

CHEESE	DESCRIPTION	SUBSTITUTIONS
American	Processed cheese with white or orange color; mild flavor; very smooth when melted. Usually sold sliced, but blocks are available.	Cheddar, colby
Blue	White cheese streaked with bluish veins. Assertive, tangy flavor. Firm and crumbly. Gorgonzola, Danish blue, Saga, Stilton and Roquefort are a few of the varieties.	Feta has a similar tang and crumbly texture but won't duplicate the inimitable flavor of blue cheese.
Cheddar	Rich, creamy flavor that sharpens with age. Golden, orange or creamy white with smooth, firm texture; melts well.	Monterey Jack, Muenster
Colby	Similar to Cheddar but more golden with milder flavor.	Cheddar, Monterey Jack
Feta	Sheep's milk cheese that is tart and salty with crumbly texture. Often sold covered with water.	Goat cheese like chèvre
Monterey Jack	Semisoft and creamy with buttery, slightly tart taste. Creamy white color. Sometimes flavored with hot pepper, basil, etc.	Colby, mild Cheddar, Havarti
Mozzarella	Semisoft and creamy with a buttery, slightly tart taste. Creamy white color. Fresh mozzarella is more tender; also much more perishable.	Muenster
Neufchâtel	Soft, rich, nutty, slightly sweet with smooth, creamy texture; resembles cream cheese but has more moisture and less fat.	Regular cream cheese
Parmesan	Hard grating cheese with pale yellow color and a buttery, sweet, nutty flavor that intensifies with age.	Romano
Romano	Creamy white, hard, granular cheese with sharp, piquant flavor. Grates and melts well.	Parmesan
Swiss	Ivory colored with dime-sized eyes. Firm with mellow, buttery, nutty flavor.	Monterey Jack, mild Cheddar, Gruyèr

3

slow-cooker meals

An electric slow cooker might be the next best thing to a hired chef. You can spend a few minutes early in the day with preparations, then the slow cooker takes over and simmers away virtually unattended for hours, plus it has a hearty, hot dinner ready when you are.

Slow-Cooked Turkey Dinner, page 307

Slow-Cooker Cookware

Electric slow cookers use a steady temperature—low, but still hot enough to kill harmful bacteria. Foods cook very slowly, holding in moisture and flavor. Sizes range from a 1-quart miniature for hors d'oeuvres to a 6-quart size ideal for large families.

These recipes focus on 3½- to 4-quart cookers. Within this size range, you can choose from models that are round or oval. The oval models are useful for accommodating a whole chicken or ham.

Removable liners, which may boost the price a little, make cleaning much easier. In some models, the removable liner doubles as a table-ready serving dish.

Most models come equipped with a low and high setting; a timer to switch the settings automatically can be useful.

Slow-Cooker Success

- The slow-cooker recipes in this book have been thoroughly tested. For best results and food safety, follow each recipe exactly, including heating instructions. Refrigerate leftovers promptly after cooking.

- For food safety, meals cooked in a slow cooker need to reach a safe cooking

temperature (140°F.) within three hours. That's why it isn't a good idea to preassemble ingredients and refrigerate them or to use frozen ingredients. Thaw meat in the refrigerator or microwave, not at room temperature.

- To ensure proper cooking, cut meats and vegetables into the sizes called for in each recipe—and layer or assemble as suggested. Cook the minimum time and check for doneness. Resist the urge to lift the lid, as the cooker is slow to regain heat after the pot is uncovered. In general, cooking time is less crucial than with other types of cooking. When cooking at low temperatures, a half hour or even an hour of extra cooking time doesn't make much difference to the final results.

- Fill your slow cooker only half to three-quarters full.

- Make sure to fit the slow-cooker lid securely. A covered pot keeps the food moist.

- For cooking time conversions, one hour on the high setting generally equals two hours on the low setting.

- To reduce the amount of liquid or stock in the recipe, turn the setting to high and cook uncovered for one hour.

- Colors fade during long cooking, so dress up slow-cooked dishes with colorful garnishes. Some vegetables, like green onions, tend to retain more flavor and texture if added toward the end of cooking time. For more intense fresh herb flavor and color impact, add some fresh herbs at the beginning and add more just before serving.

Finishing Touches

Even though meals made in a slow cooker can be served right from the pot, you may want to make them a bit more special. If the dish calls for rice or noodles, spoon the contents of the slow cooker over them.

Sprinkling the entree with fresh herbs, chopped green onions, grated cheese, french-fried onions or crumbled, cooked bacon adds to its appearance, appeal and flavor.

Kids' Favorites

Children love familiar flavors such as hot dogs, ground beef and noodles:

Slow-Cooked Hamburger and Noodle Soup, page 260

Tried and True Family Favorites

The comforts of home come through in these nourishing slow-cooked meals:

Slow-Cooked Beef Burgundy, page 284

Easy Entertaining

**Chilies, barbecue-style meats and other
specialties are exactly right for casual gatherings:**

Slow-Cooked Barbecued Pork in Buns, page 277

Spicy Southwest Beef and Bean Chili

Prep Time: 15 minutes (Ready in 8 hours 15 minutes)

Yield: 6 (1½-cup) servings

1	medium onion, chopped
1½	lb. boneless beef round steak (½ inch thick), cut into ¾ x ¾-inch pieces
4	(8-oz.) cans no-salt-added tomato sauce
1	(15¼-oz.) can whole kernel corn, drained
1	(15-oz.) can black beans, drained, rinsed
1	(4½-oz.) can chopped green chiles
2	tablespoons chili powder

1. In 3½- to 4-quart slow cooker, combine all ingredients; mix well.
2. Cover; cook on low setting for at least 8 hours.

Nutrition Information Per Serving: Serving Size: 1½ Cups • Calories 300 • Calories from Fat 60 • % Daily Value • Total Fat 7 g 11% • Saturated 2 g 10% • Cholesterol 55 mg 18% • Sodium 430 mg 18% • Total Carbohydrate 31 g 10% • Dietary Fiber 6 g 24% • Sugars 10 g • Protein 29 g • Vitamin A 20% • Vitamin C 40% • Calcium 6% • Iron 20%
Dietary Exchanges: 1½ Starch, 1 Vegetable, 3 Lean Meat OR 1½ Carbohydrate, 1 Vegetable, 3 Lean Meat

Four-Can Chili

Prep Time: 10 minutes (Ready in 4 hours 10 minutes)

Yield: 4 (1½-cup) servings

CHILI

1	(14½- or 16-oz.) can whole tomatoes, undrained, cut up
1	(15-oz.) can chili without beans
1	(15½- or 15-oz.) can pinto beans, drained
1	(15½- or 15-oz.) can red kidney beans, drained
¼	cup barbecue sauce
½	teaspoon chili powder

TOPPINGS

4	oz. (1 cup) shredded Cheddar cheese
½	cup chopped onion
¼	cup sour cream

1. In 3½- to 4-quart slow cooker, combine all chili ingredients; mix well.
2. Cover; cook on high setting for 2 to 4 hours to blend flavors. Or, cook 1 hour on high setting; reduce heat to low setting and cook 8 to 9 hours. Serve with toppings.

Nutrition Information Per Serving: Serving Size: 1½ Cups • Calories 480 • Calories from Fat 180 • % Daily Value • Total Fat 20 g 31% • Saturated 11 g 55% • Cholesterol 60 mg 20% • Sodium 1190 mg 50% • Total Carbohydrate 47 g 16% • Dietary Fiber 11 g 44% • Sugars 9 g • Protein 27 g • Vitamin A 50% • Vitamin C 25% • Calcium 40% • Iron 25%
Dietary Exchanges: 2½ Starch, ½ Fruit, 3 Lean Meat, 2 Fat OR 3 Carbohydrate, 3 Lean Meat, 2 Fat

Three-Bean Chili

Prep Time: 15 minutes (Ready in 5 hours 45 minutes)

Yield: 7 (1½-cup) servings

½ lb. ground beef or ground turkey
1 cup chopped onions
½ cup chopped green bell pepper
1 (28-oz.) can whole tomatoes, undrained, cut up
1 (15-oz.) can tomato sauce
1 (10¾-oz.) can condensed tomato soup
1 (1¼-oz.) pkg. taco seasoning mix
1 (15½- or 15-oz.) can dark red kidney beans, drained
1 (15½-oz.) can great northern beans, drained
1 (15½-oz.) can butter beans, undrained*

1. In medium skillet, brown ground beef with onions and bell pepper until beef is thoroughly cooked. Drain.

2. In 3½- to 4-quart slow cooker, combine cooked ground beef mixture, tomatoes, tomato sauce, soup and taco seasoning mix; mix well.

3. Cover; cook on high setting for 30 minutes.

4. Stir in beans. Reduce heat to low setting; cover and cook an additional 4 to 5 hours or until thoroughly heated.

Tip: *For a thicker chili, drain butter beans.

Nutrition Information Per Serving: Serving Size: 1½ Cups • Calories 300 • Calories from Fat 50 • % Daily Value • Total Fat 6 g 9% • Saturated 2 g 10% • Cholesterol 20 mg 7% • Sodium 1540 mg 64% • Total Carbohydrate 45 g 15% • Dietary Fiber 10 g 40% • Sugars 10 g • Protein 17 g • Vitamin A 40% • Vitamin C 80% • Calcium 30% • Iron 45%
Dietary Exchanges: 2½ Starch, 1 Vegetable, 1 Medium-Fat Meat OR 2½ Carbohydrate, 1 Vegetable, 1 Medium-Fat Meat

Six-Can Slow-Cooked Chili

Prep Time: 10 minutes (Ready in 4 hours 10 minutes)

Yield: 8 (1½-cup) servings

¼ cup cornmeal
1 teaspoon paprika
½ cup barbecue sauce
1 (28-oz.) can whole tomatoes, undrained, cut up
2 (15-oz.) cans chili without beans
1 (15½- or 15-oz.) can pinto or red kidney beans, undrained
1 (15-oz.) can spicy chili beans, undrained
1 (10¾-oz.) can condensed French onion soup

1. In 3½- to 4-quart slow cooker, combine all ingredients; mix well.

2. Cover; cook on high setting for 2 to 4 hours or on low setting for 8 to 9 hours or until thoroughly heated.

Tip: For hotter chili flavor, add 2 teaspoons chili powder.

Nutrition Information Per Serving: Serving Size: 1½ Cups • Calories 250 • Calories from Fat 45 • % Daily Value • Total Fat 5 g 8% • Saturated 1 g 5% • Cholesterol 15 mg 5% • Sodium 1320 mg 55% • Total Carbohydrate 36 g 12% • Dietary Fiber 7 g 28% • Sugars 6 g • Protein 15 g • Vitamin A 35% • Vitamin C 15% • Calcium 10% • Iron 20%
Dietary Exchanges: 2½ Starch, 1 Lean Meat OR 2½ Carbohydrate, 1 Lean Meat

Chili Toppings

Let each diner personalize the chili by choosing from among a selection of toppings, such as:

Chopped onions or green onions

Shredded Cheddar or Monterey Jack cheese

Sliced ripe olives

Minced jalapeños

Sour cream (or plain nonfat yogurt)

Shredded lettuce

Chopped fresh tomatoes

Crumbled cooked bacon

Diced roasted bell pepper

Slow-Cooked Chili

Prep Time: 20 minutes (Ready in 8 hours 20 minutes)
Yield: 6 (1½-cup) servings

1	lb. lean ground beef
½	lb. bulk Italian sausage
½	cup chopped onion
1	(28-oz.) can whole tomatoes, undrained, cut up
1	(15-oz.) can tomato sauce
1	teaspoon sugar
1	to 1½ teaspoons cumin
2	teaspoons chili powder
1	teaspoon dried oregano leaves
1	(15-oz.) can spicy chili beans, undrained
1	(15-oz.) can garbanzo beans, drained, rinsed

1. In large skillet, cook ground beef, sausage and onion until beef is browned and thoroughly cooked. Drain.

2. In 3½- to 4-quart slow cooker, combine browned meat and onion with all remaining ingredients; mix well.

3. Cover; cook on low setting for 7 to 8 hours or until thoroughly heated.

Nutrition Information Per Serving: Serving Size: 1½ Cups • Calories 420 • Calories from Fat 170 • % Daily Value • Total Fat 19 g 29% • Saturated 7 g 35% • Cholesterol 70 mg 23% • Sodium 1300 mg 54% • Total Carbohydrate 35 g 12% • Dietary Fiber 9 g 36% • Sugars 8 g • Protein 28 g • Vitamin A 40% • Vitamin C 35% • Calcium 10% • Iron 30%
Dietary Exchanges: 2 Starch, 1 Vegetable, 3 Lean Meat, 1½ Fat OR 2 Carbohydrate, 1 Vegetable, 3 Lean Meat, 1½ Fat

Slow-Cooked Chili

Hearty Home-Style Chili

Prep Time: 20 minutes (Ready in 4 hours 20 minutes)

Yield: 6 (1¾-cup) servings

2	lb. lean ground beef
1	medium onion, chopped
1	cup sliced celery
½	cup chopped green bell pepper
½	cup chopped red bell pepper
1	(28-oz.) can whole tomatoes, undrained, cut up
1	(6-oz.) can tomato paste
4	garlic cloves, minced
1	teaspoon salt
1	teaspoon cumin
2	teaspoons chili powder
1	teaspoon ground red pepper (cayenne)
½	teaspoon pepper
2	(15½- or 15-oz.) cans kidney beans, drained, rinsed

1. In large skillet, cook ground beef and onion until beef is thoroughly cooked. Drain.

2. In 3½- to 4-quart slow cooker, combine ground beef, onion and all remaining ingredients; mix well.

3. Cover; cook on high setting for 3 to 4 hours or until thoroughly heated.

Nutrition Information Per Serving: Serving Size: 1¾ Cups • Calories 470 • Calories from Fat 190 • % Daily Value • Total Fat 21 g 32% • Saturated 8 g 40% • Cholesterol 95 mg 32% • Sodium 1050 mg 44% • Total Carbohydrate 35 g 12% • Dietary Fiber 9 g 36% • Sugars 7 g • Protein 36 g • Vitamin A 50% • Vitamin C 70% • Calcium 15% • Iron 30%
Dietary Exchanges: 2 Starch, 1 Vegetable, 4 Lean Meat, 1½ Fat OR 2 Carbohydrate, 1 Vegetable, 4 Lean Meat, 1½ Fat

About Tomato Paste

Tomato paste is made from tomatoes that have been cooked for several hours, strained and reduced to a thick, deep-red and richly flavored concentrate. Paste is the most concentrated of tomato products, and a little goes a long way. It adds strong tomato flavor to foods and thickens sauces naturally. Paste is available in cans or tubes; tubes are especially convenient because you can refrigerate the remainder for up to three months. If you have extra tomato paste from a can, you can place it by tablespoons on a waxed-paper-lined baking sheet, freeze them, then store the portions in a resealable plastic bag until needed.

Texas Two-Meat Slow-Cooked Chili

Prep Time: 20 minutes (Ready in 9 hours 20 minutes)

Yield: 6 (1½-cup) servings

1	lb. boneless beef chuck steak, cut into 1-inch pieces
1	lb. pork tenderloin, cut into 1-inch pieces
¼	cup all-purpose flour
1	tablespoon oil
2	(10-oz.) cans tomatoes and green chiles, undrained
1	(15½- or 15-oz.) can pinto beans, undrained
1	(12-oz.) can beer
½	cup chopped red onion
2	tablespoons chili powder
1	teaspoon cumin
½	teaspoon garlic powder
½	teaspoon salt
⅛	teaspoon cinnamon

1. In large bowl, combine beef, pork and flour; toss to coat evenly. Heat oil in large skillet over medium-high heat until hot. Add beef and pork; cook and stir until no longer pink.

2. In 3½- to 4-quart slow cooker, combine browned beef and pork and all remaining ingredients; mix well.

3. Cover; cook on low setting for 7 to 9 hours or until beef and pork are fork-tender.

Nutrition Information Per Serving: Serving Size: 1½ Cups • Calories 350 • Calories from Fat 90 • % Daily Value • Total Fat 10 g 15% • Saturated 3 g 15% • Cholesterol 95 mg 32% • Sodium 930 mg 39% • Total Carbohydrate 24 g 8% • Dietary Fiber 6 g 24% • Sugars 4 g • Protein 38 g • Vitamin A 20% • Vitamin C 8% • Calcium 10% • Iron 25%
Dietary Exchanges: 1½ Starch, 5 Very Lean Meat, 1 Fat OR 1½ Carbohydrate, 5 Very Lean Meat, 1 Fat

Spicy Three-Bean Slow-Cooked Chili

Prep Time: 20 minutes (Ready in 9 hours 20 minutes)

Yield: 6 (1½-cup) servings

CHILI

- 1 (28-oz.) can crushed tomatoes, undrained
- 1 (15½-oz.) can great northern beans, drained, rinsed
- 1 (15½- or 15-oz.) can kidney beans, drained, rinsed
- 1 (15-oz.) can black beans, drained, rinsed
- 1 (10-oz.) can mild enchilada sauce
- 1 (8-oz.) can tomato sauce
- 1 (4½-oz.) can chopped green chiles
- 1 red bell pepper, cut into ½-inch pieces
- ½ cup chopped onion
- 2 to 3 teaspoons chili powder
- 1 teaspoon dried oregano leaves
- ½ teaspoon cumin

TOPPING

- 3 purchased corn muffins, crumbled
- 3 oz. (¾ cup) shredded Cheddar cheese

1. In 3½- to 4-quart slow cooker, combine all chili ingredients; mix well.

2. Cover; cook on low setting for at least 9 hours.

3. Before serving, heat oven to 375° F. Arrange crumbled corn muffins in single layer on ungreased cookie sheet. Bake at 375° F. for 5 to 8 minutes or until light brown and crisp.

4. To serve, ladle chili into individual soup bowls. Sprinkle each with toasted corn muffin crumbs and cheese.

Nutrition Information Per Serving: Serving Size: 1½ Cups • Calories 390 • Calories from Fat 80 • % Daily Value • Total Fat 9 g 14% • Saturated 4 g 20% • Cholesterol 20 mg 7% • Sodium 1210 mg 50% • Total Carbohydrate 58 g 19% • Dietary Fiber 13 g 52% • Sugars 12 g • Protein 18 g • Vitamin A 60% • Vitamin C 60% • Calcium 30% • Iron 25%
Dietary Exchanges: 2½ Starch, 1 Fruit, 1 Vegetable, 1 Lean Meat, 1 Fat OR 3½ Carbohydrate, 1 Vegetable, 1 Lean Meat, 1 Fat

Spicy Three-Bean Slow-Cooked Chili

Provençal Beef Stew

Prep Time: 15 minutes (Ready in 10 hours 15 minutes)
Yield: 6 (1½-cup) servings

1¼	lb. beef stew meat
4	slices bacon, cut into 1-inch pieces
1	(18-oz.) jar brown gravy
1	(14½-oz.) can diced tomatoes, undrained
1	teaspoon dried thyme leaves
½	teaspoon salt
¼	teaspoon pepper
1	(1-lb.) pkg. fresh baby carrots
8	new red potatoes, quartered
2	small onions, cut into eighths
1	(8-oz.) pkg. fresh whole mushrooms

1. In large skillet, cook beef and bacon over medium-high heat until beef is browned. Drain.

2. In 3½- to 4-quart slow cooker, combine gravy, tomatoes, thyme, salt and pepper; mix well. Add browned beef, bacon and all remaining ingredients; stir gently to mix.

3. Cover; cook on low setting for 8 to 10 hours or until beef and vegetables are tender.

Nutrition Information Per Serving: Serving Size: 1½ Cups • Calories 360 • Calories from Fat 90 • % Daily Value • Total Fat 10 g 15% • Saturated 4 g 20% • Cholesterol 70 mg 23% • Sodium 900 mg 38% • Total Carbohydrate 37 g 12% • Dietary Fiber 6 g 24% • Sugars 8 g • Protein 30 g • Vitamin A 430% • Vitamin C 0% • Calcium 8% • Iron 30%
Dietary Exchanges: 2 Starch, 1 Vegetable, 3 Lean Meat OR 2 Carbohydrate, 1 Vegetable, 3 Lean Meat

Reducing Fat in Slow-Cooker Meals

Purchase lean cuts of meat and trim off all visible fat before cooking. The slow, moist cooking will help tenderize lean cuts that might otherwise be tough. For fatty meats, brown the meat and discard the drippings before adding the meat to the slow cooker. After cooking, spoon off excess fat with a large spoon.

Easy Slow-Cooker Stew

Prep Time: 10 minutes (Ready in 7 hours 10 minutes)

Yield: 12 (1-cup) servings

3   lb. beef stew meat
3   large onions, cut into eighths
1   (14½- or 16-oz.) can whole
     tomatoes, undrained,
     cut up
2   cups water
¼   cup instant tapioca or
     cornstarch
1   tablespoon beef-flavor
     instant bouillon
1   tablespoon brown sugar
2   teaspoons salt
1   teaspoon pepper
2   bay leaves
1   (1-lb.) pkg. fresh baby
     carrots
1   (1-lb.) pkg. frozen cut green
     beans

1. In 3½- to 4-quart slow cooker, combine all ingredients except carrots and green beans; mix well.

2. Cover; cook on high setting for 6 to 7 hours, stirring occasionally and adding carrots and green beans during last hour of cooking time. Before serving, remove and discard bay leaves.

Nutrition Information Per Serving: Serving Size: 1 Cup • Calories 320 • Calories from Fat 100 • % Daily Value • Total Fat 11 g 17% • Saturated 4 g 20% • Cholesterol 95 mg 32% • Sodium 670 mg 28% • Total Carbohydrate 18 g 6% • Dietary Fiber 3 g 12% • Sugars 6 g • Protein 36 g • Vitamin A 70% • Vitamin C 20% • Calcium 4% • Iron 20%
Dietary Exchanges: 3 Vegetable, 4½ Lean Meat

Old-Fashioned Beef Stew

Prep Time: 20 minutes (Ready in 10 hours 20 minutes)

Yield: 5 (1½-cup) servings

1   tablespoon oil
1½   lb. beef stew meat, cut into
     ¾-inch cubes
4   medium carrots, cut into
     ½-inch slices
3   medium red potatoes,
     unpeeled, cut into ½-inch
     cubes
1½   cups frozen pearl onions
     (from 16-oz. pkg.)
3   cups vegetable juice cocktail
3   tablespoons quick-cooking
     tapioca
1   teaspoon beef-flavor instant
     bouillon
2   teaspoons Worcestershire
     sauce
1½   teaspoons monosodium
     glutamate
¼   teaspoon pepper

1. Heat oil in large skillet or Dutch oven over medium-high heat until hot. Add beef; cook and stir 4 to 6 minutes or until browned.

2. In 3½- to 4-quart slow cooker, combine browned beef and all remaining ingredients; mix well.

3. Cover; cook on low setting for 9 to 10 hours or until beef and vegetables are tender.

Nutrition Information Per Serving: Serving Size: 1½ Cups • Calories 410 • Calories from Fat 100 • % Daily Value • Total Fat 11 g 17% • Saturated 3 g 15% • Cholesterol 90 mg 30% • Sodium 690 mg 29% • Total Carbohydrate 43 g 14% • Dietary Fiber 6 g 24% • Sugars 13 g • Protein 34 g • Vitamin A 360% • Vitamin C 70% • Calcium 6% • Iron 30%
Dietary Exchanges: 2 Starch, 2 Vegetable, 3½ Lean Meat OR 2 Carbohydrate, 2 Vegetable, 3½ Lean Meat

Slow-Cooked Beef Stew

Prep Time: 25 minutes (Ready in 8 hours 25 minutes)

Yield: 4 (2-cup) servings

1   lb. medium new red
    potatoes, cut into eighths
4   medium carrots, sliced
    (2 cups)
1   onion, cut in half lengthwise,
    thinly sliced
¾   lb. beef top round steak,
    trimmed, cut into ¾-inch
    cubes
1   cup beef broth
3   tablespoons tomato paste
2   teaspoons paprika
¼   teaspoon caraway seed
1   garlic clove, minced
2   tablespoons water
2   tablespoons cornstarch

1. In 3½- to 4-quart slow cooker, layer potatoes, carrots, onion and beef cubes. In small bowl, combine broth, tomato paste, paprika, caraway seed and garlic; blend well. Add to slow cooker.

2. Cover; cook on low setting for at least 8 hours.

3. Before serving, in small bowl, combine water and cornstarch; blend until smooth. With slotted spoon, remove beef and vegetables from broth; cover to keep warm. Stir cornstarch mixture into broth mixture in slow cooker.

4. Increase heat to high setting; cover and cook an additional 5 to 10 minutes or until thickened. Serve broth mixture over beef and vegetables.

Nutrition Information Per Serving: Serving Size: 2 Cups • Calories 300 • Calories from Fat 25 • % Daily Value • Total Fat 3 g 5% • Saturated 1 g 5% • Cholesterol 45 mg 15% • Sodium 350 mg 15% • Total Carbohydrate 45 g 15% • Dietary Fiber 6 g 24% • Sugars 7 g • Protein 23 g • Vitamin A 420% • Vitamin C 35% • Calcium 6% • Iron 25%
Dietary Exchanges: 3 Starch, 1 Lean Meat OR 3 Carbohydrate, 1 Lean Meat

Slow-Cooked Beef Stew

Italian Ravioli Stew

Prep Time: 25 minutes (Ready in 6 hours 25 minutes)

Yield: 8 (1⅓-cup) servings

2 cups sliced fresh carrots
1 cup chopped onions
2 (14½-oz.) cans ready-to-
   serve chicken broth
2 (14½-oz.) cans Italian-style
   diced tomatoes, undrained
1 (19-oz.) can white kidney or
   cannellini beans, drained
2 teaspoons dried basil leaves
1 (9-oz.) pkg. refrigerated
   Italian sausage- or cheese-
   filled ravioli

1. In 3½- to 4-quart slow cooker, combine all ingredients except ravioli; mix well.

2. Cover; cook on low setting for 6 hours or until vegetables are tender.

3. Before serving, increase heat to high setting. Add ravioli; cover and cook an additional 8 minutes or until ravioli are tender.

Nutrition Information Per Serving: Serving Size: 1⅓ Cups • Calories 210 • Calories from Fat 35 • % Daily Value • Total Fat 4 g 6% • Saturated 2 g 10% • Cholesterol 15 mg 5% • Sodium 790 mg 33% • Total Carbohydrate 34 g 11% • Dietary Fiber 6 g 24% • Sugars 6 g • Protein 10 g • Vitamin A 180% • Vitamin C 20% • Calcium 10% • Iron 15%
Dietary Exchanges: 2 Starch, 1 Vegetable, ½ Medium-Fat Meat OR 2 Carbohydrate, 1 Vegetable, ½ Medium-Fat Meat

Squash "Bowls" for Stew

To prepare the squash, rinse the skin, then cut the squash in half through the stem. Scoop out the seeds. Cut a small slice from the rounded part of each half to steady it on the plate. Rub the cut edges with oil, then invert the squash halves on a microwave-safe dinner plate or baking tray and microwave on HIGH until tender, about eight minutes for two halves, or bake in a pre-heated 350° F. oven for about an hour. For extra flavor, tuck a couple of garlic cloves (peeling not required) or herb sprigs under the squash halves before cooking.

Set the cooked squash halves on a bowl or plate to contain any spills. Ladle stew into squash "bowls" and serve.

Green Chile Stew

Prep Time: 20 minutes (Ready in 6 hours 20 minutes)

Yield: 6 (1½-cup) servings

1½ lb. boneless pork loin, cut into cubes
2 (4-oz.) cans whole green chiles, drained, cut into strips
1 (20-oz.) jar chunky-style salsa
1 (15¼-oz.) can whole kernel corn, drained
1 (15-oz.) can garbanzo beans, drained, rinsed
1 medium onion, chopped
1 cup chicken broth
3 teaspoons chili powder
3 teaspoons dried cilantro leaves, if desired
2 teaspoons sugar

1. In 3½- to 4-quart slow cooker, combine all ingredients; mix well.

2. Cover; cook on low setting for 6 hours or until pork is tender.

Nutrition Information Per Serving: Serving Size: 1½ Cups • Calories 340 • Calories from Fat 90 • % Daily Value • Total Fat 10 g 15% • Saturated 3 g 15% • Cholesterol 70 mg 23% • Sodium 1370 mg 57% • Total Carbohydrate 33 g 11% • Dietary Fiber 6 g 24% • Sugars 9 g • Protein 30 g • Vitamin A 20% • Vitamin C 15% • Calcium 6% • Iron 10%
Dietary Exchanges: 2 Starch, 1 Vegetable, 3 Lean Meat OR 2 Carbohydrate, 1 Vegetable, 3 Lean Meat

Tomato-Bean Stew

Prep Time: 15 minutes (Ready in 12 hours 45 minutes)

Yield: 6 (1½-cup) servings

4   slices bacon
8   oz. (1¼ cups) dried bean
     blend
½   cup sliced celery
½   cup chopped onion
3   cups water
1   (15¼-oz.) can whole kernel
     corn, undrained
1   (1¼-oz.) pkg. taco seasoning
     mix
1   (28-oz.) can whole tomatoes,
     undrained, cut up
2   teaspoons sugar

1. Cook bacon until crisp. Drain on paper towels; crumble. Sort bean blend. Rinse well; drain.

2. In 3½- to 4-quart slow cooker, combine cooked bacon, bean blend and all remaining ingredients except tomatoes and sugar; mix well.

3. Cover; cook on low setting for 10 to 12 hours or until beans are tender.

4. Add tomatoes and sugar; mix well. Cover; cook on low setting for an additional 30 minutes or until thoroughly heated.

Nutrition Information Per Serving: Serving Size: 1½ Cups • Calories 250 • Calories from Fat 20 • % Daily Value • Total Fat 2 g 3% • Saturated 1 g 5% • Cholesterol 4 mg 1% • Sodium 1140 mg 48% • Total Carbohydrate 47 g 16% • Dietary Fiber 15 g 60% • Sugars 10 g • Protein 12 g • Vitamin A 20% • Vitamin C 15% • Calcium 8% • Iron 10%
Dietary Exchanges: 3 Starch, ½ Very Lean Meat OR 3 Carbohydrate, ½ Very Lean Meat

Easy Breads for Soups and Stews

Crackers are traditional with soup; biscuits are a favorite with stew. Some other ideas include:

Warmed pita triangles

Baked refrigerated biscuits

Squares of homemade or purchased cornbread

Hard rolls

Whole-grain toast

Plain or seeded breadsticks

Wedges of baked purchased pizza dough or prebaked pizza bread crust

Toasted, split English muffins spread with cream cheese

Tomato-Bean Stew

Chicken Ratatouille Stew

Prep Time: 20 minutes (Ready in 10 hours 20 minutes)

Yield: 6 (1¾-cup) servings

4   boneless, skinless chicken breast halves, cut into 1-inch pieces
1   (28- to 30-oz.) jar spaghetti sauce
1   medium eggplant, peeled, coarsely chopped
2   tomatoes, coarsely chopped
2   small zucchini, sliced
1   green bell pepper, cut into 1-inch pieces
1   large onion, chopped
3   garlic cloves, minced
1   teaspoon dried basil leaves
1   teaspoon dried oregano leaves

1. In 3½- to 4-quart slow cooker, combine all ingredients; mix well.

2. Cover; cook on low setting for 8 to 10 hours or until chicken is no longer pink.

Nutrition Information Per Serving: Serving Size: 1¾ Cups • Calories 220 • Calories from Fat 45 • % Daily Value • Total Fat 5 g 8% • Saturated 1 g 5% • Cholesterol 50 mg 17% • Sodium 630 mg 26% • Total Carbohydrate 21 g 7% • Dietary Fiber 5 g 20% • Sugars 4 g • Protein 22 g • Vitamin A 25% • Vitamin C 45% • Calcium 8% • Iron 15%
Dietary Exchanges: 1 Starch, 1 Vegetable, 2½ Very Lean Meat, ½ Fat OR 1 Carbohydrate, 1 Vegetable, 2½ Very Lean Meat, ½ Fat

Hunter's Stew with Chicken

Prep Time: 15 minutes (Ready in 6 hours 15 minutes)

Yield: 4 (1½-cup) servings

1   medium onion, thinly sliced
1   medium green bell pepper, cut into 1-inch pieces
3   boneless, skinless chicken breast halves, cut into 2 x 1-inch pieces
1   (15-oz.) can garbanzo beans, drained
1   (14-oz.) jar spaghetti sauce
1   (8-oz.) can mushroom pieces and stems, drained

1. In 3½- to 4-quart slow cooker, combine all ingredients; mix well.

2. Cover; cook on low setting for at least 6 hours.

Nutrition Information Per Serving: Serving Size: 1½ Cups • Calories 290 • Calories from Fat 50 • % Daily Value • Total Fat 6 g 9% • Saturated 1 g 5% • Cholesterol 55 mg 18% • Sodium 790 mg 33% • Total Carbohydrate 30 g 10% • Dietary Fiber 9 g 36% • Sugars 3 g • Protein 29 g • Vitamin A 10% • Vitamin C 30% • Calcium 8% • Iron 15%
Dietary Exchanges: 2 Starch, 3 Very Lean Meat, ½ Fat OR 2 Carbohydrate, 3 Very Lean Meat, ½ Fat

Italian Chicken Stew

Prep Time: 20 minutes (Ready in 10 hours 20 minutes)

Yield: 4 (1¾-cup) servings

4   boneless, skinless chicken breast halves, cut into 1½-inch pieces

1   (19-oz.) can white kidney or cannellini beans, drained, rinsed

1   (15½- or 15-oz.) can red kidney beans, drained, rinsed

1   (14½-oz.) can diced tomatoes, undrained

1   cup chopped celery

1   cup sliced fresh carrots

2   small garlic cloves, coarsely chopped

1   cup water

½   cup dry red wine

3   tablespoons tomato paste

1   tablespoon sugar

1½   teaspoons dried Italian seasoning

1. In 3½- to 4-quart slow cooker, combine chicken, cannellini beans, kidney beans, tomatoes, celery, carrots and garlic; mix well.

2. In medium bowl, combine all remaining ingredients; mix well. Pour over chicken and vegetables; mix well.

3. Cover; cook on low setting for 8 to 10 hours or on high setting for 5 to 6 hours or until vegetables are tender.

Nutrition Information Per Serving: Serving Size: 1¾ Cups • Calories 410 • Calories from Fat 35 • % Daily Value • Total Fat 4 g 6% • Saturated 1 g 5% • Cholesterol 75 mg 25% • Sodium 690 mg 29% • Total Carbohydrate 50 g 17% • Dietary Fiber 12 g 48% • Sugars 9 g • Protein 39 g • Vitamin A 190% • Vitamin C 25% • Calcium 15% • Iron 30%
Dietary Exchanges: 3 Starch, 1 Vegetable, 4 Very Lean Meat OR 3 Carbohydrate, 1 Vegetable, 4 Very Lean Meat

Slow-Cooked Chicken and Sausage Stew

Prep Time: 25 minutes (Ready in 8 hours 25 minutes)

Yield: 4 (1½-cup) servings

½   lb. kielbasa sausage, cut into ¼-inch slices

2   boneless, skinless chicken breast halves, cut into thin bite-sized strips

½   cup thinly sliced fresh carrot

1   medium onion, thinly sliced, separated into rings

1   (16-oz.) can baked beans, undrained

2   tablespoons brown sugar

1   teaspoon dry mustard

½   cup ketchup

1   tablespoon vinegar

1½   cups frozen cut green beans, thawed, drained*

1. In 3½- to 4-quart slow cooker, combine all ingredients except green beans; mix well.

2. Cover; cook on low setting for at least 8 hours.

3. Before serving, stir in green beans. Increase heat to high setting; cover and cook an additional 10 minutes or until green beans are crisp-tender.

Tip: *To quickly thaw green beans, place in colander or strainer; rinse with warm water until thawed. Drain well.

Nutrition Information Per Serving: Serving Size: 1½ Cups • Calories 460 • Calories from Fat 160 • % Daily Value • Total Fat 18 g 28% • Saturated 6 g 30% • Cholesterol 75 mg 25% • Sodium 1520 mg 63% • Total Carbohydrate 47 g 16% • Dietary Fiber 8 g 32% • Sugars 20 g • Protein 28 g • Vitamin A 100% • Vitamin C 20% • Calcium 15% • Iron 15%
Dietary Exchanges: 2 Starch, 1 Fruit, 1 Vegetable, 3 Lean Meat, 1 Fat OR 3 Carbohydrate, 1 Vegetable, 3 Lean Meat, 1 Fat

focus on soups

Soups are among the most satisfying of dishes to make because they are nutritious, heart-warming and practically foolproof. While deviating from a cake or pastry recipe may result in disaster, soup recipes are very tolerant. Variations in quantity or even substituted ingredients may change the character of the soup—but it probably will still be good.

Soup starts with water, canned or homemade broth or even cans of condensed soup. For part of the liquid you can substitute wine, beer, tomato juice or sauce, or liquid left from cooking vegetables or potatoes. For slow-cooker soups it is important to keep the overall quantity of liquid the same as that specified in the recipe.

In soup recipes that use rice or noodles, you should usually stir them in toward the end of the cooking time to prevent the starch from absorbing too much of the liquid and turning the mixture gummy. Dairy products (milk, cream, cheese, sour cream or yogurt) should also be stirred in shortly before serving to prevent curdling.

Substitute ingredients as your pantry and preferences dictate. Use green onions in place of regular onions, for example; substitute corn for green peas or any kind of canned beans for another. Turkey can stand in for chicken in any soup recipe.

Golden Pea Soup, page 262

How to Defat Soups

Removing the unwanted extra fat from your recipe is surprisingly simple. There are two ways to defat soups: the refrigeration method and the brown and drain method. Just follow these easy steps:

The Refrigeration Method

STEP 1
Prepare soup or broth as directed in the recipe. Cool uncovered in the refrigerator. Then cover and refrigerate 4 to 6 hours, or overnight.

STEP 2
Remove and discard the fat layer that has formed on top. Add any remaining ingredients to the soup and continue as directed in the recipe.

The Brown and Drain Method

STEP 1
Brown meat as directed in the recipe.

STEP 2
Drain meat in a strainer or remove meat from the pan with a slotted spoon, discarding the fat. Continue as directed in the recipe.

Slow-Cooked Chili Soup

Prep Time: 15 minutes (Ready in 7 hours)

Yield: 7 (1⅓-cup) servings

1	tablespoon oil
1½	lb. boneless beef round steak, cut into ½-inch cubes
1	cup chopped onions
1	cup chopped green bell pepper
1	cup chopped carrots
3	to 6 teaspoons chili powder
¼	teaspoon salt
¼	teaspoon garlic powder
¼	teaspoon ground red pepper (cayenne)
¼	teaspoon pepper
1	cup water
2	(14½-oz.) cans diced tomatoes, undrained
1	(15-oz.) can tomato sauce
2	(15½- or 15-oz.) cans dark red kidney beans, drained

1. Heat oil in large skillet over medium-high heat until hot. Add beef and onions; cook and stir until beef is browned.

2. In 3½- to 4-quart slow cooker, combine browned beef and onions and all remaining ingredients except kidney beans; mix well.

3. Cover; cook on high setting for 1 hour.

4. Reduce heat to low setting; cook 4 to 5 hours or until beef and vegetables are tender.

5. Stir in beans. Cover; cook on low setting for an additional 30 to 45 minutes or until thoroughly heated.

Nutrition Information Per Serving: Serving Size: 1⅓ Cups • Calories 310 • Calories from Fat 70 • % Daily Value • Total Fat 8 g 12% • Saturated 2 g 10% • Cholesterol 50 mg 17% • Sodium 830 mg 35% • Total Carbohydrate 32 g 11% • Dietary Fiber 9 g 36% • Sugars 9 g • Protein 27 g • Vitamin A 140% • Vitamin C 50% • Calcium 10% • Iron 25%
Dietary Exchanges: 2 Starch, 1 Vegetable, 2½ Lean Meat OR 2 Carbohydrate, 1 Vegetable, 2½ Lean Meat

Thickening Soups or Stews

A little cream stirred in just before serving is a traditional way to give soup or stew a little more body. You can also puree some of the soup broth and vegetables in a blender, then stir the puree back into the soup, or stir in one of the following:

Tomato puree

Mashed or pureed sweet or white potatoes or potato flakes

Pureed butternut squash

Pureed parsnips, turnips or celery root

Slow-Cooked Cabbage Soup

Prep Time: 15 minutes (Ready in 5 hours 15 minutes)
Yield: 6 (1½-cup) servings

1 lb. extra-lean ground beef
1 medium onion, chopped
     (½ cup)
2 cups tomato juice
1 cup water
1 (16-oz.) pkg. coleslaw blend
1 (15-oz.) can chunky salsa or
     tomato sauce
1 (11-oz.) can vacuum-packed
     whole kernel corn, drained
1 teaspoon dried Italian
     seasoning
3 tablespoons light sour
     cream, if desired

1. In large nonstick skillet, cook ground beef and onion over medium heat for 5 minutes or until beef is thoroughly cooked, stirring occasionally. Drain.

2. Place beef mixture in 3½- to 4-quart slow cooker. Add all remaining ingredients except sour cream; stir to combine.

3. Cover; cook on low setting for at least 5 hours. Serve with sour cream if desired.

Nutrition Information Per Serving: Serving Size: 1½ Cups • Calories 280 • Calories from Fat 100 • % Daily Value • Total Fat 11 g 17% • Saturated 4 g 20% • Cholesterol 50 mg 17% • Sodium 900 mg 38% • Total Carbohydrate 27 g 9% • Dietary Fiber 3 g 12% • Sugars 14 g • Protein 18 g • Vitamin A 70% • Vitamin C 60% • Calcium 8% • Iron 15%
Dietary Exchanges: 1 Starch, ½ Fruit, 1 Vegetable, 2 Lean Meat, 1 Fat OR 1½ Carbohydrate, 1 Vegetable, 2 Lean Meat, 1 Fat

Slow-Cooked Hamburger and Noodle Soup

Prep Time: 10 minutes (Ready in 8 hours 30 minutes)

Yield: 5 (1½-cup) servings

Photo at right, pages v and 236 and on back jacket

1   lb. lean or extra-lean ground beef
1   medium onion, coarsely chopped
1   stalk celery, cut into ¼-inch slices
1   (1.15-oz.) pkg. dry beefy mushroom recipe soup mix
1   (14½-oz.) can diced tomatoes, undrained
3   cups water
2   cups frozen mixed vegetables, thawed, drained*
2   oz. (1 cup) uncooked fine egg noodles

1. In large skillet, brown ground beef until thoroughly cooked. Drain well.

2. In 3½- to 4-quart slow cooker, combine cooked ground beef and all remaining ingredients except mixed vegetables and noodles; mix well.

3. Cover; cook on low setting for 6 to 8 hours or until onion is tender.

4. Stir in thawed vegetables and egg noodles. Increase heat to high setting; cover and cook an additional 15 to 20 minutes or until vegetables are crisp-tender and noodles are tender.

Tip: *To quickly thaw mixed vegetables, place in colander or strainer; rinse with warm water until thawed. Drain well.

Nutrition Information Per Serving: Serving Size: 1½ Cups • Calories 310 • Calories from Fat 120 • % Daily Value • Total Fat 13 g 20% • Saturated 5 g 25% • Cholesterol 65 mg 22% • Sodium 700 mg 29% • Total Carbohydrate 26 g 9% • Dietary Fiber 4 g 16% • Sugars 6 g • Protein 21 g • Vitamin A 25% • Vitamin C 15% • Calcium 6% • Iron 15%
Dietary Exchanges: 1 Starch, 2 Vegetable, 2 Lean Meat, 1½ Fat OR 1 Carbohydrate, 2 Vegetable, 2 Lean Meat, 1½ Fat

Slow-Cooked Hamburger and Noodle Soup

Golden Pea Soup

Prep Time: 10 minutes (Ready in 5 hours 10 minutes)

Yield: 6 (1⅓-cup) servings

Photo page 256

1	(16-oz.) pkg. dried yellow split peas
2	cups diced cooked ham
2	carrots, diced
½	cup finely chopped onion
1	tablespoon chicken-flavor instant bouillon
1	teaspoon celery salt
1	teaspoon dry mustard
½	teaspoon hot pepper sauce
6	cups boiling water

1. Sort peas. Rinse well; drain. In 3½- to 4-quart slow cooker, combine all ingredients; mix well.

2. Cover; cook on high setting for 1 hour.

3. Reduce heat to low setting; cook an additional 3 to 4 hours or until peas are very soft.

Nutrition Information Per Serving: Serving Size: 1⅓ Cups • Calories 350 • Calories from Fat 35 • % Daily Value • Total Fat 4 g 6% • Saturated 1 g 5% • Cholesterol 20 mg 7% • Sodium 1470 mg 61% • Total Carbohydrate 50 g 17% • Dietary Fiber 20 g 80% • Sugars 4 g • Protein 29 g • Vitamin A 140% • Vitamin C 6% • Calcium 6% • Iron 20%
Dietary Exchanges: 3½ Starch, 2½ Very Lean Meat OR 3½ Carbohydrate, 2½ Very Lean Meat

Smoky Bean and Cabbage Soup

Prep Time: 30 minutes (Ready in 10 hours 30 minutes)

Yield: 6 (1⅔-cup) servings

2½	cups coarsely chopped cabbage
1	cup chopped onions
2	medium carrots, cut into ¼-inch slices
1	medium turnip, peeled, chopped (1 cup)
2	(15-oz.) cans navy beans, drained, rinsed
1	teaspoon dried marjoram leaves
¼	teaspoon pepper
1	bay leaf
6	cups water
1	(1-lb.) smoked ham shank, trimmed of fat

1. In 3½- to 4-quart slow cooker, combine all ingredients except ham shank; stir gently to mix. Add ham shank.

2. Cover; cook on low setting for at least 10 hours.

3. Remove and discard bay leaf. Remove ham shank; cool slightly. Remove meat from bone; coarsely chop. Add meat to soup.

Nutrition Information Per Serving: Serving Size: 1⅔ Cups • Calories 270 • Calories from Fat 25 • % Daily Value • Total Fat 3 g 5% • Saturated 1 g 5% • Cholesterol 25 mg 8% • Sodium 960 mg 40% • Total Carbohydrate 37 g 12% • Dietary Fiber 10 g 40% • Sugars 8 g • Protein 24 g • Vitamin A 140% • Vitamin C 20% • Calcium 10% • Iron 20%
Dietary Exchanges: 2 Starch, 1 Vegetable, 2½ Very Lean Meat OR 2 Carbohydrate, 1 Vegetable, 2½ Very Lean Meat

Confetti Yellow Pea Soup

Prep Time: 10 minutes (Ready in 9 hours 40 minutes)

Yield: 6 (1½-cup) servings

1   (16-oz.) pkg. dried yellow split peas
1   quart (4 cups) water
1   (10½-oz.) can condensed chicken broth
1   cup julienne-cut (2 x ⅛ x ⅛-inch) carrots
6   oz. chorizo sausage, casing removed, cut into ¼-inch slices
¼   teaspoon salt
¼   teaspoon pepper
½   cup sliced green onions
1   (11-oz.) can vacuum-packed whole kernel corn with red and green peppers, undrained

1. Sort peas. Rinse well; drain. In 3½- to 4-quart slow cooker, combine all ingredients except green onions and corn; stir gently to mix.

2. Cover; cook on low setting for 7 to 9 hours or until peas are soft.

3. Stir in green onions and corn. Cover; cook on low setting for an additional 30 minutes or until corn is thoroughly heated.

Nutrition Information Per Serving: Serving Size: 1½ Cups • Calories 430 • Calories from Fat 90 • % Daily Value • Total Fat 10 g 15% • Saturated 3 g 15% • Cholesterol 20 mg 7% • Sodium 970 mg 40% • Total Carbohydrate 59 g 20% • Dietary Fiber 21 g 84% • Sugars 7 g • Protein 27 g • Vitamin A 120% • Vitamin C 6% • Calcium 6% • Iron 25%
Dietary Exchanges: 4 Starch, 2 Lean Meat OR 4 Carbohydrate, 2 Lean Meat

Julienne Vegetables

"Julienne" sounds more romantic than "matchstick cut" but that's exactly what it means. To cut zucchini, carrots and other ingredients into julienne (matchstick-sized pieces), rinse, trim and peel the vegetable. Next, cut the ingredient lengthwise into planks about ⅛ inch thick. Stack the planks and cut them into strips about ⅛ inch wide. Finally, cut the strips into pieces of the desired length (usually about 2 inches long).

Easy Italian Sausage-Vegetable Soup

Prep Time: 15 minutes (Ready in 9 hours 45 minutes)

Yield: 7 (1½-cup) servings

½ lb. bulk Italian pork sausage
1 cup sliced fresh carrots
1 large baking potato, peeled,
 cut into ½-inch cubes
1 garlic clove, minced
2 (14½-oz.) cans ready-to-
 serve beef broth
1 (15-oz.) can garbanzo beans,
 drained
1 (14½-oz.) can pasta-style
 chunky tomatoes,
 undrained
1½ cups water
½ teaspoon dried Italian
 seasoning
1 bay leaf
1 cup julienne-cut (2 x ⅛ x ⅛-
 inch) zucchini
 Grated fresh Parmesan
 cheese

1. Brown sausage in large skillet. Drain. In 3½- to 4-quart slow cooker, combine cooked sausage and all remaining ingredients except zucchini and cheese; stir gently to mix.

2. Cover; cook on low setting for 7 to 9 hours.

3. Remove and discard bay leaf. Gently stir in zucchini. Cover; cook on low setting for an additional 30 minutes or until zucchini is tender.

4. To serve, ladle soup into bowls; sprinkle with cheese.

Nutrition Information Per Serving: Serving Size: 1½ Cups • Calories 220 • Calories from Fat 80 • % Daily Value • Total Fat 9 g 14% • Saturated 3 g 15% • Cholesterol 20 mg 7% • Sodium 910 mg 38% • Total Carbohydrate 22 g 7% • Dietary Fiber 5 g 20% • Sugars 3 g • Protein 12 g • Vitamin A 110% • Vitamin C 15% • Calcium 10% • Iron 10%
Dietary Exchanges: 1½ Starch, 1 High-Fat Meat OR 1½ Carbohydrate, 1 High-Fat Meat

Easy Italian Sausage-Vegetable Soup

Chicken-Vegetable Chowder

Prep Time: 10 minutes (Ready in 9 hours 40 minutes)

Yield: 5 (1½-cup) servings

1 lb. boneless, skinless chicken thighs, cut into 1-inch pieces
1 cup fresh baby carrots, cut in half lengthwise
1 cup sliced fresh mushrooms
½ cup chopped onion
½ cup water
¼ teaspoon garlic powder
⅛ teaspoon dried thyme leaves
1 (14½-oz.) can ready-to-serve chicken broth
1 (10¾-oz.) can condensed 98% fat-free cream of chicken and broccoli soup with 30% less sodium
½ cup milk
3 tablespoons all-purpose flour
1 (9-oz.) pkg. cut broccoli in a pouch, thawed, drained*

1. In 3½- to 4-quart slow cooker, combine chicken, carrots, mushrooms, onion, water, garlic powder, thyme and broth; mix well.

2. Cover; cook on low setting for 7 to 9 hours or until chicken is no longer pink.

3. In small bowl, combine soup, milk and flour; beat with wire whisk until smooth. Add soup mixture and broccoli to chicken mixture.

4. Cover; cook on low setting for an additional 30 minutes or until broccoli is tender.

Tip: *To quickly thaw broccoli, remove broccoli from pouch; place in colander or strainer. Rinse with warm water until thawed; drain well. Or cut small slit in center of pouch; microwave on HIGH for 2 to 3 minutes or until thawed. Remove broccoli from pouch; drain well.

Nutrition Information Per Serving: Serving Size: 1½ Cups • Calories 240 • Calories from Fat 80 • % Daily Value • Total Fat 9 g 14% • Saturated 3 g 15% • Cholesterol 60 mg 20% • Sodium 670 mg 28% • Total Carbohydrate 17 g 6% • Dietary Fiber 3 g 12% • Sugars 5 g • Protein 22 g • Vitamin A 150% • Vitamin C 35% • Calcium 8% • Iron 10%
Dietary Exchanges: 1 Starch, ½ Vegetable, 2½ Lean Meat OR 1 Carbohydrate, ½ Vegetable, 2½ Lean Meat

Slow-Cooked Two-Bean Minestrone

Prep Time: 10 minutes (Ready in 10 hours 30 minutes)

Yield: 6 (1½-cup) servings

1	medium onion, halved crosswise, cut into thin wedges
1	garlic clove, minced
1	stalk celery, coarsely chopped
2	medium carrots, cut into ½-inch slices
2	(14½-oz.) cans ready-to-serve chicken broth
1	(19-oz.) can white kidney or cannellini beans, drained, rinsed
1	(15½- or 15-oz.) can red kidney beans, drained, rinsed
1	(14½-oz.) can Italian-seasoned stewed tomatoes, undrained, cut up
½	teaspoon salt
⅛	teaspoon pepper
1	cup frozen cut leaf spinach, thawed, squeezed to drain*
3	oz. uncooked spaghetti, broken into thirds (¾ cup)

1. In 3½- to 4-quart slow cooker, combine all ingredients except spinach and spaghetti; mix well.

2. Cover; cook on low setting for 7 to 10 hours or until vegetables are tender.

3. Stir in thawed spinach and spaghetti. Increase heat to high setting; cover and cook an additional 15 to 20 minutes or until spaghetti is tender.

Tip: *To quickly thaw spinach, place in colander or strainer; rinse with warm water until thawed. Squeeze dry with paper towels.

Nutrition Information Per Serving: Serving Size: 1½ Cups • Calories 240 • Calories from Fat 20 • % Daily Value • Total Fat 2 g 3% • Saturated 0 g 0% • Cholesterol 0 mg 0% • Sodium 970 mg 40% • Total Carbohydrate 43 g 14% • Dietary Fiber 9 g 36% • Sugars 5 g • Protein 13 g • Vitamin A 160% • Vitamin C 15% • Calcium 10% • Iron 20%
Dietary Exchanges: 2½ Starch, 1 Vegetable, ½ Very Lean Meat OR 2½ Carbohydrate, 1 Vegetable, ½ Very Lean Meat

Confetti Wild Rice Soup

Prep Time: 20 minutes (Ready in 8 hours 20 minutes)
Yield: 6 servings

⅔ cup uncooked wild rice, rinsed, drained
½ cup chopped onion
3 (14½-oz.) cans ready-to-serve chicken broth
2 medium carrots, thinly sliced (1 cup)
½ teaspoon dried marjoram leaves
⅛ teaspoon pepper
2 boneless, skinless chicken breast halves, cut into ½-inch pieces
1½ cups frozen whole kernel corn, thawed, drained*
1 cup frozen cut broccoli, thawed, drained*

1. In 3½- to 4-quart slow cooker, combine all ingredients except corn and broccoli; mix well.

2. Cover; cook on low setting for at least 8 hours.

3. Before serving, stir in corn and broccoli. Increase heat to high setting; cover and cook an additional 5 minutes or until vegetables are crisp-tender.

Tip: *To quickly thaw corn and broccoli, place in colander or strainer; rinse with warm water until thawed. Drain well.

Nutrition Information Per Serving: Serving Size: ⅙ of Recipe • Calories 200 • Calories from Fat 25 • % Daily Value • Total Fat 3 g 5% • Saturated 1 g 5% • Cholesterol 25 mg 8% • Sodium 690 mg 29% • Total Carbohydrate 25 g 8% • Dietary Fiber 3 g 12% • Sugars 4 g • Protein 17 g • Vitamin A 140% • Vitamin C 10% • Calcium 4% • Iron 8%
Dietary Exchanges: 1½ Starch, 2 Very Lean Meat OR 1½ Carbohydrate, 2 Very Lean Meat

Confetti Wild Rice Soup

Vegetarian Navy Bean Soup

Vegetarian Navy Bean Soup

Prep Time: 20 minutes (Ready in 8 hours 20 minutes)

Yield: 7 (1½-cup) servings

1 cup finely chopped carrots
1 cup finely chopped celery, including leaves
½ cup finely chopped onion
1 (16-oz.) pkg. dried navy beans, rinsed
2 quarts (8 cups) water
1 cup vegetable juice cocktail
1 tablespoon chicken-flavor instant bouillon, if desired
⅛ teaspoon crushed red pepper flakes

1. In 3½- to 4-quart slow cooker, combine all ingredients; mix well.

2. Cover; cook on low setting for at least 8 hours.

3. If desired, in blender container or food processor bowl with metal blade, puree part or all of soup until smooth.

Nutrition Information Per Serving: Serving Size: 1½ Cups • Calories 240 • Calories from Fat 10 • % Daily Value • Total Fat 1 g 2% • Saturated 0 g 0% • Cholesterol 0 mg 0% • Sodium 540 mg 23% • Total Carbohydrate 44 g 15% • Dietary Fiber 11 g 44% • Sugars 7 g • Protein 14 g • Vitamin A 110% • Vitamin C 15% • Calcium 15% • Iron 20%
Dietary Exchanges: 2½ Starch, 1 Very Lean Meat OR 2½ Carbohydrate, 1 Very Lean Meat

Mediterranean Stew

Prep Time: 25 minutes (Ready in 9 hours 25 minutes)
Yield: 6 servings

2	cups cubed peeled buttercup squash
1½	cups julienne-cut (2 x ⅛ x ⅛-inch) carrots
1	cup cubed unpeeled eggplant
1	cup onion wedges
1	cup sliced zucchini
1	(28-oz.) can Italian-style plum tomatoes, undrained, cut up
1	(15-oz.) can garbanzo beans, drained
1	(14½-oz.) can ready-to-serve chicken broth
1	garlic clove, minced
1	teaspoon cumin
½	teaspoon salt
¾	teaspoon allspice
¼	teaspoon pepper
2	cups uncooked couscous
½	cup raisins

1. In 3½- to 4-quart slow cooker, combine all ingredients except couscous and raisins; mix well.

2. Cover; cook on low setting for 7 to 9 hours or until vegetables are tender.

3. Before serving, cook couscous as directed on package; stir in raisins. To serve, spoon 1 cup couscous into each individual soup plate. Spoon stew over couscous.

Nutrition Information Per Serving: Serving Size: ⅙ of Recipe • Calories 410 • Calories from Fat 20 • % Daily Value • Total Fat 2 g 3% • Saturated 0 g 0% • Cholesterol 0 mg 0% • Sodium 760 mg 32% • Total Carbohydrate 83 g 28% • Dietary Fiber 10 g 40% • Sugars 18 g • Protein 16 g • Vitamin A 220% • Vitamin C 30% • Calcium 10% • Iron 15%
Dietary Exchanges: 4 Starch, 1 Fruit, 1½ Vegetable OR 5 Carbohydrate, 1½ Vegetable

Butternut vs. Buttercup

Both of these similar-sounding winter squashes are economical and keep well. Butternut has tan skin and a distinctive pear shape. The bright orange flesh, high water content and super-smooth texture make it ideal for puree or soup. Buttercup, on the other hand, is akin to acorn squash. Buttercup has a dark green exterior and golden flesh that's smoother than acorn squash, which tends to be stringy, and drier and fluffier than the flesh of butternut. Buttercup is a good choice for recipes in which the squash is cubed, since it retains its shape.

Italian Tortellini Stew

Prep Time: 15 minutes (Ready in 6 hours 35 minutes)

Yield: 8 (1¼-cup) servings

1　medium onion, chopped
2　medium zucchini, cut into
　　1-inch cubes
2　(14½-oz.) cans ready-to-
　　serve vegetable or chicken
　　broth
1　(28-oz.) can crushed
　　tomatoes, undrained
1　(15½-oz.) can great northern
　　beans, drained, rinsed
2　tablespoons dried basil
　　leaves
¼　teaspoon salt
¼　teaspoon pepper
1　(8-oz.) pkg. uncooked dry
　　cheese-filled tortellini

1. In 3½- to 4-quart slow cooker, combine all ingredients except tortellini; mix well.

2. Cover; cook on low setting for at least 6 hours.

3. Before serving, increase heat to high setting. Add tortellini; cover and cook an additional 20 minutes or until tortellini are tender.

Nutrition Information Per Serving: Serving Size: 1¼ Cups • Calories 230 • Calories from Fat 35 • % Daily Value • Total Fat 4 g 6% • Saturated 2 g 10% • Cholesterol 10 mg 3% • Sodium 910 mg 38% • Total Carbohydrate 36 g 12% • Dietary Fiber 6 g 24% • Sugars 6 g • Protein 12 g • Vitamin A 20% • Vitamin C 25% • Calcium 15% • Iron 20%
Dietary Exchanges: 2 Starch, 1 Vegetable, ½ Medium-Fat Meat OR 2 Carbohydrate, 1 Vegetable, ½ Medium-Fat Meat

Moroccan Lentil Stew

Prep Time: 30 minutes (Ready in 10 hours 30 minutes)

Yield: 6 (1½-cup) servings

1　cup dried lentils, rinsed
1　(1-lb.) butternut squash,
　　peeled, cut into ¾-inch
　　cubes
8　small new red potatoes, cut
　　into ¾-inch cubes
1　medium onion, chopped
1　(28-oz.) can crushed
　　tomatoes, undrained
3　teaspoons curry powder
½　teaspoon salt
2　cups water
1　(8-oz.) pkg. frozen cut green
　　beans in a pouch, thawed,
　　drained*

1. In 3½- to 4-quart slow cooker, combine all ingredients except green beans; stir gently to mix.

2. Cover; cook on low setting for 8 to 10 hours or on high setting for 5 to 6 hours or until lentils and potatoes are tender.

3. Before serving, stir in thawed green beans. Increase heat to high setting; cover and cook an additional 10 to 15 minutes or until beans are tender.

Tip: *To quickly thaw green beans, remove green beans from pouch; place in colander or strainer. Rinse with warm water until thawed; drain well. Or cut small slit in center of pouch; microwave on HIGH for 2 to 3 minutes or until thawed. Remove green beans from pouch; drain well.

Nutrition Information Per Serving: Serving Size: 1½ Cups • Calories 270 • Calories from Fat 10 • % Daily Value • Total Fat 1 g 2% • Saturated 0 g 0% • Cholesterol 0 mg 0% • Sodium 530 mg 22% • Total Carbohydrate 53 g 18% • Dietary Fiber 15 g 60% • Sugars 8 g • Protein 13 g • Vitamin A 120% • Vitamin C 50% • Calcium 10% • Iron 30%
Dietary Exchanges: 3 Starch, 1 Vegetable, ½ Very Lean Meat OR 3 Carbohydrate, 1 Vegetable, ½ Very Lean Meat

Hot Beef Sandwiches au Jus

Prep Time: 10 minutes (Ready in 4 hours 10 minutes)
Yield: 16 sandwiches

1	(4 to 5-lb.) beef rump roast
1	(1-oz.) pkg. dry onion soup mix
2	teaspoons sugar
1	teaspoon dried oregano leaves
2	(10½-oz.) cans condensed beef broth
1	(12-oz.) can beer
2	garlic cloves, finely chopped
16	crusty French rolls, split

1. Place beef roast in 3½- to 4-quart slow cooker. In medium bowl, combine all remaining ingredients except rolls; mix well. Pour over roast.

2. Cover; cook on high setting for 4 hours or until beef is very tender.

3. Slice or shred beef. Serve in rolls. If desired, skim fat from juices. Serve sandwiches with individual portions of meat juices for dipping.

Nutrition Information Per Serving: Serving Size: 1 Sandwich • Calories 320 • Calories from Fat 110 • % Daily Value • Total Fat 12 g 18% • Saturated 4 g 20% • Cholesterol 75 mg 25% • Sodium 650 mg 27% • Total Carbohydrate 23 g 8% • Dietary Fiber 1 g 4% • Sugars 1 g • Protein 29 g • Vitamin A 0% • Vitamin C 0% • Calcium 4% • Iron 20%
Dietary Exchanges: 1½ Starch, 3½ Lean Meat OR 1½ Carbohydrate, 3½ Lean Meat

Slow-Cooked Sloppy Joes

Prep Time: 15 minutes (Ready in 5 hours 15 minutes)
Yield: 21 sandwiches

3	lb. lean ground beef
1	cup chopped onions
1	cup chopped celery
½	cup chopped green bell pepper
1	(12-oz.) bottle chili sauce
1	(6-oz.) can tomato paste
2	to 3 tablespoons brown sugar
2	tablespoons Worcestershire sauce
¼	teaspoon pepper
21	sandwich buns, split

1. In large skillet, brown ground beef, onions, celery and bell pepper until beef is thoroughly cooked. Drain.

2. Place ground beef mixture in 3½- to 4-quart slow cooker. Stir in all remaining ingredients except buns.

3. Cover; cook on low setting for 3 to 5 hours, stirring occasionally. Serve in buns.

Nutrition Information Per Serving: Serving Size: 1 Sandwich • Calories 280 • Calories from Fat 100 • % Daily Value • Total Fat 11 g 17% • Saturated 4 g 20% • Cholesterol 40 mg 13% • Sodium 580 mg 24% • Total Carbohydrate 30 g 10% • Dietary Fiber 2 g 8% • Sugars 10 g • Protein 16 g • Vitamin A 8% • Vitamin C 0% • Calcium 8% • Iron 15%
Dietary Exchanges: 1 Starch, 1 Fruit, 2 Medium-Fat Meat OR 2 Carbohydrate, 2 Medium-Fat Meat

Hot Beef Sandwiches au Jus

Zesty Beef and Corn Sandwiches

Prep Time: 10 minutes (Ready in 4 hours 10 minutes)

Yield: 21 sandwiches

3	lb. ground beef
1	cup chopped onions
1	medium green bell pepper, chopped
1	(12-oz.) bottle spicy barbecue sauce
1	to 2 tablespoons prepared mustard
1	(11-oz.) can whole kernel corn
21	sandwich buns, split

1. In large skillet, brown ground beef until thoroughly cooked. Drain.

2. In 3½- to 4-quart slow cooker, combine browned ground beef, onions, bell pepper, barbecue sauce and mustard; blend well.

3. Cover; cook on low setting for about 4 hours, stirring in corn during last hour of cooking time. Serve in buns.

Nutrition Information Per Serving: Serving Size: 1 Sandwich • Calories 280 • Calories from Fat 110 • % Daily Value • Total Fat 12 g 18% • Saturated 4 g 20% • Cholesterol 40 mg 13% • Sodium 470 mg 20% • Total Carbohydrate 27 g 9% • Dietary Fiber 2 g 8% • Sugars 6 g • Protein 15 g • Vitamin A 4% • Vitamin C 6% • Calcium 8% • Iron 15%
Dietary Exchanges: 1½ Starch, ½ Fruit, 1½ Medium-Fat Meat, ½ Fat OR 2 Carbohydrate, 1½ Medium-Fat Meat, ½ Fat

Slow-and-Easy Barbecued Beef Sandwiches

Prep Time: 25 minutes (Ready in 6 hours 45 minutes)

Yield: 24 sandwiches

4	lb. boneless beef round steak (¾ inch thick)
2	cups ketchup
1	cup cola-flavored carbonated beverage
1	tablespoon prepared horseradish
1	medium onion, chopped
2	garlic cloves, minced
24	sandwich buns, split

1. Trim all fat from beef; cut into pieces to fit in 3½- to 4-quart slow cooker. Arrange beef in slow cooker. Add all remaining ingredients except buns.

2. Cover; cook on high setting for 5 to 6 hours or until beef is very tender and falls apart.

3. Remove beef from slow cooker; place on cutting board. With 2 forks, shred beef. Return beef to juices in slow cooker.

4. Cover; cook on high setting for an additional 20 minutes or until beef is moistened and thoroughly heated.

5. With slotted spoon, spoon about ⅓ cup mixture into each bun. Mixture can be kept warm for several hours on low setting.

Nutrition Information Per Serving: Serving Size: 1 Sandwich • Calories 250 • Calories from Fat 50 • % Daily Value • Total Fat 6 g 9% • Saturated 2 g 10% • Cholesterol 40 mg 13% • Sodium 520 mg 22% • Total Carbohydrate 29 g 10% • Dietary Fiber 2 g 8% • Sugars 8 g • Protein 20 g • Vitamin A 4% • Vitamin C 4% • Calcium 6% • Iron 15%
Dietary Exchanges: 1½ Starch, ½ Fruit, 2 Lean Meat OR 2 Carbohydrate, 2 Lean Meat

Tangy Barbecued Beef Sandwiches

Prep Time: 15 minutes (Ready in 6 hours 15 minutes)

Yield: 22 sandwiches

1	(3½- to 4-lb.) boneless beef chuck roast, cut crosswise into ¼-inch slices*
1	cup chopped onions
4	garlic cloves, minced
½	cup firmly packed brown sugar
2	teaspoons dry mustard
1	teaspoon chili powder
1	teaspoon paprika
⅓	cup vinegar
⅓	cup Worcestershire sauce
3	tablespoons lemon juice
1¾	cups ketchup
22	sandwich buns, split

1. In 3½- to 4-quart slow cooker, combine all ingredients except buns; mix well.

2. Cover; cook on low setting for 5 to 6 hours or until beef is tender, stirring occasionally. Serve in buns.

Tip: *To make slicing beef easier, freeze 20 to 30 minutes or until firm but not frozen.

Nutrition Information Per Serving: Serving Size: 1 Sandwich • Calories 270 • Calories from Fat 50 • % Daily Value • Total Fat 6 g 9% • Saturated 2 g 10% • Cholesterol 45 mg 15% • Sodium 570 mg 24% • Total Carbohydrate 34 g 11% • Dietary Fiber 2 g 8% • Sugars 13 g • Protein 19 g • Vitamin A 6% • Vitamin C 6% • Calcium 8% • Iron 20%
Dietary Exchanges: 2 Starch, 2 Lean Meat OR 2 Carbohydrate, 2 Lean Meat

Southwest Beef Sandwiches

Prep Time: 15 minutes (Ready in 4 hours 15 minutes)

Yield: 8 sandwiches

1½	cups chopped onions
1½	cups chunky-style salsa
3	tablespoons chopped fresh cilantro
3	garlic cloves, minced
2	teaspoons cumin
2	teaspoons chili powder
¼	teaspoon salt
1½	lb. beef flank steak, cut into 6 pieces
8	sandwich buns, split

1. In 3½- to 4-quart slow cooker, combine all ingredients except beef and buns. Add beef; mix well.

2. Cover; cook on high setting for 4 hours or on low setting for at least 8 hours or until beef is tender.

3. Remove beef from slow cooker. Shred beef; return to slow cooker and mix well.

4. To serve, spoon ⅓ to ½ cup beef mixture into each bun. If desired, top with shredded cheese or sour cream.

Nutrition Information Per Serving: Serving Size: 1 Sandwich • Calories 250 • Calories from Fat 70 • % Daily Value • Total Fat 8 g 12% • Saturated 3 g 15% • Cholesterol 35 mg 12% • Sodium 560 mg 23% • Total Carbohydrate 28 g 9% • Dietary Fiber 2 g 8% • Sugars 8 g • Protein 17 g • Vitamin A 8% • Vitamin C 10% • Calcium 8% • Iron 20%
Dietary Exchanges: 2 Starch, 1½ Lean Meat OR 2 Carbohydrate, 1½ Lean Meat

Slow-Cooked Barbecued Pork in Buns

Prep Time: 20 minutes (Ready in 8 hours 20 minutes)

Yield: 18 sandwiches

Photo at left and page 237

1   (3-lb.) boneless pork roast, cut into thin strips
¾   cup chopped onions
¼   cup cornstarch
¼   cup firmly packed brown sugar
2   teaspoons dry mustard
½   teaspoon salt
¼   teaspoon garlic powder
¼   teaspoon ground red pepper (cayenne)
1½   cups ketchup
2   tablespoons Worcestershire sauce
18   sandwich buns, split

1. In 3½- to 4-quart slow cooker, combine all ingredients except buns; mix well.

2. Cover; cook on low setting for 6 to 8 hours or until pork is tender.

3. Spoon about ⅓ cup pork mixture into each bun.

Nutrition Information Per Serving: Serving Size: 1 Sandwich • Calories 270 • Calories from Fat 60 • % Daily Value • Total Fat 7 g 11% • Saturated 2 g 10% • Cholesterol 40 mg 13% • Sodium 580 mg 24% • Total Carbohydrate 33 g 11% • Dietary Fiber 2 g 8% • Sugars 10 g • Protein 18 g • Vitamin A 4% • Vitamin C 4% • Calcium 8% • Iron 10%
Dietary Exchanges: 1½ Starch, ½ Fruit, 2 Lean Meat OR 2 Carbohydrate, 2 Lean Meat

Let the Bun Match the Barbecue

Slow-cooked barbecued meats, tender and bathed in rich, thick sauce, make a hearty sandwich. Choose your bread carefully. If you intend to pick up the barbecue and eat it like a sandwich, choose a substantial hard roll or sub roll with a fairly durable crust. Otherwise you can hand out forks and make the gravy-soaked bread part of the experience, using soft hamburger buns, baking powder biscuits or squares of cornbread.

Beef and Pork Barbecue

Prep Time: 20 minutes (Ready in 10 hours 20 minutes)

Yield: 16 sandwiches

1½	lb. beef stew meat
1½	lb. cubed pork
2	cups chopped onions
2	cups chopped green bell peppers
½	cup firmly packed brown sugar
2	teaspoons salt
1	teaspoon dry mustard
3	teaspoons chili powder
¼	cup vinegar
2	teaspoons Worcestershire sauce
1	(6-oz.) can tomato paste
16	sandwich buns, split

1. In 3½- to 4-quart slow cooker, combine all ingredients except buns.

2. Cover; cook on high setting for 1 hour.

3. Reduce heat to low setting; cook 7 to 9 hours or until meat is tender.

4. With fork, stir barbecue mixture to break up meat pieces. Serve in buns.

Nutrition Information Per Serving: Serving Size: 1 Sandwich • Calories 280 • Calories from Fat 70 • % Daily Value • Total Fat 8 g 12% • Saturated 3 g 15% • Cholesterol 50 mg 17% • Sodium 640 mg 27% • Total Carbohydrate 33 g 11% • Dietary Fiber 2 g 8% • Sugars 13 g • Protein 19 g • Vitamin A 10% • Vitamin C 20% • Calcium 8% • Iron 20%
Dietary Exchanges: 2 Starch, 2 Lean Meat OR 2 Carbohydrate, 2 Lean Meat

Turkey Barbecue

Prep Time: 15 minutes (Ready in 10 hours 15 minutes)

Yield: 16 sandwiches

3	lb. fresh turkey breast tenderloins, cut crosswise into ¼-inch slices*
2	cups chopped onions
2	cups chopped green bell peppers
½	cup firmly packed brown sugar
2	tablespoons all-purpose flour
1	teaspoon salt
1	teaspoon dry mustard
3	teaspoons chili powder
¼	cup vinegar
2	teaspoons Worcestershire sauce
1	(6-oz.) can tomato paste
16	sandwich buns, split

1. In 3½- to 4-quart slow cooker, combine all ingredients except buns; mix well.

2. Cover; cook on high setting for 1 hour.

3. Reduce heat to low setting; cook an additional 7 to 9 hours or until turkey is tender.** Serve in buns.

Tips: *Freeze turkey slightly for ease in slicing.

**If thicker mixture is desired, uncover and cook on high setting during last 45 minutes of cooking time.

Nutrition Information Per Serving: Serving Size: 1 Sandwich • Calories 260 • Calories from Fat 25 • % Daily Value • Total Fat 3 g 5% • Saturated 1 g 5% • Cholesterol 55 mg 18% • Sodium 510 mg 21% • Total Carbohydrate 34 g 11% • Dietary Fiber 2 g 8% • Sugars 13 g • Protein 25 g • Vitamin A 10% • Vitamin C 20% • Calcium 8% • Iron 15% •
Dietary Exchanges: 1½ Starch, 1 Fruit, 3 Very Lean Meat OR 2½ Carbohydrate, 3 Very Lean Meat

Make-Your-Own Taco Salad

Prep Time: 20 minutes (Ready in 2 hours 20 minutes)

Yield: 8 servings

MEAT SAUCE

1   lb. ground beef, crumbled
1   (1¼-oz.) pkg. taco seasoning
      mix
1   (16-oz.) can tomato puree
1   (15½- or 15-oz.) can pinto
      beans, drained
1   medium onion, chopped
⅛   teaspoon pepper, if desired

SALAD

12   oz. (8 cups) corn chips
4   to 6 cups shredded lettuce
1   to 2 tomatoes, chopped
1   avocado, chopped
4   oz. (1 cup) shredded
      American or Cheddar
      cheese
      Purchased ranch salad
      dressing or salsa

1. In 3½- to 4-quart slow cooker, combine all meat sauce ingredients; mix well.

2. Cover; cook on high setting for 2 hours or on low setting for 6 to 8 hours or until beef is thoroughly cooked and mixture is thoroughly heated.

3. To serve, place corn chips in individual bowls. Top with meat mixture, lettuce, tomatoes, avocado and cheese. Serve with salad dressing.

Nutrition Information Per Serving: Serving Size: ⅛ of Recipe • Calories 710 • Calories from Fat 440 • % Daily Value • Total Fat 49 g 75% • Saturated 11 g 55% • Cholesterol 55 mg 18% • Sodium 1380 mg 58% • Total Carbohydrate 47 g 16% • Dietary Fiber 8 g 32% • Sugars 8 g • Protein 20 g • Vitamin A 35% • Vitamin C 40% • Calcium 30% • Iron 35%
Dietary Exchanges: 3 Starch, 1 Vegetable, 1½ Lean Meat, 8 Fat OR 3 Carbohydrate, 1 Vegetable, 1½ Lean Meat, 8 Fat

Quick Desserts for Slow-Cooked Meals

Purchased pound cake or angel food cake is easy to dress up:

♦ Top slices of cake with thawed frozen berries and a spritz of whipped cream or whipped topping.

♦ In a clear glass bowl, fold together chunks of cake, prepared vanilla pudding and chopped fresh fruit or canned pineapple chunks or mandarin orange segments. Spike the mixture with a splash of rum or liqueur, if desired.

♦ Toast slices of day-old pound cake in the toaster oven and spread with jam.

♦ Drizzle the cake with chocolate syrup or hot fudge sauce.

Tacoloaf Dinner

Prep Time: 15 minutes (Ready in 8 hours 15 minutes)
Yield: 6 servings

2	(15-oz.) cans spicy chili beans, undrained
1	(11-oz.) can vacuum-packed whole kernel corn, undrained
1½	lb. lean ground beef
1	cup crushed corn chips
⅓	cup thick and chunky salsa
1	(1¼-oz.) pkg. taco seasoning mix
1	egg, slightly beaten
¼	cup chunky-style picante sauce

1. In 3½- to 4-quart slow cooker, combine beans and corn; mix well.

2. In large bowl, combine ground beef, corn chips, salsa, taco seasoning mix and egg; mix well. Shape into flat round loaf. Place in slow cooker over beans and corn. Top with picante sauce.

3. Cover; cook on low setting for at least 8 hours.

4. Remove loaf from slow cooker; place on serving platter. Cut into wedges. With slotted spoon, place beans and corn in serving bowl. If desired, remaining sauce in slow cooker can be spooned over tacoloaf wedges.

Nutrition Information Per Serving: Serving Size: ⅙ of Recipe • Calories 500 • Calories from Fat 200 • % Daily Value • Total Fat 22 g 34% • Saturated 7 g 35% • Cholesterol 105 mg 35% • Sodium 1500 mg 63% • Total Carbohydrate 47 g 16% • Dietary Fiber 8 g 32% • Sugars 6 g • Protein 29 g • Vitamin A 10% • Vitamin C 4% • Calcium 8% • Iron 25%
Dietary Exchanges: 2½ Starch, ½ Fruit, 3 Lean Meat, 2½ Fat OR 3 Carbohydrate, 3 Lean Meat, 2½ Fat

Tacoloaf Dinner

Four-Bean Casserole

Prep Time: 20 minutes (Ready in 8 hours 20 minutes)
Yield: 6 (1⅓-cup) servings

½	lb. bacon, cut into 1-inch pieces
1	lb. ground beef
½	cup chopped onion
⅓	cup firmly packed brown sugar
½	cup ketchup
¼	cup molasses
1	tablespoon prepared mustard
2	teaspoons Worcestershire sauce
1	(16-oz.) can pork and beans in tomato sauce, undrained
1	(15½- or 15-oz.) can light red kidney beans, undrained
1	(15½-oz.) can butter beans, drained
1	(15-oz.) can lima beans, drained

1. Cook bacon in large skillet until lightly browned. Remove from skillet; drain on paper towels. In same skillet, brown ground beef and onion until beef is thoroughly cooked. Drain.

2. In 3½- to 4-quart slow cooker, combine cooked bacon, cooked ground beef and onion, and all remaining ingredients; mix well. Cover; cook on low setting for 7 to 8 hours.

Nutrition Information Per Serving: Serving Size: 1⅓ Cups • Calories 580 • Calories from Fat 160 • % Daily Value • Total Fat 18 g 28% • Saturated 7 g 35% • Cholesterol 60 mg 20% • Sodium 1410 mg 59% • Total Carbohydrate 74 g 25% • Dietary Fiber 14 g 56% • Sugars 34 g • Protein 31 g • Vitamin A 6% • Vitamin C 6% • Calcium 15% • Iron 35%
Dietary Exchanges: 3 Starch, 2 Fruit, 3 Lean Meat, 1½ Fat OR 5 Carbohydrate, 3 Lean Meat, 1½ Fat

French Onion Beef

Prep Time: 30 minutes (Ready in 10 hours 30 minutes)

Yield: 6 servings

1¼ lb. boneless beef round steak (½ to ¾ inch thick)
1 (8-oz.) pkg. (3 cups) sliced fresh mushrooms
1 large onion, sliced, separated into rings
1 (10¾-oz.) can condensed French onion soup
1 (6-oz.) pkg. 10-minute herb stuffing mix
¼ cup margarine or butter, melted
4 oz. (1 cup) shredded mozzarella cheese

1. Cut beef into 6 serving-sized pieces. Layer half each of beef, mushrooms and onion in 3½- to 4-quart slow cooker; repeat layers. Pour soup over ingredients in slow cooker.

2. Cover; cook on low setting for 8 to 10 hours or until beef is tender and no longer pink.

3. Before serving, in medium bowl, combine stuffing mix, contents of seasoning packet, melted margarine and ½ cup liquid from slow cooker; toss to mix. Place stuffing on top of contents in slow cooker.

4. Increase heat to high setting. Cover; cook an additional 10 minutes or until stuffing is fluffy. Sprinkle with cheese. Cover; cook until cheese is melted.

Nutrition Information Per Serving: Serving Size: ⅙ of Recipe • Calories 390 • Calories from Fat 150 • % Daily Value • Total Fat 17 g 26% • Saturated 5 g 25% • Cholesterol 60 mg 20% • Sodium 1080 mg 45% • Total Carbohydrate 31 g 10% • Dietary Fiber 3 g 12% • Sugars 5 g • Protein 29 g • Vitamin A 10% • Vitamin C 4% • Calcium 20% • Iron 20%
Dietary Exchanges: 2 Starch, 3½ Lean Meat, 1 Fat OR 2 Carbohydrate, 3½ Lean Meat, 1 Fat

To Brown or Not to Brown

Food does not brown in a slow cooker. Some people prefer the color and flavor of browned meats, poultry, onions and other vegetables. If you decide to brown ingredients before adding them to the slow cooker, remember that browning can reduce the fat and liquid from meats as well as the liquid from vegetables.

Slow-Cooked Beef Burgundy

Prep Time: 45 minutes (Ready in 7 hours 45 minutes)

Yield: 8 servings

Photo below and page 236

4	slices bacon
2	lb. beef stew meat, cut into 1½-inch cubes
2	large carrots, cut into 1-inch chunks
1	medium onion, sliced
½	cup all-purpose flour
½	teaspoon dried marjoram leaves
¼	teaspoon pepper
¼	teaspoon garlic powder
1	(10½-oz.) can condensed beef broth
½	cup burgundy or dry red wine
1	tablespoon Worcestershire sauce
1	(8-oz.) pkg. (3 cups) sliced fresh mushrooms
1	(16-oz.) pkg. uncooked egg noodles
2	tablespoons chopped fresh parsley

1. Cook bacon until crisp. Drain on paper towels; crumble. In 3½- to 4-quart slow cooker, combine cooked bacon, beef, carrots and onion.

2. In small bowl, combine flour, marjoram, pepper and garlic powder. With wire whisk, stir in broth, wine and Worcestershire sauce until smooth. Add to mixture in slow cooker; stir to combine.

3. Cover; cook on high setting for 1 hour.

4. Reduce heat to low setting; cook an additional 5 to 6 hours or until beef is tender.

5. Stir in mushrooms. Increase heat to high setting; cover and cook an additional 30 minutes or until mushrooms are tender. Meanwhile, cook noodles to desired doneness as directed on package. Drain. Serve beef mixture over noodles; sprinkle with parsley.

Nutrition Information Per Serving: Serving Size: ⅛ of Recipe • Calories 480 • Calories from Fat 110 • % Daily Value • Total Fat 12 g 18% • Saturated 4 g 20% • Cholesterol 125 mg 42% • Sodium 340 mg 14% • Total Carbohydrate 53 g 18% • Dietary Fiber 3 g 12% • Sugars 5 g • Protein 37 g • Vitamin A 160% • Vitamin C 6% • Calcium 4% • Iron 35%
Dietary Exchanges: 3 Starch, 3½ Lean Meat OR 3 Carbohydrate, 3½ Lean Meat

Slow-Cooked Beef Burgundy

Slow-Cooked Corned Beef Dinner

Slow-Cooked Corned Beef Dinner

Prep Time: 15 minutes (Ready in 10 hours 15 minutes)
Yield: 6 servings

6	carrots, cut into 1-inch pieces
4	medium potatoes, unpeeled, cut into 1-inch cubes
1	large onion, cut into thin wedges
1	(2- to 2½-lb.) corned beef brisket
4	to 5 cups water
¼	teaspoon coarsely ground black pepper
6	whole cloves
1	bay leaf

1. In 3½- to 4-quart slow cooker, combine carrots, potatoes and onion; mix well.

2. If necessary, cut brisket to fit into slow cooker. Place brisket over vegetables. Add enough of the water to cover. If brisket is packaged with spice packet, add contents of spice packet and omit pepper, cloves and bay leaf. If not, add pepper, cloves and bay leaf.

3. Cover; cook on low setting for 10 to 12 hours or until brisket and vegetables are tender. Remove and discard bay leaf. Cut brisket into thin slices.

Nutrition Information Per Serving: Serving Size: ⅙ of Recipe • Calories 370 • Calories from Fat 160 • % Daily Value • Total Fat 18 g 28% • Saturated 6 g 30% • Cholesterol 90 mg 30% • Sodium 1070 mg 45% • Total Carbohydrate 31 g 10% • Dietary Fiber 5 g 20% • Sugars 7 g • Protein 20 g • Vitamin A 410% • Vitamin C 20% • Calcium 4% • Iron 20%
Dietary Exchanges: 2 Starch, 2 High-Fat Meat OR 2 Carbohydrate, 2 High-Fat Meat

Slow-Cooked Pot Roast and Vegetables

Prep Time: 25 minutes (Ready in 10 hours 25 minutes)

Yield: 4 servings

1	tablespoon all-purpose flour
½	teaspoon salt
⅛	teaspoon pepper
1	lb. boneless beef top round steak (½ inch thick), cut into serving-sized pieces
4	medium potatoes, peeled, each cut into 6 pieces
4	large carrots, cut into 1-inch pieces
1	onion, thinly sliced
1	bay leaf
1	(14½-oz.) can ready-to-serve beef broth
1	teaspoon Worcestershire sauce
2	tablespoons cornstarch

1. In shallow bowl, combine flour, salt and pepper; mix well. Add round steak pieces to flour mixture; turn to coat both sides.

2. Spray large nonstick skillet with nonstick cooking spray. Heat over medium-high heat until hot. Add beef; cook 2 to 3 minutes on each side or until browned. Remove from skillet; cover to keep warm.

3. In 3½- to 4-quart slow cooker, combine potatoes, carrots and onion; mix well. Add bay leaf. Place browned beef over vegetables.

4. In small bowl, combine 1½ cups of the broth and Worcestershire sauce. Pour over beef.

5. Cover; cook on low setting for 8 to 10 hours or until beef is tender.

6. With slotted spoon, remove beef and vegetables from slow cooker; place on serving platter. Cover to keep warm.

7. Pour liquid from slow cooker into medium saucepan; remove and discard bay leaf. In small bowl, combine remaining broth and cornstarch; blend until smooth. Add to liquid in saucepan. Bring to a boil over medium-high heat, stirring constantly. Boil 1 minute. Serve sauce with beef and vegetables.

Nutrition Information Per Serving: Serving Size: ¼ of Recipe • Calories 340 • Calories from Fat 35 • % Daily Value • Total Fat 4 g 6% • Saturated 1 g 5% • Cholesterol 60 mg 20% • Sodium 680 mg 28% • Total Carbohydrate 46 g 15% • Dietary Fiber 6 g 24% • Sugars 7 g • Protein 29 g • Vitamin A 410% • Vitamin C 30% • Calcium 4% • Iron 25%
Dietary Exchanges: 2½ Starch, 1 Vegetable, 3 Very Lean Meat OR 2½ Carbohydrate, 1 Vegetable, 3 Very Lean Meat

Keeping Potato Appeal

Peeled potatoes discolor and turn a dingy shade of gray after just a few minutes of exposure to air. To maintain the original color, keep cut potatoes covered with cold water until you are ready to use them.

Hearty Italian Spaghetti Dinner

Prep Time: 30 minutes (Ready in 7 hours 30 minutes)

Yield: 6 servings

3	(4-oz.) boneless pork loin chops, trimmed of fat, cut into 1 x ¼-inch strips
1	cup finely chopped onions
½	cup sun-dried tomatoes, cut up
1	tablespoon dried parsley flakes
1	tablespoon dried Italian seasoning
½	teaspoon salt
4	garlic cloves, minced
1	(28-oz.) can crushed tomatoes, undrained
1	(8-oz.) can tomato sauce
12	oz. uncooked spaghetti

1. In 3½- to 4-quart slow cooker, combine all ingredients except spaghetti; mix well.

2. Cover; cook on low setting for at least 7 hours.

3. Before serving, cook spaghetti to desired doneness as directed on package. Drain. Serve pork mixture over spaghetti.

Nutrition Information Per Serving: Serving Size: ⅙ of Recipe • Calories 350 • Calories from Fat 35 • % Daily Value • Total Fat 4 g 6% • Saturated 1 g 5% • Cholesterol 25 mg 8% • Sodium 720 mg 30% • Total Carbohydrate 57 g 19% • Dietary Fiber 5 g 20% • Sugars 9 g • Protein 21 g • Vitamin A 25% • Vitamin C 35% • Calcium 8% • Iron 25%
Dietary Exchanges: 3½ Starch, 1 Vegetable, 1 Lean Meat OR 3½ Carbohydrate, 1 Vegetable, 1 Lean Meat

Scalloped Potatoes, Tomatoes and Ham

Prep Time: 15 minutes (Ready in 7 hours 15 minutes)

Yield: 6 (1⅓-cup) servings

6	cups thinly sliced, peeled potatoes (about 6 medium)
½	cup chopped onion
2	tablespoons all-purpose flour
1	teaspoon salt
¼	teaspoon pepper
2	cups chopped cooked ham
1	(14½- or 16-oz.) can whole tomatoes, undrained, cut up
2	tablespoons margarine or butter, cut into small pieces

1. Spray inside of 3½- to 4-quart slow cooker with nonstick cooking spray. In sprayed slow cooker, layer half of each ingredient in order listed. Repeat layers.

2. Cover; cook on high setting for 1 hour.

3. Reduce heat to low setting; cook an additional 5 to 6 hours or until potatoes are tender. Stir before serving.

Nutrition Information Per Serving: Serving Size: 1⅓ Cups • Calories 270 • Calories from Fat 60 • % Daily Value • Total Fat 7 g 11% • Saturated 2 g 10% • Cholesterol 20 mg 7% • Sodium 1080 mg 45% • Total Carbohydrate 38 g 13% • Dietary Fiber 4 g 16% • Sugars 4 g • Protein 13 g • Vitamin A 10% • Vitamin C 30% • Calcium 2% • Iron 8%
Dietary Exchanges: 2½ Starch, 1 Very Lean Meat, 1 Fat OR 2½ Carbohydrate, 1 Very Lean Meat, 1 Fat

Pork Chops with Corn Stuffing

Prep Time: 20 minutes (Ready in 6 hours 20 minutes)

Yield: 6 servings

1	tablespoon oil
6	(4-oz.) boneless pork loin chops (about ¾ inch thick)
1½	teaspoons dried pork seasoning
4	cups cornbread stuffing mix
½	cup chopped celery
¼	cup chopped onion
¼	teaspoon dried sage leaves, crushed
1	(14½-oz.) can ready-to-serve chicken broth
1	(11-oz.) can vacuum-packed whole kernel corn with red and green peppers, drained
1	egg, beaten

1. Heat oil in large skillet over medium heat until hot. Add pork chops; cook until browned on both sides. Drain. Sprinkle pork with pork seasoning. In large bowl, combine all remaining ingredients; mix well.

2. Spray inside of 3½- to 4-quart slow cooker with nonstick cooking spray. Spoon stuffing mixture into sprayed slow cooker. Arrange browned pork chops in 2 layers over stuffing.

3. Cover; cook on low setting for 5 to 6 hours or until pork is no longer pink in center.

Nutrition Information Per Serving: Serving Size: ⅙ of Recipe • Calories 410 • Calories from Fat 130 • % Daily Value • Total Fat 14 g 22% • Saturated 4 g 20% • Cholesterol 105 mg 35% • Sodium 920 mg 38% • Total Carbohydrate 40 g 13% • Dietary Fiber 7 g 28% • Sugars 5 g • Protein 32 g • Vitamin A 4% • Vitamin C 4% • Calcium 6% • Iron 15%
Dietary Exchanges: 2½ Starch, 3½ Lean Meat, ½ Fat OR 2½ Carbohydrate, 3½ Lean Meat, ½ Fat

Corn, Ham and Potato Scallop

Prep Time: 15 minutes (Ready in 9 hours 15 minutes)

Yield: 6 (1½-cup) servings

6	cups cubed (1-inch) peeled baking potatoes
1½	cups cubed cooked ham
1	(15¼-oz.) can whole kernel corn, drained
¼	cup chopped green bell pepper
2	teaspoons instant minced onion
1	(10¾-oz.) can condensed Cheddar cheese soup
½	cup milk
2	tablespoons all-purpose flour

1. In 3½- to 4-quart slow cooker, combine potatoes, ham, corn, bell pepper and onion; mix well.

2. In small bowl, combine soup, milk and flour; beat with wire whisk until smooth. Pour soup mixture over potato mixture; stir gently to mix.

3. Cover; cook on low setting for 7 to 9 hours or until potatoes are tender.

Nutrition Information Per Serving: Serving Size: 1½ Cups • Calories 320 • Calories from Fat 60 • % Daily Value • Total Fat 7 g 11% • Saturated 4 g 20% • Cholesterol 30 mg 10% • Sodium 1010 mg 42% • Total Carbohydrate 49 g 16% • Dietary Fiber 5 g 20% • Sugars 6 g • Protein 14 g • Vitamin A 10% • Vitamin C 25% • Calcium 10% • Iron 15%
Dietary Exchanges: 3½ Starch, ½ Lean Meat, ½ Fat OR 3½ Carbohydrate, ½ Lean Meat, ½ Fat

Pork Chops with Corn Stuffing

Au Gratin Potatoes and Ham

Prep Time: 20 minutes (Ready in 9 hours 20 minutes)

Yield: 7 (1-cup) servings

6 cups (6 medium) sliced peeled potatoes
1 medium onion, coarsely chopped
1½ cups cubed cooked ham
4 oz. (1 cup) shredded American cheese
1 (10¾-oz.) can condensed 98% fat-free cream of mushroom soup with 30% less sodium
½ cup milk
¼ to ½ teaspoon dried thyme leaves

1. In 3½- to 4-quart slow cooker, layer half each of the potatoes, onion, ham and cheese; repeat layers. In small bowl, combine soup, milk and thyme; pour over top.

2. Cover; cook on high setting for 1 hour.

3. Reduce heat to low setting; cook 6 to 8 hours or until potatoes are tender.

Nutrition Information Per Serving: Serving Size: 1 Cup • Calories 350 • Calories from Fat 70 • % Daily Value • Total Fat 8 g 12% • Saturated 4 g 20% • Cholesterol 30 mg 10% • Sodium 860 mg 36% • Total Carbohydrate 55 g 18% • Dietary Fiber 9 g 36% • Sugars 4 g • Protein 15 g • Vitamin A 4% • Vitamin C 20% • Calcium 20% • Iron 45%
Dietary Exchanges: 3½ Starch, ½ Lean Meat, 1 Fat OR 3½ Carbohydrate, ½ Lean Meat, 1 Fat

Cheesy Ham au Gratin

Prep Time: 10 minutes (Ready in 8 hours 10 minutes)

Yield: 4 (1³/₄-cup) servings

2 cups diced cooked ham
2 cups milk
1 cup boiling water
2 (11-oz.) cans vacuum-packed whole kernel corn with red and green peppers, drained
1 (10¾-oz.) can condensed Cheddar cheese soup
1 (7.8-oz.) pkg. cheesy scalloped potato mix

1. In 3½- to 4-quart slow cooker, combine all ingredients; mix well, making sure potato slices are covered with sauce.

2. Cover; cook on low setting for at least 8 hours.

Nutrition Information Per Serving: Serving Size: 1¾ Cups • Calories 590 • Calories from Fat 140 • % Daily Value • Total Fat 16 g 25% • Saturated 7 g 35% • Cholesterol 60 mg 20% • Sodium 3060 mg 128% • Total Carbohydrate 84 g 28% • Dietary Fiber 6 g 24% • Sugars 18 g • Protein 28 g • Vitamin A 20% • Vitamin C 6% • Calcium 30% • Iron 15%
Dietary Exchanges: 5½ Starch, 1½ Lean Meat, 1½ Fat OR 5½ Carbohydrate, 1½ Lean Meat, 1½ Fat

Slow Cooker-to-Grill Ribs

Prep Time: 35 minutes (Ready in 8 hours 35 minutes)

Yield: 4 servings

RIBS

4   lb. country-style pork ribs
1   medium onion, sliced
     Boiling water

SAUCE

½   cup prepared barbecue
     sauce
¼   cup grape jelly
¼   to ½ teaspoon liquid smoke

1. <u>SLOW COOKER TO GRILL DIRECTIONS:</u> Arrange ribs and onion in 3½- to 4-quart slow cooker. Add enough boiling water to just cover ribs.

2. Cover; cook on low setting for 7 to 8 hours. Drain.*

3. Heat grill. In small saucepan, combine all sauce ingredients. Cook and stir over medium heat just until jelly is melted.

4. When ready to grill, carefully oil grill rack. Place ribs on gas grill over low heat or on charcoal grill 4 to 6 inches from medium coals. Brush ribs generously with sauce. Cook 20 minutes or until browned, turning occasionally and brushing with sauce. Discard any remaining sauce.

Tip: *To make ahead, prepare as directed to this point. Place ribs in baking dish. Prepare sauce as directed; pour over ribs, coating each rib. Cool 30 minutes. Cover; refrigerate up to 24 hours. Grill as directed above.

Nutrition Information Per Serving: Serving Size: ¼ of Recipe • Calories 870 • Calories from Fat 560 • % Daily Value • Total Fat 62 g 95% • Saturated 22 g 110% • Cholesterol 220 mg 73% • Sodium 390 mg 16% • Total Carbohydrate 20 g 7% • Dietary Fiber 1 g 4% • Sugars 10 g • Protein 57 g • Vitamin A 6% • Vitamin C 6% • Calcium 8% • Iron 15%
Dietary Exchanges: 1½ Fruit, 8 High-Fat Meat OR 1½ Carbohydrate, 8 High-Fat Meat

Autumn Pork Roast Dinner

Prep Time: 15 minutes (Ready in 8 hours 15 minutes)

Yield: 6 servings

1   (1¾- to 2-lb.) boneless
     rolled pork loin roast
¼   teaspoon salt
⅛   teaspoon pepper
3   large sweet potatoes, peeled,
     thinly sliced
1   medium onion, sliced,
     separated into rings
¾   teaspoon dried thyme leaves
1   quart (4 cups) apple juice

1. Sprinkle pork roast with salt and pepper; place in 3½- to 4-quart slow cooker. Place sliced sweet potatoes around and on top of roast. Top with onion; sprinkle with thyme. Pour apple juice over onion.

2. Cover; cook on low setting for at least 8 hours.

Nutrition Information Per Serving: Serving Size: ⅙ of Recipe • Calories 380 • Calories from Fat 100 • % Daily Value • Total Fat 11 g 17% • Saturated 4 g 20% • Cholesterol 90 mg 30% • Sodium 170 mg 7% • Total Carbohydrate 37 g 12% • Dietary Fiber 2 g 8% • Sugars 21 g • Protein 34 g • Vitamin A 260% • Vitamin C 20% • Calcium 6% • Iron 15%
Dietary Exchanges: 1½ Starch, 1 Fruit, 4 Lean Meat OR 2½ Carbohydrate, 4 Lean Meat

Maple-Mustard Country-Style Ribs

Prep Time: 10 minutes (Ready in 8 hours 10 minutes)

Yield: 4 servings

1 large onion, cut into ¼-inch slices, separated into rings
⅓ cup maple-flavored syrup
¼ cup spicy brown mustard or country-style Dijon mustard
2½ to 3 lb. country-style pork ribs, trimmed of fat, cut into 3-inch pieces

1. Place onion rings in 3½- to 4-quart slow cooker. In small bowl, combine syrup and mustard; mix well. Spread evenly over ribs. Place coated ribs over onion.

2. Cover; cook on low setting for at least 8 hours. If desired, serve with additional mustard.

Nutrition Information Per Serving: Serving Size: ¼ of Recipe • Calories 680 • Calories from Fat 420 • % Daily Value • Total Fat 47 g 72% • Saturated 18 g 90% • Cholesterol 165 mg 55% • Sodium 370 mg 15% • Total Carbohydrate 21 g 7% • Dietary Fiber 1 g 4% • Sugars 12 g • Protein 43 g • Vitamin A 0% • Vitamin C 4% • Calcium 6% • Iron 10%
Dietary Exchanges: 1½ Fruit, 6 High-Fat Meat OR 1½ Carbohydrate, 6 High-Fat Meat

Maple-Mustard Country-Style Ribs

Double Duty for Your Slow Cooker

Slow cookers are handy, but they take up counter space when they are idle. Take advantage of the interior by using it to conceal cookie cutters, other miscellaneous small kitchen items or even a package of cookies. Consolidate loose items in a plastic bag for easy removal when the appliance is needed for cooking.

Slow-Cooked Cassoulet

Prep Time: 15 minutes (Ready in 9 hours 15 minutes)
Yield: 6 (1-cup) servings

½ cup chopped onion
½ cup thinly sliced fresh carrots
1 lb. cocktail-sized smoked link sausages
1 (16-oz.) can baked beans, undrained
1 (9-oz.) pkg. frozen baby lima beans in a pouch
1 (8-oz.) pkg. frozen cut green beans in a pouch
½ cup firmly packed brown sugar
½ cup ketchup
1 tablespoon vinegar
1 teaspoon prepared mustard

1. In 3½- to 4-quart slow cooker, combine all ingredients; mix well.

2. Cover; cook on high setting for 1 hour.

3. Reduce heat to low setting; cook 4 to 8 hours or until carrots are tender and mixture is thoroughly heated.

Nutrition Information Per Serving: Serving Size: 1 Cup • Calories 510 • Calories from Fat 220 • % Daily Value • Total Fat 24 g 37% • Saturated 8 g 40% • Cholesterol 55 mg 18% • Sodium 1300 mg 54% • Total Carbohydrate 56 g 19% • Dietary Fiber 8 g 32% • Sugars 28 g • Protein 18 g • Vitamin A 70% • Vitamin C 20% • Calcium 10% • Iron 20%
Dietary Exchanges: 2 Starch, 1½ Fruit, 1½ Medium-Fat Meat, 3 Fat OR 3½ Carbohydrate, 1½ Medium-Fat Meat, 3 Fat

Mom's Baked Lima Beans

Prep Time: 25 minutes (Ready in 19 hours)

Yield: 8 (1-cup) servings

1½	lb. (3 cups) dried lima beans
2	quarts (8 cups) water
¼	lb. salt pork or bacon, cut into ¼-inch pieces
½	cup chopped green bell pepper
1	medium onion, chopped
¼	cup molasses
¼	to ½ cup dark corn syrup
1	teaspoon pepper
½	teaspoon salt
¼	teaspoon paprika
1	(2-oz.) jar chopped pimientos, drained

1. Sort beans. Rinse well; drain. In Dutch oven or large saucepan, cover beans with water. Soak at least 12 hours or overnight.

2. Do not drain beans. Bring to a boil. Reduce heat; cover and simmer about 30 minutes or until beans are almost tender.

3. Drain beans, reserving liquid. Place beans in 3½- to 4-quart slow cooker. Combine ¾ cup reserved liquid with all remaining ingredients; mix well. Pour over beans; stir to mix.

4. Cover; cook on high setting for 5 to 6 hours or on low setting for 10 to 12 hours or until beans are tender and mixture is thoroughly heated.

Nutrition Information Per Serving: Serving Size: 1 Cup • Calories 450 • Calories from Fat 110 • % Daily Value • Total Fat 12 g 18% • Saturated 4 g 20% • Cholesterol 10 mg 3% • Sodium 370 mg 15% • Total Carbohydrate 68 g 23% • Dietary Fiber 15 g 60% • Sugars 19 g • Protein 17 g • Vitamin A 6% • Vitamin C 20% • Calcium 6% • Iron 30%
Dietary Exchanges: 3½ Starch, 1 Fruit, 1 Very Lean Meat, 2 Fat OR 4½ Carbohydrate, 1 Very Lean Meat, 2 Fat

Slow-Cooked Beans

Prep Time: 15 minutes (Ready in 8 hours 15 minutes)

Yield: 18 (½-cup) servings

½	lb. bacon, diced
½	cup firmly packed brown sugar
¼	cup cornstarch
1	teaspoon dry mustard
½	cup molasses
1	tablespoon vinegar
4	(16-oz.) cans baked beans
1	medium onion, chopped
1	green bell pepper, chopped

1. In large skillet, cook bacon over medium heat until crisp. Drain, reserving 2 tablespoons drippings.

2. In 3½- to 4-quart slow cooker, combine cooked bacon, reserved 2 tablespoons drippings and all remaining ingredients; mix well.

3. Cover; cook on high setting for 1 hour.

4. Reduce heat to low setting; cook an additional 5 to 7 hours or until thoroughly heated.

Nutrition Information Per Serving: Serving Size: ½ Cup • Calories 200 • Calories from Fat 35 • % Daily Value • Total Fat 4 g 6% • Saturated 1 g 5% • Cholesterol 4 mg 1% • Sodium 460 mg 19% • Total Carbohydrate 35 g 12% • Dietary Fiber 5 g 20% • Sugars 17 g • Protein 6 g • Vitamin A 4% • Vitamin C 8% • Calcium 8% • Iron 6%
Dietary Exchanges: 2 Starch, ½ Fruit, ½ Fat OR 2½ Carbohydrate, ½ Fat

Beans 'n Wieners

Prep Time: 15 minutes (Ready in 4 hours 15 minutes)

Yield: 8 (1-cup) servings

1	lb. wieners, cut into fourths
3	(16-oz.) cans pork and beans in tomato sauce
½	cup ketchup
¼	cup chopped onion
¼	cup molasses
2	teaspoons prepared mustard

1. In 3½- to 4-quart slow cooker, combine all ingredients; mix well.

2. Cover; cook on low setting for 3 to 4 hours or until thoroughly heated.*

Tip: *Four slices bacon, crisply cooked and crumbled, can be added the last hour of cooking time.

Nutrition Information Per Serving: Serving Size: 1 Cup • Calories 420 • Calories from Fat 170 • % Daily Value • Total Fat 19 g 29% • Saturated 7 g 35% • Cholesterol 40 mg 13% • Sodium 1540 mg 64% • Total Carbohydrate 47 g 16% • Dietary Fiber 10 g 40% • Sugars 21 g • Protein 16 g • Vitamin A 10% • Vitamin C 6% • Calcium 10% • Iron 25%
Dietary Exchanges: 2 Starch, 1 Fruit, 1½ High-Fat Meat, 1 Fat OR 3 Carbohydrate, 1½ High-Fat Meat, 1 Fat

Slow-Cooked Pasta Jambalaya

Prep Time: 35 minutes (Ready in 9 hours 35 minutes)

Yield: 6 (1⅓-cup) servings

1	lb. boneless, skinless chicken thighs, cut into 2 x 1-inch pieces
2	stalks celery, cut into ¼-inch slices
1	medium green bell pepper, cut into 1-inch pieces
1	medium onion, coarsely chopped
2	garlic cloves, minced
1	(28-oz.) can crushed tomatoes, undrained
1	tablespoon sugar
½	teaspoon salt
½	teaspoon dried Italian seasoning
⅛	to ¼ teaspoon ground red pepper (cayenne)
1	bay leaf
3½	oz. (½ cup) uncooked orzo or rosamarina (rice-shaped pasta)
1	lb. shelled, deveined, cooked shrimp

1. In 3½- to 4-quart slow cooker, combine all ingredients except orzo and shrimp; mix well.

2. Cover; cook on low setting for 7 to 9 hours or until chicken is no longer pink. Remove and discard bay leaf.

3. Stir in orzo. Increase heat to high setting; cover and cook 15 minutes or until orzo is tender.

4. Stir in shrimp; cover and cook on high setting for an additional 2 minutes or until shrimp are thoroughly heated.

Nutrition Information Per Serving: Serving Size: 1⅓ Cups • Calories 300 • Calories from Fat 60 • % Daily Value • Total Fat 7 g 11% • Saturated 2 g 10% • Cholesterol 195 mg 65% • Sodium 610 mg 25% • Total Carbohydrate 26 g 9% • Dietary Fiber 3 g 12% • Sugars 8 g • Protein 34 g • Vitamin A 20% • Vitamin C 35% • Calcium 10% • Iron 30%
Dietary Exchanges: 1½ Starch, 1 Vegetable, 4 Very Lean Meat, ½ Fat OR 1½ Carbohydrate, 1 Vegetable, 4 Very Lean Meat, ½ Fat

Twenty-Garlic Chicken Dinner

Prep Time: 15 minutes (Ready in 7 hours 15 minutes)

Yield: 4 servings

1	(3- to 3½-lb.) whole frying chicken
1	teaspoon salt
1	teaspoon paprika
½	teaspoon pepper
1	teaspoon olive oil
1	large onion, sliced
1	medium bulb garlic (about 20 cloves)
4	servings instant mashed potatoes

1. Remove giblets from chicken; remove as much fat as possible. Rinse and drain chicken. Pat dry inside and out with paper towels.

2. In small bowl, combine salt, paprika, pepper and oil; mix to form paste. Spread evenly over chicken.

3. Place onion slices in 3½- to 4-quart slow cooker. Place chicken, breast side up, over onion. Separate garlic into cloves; do not peel cloves. Place garlic cloves in and around chicken.

4. Cover; cook on low setting for at least 7 hours.

5. Before serving, prepare mashed potatoes as directed on package.

6. With slotted spoon, remove chicken, onion and garlic from slow cooker. Cut chicken into pieces and serve. Squeeze 4 cooked garlic cloves onto mashed potatoes; mix well. Reserve remaining cooked garlic cloves to spread on bread or vegetables.

Nutrition Information Per Serving: Serving Size: ¼ of Recipe • Calories 570 • Calories from Fat 260 • % Daily Value • Total Fat 29 g 45% • Saturated 8 g 40% • Cholesterol 140 mg 47% • Sodium 930 mg 39% • Total Carbohydrate 30 g 10% • Dietary Fiber 3 g 12% • Sugars 4 g • Protein 47 g • Vitamin A 20% • Vitamin C 10% • Calcium 10% • Iron 15%
Dietary Exchanges: 2 Starch, 6 Lean Meat, 2 Fat OR 2 Carbohydrate, 6 Lean Meat, 2 Fat

Twenty-Garlic Chicken Dinner

Long, slow cooking brings out the natural sweetness in many fruits and vegetables. To enhance the sweetness, many slow-cooker recipes include a bit of brown or white sugar, molasses or ketchup.

Cassoulet

Prep Time: 20 minutes (Ready in 15 hours 20 minutes)

Yield: 10 (1-cup) servings

1	(16-oz.) pkg. dried navy beans
1	quart (4 cups) water
4	boneless, skinless chicken breast halves, cut into 1-inch pieces
½	lb. cooked ham, cut into 1-inch pieces
3	large carrots, sliced
2	medium onions, coarsely chopped
1	rib celery, sliced
¼	cup firmly packed brown sugar
½	teaspoon salt
¼	teaspoon dry mustard
¼	teaspoon pepper
1	(8-oz.) can tomato sauce
2	tablespoons molasses

1. Sort beans. Rinse well; drain. In 3½- to 4-quart slow cooker, combine beans and water. Soak at least 8 hours or overnight.

2. Cover; cook on high setting for 3 hours.

3. Add remaining ingredients; mix well. Cover; cook on high setting for an additional 3 to 4 hours or until beans are tender and chicken is no longer pink.

Nutrition Information Per Serving: Serving Size: 1 Cup • Calories 300 • Calories from Fat 25 • % Daily Value • Total Fat 3 g 5% • Saturated 1 g 5% • Cholesterol 40 mg 13% • Sodium 610 mg 25% • Total Carbohydrate 43 g 14% • Dietary Fiber 8 g 32% • Sugars 15 g • Protein 25 g • Vitamin A 190% • Vitamin C 10% • Calcium 10% • Iron 20%
Dietary Exchanges: 3 Starch, 2 Very Lean Meat OR 3 Carbohydrate, 2 Very Lean Meat

Slow-Cooked Chicken Cacciatore

Prep Time: 20 minutes (Ready in 6 hours 20 minutes)

Yield: 4 servings

4   chicken thighs, skin removed
    if desired
4   chicken legs, skin removed if
    desired
1   (15-oz.) can chunky Italian-
    style tomato sauce
1   (4½-oz.) jar whole
    mushrooms, drained
1   teaspoon dried oregano
    leaves
1   small onion, sliced
1   small green bell pepper, cut
    into 1-inch pieces
2   garlic cloves, minced
¼   cup water
2   tablespoons all-purpose flour

1. In 3½- to 4-quart slow cooker, combine all ingredients except water and flour; mix gently.

2. Cover; cook on low setting for 6 hours or until chicken is fork-tender and juices run clear.

3. With slotted spoon, remove chicken and vegetables from slow cooker; place in serving bowl. Cover to keep warm.

4. In small bowl, combine water and flour; blend well. Stir into liquid in slow cooker. Increase heat to high setting; cover and cook an additional 5 to 10 minutes or until thickened. Stir well; spoon mixture over chicken.

Nutrition Information Per Serving: Serving Size: ¼ of Recipe • Calories 260 • Calories from Fat 90 • % Daily Value • Total Fat 10 g 15% • Saturated 2 g 10% • Cholesterol 90 mg 30% • Sodium 670 mg 28% • Total Carbohydrate 14 g 5% • Dietary Fiber 3 g 12% • Sugars 8 g • Protein 29 g • Vitamin A 10% • Vitamin C 15% • Calcium 10% • Iron 15%
Dietary Exchanges: ½ Starch, 1 Vegetable, 3½ Lean Meat

Easy Sweet 'n Sour Chicken

Prep Time: 25 minutes (Ready in 10 hours 25 minutes)

Yield: 6 servings

2   lb. (about 12) boneless,
    skinless chicken thighs,
    cut into 1½-inch pieces
1   (25- to 28-oz.) jar sweet-
    and-sour simmer sauce
1   (1-lb.) pkg. frozen broccoli
    florets, carrots and water
    chestnuts, thawed,
    drained*
3   cups uncooked instant rice
3   cups water

1. In 3½- to 4-quart slow cooker, combine chicken and simmer sauce; stir gently to mix.

2. Cover; cook on low setting for 8 to 10 hours or until chicken is no longer pink.

3. Before serving, stir in thawed vegetables. Increase heat to high setting; cover and cook an additional 15 minutes or until vegetables are crisp-tender. Meanwhile, cook rice in water as directed on package. Serve chicken mixture over rice.

Tip: *To quickly thaw vegetables, place in colander or strainer; rinse with warm water until thawed. Drain well.

Nutrition Information Per Serving: Serving Size: ⅙ of Recipe • Calories 570 • Calories from Fat 110 • % Daily Value • Total Fat 12 g 18% • Saturated 3 g 15% • Cholesterol 95 mg 32% • Sodium 860 mg 36% • Total Carbohydrate 84 g 28% • Dietary Fiber 2 g 8% • Sugars 30 g • Protein 32 g • Vitamin A 40% • Vitamin C 15% • Calcium 4% • Iron 20%
Dietary Exchanges: 3 Starch, 2 Fruit, 1 Vegetable, 3 Lean Meat OR 5 Carbohydrate, 1 Vegetable, 3 Lean Meat

Barbecued Turkey and Vegetables

Prep Time: 20 minutes (Ready in 9 hours 20 minutes)

Yield: 4 servings

1	cup barbecue sauce
½	cup hot water
2	turkey thighs (2 lb.), skin removed, cut in half
3	medium potatoes, unpeeled, cut into 8 pieces each
6	medium carrots, cut into 2½ x ½-inch sticks

1. In medium bowl, combine barbecue sauce and water; mix well. Layer turkey, potatoes and carrots in 3½- to 4-quart slow cooker. Pour sauce mixture over top.

2. Cover; cook on low setting for at least 9 hours.

3. Remove turkey and vegetables with slotted spoon; place on serving platter. Serve cooking juices over turkey and vegetables.

Nutrition Information Per Serving: Serving Size: ¼ of Recipe • Calories 380 • Calories from Fat 80 • % Daily Value • Total Fat 9 g 14% • Saturated 3 g 15% • Cholesterol 85 mg 28% • Sodium 630 mg 26% • Total Carbohydrate 42 g 14% • Dietary Fiber 6 g 24% • Sugars 8 g • Protein 33 g • Vitamin A 620% • Vitamin C 30% • Calcium 8% • Iron 25%
Dietary Exchanges: 2 Starch, ½ Fruit, 1 Vegetable, 3½ Lean Meat OR 2½ Carbohydrate, 1 Vegetable, 3½ Lean Meat

Barbecued Turkey and Vegetables

Scalloped Potatoes and Turkey

Scalloped Potatoes and Turkey

Prep Time: 15 minutes (Ready in 7 hours 15 minutes)

Yield: 6 (1¼-cup) servings

1	lb. ground turkey breast
½	teaspoon ground thyme
⅛	teaspoon pepper
1	(7.8-oz.) pkg. cheesy scalloped potato mix
2	tablespoons margarine or butter
2½	cups boiling water
1½	cups skim milk
1	medium red bell pepper, chopped
1	medium onion, thinly sliced

1. Spray large skillet with nonstick cooking spray. Heat over medium-high heat until hot. Add ground turkey; cook until browned and no longer pink. Stir in thyme and pepper.

2. In large bowl, combine contents of sauce packet from potato mix, potato slices and margarine. Add boiling water; stir until margarine melts. Add milk; mix well.

3. Stir in browned turkey, bell pepper and onion. Spoon mixture into 3½- to 4-quart slow cooker. With back of spoon, press down potatoes until covered with sauce.

4. Cover; cook on low setting for at least 7 hours.

Nutrition Information Per Serving: Serving Size: 1¼ Cups • Calories 330 • Calories from Fat 120 • % Daily Value • Total Fat 13 g 20% • Saturated 3 g 15% • Cholesterol 60 mg 20% • Sodium 800 mg 33% • Total Carbohydrate 34 g 11% • Dietary Fiber 3 g 12% • Sugars 6 g • Protein 20 g • Vitamin A 20% • Vitamin C 30% • Calcium 15% • Iron 10%

Dietary Exchanges: 2½ Starch, 1½ Very Lean Meat, 2 Fat OR 2½ Carbohydrate, 1½ Very Lean Meat, 2 Fat

Cajun Turkey Loaf

Prep Time: 15 minutes (Ready in 8 hours 15 minutes)
Yield: 6 servings

2   slices whole wheat bread
1   to 1¼ lb. lean ground turkey
½   teaspoon cumin
¼   teaspoon allspice
¼   teaspoon ground red pepper
       (cayenne)
1   garlic clove, minced
1   egg, slightly beaten
1   (14½-oz.) can Cajun-style or
       plain stewed tomatoes,
       undrained, large pieces
       cut up if necessary
½   green bell pepper, cut into
       thin strips

1. Tear bread into small pieces. In food processor bowl with metal blade, process bread pieces until crumbs form.

2. In large bowl, combine bread crumbs, ground turkey, cumin, allspice, ground red pepper, garlic, egg and ⅓ cup of the stewed tomatoes; mix well. Shape into flat round loaf. Place in 3½- to 4-quart slow cooker. Pour remaining stewed tomatoes over loaf; top with bell pepper.

3. Cover; cook on low setting for at least 8 hours or until meat thermometer inserted into loaf reaches at least 165°F.

4. With 2 slotted pancake turners, carefully lift loaf from slow cooker; place on serving platter. Cut into slices.

Nutrition Information Per Serving: Serving Size: ⅙ of Recipe • Calories 220 • Calories from Fat 90 • % Daily Value • Total Fat 10 g 15% • Saturated 3 g 15% • Cholesterol 105 mg 35% • Sodium 290 mg 12% • Total Carbohydrate 10 g 3% • Dietary Fiber 2 g 8% • Sugars 2 g • Protein 22 g • Vitamin A 10% • Vitamin C 15% • Calcium 6% • Iron 15%
Dietary Exchanges: ½ Starch, 3 Lean Meat OR ½ Carbohydrate, 3 Lean Meat

Ground Turkey

Ground turkey, available in the poultry section of the supermarket, makes a good lower-fat substitute for ground beef or pork. Some people find that the lower fat content makes the end product less juicy, but the slow cooker can compensate for this. Long, gentle cooking holds in natural moisture. As with other ground meats, the greater surface area increases the perishability and potential for contamination, so use or freeze all ground turkey within a day of purchase.

Turkey Breast with Cranberry-Onion Gravy

Prep Time: 15 minutes (Ready in 10 hours 15 minutes)

Yield: 8 servings

1	(4-lb.) fresh or frozen turkey breast, thawed
1	(15-oz.) can jellied cranberry sauce
1	(1-oz.) pkg. dry onion soup mix
1	tablespoon prepared mustard
½	teaspoon salt
¼	cup water
3	tablespoons cornstarch

1. Remove and discard skin from turkey breast. Place turkey in 3½- to 4-quart slow cooker.

2. In small bowl, combine cranberry sauce, soup mix, mustard and salt; blend well. Pour over turkey.

3. Cover; cook on low setting for 8 to 10 hours or until thermometer inserted into thickest portion of turkey breast reaches 165 to 170°F.

4. Remove turkey from slow cooker; cover to keep warm. Place fine strainer over medium saucepan. Carefully pour liquid from slow cooker through strainer into saucepan.

5. In small bowl, combine water and cornstarch; blend until smooth. Add to strained liquid in saucepan. Bring to a boil over medium-high heat, stirring constantly. Boil 1 minute.

6. To serve, slice turkey; arrange on serving platter. Spoon about ½ cup gravy over turkey. Serve with remaining gravy.

Nutrition Information Per Serving: Serving Size: ⅛ of Recipe • Calories 310 • Calories from Fat 20 • % Daily Value • Total Fat 2 g 3% • Saturated 1 g 5% • Cholesterol 130 mg 43% • Sodium 570 mg 24% • Total Carbohydrate 25 g 8% • Dietary Fiber 1 g 4% • Sugars 20 g • Protein 47 g • Vitamin A 0% • Vitamin C 0% • Calcium 2% • Iron 15%
Dietary Exchanges: ½ Starch, 1 Fruit, 6½ Very Lean Meat OR 1½ Carbohydrate, 6½ Very Lean Meat

Turkey Loaf Teriyaki

Prep Time: 10 minutes (Ready in 8 hours 10 minutes)
Yield: 6 servings

4	tablespoons purchased teriyaki baste and glaze
1½	lb. lean ground turkey
¾	cup unseasoned dry bread crumbs
¼	cup chopped green onions
1	(2-oz.) jar diced pimientos, drained
1	egg

1. Reserve 2 tablespoons of the teriyaki glaze for topping. In medium bowl, combine remaining 2 tablespoons teriyaki glaze and all remaining ingredients; mix well. Shape into flat round loaf.

2. Cut 20 x 12-inch strip of foil; cut lengthwise in half. Fold each strip lengthwise in half twice, forming two 20 x 1½-inch strips. Crisscross strips; place loaf on center of strips.

3. Lift ends of strips to transfer loaf to 3½- to 4-quart slow cooker; fold ends of foil over top edge of slow cooker (see diagram). Press loaf away from sides of slow cooker. Spread reserved 2 tablespoons teriyaki glaze over loaf.

4. Cover; cook on low setting for at least 8 hours.

5. To remove loaf from slow cooker, lift with foil strips; place on serving plate. If desired, serve with additional teriyaki glaze.

Nutrition Information Per Serving: Serving Size: ⅙ of Recipe • Calories 270 • Calories from Fat 110 • % Daily Value • Total Fat 12 g 18% • Saturated 3 g 15% • Cholesterol 120 mg 40% • Sodium 470 mg 20% • Total Carbohydrate 14 g 5% • Dietary Fiber 1 g 3% • Sugars 4 g • Protein 26 g • Vitamin A 8% • Vitamin C 20% • Calcium 6% • Iron 15%
Dietary Exchanges: 1 Starch, 3½ Lean Meat OR 1 Carbohydrate, 3½ Lean Meat

Turkey Loaf Teriyaki

Sausage and Sauerkraut Dinner

Prep Time: 10 minutes (Ready in 8 hours 10 minutes)

Yield: 4 (2-cup) servings

6   small red potatoes,
    unpeeled, quartered
8   fresh baby carrots, cut into
    ¼-inch slices
1   medium onion, cut into thin
    wedges
1   tablespoon brown sugar
1   tablespoon spicy brown
    mustard
1   teaspoon caraway seed
1   (15-oz.) can sauerkraut
1   lb. fully cooked turkey
    kielbasa, cut into 1-inch
    slices

1. In 3½- to 4-quart slow cooker, combine potatoes, carrots and onion.

2. In medium bowl, combine brown sugar, mustard and caraway seed; mix well. Stir in sauerkraut and kielbasa. Spoon sauerkraut mixture over vegetables in slow cooker.

3. Cover; cook on low setting for at least 8 hours.

Nutrition Information Per Serving: Serving Size: 2 Cups • Calories 360 • Calories from Fat 60 • % Daily Value • Total Fat 7 g 11% • Saturated 1 g 5% • Cholesterol 70 mg 23% • Sodium 2040 mg 85% • Total Carbohydrate 51 g 17% • Dietary Fiber 7 g 28% • Sugars 8 g • Protein 23 g • Vitamin A 110% • Vitamin C 60% • Calcium 15% • Iron 30%
Dietary Exchanges: 3 Starch, 1 Vegetable, 2 Lean Meat OR 3 Carbohydrate, 1 Vegetable, 2 Lean Meat

Slow-Cooked Bean Cassoulet

Prep Time: 15 minutes (Ready in 8 hours 15 minutes)

Yield: 6 (1¼-cup) servings

1   (16-oz.) can vegetarian
    baked beans, undrained
1   (15½-oz.) can butter beans,
    drained, rinsed
1   (15½- or 15-oz.) can red
    kidney beans, drained,
    rinsed
1   (14½-oz.) can Italian-
    seasoned stewed
    tomatoes, undrained,
    cut up
1   (9-oz.) pkg. frozen baby lima
    beans in a pouch
1   cup thinly sliced fresh
    carrots
1   cup chopped onions
½   teaspoon garlic salt
⅛   teaspoon fennel seed,
    crushed
⅛   teaspoon ground red pepper
    (cayenne)

1. In 3½- to 4-quart slow cooker, combine all ingredients; mix well.

2. Cover; cook on low setting for at least 8 hours.

Nutrition Information Per Serving: Serving Size: 1¼ Cups • Calories 260 • Calories from Fat 10 • % Daily Value • Total Fat 1 g 2% • Saturated 0 g 0% • Cholesterol 0 mg 0% • Sodium 920 mg 38% • Total Carbohydrate 50 g 17% • Dietary Fiber 12 g 48% • Sugars 9 g • Protein 13 g • Vitamin A 130% • Vitamin C 20% • Calcium 15% • Iron 15%
Dietary Exchanges: 3 Starch, 1 Vegetable OR 3 Carbohydrate, 1 Vegetable

Slow-Cooked Turkey Dinner

Prep Time: 15 minutes (Ready in 7 hours 45 minutes)

Yield: 4 servings

Photo page 232

6	small red potatoes (about 2½ inches in diameter), unpeeled, quartered
2	cups sliced fresh carrots
1½	lb. turkey thighs, skinned
¼	cup all-purpose flour
2	tablespoons dry onion soup mix
⅓	cup chicken broth or water
1	(10¾-oz.) can condensed 98% fat-free cream of mushroom soup with 30% less sodium

1. Place potatoes and carrots in 3½- to 4-quart slow cooker. Place turkey thighs over vegetables.

2. In medium bowl, combine all remaining ingredients; blend well. Pour over turkey.

3. Cover; cook on high setting for 30 minutes.

4. Reduce heat to low setting; cook at least 7 hours.

Nutrition Information Per Serving: Serving Size: ¼ of Recipe • Calories 410 • Calories from Fat 70 • % Daily Value • Total Fat 8 g 12% • Saturated 3 g 15% • Cholesterol 65 mg 22% • Sodium 1130 mg 47% • Total Carbohydrate 57 g 19% • Dietary Fiber 6 g 24% • Sugars 9 g • Protein 28 g • Vitamin A 340% • Vitamin C 30% • Calcium 15% • Iron 25%
Dietary Exchanges: 3½ Starch, 1 Vegetable, 2 Lean Meat OR 3½ Carbohydrate, 1 Vegetable, 2 Lean Meat

Three-Bean Cassoulet

Prep Time: 15 minutes (Ready in 6 hours 45 minutes)

Yield: 6 (1-cup) servings

1	(15½-oz.) can butter beans, drained
1	(15½-oz.) can great northern beans, drained
1	(15-oz.) can garbanzo beans, drained
1	(14½-oz.) can stewed tomatoes, undrained, cut up
1	cup finely chopped carrots
1	cup chopped onions
2	garlic cloves, minced
2	teaspoons dried parsley flakes
1	teaspoon dried basil leaves
½	teaspoon dried thyme leaves
½	teaspoon salt
⅛	teaspoon pepper
1	bay leaf

1. In 3½- to 4-quart slow cooker, combine all ingredients; mix well.

2. Cover; cook on high setting for 30 minutes.

3. Reduce heat to low setting; cook an additional 5 to 6 hours or until vegetables are tender. Remove and discard bay leaf.

Nutrition Information Per Serving: Serving Size: 1 Cup • Calories 210 • Calories from Fat 20 • % Daily Value • Total Fat 2 g 3% • Saturated 0 g 0% • Cholesterol 0 mg 0% • Sodium 690 mg 29% • Total Carbohydrate 37 g 12% • Dietary Fiber 10 g 40% • Sugars 5 g • Protein 11 g • Vitamin A 120% • Vitamin C 15% • Calcium 15% • Iron 15%
Dietary Exchanges: 2 Starch, 1 Vegetable, ½ Very Lean Meat OR 2 Carbohydrate, 1 Vegetable, ½ Very Lean Meat

Slow and Smoky Baked Beans

Slow and Smoky Baked Beans

Prep Time: 15 minutes (Ready in 12 hours 15 minutes)

Yield: 12 (½-cup) servings

1	(16-oz.) pkg. dried navy beans
½	cup finely chopped onion
½	cup chopped peeled apple
2	quarts (8 cups) water
½	cup hickory smoke flavor barbecue sauce
¼	cup chili sauce
1	teaspoon seasoned salt
½	teaspoon dry mustard

1. Sort beans. Rinse well; drain. In large saucepan or Dutch oven, combine beans, onion, apple and water. Bring to a boil. Boil 30 minutes; remove from heat. Let stand 1½ hours or until beans are tender.

2. If necessary, drain bean mixture. In 3½- to 4-quart slow cooker, combine bean mixture and all remaining ingredients; mix well.

3. Cover; cook on low setting for 8 to 10 hours or until beans are very tender and a deep rich brown color. If desired, stir occasionally.

Nutrition Information Per Serving: Serving Size: ½ Cup • Calories 150 • Calories from Fat 10 • % Daily Value • Total Fat 1 g 2% • Saturated 0 g 0% • Cholesterol 0 mg 0% • Sodium 290 mg 12% • Total Carbohydrate 27 g 9% • Dietary Fiber 6 g 24% • Sugars 5 g • Protein 8 g • Vitamin A 6% • Vitamin C 4% • Calcium 6% • Iron 15%
Dietary Exchanges: 1½ Starch, ½ Fruit, ½ Very Lean Meat OR 2 Carbohydrate, ½ Very Lean Meat

Mexican Rice and Bean Casserole

Prep Time: 15 minutes (Ready in 5 hours 15 minutes)

Yield: 4 (1½-cup) servings

1	cup uncooked regular long-grain white rice
⅔	cup frozen whole kernel corn
½	cup chopped onion
¼	teaspoon turmeric
2	garlic cloves, minced
1	(15-oz.) can spicy chili beans, undrained
1	(14½-oz.) can stewed tomatoes, undrained, cut up
1	(14½-oz.) can ready-to-serve fat-free chicken broth with ⅓ less sodium
1	(4½-oz.) can chopped green chiles
2	oz. (½ cup) shredded Cheddar cheese

1. Spray large skillet with nonstick cooking spray. Heat over medium-high heat until hot. Add rice; cook and stir 5 to 7 minutes or until light golden brown.

2. In 3½- to 4-quart slow cooker, combine browned rice and all remaining ingredients except cheese; mix well. Cover; cook on low setting for at least 5 hours.

3. Stir mixture; sprinkle with cheese. Cover; cook until cheese is melted.

Nutrition Information Per Serving: Serving Size: 1½ Cups • Calories 390 • Calories from Fat 50 • % Daily Value • Total Fat 6 g 9% • Saturated 3 g 15% • Cholesterol 15 mg 5% • Sodium 1080 mg 45% • Total Carbohydrate 69 g 23% • Dietary Fiber 8 g 32% • Sugars 6 g • Protein 15 g • Vitamin A 20% • Vitamin C 25% • Calcium 25% • Iron 25%
Dietary Exchanges: 4 Starch, 1 Vegetable, 1 Fat OR 4 Carbohydrate, 1 Vegetable, 1 Fat

Mexican Rice and Bean
Casserole

How to Use the Nutrition Information

The nutrition information for each recipe can help you estimate how the recipe contributes to your daily food needs. The information includes calories, fat, cholesterol, sodium, carbohydrate, dietary fiber, sugars, protein, vitamins A and C, calcium and iron.

Percent Daily Values tell you how much the nutrients in one serving of food contribute to a 2,000-calorie diet. For example, if the Percent Daily Value for total fat is 10%, one serving contributes 10% of the daily total fat suggested for a person on a 2,000-calorie-a-day diet. (U.S. officials have chosen 2,000 calories as an average level. It's about right for most moderately active women, teenage girls and sedentary men. Older adults, sedentary women and children need less; many men, teenage boys and active women need more.)

Dietary exchanges are the nutritional accounting system commonly used by people with diabetes. This information is based on *1995 Exchange Lists for Meal Planning* by the American Diabetes Association and the American Dietetic Association. This information is not the same as Weight Watchers exchanges. For many recipes, two lists of exchanges are provided: The first uses the traditional method and the second reflects the newer system of carbohydrate counting. Consult your doctor or registered dietitian if you have questions, or contact the American Dietetic Association at 1-800-366-1655. You can also visit their Web site, **www. eatright.org.**

Nutrition Information for Recipe Variations

- **When a recipe gives alternative ingredients, the nutrition analysis uses the first one mentioned. For example, if "egg substitute or egg" is listed, the nutrition information is based on egg substitute.**
- **When a recipe lists a range of amounts for an ingredient, the nutrition information uses the larger amount.**

- **Garnishes and optional ingredients are included in the analysis if they are named in the ingredient list for the recipe.**
- **When a recipe uses a marinade, the nutrition analysis includes the estimated amount of marinade absorbed during preparation.**

Our Experts Behind the Scenes

The Pillsbury team of nutrition professionals, including registered dietitians and home economists, is dedicated to delivering comprehensive nutrition information. We continually update our nutrition database to include new information from the USDA and food manufacturers.

Your Daily Nutritional Requirements

These average daily nutritional needs are for healthy adults age 25 to 50. Since your age, size, activity level and health all affect dietary needs, your requirements may differ.

	MEN	WOMEN
Calories	2,400	1,850
Total fat	80 g or less	62 g or less
Saturated fat	27 g or less	20 g or less
Cholesterol	300 mg or less	300 mg or less
Sodium	2,400 mg	2,400 mg
Total carbohydrate	360 g	275 g
Dietary fiber	20 to 30 g	20 to 30 g
Protein	63 g	50 g
Calcium	1,000 mg	1,000 mg
Iron	10 mg	15 mg

SOURCE: National Academy of Sciences, National Research Council, Recommended Dietary Allowances (10th edition, 1989).

index

Page numbers in *italics* are photographs.

Other Titles by Pillsbury

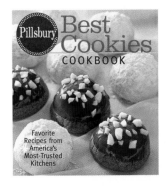

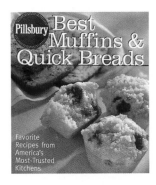

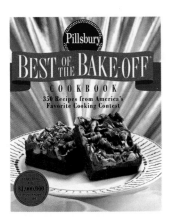

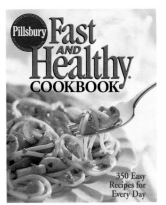

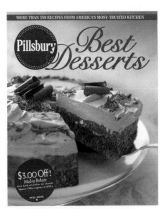

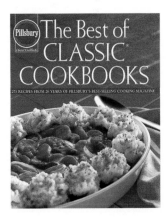

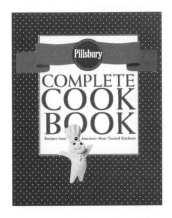

Coming Spring 2000

conversion chart

American cooks use standard containers, the 8-ounce cup and a tablespoon that takes exactly 16 level fillings to fill that cup level. Measuring by cup makes it very difficult to give weight equivalents, as a cup of densely packed butter will weigh considerably more than a cup of flour. The easiest way therefore to deal with cup measurements in recipes is to take the amount by volume rather than by weight. Thus the equation reads:

1 cup = 240 ml = 8 fl. oz.   ½ cup = 120 ml = 4 fl. oz.

It is possible to buy a set of American cup measures in major stores around the world.

In the States, butter is often measured in sticks. One stick is the equivalent of 8 tablespoons. One tablespoon of butter is therefore the equivalent to ½ ounce/15 grams.

Liquid Measures

Fluid Ounces	U.S.	Imperial	Milliliters
	1 teaspoon	1 teaspoon	5
¼	2 teaspoons	1 dessertspoon	10
½	1 tablespoon	1 tablespoon	14
1	2 tablespoons	2 tablespoons	28
2	¼ cup	4 tablespoons	56
4	½ cup		110
5		¼ pint or 1 gill	140
6	¾ cup		170
8	1 cup		225
9			250, ¼ liter
10	1¼ cups	½ pint	280
12	1½ cups		340
15		¾ pint	420
16	2 cups		450
18	2¼ cups		500, ½ liter
20	2½ cups	1 pint	560

Solid Measures

U.S. and Imperial Measures		Metric Measures	
Ounces	Pounds	Grams	Kilos
1		28	
2		56	
3½		100	
4	¼	112	
5		140	
6		168	
8	½	225	
9		250	¼
12	¾	340	
16	1	450	

Oven Temperature Equivalents

Fahrenheit	Celsius	Gas Mark	Description
225	110	¼	Cool
250	130	½	
275	140	1	Very Slow
300	150	2	
325	170	3	Slow
350	180	4	Moderate
375	190	5	
400	200	6	Moderately Hot
425	220	7	Fairly Hot
450	230	8	Hot
475	240	9	Very Hot
500	250	10	Extremely Hot

Any broiling recipes can be used with the grill of the oven, but beware of high-temperature grills.

Equivalents for Ingredients

all-purpose flour—plain flour
arugula—rocket
beet—beetroot
coarse salt—kitchen salt
cornstarch—cornflour
eggplant—aubergine
fava beans—broad beans
lima beans—broad beans

scallion—spring onion
shortening—white fat
snow pea—mangetout
squash—courgettes or marrow
unbleached flour—strong, white flour
vanilla bean—vanilla pod
zest—rind
zucchini—courgettes or marrow

light cream—single cream
heavy cream—double cream
half and half—12% fat milk
buttermilk—ordinary milk

cheesecloth—muslin
parchment paper—greaseproof paper
plastic wrap—cling film